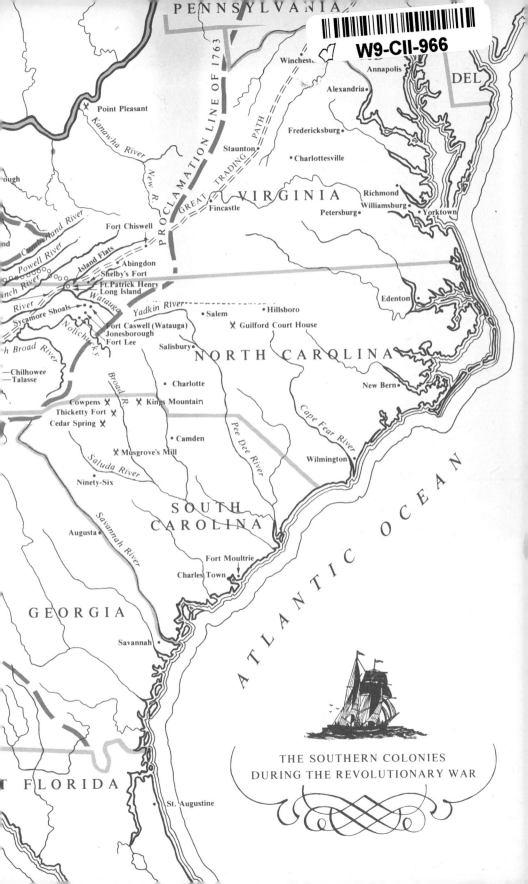

PENNSYLVANIA

W9-CII-966

DEL

Winchester
Annapolis
Alexandria

Point Pleasant

Fredericksburg

Staunton
Charlottesville

VIRGINIA

Richmond
Williamsburg
Yorktown

Fincastle
Petersburg

Fort Chiswell

Island Flats
Abingdon
Shelby's Fort
Ft. Patrick Henry
Long Island

Edenton

Sycamore Shoals

Yadkin River

Salem
Hillsboro

Fort Caswell (Watauga)
Jonesborough
Fort Lee

Guilford Court House

Salisbury

NORTH CAROLINA

Chilhowee
Talasse

Charlotte

New Bern

Cowpens
Kings Mountain
Thicketty Fort
Cedar Spring

Camden

Wilmington

Musgrove's Mill

Saluda River

Ninety-Six

SOUTH
CAROLINA

Augusta

Fort Moultrie

ATLANTIC OCEAN

Charles Town

GEORGIA

Savannah

FLORIDA

St. Augustine

THE SOUTHERN COLONIES
DURING THE REVOLUTIONARY WAR

PROCLAMATION LINE OF 1763

GREAT TRADING PATH

Kanawha River

New R.

Cumberland River

Powell River

Clinch River

Watauga

Nolichucky

Broad River

Broad R.

Pee Dee River

Cape Fear River

Savannah River

TENNESSEE
During the
REVOLUTIONARY WAR

PUBLISHED UNDER AUSPICES OF
*The Tennessee American Revolution
Bicentennial Commission*

TENNESSEE
During the
REVOLUTIONARY
WAR
by
Samuel Cole Williams

WITH AN INTRODUCTION BY

FRANK B. WILLIAMS, JR.

AND INDEX BY MURIEL C. SPODEN

The University of Tennessee Press

Knoxville

COPYRIGHT © 1944 BY THE TENNESSEE HISTORICAL COMMISSION. SPECIAL CONTENTS OF THIS EDITION COPYRIGHT © 1974 BY THE UNIVERSITY OF TENNESSEE PRESS. ALL RIGHTS RESERVED. MANUFACTURED IN THE UNITED STATES OF AMERICA.

Library of Congress Cataloging in Publication Data

Williams, Samuel Cole, 1864–1947.
  Tennessee during the Revolutionary War.

  Reprint of the ed. published by Tennessee Historical Commission with new introd., maps, and index.
  "A bibliography of the historical writings of Samuel Cole Williams, compiled by Pollyanna Creekmore": p.
  1. Tennessee—History—Revolution, 1775–1783.
I. Title.
E263.T4W54   1974   976.8'03   74-4377
ISBN 0-87049-155-5

INTRODUCTION TO THE NEW EDITION

The republication of this volume under auspices of the Tennessee American Revolution Bicentennial Commission is more than a memorial to Samuel Cole Williams, one of the state's most prodigious historians. *Tennessee During the Revolutionary War* is the only book-length treatment of this important era and locale; and despite the scholarly shortcomings that are visible to contemporary historians, the work constitutes a valuable historical record. It has long been out of print and is increasingly rare.

The new material found in the present edition will, we hope, enhance the value of the book even more. In addition to this introduction, in which the Judge's life and this particular book are surveyed, new contributions include a corrected and expanded index, a bibliography of Judge Williams' writings, and two new maps. Muriel C. (Mrs. Hal T.) Spoden of Kingsport, who had earlier produced a separate supplement to the original index, consented to prepare an entirely new index for the present work. It is an excellent addition. The helpful bibliography that follows the introduction is the work of Pollyanna Creekmore, documents librarian of East Tennessee State University; it appeared initially in the East Tennessee Historical Society's *Publications* 20 (1948), 9–15, and is reprinted here with permission of the editors. The most important illustrations of the original edition have been retained and in some cases expanded. For instance, the rough map by Colonel Christian, facing page 54, is reproduced here in its entirety; and in Appendix B will be found all three pages, rather than just two, of Nathaniel Gist's talk to the Cherokee chiefs. Of particular value to the present-day reader, however, are the maps added: the large map appearing on the end sheets and following page 82, prepared especially for this publication, and the Kings Mountain map following page 142. Finally, the volume has, in this republication, been given an attractive new cover and jacket. In terms of the basic text, however, the owner of the present edition holds a facsimile of the original work.

When the Tennessee Historical Commission published Samuel Cole Williams' *Tennessee During the Revolutionary War* in 1944, the eighty-year-old author already had written scores of articles and thirteen books, and he had directed the compilation of the authoritative *Annotated Code of Tennessee* published in eight volumes. In the next three years he wrote eight articles, revised his book on William Tatham, and almost completed his account of the Southwest Territory, the projected fourth volume of his studies in the history of Tennessee to 1796.[1] Williams' success as a historian capped a career that included his rise to eminence in his chosen profession of law, appointment as associate justice of the Supreme Court of Tennessee, involvement in business and civic affairs of upper East Tennessee, and designation as first dean of the Lamar School of Law of Emory University.

Born in Gibson County, Tennessee, January 15, 1864, Williams received his early education in the schools of Humboldt. Encouraged by Judge (later Justice) Horace Lurton, a friend of the family, young Williams enrolled in the Vanderbilt University School of Law and received his degree in 1884. The same year he began practice with the firm of Sam Kirkpatrick and John H. Bowman in Jonesboro, Tennessee. The firm's clients included some of the more prosperous businessmen and corporations in southwest Virginia, western North Carolina, and eastern Tennessee. After the death of his partners, Williams moved to Johnson City which, in 1892, was in the process of becoming the hub of economic activity in the tri-state area.[2]

Williams' practice grew and with it his reputation. In 1913, for example, he served on a planning committee of the American Bar Association. During these years, like many successful lawyers, he took advantage of opportunities to invest in real estate and established enterprises. On occasion he took the lead in

---

[1] Interview with Mrs. Robert R. Miller, daughter of Judge Williams, Johnson City, July 3, 1973. Other books in the series were *Dawn of Tennessee Valley and Tennessee History* (Johnson City: The Watauga Press, 1937); *History of the Lost State of Franklin* (Johnson City: The Watauga Press, 1924); and *Tennessee During the Revolutionary War* (Nashville: Tennessee Historical Commission, 1944).

[2] Billy Joe Crouch, "Judge Samuel Cole Williams, Businessman, Lawyer-Jurist, Dean, and Historian" (master's thesis, East Tennessee State College, 1956), 1–2.

launching new businesses and banks.[3] In short, Williams became both a successful lawyer and a successful businessman. His reputation as a lawyer stemmed from thorough preparation. He knew the law, the precedents, his clients, and his opposition. W. F. Guinn recalled that the judge spent hours trying to anticipate the points opposing counsel would bring up, and rarely did he lack a counter argument. Williams concentrated on his work in court and out. He had little time for the usual small talk, exchange of gossip, ribaldry, and tall tales often associated with members of the bar. He did not engage in histrionics, badger witnesses, or try to intimidate the opposition. He asked witnesses pointed questions. He explained his case, the law, and the decisions bearing on it. His summations were concise yet comprehensive.[4]

Williams began his judicial career in 1912 when Governor Ben W. Hooper appointed him to substitute for Chancellor Hal H. Haynes of the First Chancery Division of Tennessee. The next year, after some maneuvering, Hooper appointed Williams, an "Independent Democrat" in that era of political turmoil, to fill a vacancy on the Supreme Court of Tennessee. In 1914, the judge was elected for a full term; however, he resigned before it expired.[5]

From 1919 to 1924, Williams served as dean of the Lamar School of Law of Emory University in Atlanta. Opened in 1916 under Acting Dean W. D. Thompson, the school closed during World War I. When it reopened, Dean Williams selected a competent faculty, increased the endowment, augmented the student body, and helped the school meet the standards of accrediting agencies and the American Bar Association. The aloof and dignified lawyer and judge apparently did not awe his students and faculty because they often were guests in his home where they enjoyed food and conversation. One of the students, Robert R. Miller, courted and married the dean's elder daughter, Gertrude. During the Atlanta interlude the dean bought a Fiat to replace an

---

[3] Ibid., 10–30, 38.

[4] Interview with W. F. Guinn, June 21, 1973. Guinn served as clerk in the firm of Miller and Winston in the early 1930s. He later became a member of the firm of Williams, Winston, and Guinn. Paul Fink, "Samuel Cole Williams," *East Tennessee Historical Society's Publications* 20 (1948), 3–8; Crouch, "Williams," 22.

[5] Crouch, "Williams," 28–39.

aging American-made car. Although Williams knew little about cars and avoided driving, his family relished the status symbol. "Father," Mrs. Miller explained, "did not concentrate on the road. He thought about his work."[6]

If the judge did not have a sense of humor, his family did, and, like other families, they reminded the head of the house of his vagaries. When a married couple, close friends of the Williamses, returned from an extended trip, the wife obviously was pregnant and radiantly beautiful. The judge did not notice her condition but embraced her and exclaimed, "My, how well you look. How beautiful! You must give me your recipe!" For years members of the family reminded him of his request for the recipe. In writing about life on the frontier, the judge learned that some families used deerskins to divide the one-room cabins into sleeping compartments when they had overnight guests. He wrote that "ladies retired behind the deerskins." This amused his daughters and when they wished to be excused from the family circle, they requested permission to "retire behind the deerskins."[7]

The details of how, where, when, and why the judge succumbed to the wiles of Clio seem to have gone unrecorded. He wrote in one of his prefaces that he was "startled" to discover his first note "bore the date 'October 20, 1893.' "[8] "It is fairly inferable," to use a favorite phrase of Williams, that his love affair with the muse of history began long before he resigned his deanship in 1924, at the age of sixty, and retired to Johnson City to write the history of Tennessee from earliest times to statehood. In his first article, published in 1897, he dealt with the legal history of Washington County, Tennessee. The second appeared in 1910 when he collaborated with Mrs. James Halliday McCue and N. B. Perkins.[9]

---

[6] Ibid., 41–48. Interview with Mrs. Miller, July 3, 1973.

[7] Interview with Mrs. Miller.

[8] Williams, *Dawn of Tennessee Valley*, x.

[9] Pollyanna Creekmore (comp.), "Bibliography of Historical Writings of Samuel Cole Williams," East Tennessee Historical Society's *Publications* 20 (1948), 9–15. The first article was entitled "Washington County Bar—The First Bar West of the Alleghanies," in Tennessee Bar Association *Proceedings* (1897), 95–111. The second was "The First Community of American-born Freemen and Its Dominion," contributed by Mrs. James Halliday McCue; historical record compiled by N. B. Perkins and S. C. Williams, *Journal of American History* 4 (1910), 541–551. This *Journal of American*

As becomes a competent dean residing in a community of scholars, Williams wrote several articles between 1919 and 1924, and he began collecting material for his grand design. Among his papers are bills from clerks who made copies of journals and documents which are more legible than the judge's scrawl and are easily identified. The going rate for copyists was fifteen cents per page. Had Xerox been available in those days the judge would have needed a much larger competence on which to retire, but he would have had more fun. For translations of Moravian documents he paid $29.22 and $16.15. His daughter remembered that she translated the account of the Chevalier de Lantagnac used in *Early Travels in the Tennessee Country,* and her father acknowledged her help in a footnote. Edmund C. Burnett graciously lent Williams his notes on the state of Franklin and suggested many sources he should consult. Another friend put the judge on the track of the manuscript of Sir Alexander Cuming's journal. Even at that early date a young doctoral candidate sought help in locating material for his dissertation.[10]

By 1920, if not before, Williams came across the trail of William Tatham, a young Englishman who had lived for a while in East Tennessee where he helped draft the petition that Watau-

History was published in Meridian, Connecticut, and is not to be confused with the *Journal of American History* now published by the Organization of American Historians. The article was an address by Mrs. McCue, regent of the Sycamore Shoals Chapter of the Daughters of the American Revolution. The occasion was the unveiling of a monument in memory of the men who settled in East Tennessee, formed the Watauga Association, and later fought at King's Mountain. Internal evidence strongly suggested that Judge Williams wrote most, if not all, of the article.

[10] See letters of Edward A. Henry, Univ. of Chicago Libraries, to SCW, Feb. 9, 1921; W. M. Schwarze, Moravian College and Theological Seminary, Bethlehem, Pa., to SCW, Aug. 24 and 28, and Sept. 7, 1922; Mary R. Reynolds, American Antiquarian Society of Worcester, Mass., to SCW, Aug. 14, 1922; Edmund C. Burnett, Dept. of Historical Research, Carnegie Institution, to SCW, Dec. 11, 1922; Joseph Schafer, Historical Society of Wisconsin, to SCW, June 23 and 30, 1922; Victor H. Paltsits, Chief, American History Div., New York Public Library, to SCW, Nov. 5, 1924; Worthington C. Ford to SCW, Aug. 3, 1922; A. W. Pollard, Keeper, Dept. of Printed Books, British Museum, London, to SCW, April 27 and July 31, 1922; Arthur P. Whitaker to SCW, Sept. 3, 1920. Whitaker earned his degree at Harvard and became a productive scholar. Samuel Cole Williams Papers, Manuscripts Section, Tennessee State Library and Archives, Nashville. All letters hereinafter cited are in this collection unless otherwise stated.

gans addressed to the legislature of North Carolina in 1776. Tatham had fought Indians, surveyed and mapped lands, practiced law, taught school, and made friends with influential men. Fascinated by the man, the judge spent three weeks in the British Museum in 1921 and made another visit in 1929 to do research. This activity resulted in an article, a booklet, an essay in the *Dictionary of American Biography*, and finally, in 1947, a book, *William Tatham, Wataugan*. As usually falls the lot of historians who do considerable writing, Williams became the target of a revisionist. George Melvin Herndon wrote a more realistic and detailed biography. He recognized Tatham as a man of talent, perhaps genius, who was intent on gain but never quite succeeded because he lacked determination and perseverance and an inclination to work hard.[11]

The judge, after he returned to Johnson City, devoted most of his time to historical studies. He took some legal cases that interested him, and, because of declining values of real estate and stocks during the Depression, accepted the offer to codify the laws of Tennessee. Williams, as a perusal of his bibliography attests, worked diligently and enthusiastically. He published six books, numerous articles, and worked on the *Annotated Code* over a period of eight years. He walked to and from his downtown office, and people learned to set their watches by his going and coming. He arrived promptly at nine and left at noon. He worked at home during the afternoon and evening. Descriptions of his office and library fit the stereotype picture of productive writers. Notes, papers, books, and documents cluttered the scene, and the apparent disorder made sense to no one but the creator. The judge took notes on any paper at hand. He scrawled reminders and references on backs of letters—some of his personal correspondence is preserved because he used the backs for notes —proof sheets, the yellow pads so dear to lawyers, checks, envelopes, wrapping paper, and the professional stationery of friends in whose offices he happened to be when he had an idea.

---

[11] Samuel Cole Williams, *William Tatham, Wataugan* (Johnson City: The Watauga Press, 1947), 9–10. George Melvin Herndon, *William Tatham, 1752–1819: American Versatile* (Johnson City: Research Advisory Council, East Tennessee State Univ., 1973). Williams also wrote articles on Cave Johnson and James C. Jones for *Dictionary of American Biography*. See letter of Allen Johnson, editor, to SCW, March 18, 1929.

Occasionally he used notebooks when he did research in libraries. Williams wrote his books in longhand, and his wife typed the smooth copies for the printers. Throughout the years he relied upon the usually accommodating librarians and archivists who supplied copies of letters and documents and checked sources for him.[12]

Williams published his books, with the exception of *Tennessee During the Revolutionary War,* under the colophon of The Watauga Press, which he operated from his home, and the Kingsport Press manufactured them. The printings were not large; consequently, members of the family filled the orders because he could not wrap a neat package and detested the chore. In all likelihood his sales did not cover the cost of printing because of the many complimentary copies he distributed. Although the judge could be generous with his books, he grumbled when genealogists wrote for information and did not include self-addressed stamped envelopes.[13] His forte was compiling, and like many untrained but energetic antiquarians and local historians—buffs and amateurs they are—he could not write well. "It may be well ventured," to borrow from the judge, that he had a cavalier attitude and would not take the trouble to master the scholarly minutiae of style and form. He could have afforded an editor, and he could have saved himself from many mistakes and criticisms. He, as his daughter said, liked dangling participles and resented her calling them to his attention. Some footnotes bore no relation to the texts. He failed to cite sources for quotations on occasion, and at other times he cited the sources incorrectly. The judge did not always tell readers where he found original sources; to the contrary, he resorted to a form of literary cannibalism by often citing one of his own books which contained errors. As a result, students and scholars should be careful when they use his books. Surely he did not intend to be inaccurate or to mislead; he simply was too busy collecting and writing, too happy in his work, and too sure of himself to take the trouble to polish, to check, and to double-check. This is anomalous in contrast with his legal work.

---

[12] Interview with Mrs. Miller; interview with W. F. Guinn; Williams Papers, passim. Adelaide L. Fries to SCW, March 3, 1925, and Aug. 22, 1927; Annie A. Nunns to SCW, Jan. 2, 1940; and LeRoy Reeves to SCW, Nov. 13, 1947.

[13] Interview with Mrs. Miller.

A casual reader can detect a difference in style between Williams' published articles in some of the scholarly periodicals and his books. Thanks to editors' blue pencils, the judge, like many professional historians, appeared to be a more graceful writer than he was.[14]

Elected chairman of the Tennessee Historical Commission in November 1941, Williams became interested in placing historical markers at appropriate places throughout the state and in the preservation of historic sites. He used his position to encourage people, trained and untrained, who shared his love of history, to use their local records and write the stories of their counties. The commission sponsored a number of studies. The judge received complaints and progress reports from time to time, and he prodded the slothful into greater activity. Some of the people never finished their projects. Others did, and at least two studies, written by trained historians, may serve as models for journeymen and apprentices who attempt to write local history.[15] As an example and as an aid to the people writing the histories of their counties and in observance of the sesquicentennial of Tennessee's admission to statehood, Williams wrote *Tennessee During the Revolutionary War*. Failing health necessitated the judge's retirement from the commission in 1946, but a few months before his death he voiced his concern for being left out of the deliberations. William E. Beard, the new chairman, reassured him that he was not ignored and his suggestions and presence always would be welcomed.[16]

Tennessee During the Revolutionary War is an uncritical narrative in which the judge attempted to write the truth as it had been revealed to him after many years of research. In the process he poured a lot of his old wine into a new bottle as a cursory glance at his footnotes will show. He gave some attention to the

---

[14] One editor remembered that he and a colleague "did a considerable amount of editing" on the judge's contributions. Stanley J. Folmsbee to Frank B. Williams, Jr., April 19, 1973; letter in possession of the writer.

[15] Williams Papers, passim. The model histories were Emma Inman Williams, *Historic Madison* (Jackson: Madison County Historical Society, 1946) and Robert E. Corlew, *A History of Dickson County from Earliest Times to the Present* (n.p.: Tennessee Historical Commission and the Dickson County Historical Society, 1956). See also [Daniel M. Robison] "Historical News and Notices," *Tennessee Historical Quarterly* 7 (1948), 91–92.

[16] William E. Beard to SCW, March 28, 1947.

life and manners, if not the morals, of the people about whom he wrote. He overburdened his pages with the names of so many leaders and common folk that had their progeny bought the book they would have made the Tennessee Historical Commission independent of legislative appropriations. Williams beat the drum and blew the trumpet as he recounted the brave deeds of Tennesseans who not only quelled the Indians whose lands they coveted, but also volunteered with much zest for forays into Georgia, South Carolina, Indiana country, North Carolina, and Kentucky when their services and rifles were needed.[17] He emphasized that these early settlers actually earned the name of Volunteers at the beginning of their march toward statehood and that adoption of the term much later was only delayed recognition of the fighting qualities of Tennesseans. He did not overlook the treatment of Tories on the frontier, and he seemed to appreciate the difficulties of the Cherokee. The judge followed the westward trek of James Robertson, John Donelson, and others who did not find the war a hindrance to settling on the banks of the Cumberland River albeit they still had to contend with Indians who resented their encroachment onto the dark and bloody ground.

Reviewers received *Tennessee During the Revolutionary War* with mixed reactions. Samuel M. Wilson, a personal friend of Williams, gave an effusive and highly laudatory summary of the book. St. George L. Sioussat, a professional historian, wrote a straight-forward but uncritical review. Philip M. Hamer, historian at the National Archives and a former professor at the University of Tennessee, acknowledged that the book was "a worth-while addition" to the history of the state, although the study lacked objectivity and perspective and was poorly organized. He observed that the author had not read recent publications about the war, and that footnotes were unreliable. A "conscientious reader," furthermore, could not visualize major developments in Tennessee during the war. W. Neil Franklin of the National Archives, however, cited Williams as the outstanding writer of Tennessee history and described the book as "the best comprehensive account of its subject." Even so, he said, the judge included little social and economic history, had not used

---

[17] Cf. Harriet Simpson Arnow, *Seedtime on the Cumberland* (New York: Macmillan, 1960), 192. "These men were farmers hating war . . . but if it came to a choice between blood and land, they'd risk the blood."

relevant collections, and had not accurately copied many of the quotations. The reviewers further complained about the lack of bibliography and maps.[18]

In the light of the animadversions, more specific examples of the shortcomings are in order, although the judge may be left in the position of being nibbled to death by a duck-like critic. Some historians do not agree that a majority of the early settlers were of English descent and came from Virginia. They argue in favor of Scotch-Irish and North Carolinians.[19] As has been pointed out, Williams did not always give the source of his information and left his readers in ignorance.

At other times, his documentation was contradictory. For example, in footnote 21, page 29, he gave William Tatham as authority for naming Fort Caswell in honor of Richard Caswell and cited the booklet *William Tatham, Wataugan* (1923), page 4. There he gave the source as "Ramsey page —." In the expanded edition of *Tatham* (1947), page 18, he said the same on his own authority but explained that Ramsey confused Fort Caswell with Fort Lee.

The judge, like another lawyer and jurist, John Marshall, was more careful of property rights in the practice of his profession than in his avocation. Most of the information in footnote 12, page 52, should be enclosed in quotation marks.[20] The judge confused the exact location of his quotes in footnote 11, page 77.[21]

[18] Samuel M. Wilson's review, *Tennessee Historical Quarterly* 4 (1945), 176–83; St. George L. Sioussat's review, *American Historical Review* 50 (1944–45), 547–49; Philip M. Hamer's review, *Journal of Southern History* 11 (1945), 107–108; W. Neil Franklin's review, *Mississippi Valley Historical Review* 31 (1945), 631–32.

[19] Williams, *Tennessee During the Revolutionary War*, 1–3. Cf. James K. Huhta, "Tennessee and the American Revolutionary Bicentennial," *Tennessee Historical Quarterly* 31 (1972), 309, 313–14; Stanley J. Folmsbee, Robert E. Corlew, and Enoch L. Mitchell, *Tennessee, A Short History* (Knoxville: Univ. of Tennessee Press, 1969), 48.

[20] See Lyman C. Draper, *King's Mountain and Its Heroes* (Cincinnati: Peter G. Thomson, Publisher, 1881; rpt. Nashville: Blue and Gray Press, 1971), 434.

[21] The quotation in the text is from Lewis Preston Summers, *History of Southwest Virginia, 1746–1786* (Richmond: J. L. Hill Printing, 1903), 264—not p. 265—and the quotation in the note is from p. 266. Williams seemed not to know the use of ellipses. Here and elsewhere he should have used them.

The instructions given by the Virginia Council to Colonel William Christian on August 1, 1776 (page 50) may have come from the *Official Letters of the Governors of Virginia,* Lewis Preston Summers' *History of Southwest Virginia, 1746–1786,* or another source.[22] In writing about John Rains, footnote 11, page 107, Williams cited his *Dawn of Tennessee Valley.* There he gave his source as Ramsey's *Annals,* page 95, but it is found on page 96.

Williams did not always make exact copies of his material when he took notes. His version of the petition from settlers in Fincastle County on page 17 is not a faithful transcription of the original given in facsimile opposite page 16. The excerpt from the petition Wataugans sent to the Provincial Council of North Carolina, July 5, 1776, on page 33 did not agree with the version given in the middle of page 21. The judge did not give an accurate version of Ramsey's account of Mrs. Bean's troubles on page 44. The same may be said for his copying Shelby's address to the troops at King's Mountain on page 151, and the citation from Draper in footnote 30, page 147.

The judge's penchant for egocentric regionalism may have caused him to magnify the role of the over-mountain men at King's Mountain. He can be forgiven if he overstated the case, but readers should keep in mind that the men from Sullivan and Washington counties were outnumbered by Virginians, South Carolinians, and Tarheels from yon side of the mountains.[23] Williams made a mistake when he referred to "Ferguson's repeating rifles." The piece was a single-shot breech-loader, and in all probability the Tories did not have any.[24] The judge never gave much emphasis to military history, but he did recognize

---

[22] Ibid., 240–41.

[23] George C. Mackenzie, *Kings Mountain National Military Park South Carolina,* Historical Handbook Series No. 22 (Washington: National Park Service, 1956), 11; John Richard Alden, *The South in the Revolution, 1763–1789* (Baton Rouge: Louisiana State Univ. Press, 1957), 249–50; Mayo Boatner III, *Encyclopedia of the American Revolution* (New York: David McKay, 1966), 577; Williams, *Tennessee During the Revolutionary War,* 145 and 152.

[24] Williams, *Tennessee During the Revolutionary War,* fn. 45, p. 154. Dudley Pope, *Guns* (London: Spring Books, 1962), 135–36; Boatner, *Encyclopedia of the American Revolution,* 364–65; Mackenzie, *Kings Mountain National Military Park,* 20.

innovations in frontier warfare, such as the three-pronged attack by the Cherokee on East Tennesseans in 1776.[25]

Notwithstanding his mistakes, lack of style, and other failings, Williams cannot be dismissed as an amateur. Although he did not always make as critical an inquiry as he should, obviously he was a tireless worker and by far the most productive writer of Tennessee history. He made few factual errors in proportion to the amount he wrote. He was a valuable friend for historians to have working for them in the historical societies and on the commission. He compiled an enormous amount of information from primary and secondary sources, and he used it. No historian gets the last word because new students and new scholars dig out new sources to revise old material and old interpretations. The works of Samuel Cole Williams remain for the present the point of beginning and the point of departure for those who write the history of Tennessee from the dawn virtually to statehood.

—FRANK B. WILLIAMS, JR.

A BIBLIOGRAPHY OF THE HISTORICAL WRITINGS
OF SAMUEL COLE WILLIAMS

Compiled by Pollyanna Creekmore

Unpublished Works

"Early Emancipation Movement in Tennessee." 29 p. Typewritten. Copy in McClung Collection, Lawson McGhee Library, Knoxville. A copy of notes taken by Judge Williams and placed by him in the library of the East Tennessee State College, Johnson City, Sept. 1946.

"Greeneville College: Its Founders and Early Friends." 63 p. Typewritten. McClung Collection. An address, expanded, delivered at the unveiling of a marker on the site of Greeneville College, at Tusculum commencement, June 1940. 1941.

---

[25] Williams, *Tennessee During the Revolutionary War*, 37–38. Cf. Thomas Lawrence Connelly, "Indian Warfare on the Tennessee Frontier, 1776–1794: Strategy and Tactics," East Tennessee Historical Society's *Publications* 36 (1964), 3–22.

Published Works

1. Original Works

"An Account of the Presbyterian Mission to the Cherokees, 1757–1759," *Tennessee Historical Magazine,* ser. 2, vol. 2 (1930–31), 125–38.
> Contains "An account of my proceedings since I accepted the Indian mission on October 2d, 1758, by Rev. William Richardson."

The Admission of Tennessee Into the Union. Nashville: Tennessee Historical Commission, 1945. 31 p. Reprinted from *Tennessee Historical Quarterly* 4 (1945), 291–319.

Ann Robertson: An Unsung Tennessee Heroine. Nashville: Tennessee Historical Commission, 1944. 8 p. Reprinted from *Tennessee Historical Quarterly* 3 (1944), 150–55.

The Baptists of Tennessee. Co-author with S. W. Tindell. Kingsport: Southern Publishers, 1930. 67 p.
> Foreword and "Tennessee's First Pastor" by S. C. Williams, pp. 1–18.

"Battle of King's Mountain; as Seen by the British Officers," *Tennessee Historical Magazine* 7 (1921–22), 51–66, 104–10.

Beginnings of West Tennessee, in the Land of the Chickasaws, 1541–1814. Johnson City: Watauga Press, 1930. xii, 331 p.

Brigadier-General Nathaniel Taylor. Johnson City: Watauga Press, 1940. 23 p.

"Christian Missions to the Overhill Cherokees," *Chronicles of Oklahoma* 12 (1934), 66–73.
> An address delivered at the dedication of the restored Brainerd Mission Cemetery, near Chattanooga, Nov. 1, 1933.

"Clarksville Compact of 1785," *Tennessee Historical Quarterly* 3 (1944), 237–47.

"Colonel Elijah Clarke in the Tensessee Country," *Georgia Historical Quarterly* 25 (1941), 151–58.

"Col. Joseph Williams' Battalion in Christian's Campaign," *Tennessee Historical Magazine* 9 (1925–26), 102–14.
> Contains "Col. Joseph Williams' Narrative," campaign of

Col. William Christian against the Overhill Cherokee Indians, Sept. to Nov. 1776.

"Conquest of the Old Southwest," Tennessee Historical Magazine 5 (1919–20), 212–15.
A review of Archibald Henderson's book.

Dawn of Tennessee Valley and Tennessee History. Johnson City: Watauga Press, 1937. xi, 495 p.

"Dim Figures in Our Appellate Judiciary," *Tennessee Law Review* 17 (1942), 292–307.
The figures are Howell Tatum, Thomas Emmerson, Samuel Powel, Parry W. Humphreys, William Wilcox Cooke, Archibald Roane, Henry Crabb, and Thomas Lanier Williams.

"Early Iron Works in the Tennessee Country," *Tennessee Historical Quarterly* 6 (1947), 39–46.

"The Farraguts and Tennessee," *Tennessee Historical Quarterly* 5 (1946), 320–27.

"The First Territorial Division Named for Washington," *Tennessee Historical Magazine*, ser. 2, vol. 2 (1931–32), 153–64.

"First Volunteers from the 'Volunteer State,' " *Tennessee Historical Magazine* 8 (1924–25), 132–39.
Defense of Charleston, S. C., 1776.

"A Forgotten Campaign," *Tennessee Historical Magazine* 8 (1924–25), 266–76.
Campaign of Col. John Williams, 1812.

"Fort Robinson on the Holston," East Tennessee Historical Society's *Publications* 4 (1932), 22–31.

"Founder of Tennessee's First Town: Major Jesse Walton," East Tennessee Historical Society's *Publications* 2 (1930), 70–80.
Also published as a contribution to Jonesborough's sesquicentennial, 1930. Reprinted by The Banking and Trust Company of Jonesboro.

"French and Other Intrigues in the Southwest Territory," East Tennessee Historical Society's *Publications* 13 (1941), 21–35.

"General John T. Wilder," *Indiana Magazine of History* 31 (1935), 169–203.

General John T. Wilder, Commander of the Lightning Brigade. Bloomington: Indiana Univ. Press, 1936. viii, 105 p.

"General Richard Winn's Notes, 1780," *South Carolina Historical and Genealogical Magazine* 43 (1942), 201–12; 44 (1943), 1–11.

"Generals Francis Nash and William Lee Davidson," *Tennessee Historical Quarterly* 1 (1942), 250–68.

"Genesis of the Tennessee Supreme Court," *Tennessee Law Review* 6 (1928), 75–85.

"George Farragut," East Tennessee Historical Society's *Publications* 1 (1929), 77–94.

"George Roulstone: Father of the Tennessee Press," East Tennessee Historical Society's *Publications* 17 (1945), 51–60.

"Hazard's Proposed Colony in the Tennessee Country, 1755," *Tennessee Historical Magazine*, ser. 2, vol. 2 (1931–32), 50–61.

"Henderson and Company's Purchase Within the Limits of Tennessee," *Tennessee Historical Magazine* 5 (1919–20), 5–27.

"First Community of American-born Freemen and Its Dominion," contributed by Mrs. James Halliday McCue. Historical record compiled by Williams with N. B. Perkins. *Journal of American History* 4 (1910), 541–51.

Historical Sketch and Dedicatory Address. N.p.: Holston Annual Conference, 1926.
     Dedication of a granite marker at the site of William Nelson's home and of Nelson's chapel where Bishop Asbury first preached in the Tennessee country, 1788. Erected by the S. C. Williams Bible Class of Munsey Memorial Church, Johnson City, on farm owned by Richard Carr, two miles from Johnson City.

History of Codification in Tennessee, Johnson City: Watauga Press, 1932. 51 p. Reprinted from *Tennessee Law Review* 10 (1932), 61–78, 165–79.

History of the Courts of Chancery of Tennessee. Knoxville:

Knoxville Lithographing Co., 1923. 19 p. Reprinted from *Tennessee Law Review* 2 (1923), 6–23.

History of Johnson City and Its Environs. Johnson City: Watauga Press, 1940. 31 p.

History of the Lost State of Franklin. Johnson City: Watauga Press, 1924. xiii, 371 p. Rev. ed., New York: Press of the Pioneers, 1933. xviii, 378 p.

"John Mitchel, the Irish Patriot, Resident of Tennessee," East Tennessee Historical Society's *Publications* 10 (1938), 44–56.

"Judge Horace H. Lurton," *Tennessee Law Review* 18 (1944), 242–50.

The Lincolns and Tennessee. Harrogate, Tenn.: Dept. of Lincolniana, Lincoln Memorial Univ., 1942, 33 p.
Revised edition of article appearing in *Lincoln Herald*.

"The Lincolns in Tennessee," *Lincoln Herald* 43 (Oct. 1941), 2–9; 43 (Dec. 1941), 14–19; 44 (Feb. 1942), 2–9.

"Major General Richard Winn: South Carolinian and Tennessean," *Tennessee Historical Quarterly* 1 (1942), 8–20.

"Military Career of Captain James Shelby," *Filson Club History Quarterly* 15 (1941), 227–38.

"Moses Fisk," East Tennessee Historical Society's *Publications* 20 (1948), 16–36.

"Nashville as Seen by Travelers, 1801–1821," *Tennessee Historical Magazine*, ser. 2, vol. 1 (1930–31), 182–206.

"Nathaniel Gist, Father of Sequoyah," East Tennessee Historical Society's *Publications* 5 (1933), 39–54.

"North Carolina-Tennessee Boundary Line Survey (1799)," *Tennessee Historical Magazine* 6 (1920–21), 118–29.

Phases of the History of the Supreme Court of Tennessee. Johnson City: Watauga Press, 1944. 91 p.

Phases of Southwest Territory History. Johnson City: Watauga Press, 1940. 26 p.

"The Pioneers of Carter's and Holston Valleys, by Judge Samuel C. Williams at Unveiling of Crockett Marker, July 12, 1927," in Zella Armstrong, *Notable Southern Families* (Bristol, Tenn.: King Printing, 1928), V, 493–500.

"Records of Our Earliest Courts," Tennessee Bar Association *Proceedings* 46 (1927), 96–107.

"Shelby's Fort," East Tennessee Historical Society's *Publications* 7 (1935), 28–37.

"The South's First Cotton Factory," *Tennessee Historical Quarterly* 5 (1946), 212–21.

"Stephen Holston and the Holston River," East Tennessee Historical Society's *Publications* 8 (1936), 26–34.

Tennessee During the Revolutionary War. Nashville: Tennessee Historical Commission, 1944. xi, 294 p. Rpt. Knoxville: Univ. of Tennessee Press, 1974.   p.336

"The Tennessee State Flag," *Tennessee Historical Quarterly* 2 (1943), 232–35.

"Tennessee's First Military Expedition (1803)," *Tennessee Historical Magazine* 8 (1924–25), 171–90.

"Tidence Lane—Tennessee's First Pastor," *Tennessee Historical Magazine*, ser. 2, vol. 1 (1930–31), 40–48.

"Washington County Bar—the First Bar West of the Alleghanies," Tennessee Bar Association *Proceedings* (1897), 95–111.

"Western Representation in North Carolina Assemblies, 1776–1790," East Tennessee Historical Society's *Publications* 14 (1942), 106–12.

"William Tatham, Wataugan," *Tennessee Historical Magazine* 7 (1921–22), 154–79. Also published separately. N.d. 26 p.

William Tatham, Wataugan. 2d rev. and limited ed. Johnson City: Watauga Press, 1947. 109 p.

"The Work of Goodpasture: an Appraisal," *Tennessee Historical Quarterly* 2 (1943), 58–60.

2. Edited Works

Adair's History of the American Indians. Johnson City: Watauga Press, 1930. xxxviii, 508 p.

Edited under the auspices of the National Society of the Colonial Dames of America, in Tennessee.

Early Travels in the Tennessee Country, 1540–1800. Johnson City: Watauga Press, 1928. xi, 540 p.

"Executive Journal of John Sevier," East Tennessee Historical Society's *Publications* 1 (1929), 95–153; 2 (1930), 135–49; 3 (1931), 154–82; 4 (1932), 138–67; 5 (1933), 155–77; 6 (1934), 104–28; 7 (1935), 128–64.

"Journal of Events (1825–1873) of David Anderson Deaderick," East Tennessee Historical Society's *Publications* 8 (1936), 121–37; 9 (1937), 93–110.

Lieut. Henry Timberlake's Memoirs, 1756–1765. Johnson City: Watauga Press, 1927. 197 p. Rpt. Marietta, Ga.: Continental Book Center, 1948.

CONTENTS

CHAPTER   PAGE

       PREFACE xxix

    I THE PEOPLE AND MODES OF LIFE 1

   II ONCOMING OF THE REVOLUTION 15

  III MOVES AND COUNTER MOVES—1776 24

   IV TROUBLES BEGIN—1776 32

    V THE CHEROKEE INVASION 35

  VI CHRISTIAN'S CAMPAIGN AGAINST THE CHEROKEES
       (1776) 48

  VII A YEAR BEGINNING IN TURMOIL, ENDING IN
       PEACE (1777) 61

  VIII CIVIL AFFAIRS (1777) 75

   IX A NEW COURSE CHARTED (1778) 81

    X CAMPAIGN AGAINST THE CHICKAMAUGAS (1779) 91

   XI EARLIER SETTLERS ON THE CUMBERLAND . . . 100

  XII ROBERTSON'S CUMBERLAND COLONY (1779–80) . 104

  XIII DONELSON'S "ADVENTURE" AND FLOTILLA
       (1779–80) 110

  XIV EXTENSION OF THE VIRGINIA-NORTH CAROLINA
       LINE—1779 117

   XV CIVIL AFFAIRS (1779) 123

  XVI OVER-MOUNTAIN MEN EARLY IN THE CAROLINAS
       (1780) 128

  XVII THE KING'S MOUNTAIN CAMPAIGN 138

XVIII CIVIL AFFAIRS (1780) 163

  XIX THE CUMBERLAND COMPACT 167

   XX INDIANS SEEK TO DESTROY CUMBERLAND SETTLE-
       MENTS 171

  XXI DOUBLE CALL TO ACTION—1780–1781 . . . 180

  XXII AGAIN IN THE SADDLE (1781) 193

XXIII ANOTHER CALL TO CONFRONT CORNWALLIS . . 195

XXIV TREATY AND TURMOIL (1781) 199

XXV SEVIER'S INDIAN CAMPAIGNING—1782 . . . 205

XXVI LAND BOUNTIES TO SOLDIERS 213

CHAPTER		PAGE
XXVII	The Closing Scenes of War in the East	217
XXVIII	Land Lust Rampant—1782–1783	225
XXIX	Civil Affairs (1782–1783)	232
XXX	Chickasaw Treaty at Nashborough—1783	236
XXXI	In West Tennessee	241
XXXII	The Tennessee Country in Diplomacy	245
XXXIII	Looking to the Future	252

Appendices

A. Excerpt from the *Virginia Gazette* of July 26, 1776 . . 259
B. Nathaniel Gist to the Cherokee Chiefs 260
C. Col. Russell to Col. Preston 261
D. Tatham's Indian Characters 263
E. Agent Robertson to N. C. Commissioners 271
F. Col. Wm. Campbell to Col. Wm. Preston, 1780 . . . 274
G. Gen. Greene's Appraisal of the Western Soldiery . . 275

Index 277

ILLUSTRATIONS

FOLLOWING
PAGE

Petition of Pendleton District,   16
Part of Colonel Christian's rough map, showing the
  route of his troops,   54
Map of the Southern Colonies during the Revolutionary
  War   82
Map of Kings Mountain   142
Excerpt from Virginia Gazette of July, 1776,
  Appendix A   258
Nathaniel Gist's Communication to the Cherokees
  (first and last pages), Appendix B   259

TENNESSEE

During the

Revolutionary War

BY

SAMUEL COLE WILLIAMS LL.D., L.H.D.

*Chairman of the Tennessee Historical Commission
and formerly
Associate Justice of the Supreme Court of Tennessee*

(A Contribution to the Sesquicentennial
Celebration of Tennessee Statehood in 1946)

1944

THE TENNESSEE HISTORICAL COMMISSION

NASHVILLE, TENNESSEE

IN MEMORY OF

Pearl Williams Kelley

A SISTER BELOVED WHO, AS ASSISTANT STATE LIBRARIAN,
DID THE STATE AN ESSENTIAL SERVICE IN BUILDING
UP THE COLLECTION OF MATERIALS RELATING
TO THE HISTORY OF TENNESSEE AND
THE SOUTH.

PREFACE

This volume is intended to fill the gap between the author's *Dawn of Tennessee Valley and Tennessee History* and the *History of the Lost State of Franklin;* or, to be more exact, between January 1, 1776, and the close of the year 1784. It treats of the Tennessee country *during* the Revolutionary War, not merely *in* that war—of civic affairs as well as military. The three volumes will be a record of the history of Tennessee from 1541 to the period of the Southwest Territory, 1789–1796, the last being the year in which the State of Tennessee was organized and admitted into the Union of States.

The purpose has been to treat of the period of the Revolutionary War in a detailed and definitive way. In order to do that, many of the principal archives and libraries in England and America were visited in search of materials. The scope and reach of those investigations were outlined in the Preface to the *Dawn*. They reached from the British Museum, in London, to Madison, Wisconsin, where is the invaluable Draper Collection; south to New Orleans and Charleston, as well as intermediate state capitals and other centers where important materials are to be found.

It will be apparent to the reader that the author considers the battles fought in the West by the men of the Tennessee country to be parts, and material parts, of the War of the Revolution. So far but inadequate attention has been given to the "Revolution in the West" by historians. Roosevelt and Weeks may be deemed exceptions, laying aside state historians who are so frequently quoted in these pages.

Further, it is believed that in this work there is a demonstration that the men of the western waters were efficient factors in winning the war. In this connection, perhaps it should be stated, as an aid to the reader in his appraisal of what is written and of the conclusions stated, that the author is not a descendant of any of the pioneers on the upper reaches of the Tennessee River, or on the Cumberland. However, he has lived in Washington County,

Tennessee, since August, 1889, and he began a study of the history of the region as early as 1891.

The story told in the pages which follow reveals the almost startling fact that this people volunteered and fought battles in behalf of far-distant regions during the Revolution: twice in Georgia, three times in South Carolina, once in North Carolina, once in the Indiana country and twice in the Kentucky country. They earned for their homeland the title "The Volunteer State" many decades before it was bestowed.

In the *Dawn* there was no treatment of the character or modes of life of the people, because of lack of space. What is said in Chapter 1 under that head is applicable to those who lived in the Tennessee country prior to 1776.

As was stated in the Preface of the *Dawn*, if years are spared the author, it is his intention to strike off a "History of the Southwest Territory—1789–1796." Abundant notes, made throughout many years for such a volume, are in hand, and the writer has already contributed to historical journals articles on that period which may serve as chapters, should such a volume ever reach the stage of print.

The copyright and all profits from the present book have been donated to the Tennessee Historical Commission, as a contribution to Tennessee's sesquicentennial celebration of statehood in 1946. It is published by the Commission thus far in advance in order that it may be of aid to writers of county histories in several Tennessee counties. Such histories are being fostered by the Commission as a part of the celebration.

The author is under obligation to his wife, Isabel Hayes Williams, and to his daughter, Gertrude Williams Miller, for their assistance in shaping his manuscript for the printer of this volume.

SAMUEL C. WILLIAMS

"Aquone,"
Johnson City, Tennessee,
January 15, 1944.

CHAPTER I

THE PEOPLE AND MODES OF LIFE

As the curtain was about to fall on the scenes of colonial times and to rise on those of the period of the American Revolution, the farthest westward thrust of white population at any point on the frontiers was on the upper reaches of the Tennessee River—on the Holston, the Watauga and the Nolachucky. There was to be found "the advance guard of civilization, on the farthest border yet pushed out into the western wilderness." [1]

In those settlements and by the aid of their people there was purchased from the Cherokee Indians in March, 1775, that vast domain known as Transylvania which led to the opening up of the Kentucky country and the Cumberland region around French Lick (later Nashville). Having taken a part in the last colonial war, that of Lord Dunmore in 1774, these people of the spearhead were to play a much greater part in the revolutionary struggle, the significance of which has never been fully appreciated or really grasped by historians.

Settlers in the region came in largest part from Virginia; probably seventy-five per cent migrated directly from the Old Dominion; and, if others of Virginian birth be included, the proportion would rise to eighty per cent, approximately. Nature had so dictated. Two nearly parallel mountain ranges, the Blue Ridge and the Alleghany, in Virginia and North Carolina, interposed as deterrents and near-barriers to westward migration by inhabitants of the eastern parts of those two Colonies. What is known as the Valley of Virginia west of the Blue Ridge was a trough through which emigrants flowed to our region from Pennsylvania, Maryland, and Virginia. Beginning at the point where the Shenandoah empties into the Potomac, the current of trade and migration swept up the Shenandoah to the low ridge which divided its waters from those of the upper James, the waters of which interlaced with those of the Staunton, thence to the

---

[1] Reuben G. Thwaites in *Dunmore's War*, xviii.

waters of New River and on over a divide to those of the Holston. Geographic conditions had determined the route to the southwest of an ancient Indian war-path which in turn became the Great Road of white traders to the Cherokee Indians and of emigrants who pressed farther and farther southward. The eastern escarpment of the Blue Ridge in Virginia was not as steep and forbidding as it was in North Carolina. There were numerous usable passes over it: Ashby Gap leading to Winchester in the Valley; Luray Gap leading to New Market; Swift Run Gap leading to Harrisonburg, and Afton Gap leading to Staunton. Two other gaps lower down in Virginia had a more decided influence on migration to the Tennessee country: the one through the Blue Ridge from Lynchburg to Roanoke in the Valley; the other, Fancy Gap near Hillsville leading to the Holston's upper reaches near Wytheville through both of which traveled many emigrants from Virginia "Southside" and the northern tier of counties of North Carolina. Passing down the Holston the route of travel divided after the site of Abingdon was passed. From there the main road was southwest to the Long Island of Holston (known as the Island Road). Another prong ran more southwardly to the Watauga Settlement, through Shoate's Ford of Holston (Bluff City). This road was laid out in 1773 and called "the Watauga Road."

The two mountain ranges within the limits of North Carolina were taller and steeper than they were in Virginia. At the beginning of the Revolutionary War few emigrants from upper North Carolina tried to penetrate them; the longer route through Fancy or Hillsville Gap to Chiswell's Mines and the Holston was preferred.

Virginians, in largest part coming from the Valley, settled north and west of the Holston in the Tennessee country, though some penetrated farther and settled in the region below the South Fork of Holston. This was due mainly to the fact that until 1779 Virginia exercised jurisdiction over the North of Holston Settlements, at least as far west as the Donelson line of 1771; [2] but even so on the Watauga the Virginian element was the largest.[3]

---

[2] This line began on the South Fork of Holston six miles above the Long Island and ran northwesterly. Williams, *Dawn of Tennessee Valley and Tennessee History*, 355 *et seq.*, frequently cited hereafter as the *Dawn*.

[3] The important contribution to the early settlement of the Tennessee

Next in order came the North Carolinians and then South Carolinians.

Of the Virginians those from the tidewater region in number were negligible. The introduction and rapid increase of negro slavery in that colony in the first half of the 1700's pressed many of the yeomen, the small land owning class, into the Piedmont section to the west, and the descendants of some of these found their way through the gaps mentioned above to the settlements in the region that became Tennessee. Scarcely any of such emigrants derived from the gentry of Eastern Virginia.

The racial stocks represented in the settlements were numerous: English, Scotch-Irish, Germans, Irish, Welsh, Huguenots, and at least one Pole.[4] Thus, near the beginning of civilization in the Tennessee country, there was a melting pot in miniature. The English strain undoubtedly predominated and more pronouncedly than historians have conceived. The contribution of the Scotch-Irish has been given over-emphasis.[5] The other stocks rated in the order given above. A few of the inhabitants were foreign born. Most of those of foreign strains were of the second or third generation and not direct immigrants.

country by Pittsylvania County, Virginia, is noteworthy. Emigrants from that and adjoining counties passed through Fancy Gap, as did those from the North Carolina region referred to. The last named passed through the Moravian towns into Virginia and on to the Holston. Some from North Carolina used a lower gap reaching on the way through the neighborhood of Wilkesboro and Boone. This was Boone's Gap, between Zionville, N. C., and Trade, in Johnson County.

[4] Emanuel Sandusky, on the Nolachucky.

[5] The first United States census to give the nativity of the residents of a State was that of 1850. However, the study of an expert, embodied in Rossiter's *A Century of Population Growth, 1790–1900,* led to an estimate that in 1790 there were in Tennessee: Of English origin, 26,519 or 83 per cent of the whole; Scotch-Irish, 3,574 or 11 per cent; German, 894 or 2.8 per cent; Irish (Celtic), 734 or 2.3 per cent; with a sprinkling of Welsh and Huguenot strains. This percentage of the Scotch-Irish cannot fairly be applied to the revolutionary period. The author's belief is that in that era the population had about 25 per cent of Scotch-Irish, almost all of whom came from the Valley of Virginia or from Pennsylvania through that Valley. The proportions assigned to other strains stand as correct, approximately, as applied to the population of the Tennessee country of 1776–84, except, of course, there were some increases or decreases in the several classes from time to time.

The Trek

Emigrants going out to the West in the earlier years necessarily used horses without vehicles. The women-folk and the very young children rode horseback; the men and larger children marched on foot. Packhorses carried the scanty household effects, and the boys aided the men in driving cattle and swine which brought up the rear. Not infrequently a cavalcade composed of several families journeyed together, strung out along the road in single file. Speed was impeded by the livestock, so that twelve miles was a good day's advance. Later on, when roads were cleared of trees, stumps and undergrowth (little else was done) a wagon was used to transport the household effects. At night a camp site was chosen near a spring or small stream and the evening meal, and rations for the next day, were cooked. Guns of course were carried, and the best marksmen of the party would divert from the trail or road to kill game. The carcasses were barbecued the better to preserve the meat for use in following days of the journey. Besides, a supply of cured ham and bacon was often provided at the outset, though wild game was the main dependence. This left more space in the hampers for meal for breadmaking.

However they may have traveled, utilization of all available space was a desideratum; the ingenuity of the womenfolk was taxed in the packing of essential articles. Not the least among these were fruit and vegetable seeds; and many of the wives did not fail to wrap up in bags or rags seeds of their favorite flowers. The men gave attention to providing such things as seeds of corn, wheat and tobacco.

Homes

The newcomer contented himself with a one-room log cabin with a "lean-to" in the rear, and a rude log barn for his livestock and a crib for his corn and fodder. Materials for such were immediately at hand in the widespread forests, from which seventy or eighty of the tallest and straightest small trees were felled. The men of the neighborhood assembled and freely lent aid. Commonly, the dimensions of the cabin were twenty feet long by sixteen feet in width. At each end of the logs deep notches were cut so as to hold them more securely. Many cabins at first had earthen floors, though later these were succeeded by puncheon floors. The roofs were usually of long clapboards of white-oak which, iron nails lacking, were held in place by long ridge-poles or by wooden pegs. Doors and windows were sawed out after the walls were finished, and their edges were cased with slabs to keep the wall-logs from sagging, wooden pins securing the slabs. There was no glass for the windows; wooden shutters sufficed. A huge fireplace was constructed of flat limestone, as was also the hearth. The chimneys were built of smaller flat stones or sticks, chinked with clay. All crevices in the walls were stopped up with mud or clay. The ceiling was seldom above seven feet above the floor. This left room above for a loft in which the boys of the family slept; it was reached by a rude ladder built in one corner of the main room.

During the progress of the Revolutionary War homes were much improved: the cabins were enlarged by adding duplicates to the first; or the original structure was made to serve as an outhouse and replaced by a story and a half log-house of much ampler proportions.[5]

The furnishings of such homes were quite as simple as the cabins themselves. The earlier tables were of large clapboards set on wooden legs. Some of the chairs were short sections sawed from the trunk of a tree, hickory or oak, usually; but others were but three-legged stools, though in the better homes regular chair frames with splint bottoms appeared and displaced the humbler ones. The bed frame first in use was held up at one side by supports driven into logs of the wall, on which were laid slabs of wood, and on these was placed a bedtick filled with straw or pine needles, covered by blankets of skins of the bear or other animals. Spoons, in the earlier times, were whittled out of horn or wood, and pocket or hunting knives served in some families for table use. Plates were of pewter or wood. The humble gourd served a variety of purposes. On wooden pins, inserted in the wall-logs, rested the trusty rifles and the powder horns of the father and sons. From like pegs or from the antlers of a deer were suspended the clothing of the family.

As the Revolutionary War drew towards its close, the homes of the pioneer of the better class materially improved, as did also the household equipment. Full two-story houses appeared, but

---

[5] For this development, see Williams, *History of the Lost State of Franklin*, chapter XXXIII.

they, too, were built of logs. Weatherboarding, stone and brick were yet later sometimes used in the construction of walls of the houses.

Dress

The men on the fringe of the border, such as the Wataugans of the earlier years, for dress necessarily depended largely on what the locality supplied. For this reason their costumes were much like those of the Indians. The hunting shirt was generally of dressed deer skin, and fitted loosely, open in front and so wide as to lap over a foot or more when belted, so that between the bosom and the garment there was space which could be used as a wallet for bread, jerked meat or other necessities. This shirt reached half way down the thighs and was fringed at the bottom with deer skin or cloth dyed [6] various colors. In the summer the hunting shirts were of linsey or osnaburg,[7] a coarse linen, which could also be worn in bitter winter weather beneath the deer-skin shirt or jacket. From the belt, which was tied behind, was suspended on the right side a hatchet and on the left side a hunting knife, each in a scabbard. Trousers were of the same material as the shirt. The foot-gear quite of necessity in the earlier years, was the moccasin made of dressed buckskin, the seams sewed with whang-strips of tough skin or leather.[8]   As protection against weather, briars and snakes, leggings were worn; these were wide strips of deer-skin wrapped around the legs, from ankle to a point above the calves where they were bound with thongs.

The womenfolk had a narrow range of materials for their dresses: linsey (linsey-woolsey), osnaburg, or, in exceptional cases, a finer linen. Their skill and taste were brought into play in dyeing the fabrics to produce variety. Few indeed were the jewels or objects of adornment.

---

[6] Dye-stuffs came from the bark and roots of trees and shrubs.

[7] Manufactured in Osnabruck, Prussia, imported and widely used by the borderers.

[8] The awl was an absolute necessity; it was a part of almost every kit, for use at home or on hunt or journey, in the making or repairing of moccasins. In bitter cold weather moccasins were sometimes stuffed with deer hair or moss. The sponginess of the encasing leather allowed moisture to penetrate. Rheumatism was one of the chief ills of the frontiersmen.

As the War of the Revolution progressed the population grew and the stocks of merchandise for sale in the region offered a wider range of choice. Herds of cattle increased and the tanning of leather for shoes and boots was begun. The growth of flocks of sheep gave wool for carding, spinning and knitting; also for the making of a coarse jeans for men's clothing. Throughout the period, all garments were home-made, cut by pattern by some of the more skilled of the women of the neighborhood.

Merchants

At the beginning of the revolutionary period there were only two merchants in the Tennessee country: Evan Shelby at Sapling Grove and John Carter on the Watauga; both of their establishments dated back to the early 1770's. However, before 1783 David Deaderick began merchandising at Jonesborough and his business gradually enlarged until it ranked first in the region. In the same year, Thomas Amis was engaged in merchandising on Big Creek, near the present-day Rogersville; his book of accounts is yet in the hands of a descendant in his home which is standing today in a good state of preservation. No doubt there was a small store at Greeneville, as early as 1784. In 1782 Lardner Clark began merchandising at Nashborough, as the town's "first merchant."

Slavery

Even in the years of the Watauga Association there were black slaves on the western waters. Well circumstanced men, such as William Bean, John Carter and George Lumpkin, owned slaves. Records yet in existence show this to be true. However, the average early settler was too poor to acquire that species of property. As they accumulated a degree of wealth, and cleared and cultivated more and more land, some men of this class owned a few slaves, but at all times the large majority held none. Cotton was not a crop that was suited to the soil and climate, and to its culture blacks in the Carolinas and Virginia's "Southside" had been trained. The records of the courts evidence that slaves were dealt in, even between residents. Most of the blacks were owned by farmers living in the richer valleys.

Large families being the rule, sons and in emergencies daughters in some families assisted in field work.

Agriculture and Other Pursuits

The raising of corn was the earliest and chief pursuit in agriculture. Often the planting preceded the actual removal of the family, and the corn field pressed closely on the clearing for the cabin site. Raising and reaping of wheat were difficult in the stump-studded fields, and that cereal made its way early but much more slowly. Some of the settlers who migrated from such counties in Virginia as Augusta and Botetourt had some skill in the raising and handling of hemp, which product had there received governmental encouragement by way of a subsidy. Enough was raised in the new homeland for a domestic supply. The hackling and other processing was done by the women. The thread served as warp in the home-making of woolen clothes. Hemp, however, never gained the hold in the Tennessee country that it did in Kentucky. The culture of tobacco was brought to the region by settlers who came from Virginia's "Southside" and Piedmont, but it, too, constituted only a crop for home use. The markets for the weed on or towards the Atlantic coast were too far away for economic transportation.[9]

Only one among the contemporaneous residents in the region left any account of agricultural activities and methods used there. William Tatham,[10] writing in 1800, after his return from the region to England, said: "I remember on the Nolochuckie [Nolachucky] River, in 1777, to have noticed the following course of rotation of crops: 1. Turnips in the autumn. 2. Flax sown in the spring. 3. Corn holed among the flax. All these were followed by the indigenous crab grass. I had a small meadow of timothy grass during the hard winter of 1779–80,

---

[9] The day was far-off and unforeseeable when a bright burley tobacco would become a major money crop of the region, from which cigarettes, then unknown, would be manufactured by the billions, annually.

[10] *Communications Concerning the Agriculture and Commerce of the United States,* (London, 1800). For a sketch of Tatham, see note p. 13 *post.* Tatham also commented on "a thing unknown in England: the turning of a flock of turkeys into the wheat fields, also hogs, as gleaners following the reaping of the crops;" and on lands, brought to a good state of cultivation, selling for a dollar and one-third per acre. He had a farm on the Nolachucky in 1779—seemingly acquired in 1777, near Fort Williams and the site of John Sevier's future home, "Mount Pleasant" (1780). Pp. 151–3.

which I purchased of a German . . . and it had not been sown more than two years. This grass is cultivated everywhere by the Germans and in most places by the Irish."

Water mills for the grinding of corn were early introduced; they were built and operated under a franchise from the county court, a legally fixed toll being charged—the first public service industry in the country.[11] The blacksmith and the gunsmith were held in high esteem; and essential handicrafts flourished.

Live Stock

The main reliance of the bordermen for money and merchandise was cattle, raised on the range, and feeding largely on the native grasses and the green cane that abounded along the streams. These streams were fed by never-failing springs and afforded the cattle water of the best quality.[12] Turning cattle out to range in the winter, while almost compelled by conditions, tended to the degeneracy of the herds through promiscuous and early breeding.[13] The cattle were driven to markets northward in the Valley of Virginia, and many finally reached such centers as Philadelphia and Baltimore. The horse was a prime desideratum. Those animals "were the universal means of traffic and pleasure. Every farmer's son keeps his horse of convenience, and the trade of horseswapping is as nearly unlimited as the circle of society whose occasions this noble animal accommodates." (Tatham). It is more than probable that a strain of the noted Chickasaw breed of horses found its way into the settlements during the Revolution; but not so of the Virginia thoroughbred which was introduced a few years after the close of the war.[14]

Horses, as well as cattle, were driven to markets in the East and in the Carolinas where a ready sale was found.

---

[11] These were located on creeks since the mills were small, and many of the creeks had falls sufficient to run the wheels. Before the appearance of such mills, mortars and pestles of wood were used to crush grain into coarse meal.

[12] See Isaac Shelby's remarks on the pioneers keeping livestock on the range, *post*, p.

[13] Tatham, "I remember an instance or two on the frontiers during the early settlement, in the year 1776, where a calf produced another calf at the age of 19 months. Everybody must know the unavoidable effects which must flow from such." *Ib.*, p. 96.

[14] Apparently, about 1788.

Dietary

Corn was truly the staff of life [15] throughout the period. Varieties of the common vegetables were raised largely by the women of the families. Apples, peaches, and plums gradually came into use and increasingly as orchards aged. For meat the reliance was upon wild game, large and small, until herds and flocks had time to increase; then meat from domestic animals and fowls gave variety to diet.[16] The use of wild game, however, continued general and perhaps predominant. The killing of such constituted a sport for the men and boys, and the skins were used as floor rugs, bed-covering and for many other purposes. The forests afforded a variety of nuts, wild grapes and persimmons.

Religion and Education

At the beginning of the Revolution there was only one house of worship in the entire region—Taylor's "meeting house" [17] in which all denominations worshiped. Ministers of the Gospel resident in the region were very few in number. Settlements were so sparse that it was difficult to form congregations and build churches.

Before congregations were formed and churches erected, not a few of the people yearned to hear the Gospel preached. When a Joseph Rhea, Samuel Doak, Tidence Lane or a Henry Willis did appear in their midst, the people heard him gladly. This heart hunger was felt by the women more than by the men, not for themselves only, but for their children. They did not want their off-spring to grow up uninfluenced by the religion of the Nazarene. An outstanding example was an occurrence in 1772–3, when an itinerant preacher passing through the border region was called upon by Mrs. James Robertson to baptize her own younger children and those of her neighbor, the wife of Daniel Boone.

A young Methodist preacher, Henry Ware, came into the region in 1787 and left a book of *Memoirs*. What he recorded applies to our period:

---

[15] Parched, roasting ear, in pone, mush, lye hominy, and johnny cake. The distilling of corn into spirituous liquor began about the time mills were built.

[16] Tatham was astonished at the large amount of meat consumed, and remarked on it.

[17] Built in 1773 above the site of present-day Blountville. Williams, *The Dawn*, 379, 427.

I went down to the lowest settlement on Holston. I found the people assembled in several places, in a state of great alarm, devising means of defense against an enemy from whom they expected no mercy. Many seemed struck with astonishment that I should hazard my life to visit them at such a time. They were full of kindness, heard with interest, and guarded me from place to place as I traveled about.

There were many in this circuit who manifested a desire to have Him [Christ] the God of their children, and therefore presented them to be baptized. . . . The hearts of the parents were usually touched when their children were dedicated to God. . . . There were so many children presented for baptism that I gave up the keeping of a list.

The same deterrent factors applied to education; teachers and school houses were few. The progress made along both lines is attempted to be outlined in later chapters. It was painfully slow; necessarily so under the conditions.

Character of the People

Nearly all of the inhabitants before their coming out had been frontiersmen—most of them were sons of frontiersmen—and inured to the hard conditions of border life. Fate had given very few of them even a glimpse of soft surroundings. The lesson-task set for them in a new land was but a sequel to a former one, well conned even though now less difficult.

Those who ventured out were the more daring and enterprising in the old communities. Also they were, on the average, young people possessed of buoyancy and eagerness, well suited to the conquering of a land that was itself young and full of promise for courageous souls.

In near isolation behind the ramparts of two mountain ranges, they were denied access to the sea for commerce and occupations, but to the west of them billowed away greener waves than those of the Atlantic—mountains, ridges, hills and valleys clad in tall forests which reached to the Mississippi. Here was their challenge. Here, truly, they were to make history—and on a large scale. The challenged were in boldness and resolution quite equal to the undertaking. Three foes were to be overcome: Nature's obstacles, wild animals and the Indians. All but the last, on being subjugated, gave succor to the conquerors; the Indians were to leave many a crimson scar and to give the kiss of death to a multitude of the whites before yielding up the land.

A large portion of the early settlers had been denied the privileges of an education; the percentage of illiteracy was by no means low; but few were ignorant. Worldly wisdom distilled in homely proverbs was a part of their inheritance, and common sense was a ready fulcrum. They were as a whole observant, quick-witted and inquisitive. To a high degree they were self-reliant, having faith in themselves. Realizing that they constituted an entering wedge, their entrance into the West served as a tonic. It aroused new or deepened old ambitions. A new fire coursed through their veins.

Parts of their creed were a militant individualism and a feeling of independence that bordered on fierceness. They were not disposed to hesitate or to hold to niceties of propriety, or at times even of justice when dealing with the Indians.

There was on the part of many of the early settlers an innate antipathy towards the redman. This prevented their seeing straight. On the part of the Indians, particularly the younger ones, there was nothing lacking to make the dislike mutual. The lower order of the whites were most inveterate in this regard; but this was true of every frontier in America. This class was purblind and raw-hearted in dealing with Indians, who in their view had few rights to be respected. Race antagonism led to forays and not infrequently to wars. Injuries to either side were nursed, festered and cumulated.

The thing most to be remarked about this people was the far-reach of their vision and their ability to follow through and take seizin—"to have and to hold"—qualities they transmitted to their children and grandchildren. The spirit of expansion even persisted until far-away Texas was reached and Robertson's Colony was there launched in 1826. The first generation swarmed and founded the settlements on the Cumberland and at other places in Middle Tennessee, and materially aided in the settlement of Kentucky and other States of the Old Southwest.

The virility of the stock manifested itself also in leadership and a mastery over men. Four of the early settlers of the region became brigadier-generals, two of them (Robertson and Sevier) holding that rank in the army of the United States; Isaac Shelby became the first governor of Kentucky, and John Sevier the governor of the State of Franklin and the first governor of the State of Tennessee, and William Cocke became the first senator in

Congress from the last named State. The succeeding generations furnished the first two United States senators and a governor to Missouri, the first governor and a United States senator to Arkansas, and a first senator to Indiana.

Hospitality was more than a thing of grace. One who shared it has left the best and most intimate account. A brilliant young Englishman, William Tatham,[18] a scion of a noble house (headed by the Earls of Lonsdale) appeared among this people in April, 1776. In after years he wrote:

In thirty years knowledge I have witnessed an almost universal open door to the stranger, the needy and the man of frank and inoffensive demeanor. I can also vouch for their promptitude to resent intended insult, to treat the appearance of arrogance with contemptuous roughness, and to be mulish in a refusal of what they think extorted from them by coertion or required by means of unfair traffic. . . . I scarce know a door that I could not enter as my home in the hour of distress. . . .

I personally knew the country beyond the Alleghanies from April, 1776. If I may be allowed to speak of facts which, with grateful recollection, I feel it a duty to attest, and can say with truth, and honest pride, that I owe nearly all I know to their tuition: I went among them a stranger and they took me in . . . I was homeless and they gave me one common shelter; I was bewildered in the forest; they conducted my footsteps. I believe

[18] See Williams, *William Tatham, Wataugan,* for a fairly full sketch; also another by the same writer in the *Dictionary of American Biography.* Tatham left England at the age of seventeen years; and, shortly after landing in Virginia, made his way up James River and entered the employment of the mercantile firm of Carter & Trent, in 1769. Early in 1776 he was sent by John Carter, of that firm, to his store on the site of Elizabethton. The young man took part in the defense of Fort Caswell (Watauga Fort) in 1776; drafted for the Wataugans their petition to North Carolina to be received under the government of that State; he assisted in keeping the minutes at the treaty with the Cherokees at Long Island in 1777; he aided in the defense of the region as a scout or ranger in the same year, evidently largely upon the Nolachucky, stationed, perhaps, at Fort Williams. After several years on the border and in Virginia, he returned to England, and, as a civil engineer, was placed in charge of the construction of the great Wapping Docks in the Thames at London. There he wrote several volumes on Agriculture, Political Economy, Tobacco, Canals, etc., and his writings have been of material aid in the preparation of this work. His works were consulted in the British Museum in London and the author has since acquired two of his books, all of which are rare and high-priced. It is doubted whether a complete set can be found in any American library, public or private.

the great bulk of the inhabitants to be among the most useful and orderly citizens belonging to the American States. I also am a *backwoodsman* and am present to answer.[19]

The women of this people were almost as sturdy as the men. Working at household or garden tasks, they did so in the shadow of a red threat of disaster. Deep in their sons and daughters they stamped the sigil of fortitude. There was given to infants at the breast iron-tinctured blood—that dark quintessence of manhood and womanhood that nerved to surmount difficulties and adversities without qualm or quailing.

It is the life of this folk through nine years on the outer fringe of settlement that this volume attempts to *record*, a part to rescue. In their experiences was a queer commingling of stark conflict and yet a close kinship with Dame Nature.

---

[19] Tatham, *Ib.*, 83, 151–153.

CHAPTER II

Oncoming of the Revolution

As the American Revolution was approaching crisis, the inhabitants of the Tennessee country were settled in three groups: (1) those residing north of the Holston River and east of Donelson's line; [1] (2) those west of that line whether east or west of the river, and (3) all below the Holston, whether on the south waters of that stream or on the Watauga and Nolachucky. The North of Holston settlers were deemed and treated as under the jurisdiction of Virginia until 1779, and the others were not. The first named had the protection of a treaty negotiated by Virginia with the Cherokee Indians; the two last named were not, their homes and lands being held in violation of law—the prohibiting proclamation of 1763 restrained the North of Holston settlers from extending their holdings beyond the Donelson line, and this they resented.

Strong economic reasons impelled the Tennessee people to join in the cause of independence. All desired to be free from the trammels of the proclamation and British policy. Too, all were settled within the limits of Lord Granville's grant,[2] which was owned by a non-resident noble family; this grant hung like a cloud over any title they might acquire, whether by possession or by a conveyance from the Cherokees. It was the hope of all that a revolution would remove these barriers. These incentives were joined with a genuine inclination towards the cause of America against the King and parliament of Great Britain.

The earliest action in that direction by any of the Westerners was the participation of the North of Holston settlers in the

---

[1] This line began at a point on the Holston six miles above the Long Island and ran northwestwardly towards the mouth of the Kanawha River. Williams, *Dawn of Tennessee Valley and Tennessee History*, Ch. 29. The beginning point was designed by the Cherokees to preserve to themselves the Long Island of Holston, a place much revered and tenaciously held by them.

[2] See Williams, *op. cit.*, ch. 26 and *passim*.

meeting of the Freeholders of Fincastle County, Virginia, held on January 20, 1775, which assembly approved of the Association framed by the Continental Congress in behalf of all the Colonies.[3]

Fincastle County at the time, as said, exercised actual, though extra-legal, jurisdiction over the North of Holston settlements which were really within the limits of North Carolina, and Captain Evan Shelby of Sapling Grove (the present Bristol, Tennessee) represented and spoke for his people in the Fincastle meeting. He was named a member of the Committee appointed to see that the Resolves were "carried punctually into execution."

The inhabitants south of the Holston were actually still under the independent government of the Watauga Association.[4] They feared that a war with Great Britain might bring down on them the Cherokees then under British influence. Their settlements were more exposed to a red invasion than their neighbors above the Holston, yet they moved late in 1775 (or in January following) in an adherence to the revolutionary movement and formed a committee of safety, composed of thirteen members[5] of which John Carter was chairman. In their dangerous situation, they began to feel concern for a governmental connection with Virginia or North Carolina from which aid in a time of stress might be expected. That concern was deepened by the knowledge that among them were Tories, a few on the Watauga and yet more on the Nolachucky.

West of Donelson's line and in Carter's Valley[6] the settlers preferred a connection with Virginia, though like the Wataugans they were located within the boundary of North Carolina. They, too, proceeded to organize their own committee of safety. Both committees appear to have been created early, since the Wataugans stated in their petition to North Carolina in the following year that "the purchase of the Cherokees was no sooner made (in

---

[3] The Resolves of the meeting, held at Chiswell's Mine, contained this language: "We cannot think of submitting our liberty or property to the power of a venal British Parliament or to the will of a corrupt ministry. . . . We declare that we are deliberately and resolutely determined never to surrender them to any power upon earth but at the expense of our lives."

[4] For an account of which see Williams, *Dawn*, ch. 30 and *passim*.

[5] Appended to the Petition of the Inhabitants, *post*.

[6] Tatham wrote that the settlements west and south of the Holston had not progressed beyond the mouth of Big Creek at this time.

To the Honourable, the Convention of the Colony of

Virginia

The Petition of the Inhabitants of Pendleton District
situate to the west of part of Fincastle County, humbly sheweth
that your Petitioners, being deeply impressed with the sense of the
tyranical & oppressive Measures agitated by the British ag.st the
ag.nst his allegiance to go.r Subjects in America; & more of the
Necessity of so noble a Resistance as is presently carried on by the
Colonies, think it unnatural that they tho' few, being equally int.r
ested in the common Cause should be intirely inactive while their
Brethren are brave bleeding in the field: But the best situation of
your Petitioners unhappily depriving them hitherto of the blessings
being under the Immediate Direction of any regularly constituted
Judicature; when by they would, in a proper Channel, contribute their
mite to support the glorious Cause; they have (more) themselves
into a society & after the Pattern of the several Virginia Counties
have chosen a Committee to superintend their publick affairs

there, whom to petition your Honourable Honors; praying that altho Sir afsidy has forced them, in order to provide an honest and comfortable Subsistence for themselves & Families, to settle without the Limits hitherto purchased by Government from the Indians, they may not be considered as alienated there by from their Honorable Brethren; but be incorporated into and deemed to be a Part of your respectable Colony, taken under your Protection, Direction and Jurisdiction; in default of all, by faith, promising the Strictest Attention & Obedience to all your Laws & Ordinances & a Chearful Contribution of their Quota of the general Expences,

And that your Honor may graciously receive our
Petition & the noble Cause of American Liberty to assert
with Glory and Honours, Your Petitioners shall ever
pray &c
John Coulter Chairman

At a Meeting of the Committee for Fincastle County at James McLure's on Tuesday the Twenty Third day of February 1776. Present Fifteen Members.

Petitions from sundry of the Inhabitants of Fincastle district lying to the Westward of Donaldsons Line, setting forth their strong Attachment to the American Cause, their Desire to be incorporated with this Colony Subject to the same Regulations, their Willingness to pay their proportionable part of the Publick Expences. This Committee taking the same under their Consideration are of Opinion their Petitions are Reasonable, that they ought to be prefer'd to the Next Convention by the Delegates for the County.

William Preston Chairman

Abraham Trigg Clk Committee

Copy

March, 1775) than we were alarmed by the reports of the unhappy differences between Great Britain and America, on which
report we proceeded to choose a committee, which was done
unanimously, etc." [7]

The inhabitants near the Long Island assumed for the community the name of "Pendleton District," in honor of the Virginia
patriot and statesman, Edmund Pendleton.[8]

Their petitions were sent to the revolutionary government of
Virginia. One of them, undated, was acted upon by the conven-
tion of the people of Fincastle County on February 23, 1776.
The petition contained the following:

Your Petitioners being deeply impressed with the sense of the
tyranical and oppressive measures agitated by the British Ministry against his Majesty's local subjects in America, and also of
the Necessity of so noble a Resistance as is spiritedly carried on
by the Colonies, think it unnatural that they, tho' few, being
equally interested in the common cause should be intirely inactive, while their Brethren are bravely bleeding in the Field:
But the local situation of your Petitioners unhappily depriving
them heretofore of the Blessings of being under the Immediate
Direction of any regularly constituted Judicature, whereby they
could, in a proper channel, contribute their mite to support the
glorious Cause; they have formed themselves into a Society, and
after the Pattern of several Virginia Counties, have chosen a
Committee to superintend their publick affairs thro' whom to petition our Honorable House, praying that they be made a Part of
your respectable Colony, taken under your Protective Direction
Jurisdiction in its fullest Extent promising the strictest Obedience to all your Laws and Ordinances and a cheerful Contribution of their Quota of the general Exigencies. John Coulter,
Chairman.[9]

The first petition of the Wataugans for their incorporation into
one of the Colonies on the seaboard was also sent to the government of Virginia, but it failed of bringing the desired result. A
majority of the inhabitants were natives of or migrants from
Virginia; particularly was this true of the leaders. That people

---

[7] See the Petition of the Committee, and the Inhabitants of July 5,
1776, *post*.

[8] Who owned a large boundary of land in the vicinity of the present
city of Kingsport, where his nephew, Gen. Edmund Pendleton Gaines,
successor of Andrew Jackson as major-general of the U. S. Army, was
brought up.

[9] From the manuscripts in Archives of Virginia. See illustration.

had chosen Virginia laws as the basis of their own laws, and late in 1775, or early in January, 1776,[10] they had chosen the name "Washington District" for their region, the first to be named in honor of George Washington, who had just been made commander of the American Army.[11] The substance of their petition is shown by the action of the Virginia Convention:

On May 23, 1776, a representation was received from inhabitants of some late purchases on the Rivers Wattaugah and Holston, setting forth that they are deeply impressed with a sense of the distress of their American brethren, and will, when called upon, with their lives and fortunes lend every assistance in their power; that they beg to be considered as a part of this Colony, and will readily embrace every opportunity of obeying any instructions or commands they may receive from the Convention.[12]

The fact that this application was made to Virginia escaped the historians of Tennessee, significant as it was. Discouraged by their failure in Virginia, in the first half of 1776 (probably in June) the Wataugans held a meeting at which it was determined to apply to North Carolina to be received under her protection. A petition to that end was prepared to be sent to the Provincial Council of that government. It was signed by over one hundred of the settlers. It was written by William Tatham[13] who was

[10] One of the petitions of the inhabitants of Pendleton District, evidently drafted in January, 1776, referred to the "neighbouring settlement called Washington District."

[11] Williams, "The First Territorial Division Named for Washington," in the *Tennessee Historical Magazine, Series II, Vol. II, 153–169.* A number of those whose names were appended to the petition had served as colonial soldiers of Virginia before removal to the Tennessee country; their names appear in the George Washington Manuscripts: Wm. Brooks, John Brown, James Cooper, John Davis, George Russell and Thomas Simpson. Others are listed as colonial soldiers of Virginia. Doubtless, some of these had served under Washington during the French and Indian War, and were eager to honor him so far as it lay in their power. Ramsey, indulging in surmise, says, "the name was probably suggested by John Sevier." In this instance there is some slight confirmation, in the article last cited, p. 161.

[12] Force, *American Archives* (series 4), VI, 1533–35. The words "on Holston," refer to settlers south of that river, who fell in the jurisdiction of the Watauga Association.

[13] Ramsey (*Annals*, p. 134) thought that "the document appears to be in the handwriting of one of the signers, John Sevier." Here the historian was in error. We have this statement of Tatham in a London publication *Public Characters,* of 1804: "The memorial [petition] on which the civil

serving at the time as clerk *pro tem* of the Watauga Association Court, in place of Felix Walker, the regular clerk.[13a] The petition was not dated, but Tatham in his later writings supplied the date of signing, July 5, 1776, one day after the promulgation of the Declaration of Independence in faraway Philadelphia.

The petition is a bench mark in the history of Tennessee. It not only gives the situation of affairs at its date, but also gives glimpses of their actions in preceding years. A document of such significance in the history of the West deserves to have record here in full:

To the Hon. the Provincial Council of North Carolina:
The humble petition of the inhabitants of Washington District, including the River Wataugah, Nonachuckie, &c., in committee assembled, Humbly Sheweth, that about six years ago, Col. Donelson, (in behalf of the Colony of Virginia), held a Treaty with the Cherokee Indians, in order to purchase the lands of the Western Frontiers; in consequence of which Treaty, many of your petitioners settled on the lands of the Wataugah, &c., expecting to be within the Virginia line, and consequently hold their lands by their improvements as first settlers; but to their great disappointment, when the line was run they were (contrary to their expectation) left out; finding themselves thus disappointed, and being too inconveniently situated to move back, and feeling an unwillingness to loose the labour bestowed on their plantations, they applied to the Cherokee Indians, and leased the land for a term of ten years, before the expiration of which term, it appeared that many persons of distinction were actually making purchases forever; thus yielding a precedent, (supposing many of them, who were gentlemen of the law, to be better judges of the constitution than we were,) and considering the bad consequences it must be attended with, should the reversion be purchased out of our hands, we next proceeded to make a purchase of the lands,[14]

---

and military organization of that government was founded was actually drawn up by him [Tatham]—and still is preserved in the archives of North Carolina—and at a time when he was no more than twenty-four years of age." To Ramsey we are indebted for the discovery of the petition in the archives of North Carolina, from which it seems to have disappeared since Ramsey made a copy of it.

[13a] Who was away, leading a platoon of Wataugans to Charleston.

[14] The reference is to the purchase by them at the time Judge Richard Henderson and his associates treated with the Cherokees March 17, 1775, at Sycamore Shoals of the Watauga—purchases made by the Wataugans and Jacob Brown, as to which see Williams, *The Dawn,* Ch. 32 and pp. 415, 430.

reserving those in our possession in sufficient tracts for our own use, and resolving to dispose of the remainder for the good of the community. This purchase was made and the lands acknowledged to us and our heirs forever, in an open treaty, in Wataugah Old Fields; a deed being obtained from the Chiefs of the said Cherokee nation, for themselves and their whole nation, conveying a fee simple right to the said lands. to us and our heirs forever,[15] which deed was for and in consideration of the sum of two thousand pounds sterling (paid to them in goods,) for which consideration they acknowledged themselves fully satisfied, contented and paid; and agreed for themselves, their whole nation, their heirs, &c., forever to resign, warrant and defend the said lands to us, and our heirs, &c., against themselves, their heirs, &c.

The purchase was no sooner made, than we were alarmed by the reports of the present unhappy differences between Great Britain and America, on which report, (taking the new united colonies for our guide,) we proceeded to choose a committee,[16] which was done unanimously by the consent of the people. This committee (willing to become a party in the present unhappy contest) resolved (which is now on our records) to adhere strictly to the rules and orders of the Continental Congress, and in open committee acknowledged themselves indebted to the united colonies their full proportion of the Continental expense.[17]

Finding ourselves on the Frontiers, and being apprehensive that, for the want of a proper legislature, we might become a shelter for such as endeavored to defraud their creditors; considering also the necessity for recording Deeds, Wills, and doing other public business; we, by consent of the people, formed a court [18] for the purposes above mentioned, taking (by desire of our constituents) the Virginia laws for our guide, so near as the situation of affairs would admit; this was intended for ourselves, and was done by the consent of every individual; but wherever we had to deal with people out of our district, we have ruled them to bail, to abide by our determinations, (which was, in fact, leaving the matter to reference,) otherways we dismissed their suit, lest we should in any way intrude on the legislature of the colonies. In short, we have endeavoured so strictly to do justice, that we have admitted common proof against ourselves, on accounts, &c., from the colonies, without pretending a right to require the Colony Seal.

[15] Title was taken by the Wataugan in the name of Charles Robertson, as trustee for the Watauga people. *Ib.*

[16] Committee of safety, in conformity to the procedure in Virginia, North Carolina and other Colonies, soon to become States.

[17] These records are irretrievably lost.

[18] A court of five under the Watauga Association government. *Ib.* The Wataugans for a reason understandable chose not to disclose that they had formed an independent government as early as 1772.

We therefore trust that we shall be considered as we deserve, and not, as we have (no doubt) been many times represented, as a lawless mob. It is for this very reason we can assure you that we petition; we now again repeat it, that it is for want of proper authority to try and punish felons, we can only mention to you murderers, horse thieves and robbers, and are sorry to say that some of them have escaped us for want of proper authority. We trust, however, that this will not long be the case; and we again and again repeat it, that it is for this reason we petition to this Honorable Assembly.

Above we have given you an extract of our proceedings, since our settling on Wataugah, Nonachuckie, &c., in regard to our civil affairs. We have shown you the causes of our first settling and the disappointments we have met with, the reason of our lease and of our purchase, the manner in which we purchased, and how we hold of the Indians in fee simple; the causes of our forming a committee, and the legality of its election; the same of our court and proceedings, and our reasons for petitioning in regard to our Legislature.

We will now proceed to give you some account of our military establishments, which were chosen agreeable to the rules established by convention, and officers appointed by the committee. This being done we thought it proper to raise a company on the District service, as our proportion, to act in the common cause on the sea shore. A Company of fine riflemen were accordingly enlisted, and put under Captain James Robertson, and were actually embodied, when we received sundry letters and depositions, (copies of which we now enclose you,) you will then readily judge that there was occasion for them in another place, where we daily expected an attack. We therefore thought proper to station them on our Frontiers, in defence of the common cause, at the expense and risque of our own private fortunes, till farther public orders, which we flatter ourselves will give no offence. We have enclosed you sundry proceedings at the station where our men now remain.[19]

We shall now submit the whole to your candid and impartial judgment. We pray your mature and deliberate consideration in our behalf, that you may annex us to your Province, (whether as County, district, or other division,) in such manner as may enable us to share in the glorious cause of Liberty; enforce our laws under authority, and in every respect become the best members of society; and for ourselves and constituents we hope, we may venture to assure you, that we shall adhere strictly to your determinations, and that nothing will be lacking or any thing neglected, that may add weight (in the civil or military establishments) to the glorious cause in which we are now struggling, or contribute to the welfare of our own or ages yet to come.

---

[19] See next chapters for the stations, their names and locations.

That you may strictly examine every part of this our Petition, and delay no time in annexing us to your Province, in such a manner as your wisdom shall direct, is the hearty prayer of those who, for themselves and constituents, as in duty bound, shall ever pray.

John Carter, Chn.
Charles Robertson,
James Robertson,
Zach Isbell,
John Sevier,
Jas. Smith,

Jacob Brown,
Wm. Been,
John Jones,
George Rusel,
Jacob Womack,
Robert Lucas,

The above signers are the Members in Committee assembled.
Wm. Tatham, Clerk, P. T.

Jacob Womack,
Joseph Dunham,
Rice Duncan,
Edward Hopson,
Lew. Bowyer, D.Atty,
Joseph Buller,
Andw. Greer,
        his
Jaob X Mitchell,
    mark,
Gideon Morris,
Shadrach Morris,
William Crocket,
Thos. Dedmon,
David Hickey,
Mark Mitchell,
Hugh Blair,
Elias Pebler,
Jos. Brown,
John Neave,
John Robinson,
Christopher Cunningham,
Jas. Easeley,
Ambrose Hodge,
Dan'l Morris,
Wm. Cox,
James Easley,
John Haile,
Elijah Robertson,
William Clark
        his
John X Dunham
    mark

John I. Cox,
John Cox, jr.,
Abraham Cox,
Emanuel Shote,
Thomas Houghton,
Joseph Luske,
William Reeves,
David Hughes,
Landon Carter,
John McCormick,
David Crocket,
Edward Cox,
Tho's Hughes,
William Roberson,
Henry Siler,
Frederick Calvit,
John Moore,
William Newberry,
Adam Sherrell,
Samuel Sherrell, Junr.
Samuel Sherrell, Ser.
Ossa Rose,
Henry Bates, jun.,
Jos. Grimes,
Christopher Cunningham, sen.,
Joshua Barten, sen.,
Joud. Bostin, sen.,
Henry Bates, jun.,
Will'm Dod,
Groves Morris,
Wm. Bates,
Robert Mosely,
Ge. Hartt,

Wm. Overall,
Matt. Hawkins,
John Brown,
Jos. Brown,
Job Bumper,
Isaac Wilson,
Richard Norton,
George Hutson,
Thomas Simpson,
Valentine Sevier,
Jonathan Tipton,
Robert Sevier,
Drury Goodan,
Richard Fletcher,
Allexander Greear,
Joseph Greear,
Andrew Greear, jun.,
Teeter Nave,
Lewis Jones,
Isaac Wilson,
Jno. Waddell,
Jarret Williams,
Oldham Hightower,
Abednago Hix,
Charles McCartney,
Frederick Vaughn,
Joseph McCartney,
Mark Robertson,
Joseph Calvit,
Joshua Houghton,
John Chukinbeard,
James Cooper,
William Brokees,
Julius Robertson,
John King,
Michael Hider,
John Davis,
John Barley." [20]

Washington District, as originally established, included a good portion of what is today Western North Carolina. It covered the lands acquired by the Wataugans and by Jacob Brown under deeds from the Cherokees in 1775—reaching eastward to the upper Blue Ridge rather than the Alleghany range.[21]

[20] In some instances Ramsey failed to decipher signatures; as, for example, that of Rice Duncan which he took to be "Rice Durron."

[21] When Wilkes County, N. C., was established in 1777 it was in part carved out of Washington District. North Carolina soon repented of her purpose to divide the West from her eastern parts by the real watershed, the Blue Ridge, and adopted the Alleghanies instead, with the result that Asheville and a large part of "the Land of the Sky" do not belong to the State of Tennessee. The line of the District ran to the base of Grandfather Mountain—source of New River.

CHAPTER III

MOVES AND COUNTER MOVES—1776

The authorities of Great Britain planned an attack on the three southernmost Colonies with a view to their early subjugation. It was thought that these Colonies were peculiarly vulnerable: in each there lived many who sympathized with the British, later to be called Tories; there was a large population of black slaves who might at any time give the white inhabitants grave concern, and, above all, at the back of the settlements were Indians —Cherokees or Creeks—who were under British influence and could be induced to rise in behalf of the crown.

An effort was made to veil in secrecy the plan and attack. General Henry Clinton was placed in command of the land forces, and Sir Peter Parker in command of the naval squadron which was to sail directly from England.

This design was fraught with peril to the Wataugans and all other settlers on the western waters, to the south of whom were the Overhill Cherokees, firmly attached to the British and to John Stuart the southern superintendent of that power.

In January, 1776, sixty-two Cherokees turned up at far-away St. Augustine in Florida to visit Stuart and solicit supplies of powder and lead, and the superintendent assured Lord Dartmouth of the tribe's firm attachment to the King and confidence in himself.[1]

Soon thereafter sixty horses were loaded with ammunition in Florida, and the caravan was entrusted to the leadership of Henry Stuart, the younger brother of the superintendent, for transport into the country of the Overhills. Not only were the white settlers in the West kept informed of such movements; the Continental Congress was cognizant of the perilous situation and appointed commissioners to visit the Indians, with presents, in an effort to persuade them to remain neutral in the conflict with the

---

[1] *N. C. Col. Recs.*, X, 392.

British.[2] Willie Jones of North Carolina, one of the commissioners, reported that the Overhill branch of the Cherokees refused to meet the continental commissioners in April at Fort Charlotte and, in his opinion, would soon begin hostilities against the whites.[3] Fort Charlotte, it seems, was on the site of Charlotte, N. C.

In April General Clinton with a land force of 2,800 men landed at the mouth of Cape Fear River to await the arrival of the squadron under Parker. Significantly, Superintendent John Stuart had already reached there from St. Augustine to concert with the General plans for the campaign. He learned of the efforts of the congressional commissioners to win the Indians, "notwithstanding which I do not despair of getting them to act for his Majesty's service when it becomes necessary."[4] He was ready to bring the Indians into action "in the execution of some connected plan jointly with the friends of Government, or to favor the operations of His Majesty's forces by drawing the

---

[2] The commissioners met at Salisbury in North Carolina and agreed to call the Cherokees into conference at Fort Charlotte for April 16th. *Ib.*, 392.

[3] June 2nd, 1776. "I conjecture that, whenever any one of the Southern Colonies shall be attacked on the seacoast, they will attack the same Province on the frontiers." Jones also reported the arrival of Henry Stuart in the Overhill country with thirty or forty horse-loads of ammunition. *N. C. Col. Recs*, X, 793.

[4] Stuart to Lord Germain, May 20, 1776. *N. C. Col. Recs.*, X, 607. An effort has been made by a recent historian to acquit Stuart of complicity in bringing the Cherokees to war against the white settlers; indeed, to show that Stuart tried to restrain them. This is contrary to the firm conviction of the revolutionary leaders of the South at the time. Stedman, a Briton who wrote a history of the American Revolution, had been a British officer under and with Clinton, and he says (Vol. I, 248): "British agents were again employed in engaging the Indians to make a diversion and to enter the Southern Colonies on their back and defenseless parts." Stuart and Clinton were solicitous to avoid making a record so as to escape the odium incident to being parties to such an attack by savages; and Stuart's letters and reports should be read in that light. But secret messages such as the one intercepted by the Americans in the hands of the South Carolina Tory, Moses Kirkland, disclosed the true attitude. Ramsay, *History of the American Revolution*, II, 140. The recent historian referred to, Hamer, did not reckon on finesse and suppression on the part of Stuart and his brother Henry, but he seems ready to believe that the Wataugans resorted to worse.

attention of the Rebells." [5] This is exactly what happened within a few months, as we shall see.

Deputy Henry Stuart reached the Overhill towns in April, and found there Deputy Alexander Cameron who had incurred the suspicion and detestation of the Wataugans and all settlers near the Cherokees, whether in the West, in the Carolinas or in Georgia. At once the two engaged in efforts to force the settlers on the Watauga and the Nolachucky to leave their homes and plantations and either remove to Virginia or North Carolina, or preferably to find homes in the British possessions on the lower Mississippi in the Natchez country.[6]

On May 2nd the Overhill chiefs assembled at Chota and in a talk addressed to young Stuart, almost certainly inspired and written by Cameron, they stated that any contention by the settlers on Watauga and Nolachucky that the Cherokees had sold and conveyed any lands to them in 1775 was false.[7] The desire was expressed that "you will write to the white people that settlers this side of the great boundary line to move to some other land within the white people's bounds." [8] A letter or letters were written to those settlers; but respecting the date and contents there is a dispute. Henry Stuart claimed that his letter was recopied, garbled, and his name forged by Jesse Benton, father of the Missouri statesman, "Old Bullion," and that the real letter sent was signed by both Cameron and himself, while the changed one bore his name, only, as signer. The two documents have quite dissimilar contents, and it well may be that both were written two days apart and sent to the settlers by Isaac

---

[5] Stuart to Clinton, March 15th, 1776. Pub. Rec. Office of Great Britain, C. O. 5:77, p. 209. General Gage had earlier written Stuart: "We need not be tender of calling upon the savages." Lord Dartmouth was in agreement that the Indians be induced "to take up the hatchet against his Majesty's rebellious subjects in America." *Ib.*, 5, 76, p. 381. General Gage had sent accordant orders to Stuart and Stuart cannot be supposed to have acted counter to them.

[6] John Sevier in the Franklin State convention at Greeneville in May, 1787, thus referred to this effort: "The British superintendents, Stuart and Cameron, offered them [the people south of the Holston] protection on condition that they would transplant themselves further down towards West Florida, which their abhorrence of British tyranny at that time made them refuse." Williams, *Lost State of Franklin* (2nd ed.) 157.

[7] As to their conveyances, see Williams, *Dawn*, 412, *et. seq.*

[8] *N. C. St. Recs.*, XXII, 995.

Thomas,[9] a white trader among the Overhill Cherokees; and that Henry Stuart repented of having written the second one [10] and did not disclose it to Superintendent Stuart on his return to Florida. The first letter bore date of May 7th; the other May 9th.

These communications caused much uneasiness on the part of the Wataugans. The short limit of time set for their removal called for speedy and diplomatic action. On their leader, John Carter, was placed the drafting of a reply which might result in gaining more time for consideration and action. The Stuart letter was speeded to Virginia, with appeals for military aid against the Cherokees. In his reply to young Stuart and the Cherokees Carter expressed amazement that those Indians were intent on breaking the long-lasting "chain of friendship and wash their hands of us," and the desire of the Wataugans for a continuance of peace. As to the land now in the possession of the whites, "we rely upon the contract that was made by our brothers, the Cherokees, and if it is not binding we are willing to give it up, when we are legally called upon." "As our brothers, the Cherokees, have given us such short warning to leave this place, we hope you gentlemen will give us a larger respite. . . . We pray that they will let us know by some express immediately after you receive this where we shall make an asylum for we (some of us at least) are determined to support his Majesty's crown and dignity.[11] This the majority desire me to relate to you." [12]

---

[9] Thomas was a near-giant who came into the Tennessee country from Virginia about 1774. He frequently acted as pilot or guide for the troops of Sevier and he followed the fortunes of that leader during the years of the State of Franklin. He settled and died in the present Sevier County, his large holdings of land covering the county seat, Sevierville. Isaac Thomas, a Congressman from Tennessee, born in Sevier County 1784, was his son or nephew.

[10] Brown, in *Old Frontiers*, suggests that this letter was meant for the Tories on the Nolachucky and fell into the hands of the Wataugans. p. 141.

[11] The parenthetical words, "some of us at least," refer to Tories, most of whom lived on the Nolachucky, but a few of whom were scattered on the Watauga and Holston. Carter was no doubt aware that the words might be given a wider meaning.

[12] Public Records Office of Great Britain, C. O., 5; 94, p. 105; reproduced by Hamer in *Miss. Valley Hist. Rev., XVII*, 454.

There is here a rather broad insinuation that the neutrality of the Wataugans would depend on the action of the Indians.

Such protestations did not avail. A reply was addressed to Carter, under date of Toqua, May 23rd, to the effect that the Cherokees were "unanimously resolved to recover their lands. Those on Watauga and Nolachucky seem to engross their attention most."[13] No change was made in the twenty-day period fixed for the removal of the whites.

Jacob Brown of the Nolachucky Settlement sent to Henry Stuart a statement of his own case. He expressed surprise that there was a denial of his right to the lands deeded to him by the Cherokees,[14] the boundaries of which he and Chief Little Carpenter (Attakullakulla) had jointly marked, and he enumerated the different articles he had transferred in payment.

The white settlers were firmly determined to defend their possessions should their diplomacy fail. From "Pendleton District, Long Island" (site of Kingsport) Gilbert Christian forwarded money to Col. William Preston in Virginia for ammunition and asked that men be sent to succor the inhabitants who were in great fear of the Indians. He gave information that Captain William Briscoe[15] was raising a company for defense.[16] Major Anthony Bledsoe, of the North of Holston settlement, also wrote Preston that he had learned from Isaac Thomas that the Cherokees were being instigated to rise by Cameron and Henry Stuart. Affidavits of Thomas and Bryan were enclosed, and a request for a supply of powder was made.[17]

In furtherance of the appeal for aid from Virginia, the Henry Stuart letter was speeded to the Virginia Committee of Safety at Williamsburg.[18]

The settlers south and west of Donelson's line of 1771 went to work with great energy on preparations to meet the impending blow. They strengthened and built a number of forts, some

---

[13] *Ib.*, p. 455.

[14] Williams, *Dawn*, 415, 430.

[15] Believed to have later moved on into Kentucky.

[16] Draper MSS., 4 Q Q 40 (May 16th).

[17] *Ib.*, 4 Q Q 39 (May 14). Again on May 22nd, Bledsoe wrote to Preston. John Carter sent to Preston the affidavit of John Bryan, associated with Thomas as messenger to the Cherokees, giving further information as to the activities of Cameron against the settlers.

[18] It was published in the *Virginia Gazette* of June 7th.

small, others of fair size. The farthest southwest towards the Cherokees was on Limestone Creek of Nolachucky [19] to which was given the name "Fort Lee," in honor of General Charles Lee who was then in charge of the American forces in the South.[20] The fort on the Watauga was a larger structure, and it was named "Fort Caswell," in honor of Governor-elect Richard Caswell of North Carolina.[21] This fort was under Colonel John Carter, Captain James Robertson and Lieutenant John Sevier. A small and inadequate fort was at Eaton's about five miles east of the site of Kingsport; and Shelby's Fort was on the site of the city of Bristol.[22] There was one at Jacob Womack's, two miles east of the village of Bluff City; and about three miles farther east on the Holston, John Shelby had a fortified station. The month of June was one of intense activity. The border people were inspirited by the reply received from Colonel Preston. Under date of June 3rd he wrote:

Gentlemen: Your letter of 30th ult., with the deposition of Mr. Bryan, came to hand this evening by messenger. The news is really alarming, with regard to the disposition of the Indians, who are doubtless advised to break with the white people, by the enemies to American liberty who reside among them. But I cannot conceive that you have anything to fear from their pretended invasion by British troops, by the route they mention. This must, in my opinion be a scheme purposely calculated to intimidate the inhabitants, either to abandon their plantations or turn enemies to their country, neither of which I hope it will be able to effect.

Our Convention on the 14th of May, ordered 500 lbs. of gunpowder to each of the counties of Fincastle, Botetout, Augusta and West Augusta . . . and double that quantity of lead. . . . They likewise ordered 100 men to be forthwith raised in Fincastle, to be stationed where our Committee directs for the protection of the frontier. . . . I sent the several letters and deposi-

[19] Later called Gillespie's and now Limestone Station of the Southern Railway.

[20] Ramsey (p. 150) thought Fort Lee was on the Watauga—the "Watauga Fort" or "Fort Caswell."

[21] On the authority of William Tatham, who was one of the fort's defenders during its siege. Williams, *William Tatham, Wataugan*, 4, and *Public Characters*, 1801-2 (London, 1804) being a sketch of Tatham.

[22] Ramsey (p. 146) says that Evan Shelby erected another on Beaver Creek, two miles south of the State line; if so there were two at and near Shelby's home.

tions you furnished me, from which it is reasonable to believe, that when all these shall have been examined vigorous measures will be adopted for our protection.

I have advertised our Committee to meet at Fort Chiswell on Tuesday, the 11th inst., and have directed the candidates for commissions in the new companies, to exert themselves in engaging the number of men required until then; I much expect we shall have further news from Williamsburg by the time the Committee meets. I have written to Colonel Caloway the second time for 200 lbs. of lead, which I hope he will deliver the bearer. This supply I hope will be some relief to your distressed settlement, and as I said before, should more be wanted I am convinced you will be supplied. I am fully convinced that the expense will be repaid you by the Convention of Virginia or North Carolina, on a fair representation of the case being laid before them, whichsoever of them takes your settlement under protection, as there is not the least reason that any one part of the colony should be at any extraordinary expense in the defense of the whole, and you may be assured you cannot be overstocked with that necessary article; for should it please Providence that the impending storm should blow over, and there would be no occasion to use the ammunition in the general defence, then it might be sold out to individuals, and the expense of the whole reimbursed to those who so generously contributed towards the purchase.

I am, with the most sincere wishes for the safety of your settlement, your most obedient and humble servant,

Wm. Preston.[23]

While these events were in progress there turned up in the Overhill towns, in May, a deputation of Indians from the Northern tribes: Mohawks, Ottawas, Nancutas, Delawares, Shawnees and others of the Iroquois Confederation. They came in painted black, intent on drawing the Cherokees into a combination against the American revolutionists. They told tall tales of the Kentucky country being rapidly settled by whites.[24]

It is evident that these tribes sent delegates at the behest of the British superintendent at the North in furtherance of the

---

[23] Ramsey's *Annals,* from the original which had come into the hands of Ramsey. No copy was preserved, and the original was burned when the historian's papers were destroyed by fire. It is fortunate that it was printed in full in the *Annals.*

[24] "That at a fort on Louisa River there were 1000 men assembled; and that on Green River there were 1000 men." Henry Stuart's account, in *N. C. Col. Recs.* X, 773.

policy of the British both at the North and at the South. The tribes were well chosen for the purpose. For many generations the Cherokees had looked upon the Delawares as their tutors —"grandfathers." The Iroquois and the nearby Shawnees, then under Iroquoian suzerainty, had been hereditary enemies of the Cherokees, but were now at peace, also dictated by British policy. What these tribes joined in thus advising was to the Cherokees quite as a command. In a great talk held at Chota the Overhills were told that "the King's troops would soon fall on their enemies towards the sea, and if they united and fell upon them on this side they would find them as nothing."

The concluding talk was by a deputy of the Shawnees, formerly "a noted French partisan," [25] who said: "Now is the time to begin; there is no time to be lost, and if they fought like men they might hope to enlarge their bounds; . . . they intended to carry their talks through every nation to the Southwest and that nation which should refuse to be their friends on this occasion should forever hereafter be considered their common enemy, and they would all fall on them when affairs with the white people should be settled." [26]

The talks evidenced great fear and deep hatred of the Virginians who were in the forefront of the white advance on every frontier, and these sentiments were shared by the Overhill Cherokees. The Wataugans were looked upon as Virginians or "Long Knives," and as trespassers on their land.

When Henry Stuart left the Overhills (July 12th) the Cherokees of all the towns were in readiness to march against the white settlers. Anticipating this, the military commanders in the western parts of Virginia and North Carolina were in communication as to defensive measures; [27] but the blow was to come before anything of consequence could be effected.

---

[25] Thought by some to have been the great Chief Cornstalk who led the Indian forces at the battle of Pt. Pleasant on the Ohio, in 1774.

[26] *N. C. Col. Recs.* X, 778, Henry Stuart's account.

[27] General Griffith Rutherford was to march against the Middle and Valley towns in cooperation with Williamson of South Carolina, while Col. Wm. Christian was to move with Virginia and Tennessee country forces against the towns of the Overhills. See chapter, *post.*

CHAPTER IV

Troubles Begin—1776

The first task to which the Wataugans turned was the silencing or chastisement of a nest of Tories on the Nolachucky. These British sympathizers were preparing to join the Indians as they passed on their raids against the settlers above.[1] Two companies, one from Watauga under Captain James Robertson, the other from below the Holston under Captain John Shelby,[2] marched to the Nolachucky Settlement and corralled more than seventy suspects and compelled them to take the oath of allegiance to the American cause, and to remain neutral at least. Recalcitrants were drummed out of the settlement.[3]

About the same time, around the middle of May, a Macedonian call for aid came to the Wataugans from Mecklenburg County, North Carolina, to join in meeting an attack by the British forces on Charleston. Young Felix Walker, clerk of the Watauga Association court, was then on a visit to his father east of the mountains.

From his *Memoirs*[4] it appears:

I went to Mecklenburg County, and meeting with some recruiting officers, by recommendation of General Thomas Polk I was appointed Lieutenant in Capt. Richardson's Company in the

---

[1] The plan was for Nathaniel Gist and some of the traders, then in the Overhill towns, to accompany the warriors. The traders were to divert at the bend of the Nolachucky and go to the Nolachucky Settlement and bring from there Tories to join the warriors. All Tories were to have white flags as signals in their hands to distinguish them from the Patriots. Ramsey, *Annals*, 149; *N. C. Col. Recs.* X, 606 and 781.

[2] Brother of Major (later General) Evan Shelby. See note above.

[3] Preston to Edm. Pendleton, June 15th, Draper Papers, 4 Q Q 50; Henry Stuart's account, *supra*, p. 782. "Those people do not look upon themselves as bound by the oath . . . and were resolved to avenge themselves for the affront put on them as soon as an opportunity offered." (Stuart.)

[4] In *Journal of American History*, I, 49 *et. seq.; DeBow's Review*, 1854, and Griffin, *Revolutionary Services of Col. John Walker and Family.* John was the father of Felix and settled in what is now Rutherford County, N. C. The entire *Memoirs* was reproduced from the original manuscript in the last named pamphlet.

Rifle Regiment commanded by James [Isaac] Huger,[5] then a Colonel; and was there furnished with money for the recruiting service. I returned to Watauga and on my way throughout that country, I recruited my full proportion of men,[6] and marched them to Charlestown in May, 1776, joined the Regiment and was stationed at James Island.

More than a platoon could not be spared in the delicate situation of affairs in the western country. It was to this that the inhabitants of Washington District referred in their petition to North Carolina of July 5, 1776:[7]

We thought it proper to raise a company as the District Service, as our proportion, to act in the common cause on the seashore. A company of fine riflemen were accordingly enlisted and put under Captain James Robertson, and were actually embodied when we received sundry letters and depositions (copies of which we now enclose you). You will readily judge that there was occasion for them in another place, where we daily expect an attack.

Instead of sending Robertson's entire company to the seaboard, the platoon of Walker composed of young blades was spared to aid in the defense of Charleston. The command of Colonel Gadsden and Lt. Colonel Huger was stationed between Fort Moultrie on Sullivan Island and the city, where on James Island tents were arranged for five hundred men to serve as the second line of defense. The Wataugans were at first a part of that line.

Not till June 28th was real battle joined. On the 12th Colonel Gadsden had reported to General Charles Lee that "as Colonel Huger's men are just raised, . . . none of whom have been used to cannon, they must be awkward thereat."[8] The mountain men were skilled riflemen and it is not to be doubted that they were sent to the rifle pits on Sullivan Island to aid in preventing the landing of Clinton's troops.[9]

---

[5] Isaac Huger of South Carolina was on duty as a lieutenant-colonel at Charleston, in May. There seems to have been no James Huger of military rank present. Isaac later became a brigadier-general.

[6] Walker is tantalizingly silent as to the names of those who composed his platoon, their exact number, their line of march and how they traveled, afoot or horseback. It may be well ventured that Robert Sevier and Mark Robertson, youngsters, were of the number. Both Walker and Robert Sevier married daughters of Maj. Charles Robertson.

[7] *Ante*, p. 19.

[8] *Lee Papers*, N. Y. Hist. Soc. Collection, III, 60.

[9] In these pits were other riflemen from North Carolina, Mecklenburg

The repulse of the attacks made by the land and naval forces was completely successful; so much so, that McCrady, the South Carolina historian, ranks the engagement as one of the three decisive battles of the Revolutionary War.[10]

After the repulse of the British, General Lee feared that the fleet would return to the attack and directed that damage done to Fort Moultrie be repaired. "Much is to be done for the security of the Island of Sullivan."[11] To Moultrie he wrote: "Huger's Regiment have offered themselves to work at your fort. . . . The President and Vice President [of South Carolina] prefer them."[12] In the emergency, the uplanders did not shirk such labor.

Walker's men were held at Charleston in service for some weeks longer, and there learned of a foray in force of the Cherokees against their people. Walker in his *Memoirs* wrote:

The war now becoming general through the American provinces, the British stimulating the Indians on the frontiers, the Cherokees breaking out and murdering the inhabitants of Watauga and Holstein, where my property and interests lay, I was constrained to resign my commission, contrary to the wishes of my commanding officer, and to return home to engage against the Indians.

On their return to Watauga, it was learned that much of import had transpired. Thus was begun a tradition of volunteering for martial service away from home, Province and State, so frequently repeated and so gallantly followed up as to compel the later bestowal by others of the appellation, "The Volunteer State."[13]

County. One of these, young Morgan Brown, later a Tennessean, left a detailed account: "Our rifles were in prime order, well provided and well charged; every man took deliberate aim at his object, and it really appeared that every ball took fatal effect. . . . The fire taught the enemy to lie closer behind their banks of oyster shells." *Am. Hist. Mag.* (of Nashville), VII, 369; also Williams, "The First Volunteers of the Volunteer State," *Tenn. Hist. Mag.* VIII, 136–7.

[10] *South Carolina in the Revolution.* For the participation of the overmountain men in another of these decisive battles, see Ch. XVII, *post.*

[11] *Lee Papers, Ib.,* 104; Lee to President Rutledge, July 1st.

[12] *Ib.* 105. South Carolina was not yet a State, but a Republic with a president and vice-president.

[13] In no history of Tennessee has this exploit been mentioned. It is described in more detail in Williams, "The First Volunteers of the Volunteer State," *Tenn. Hist. Mag.,* VIII, 132–140.

CHAPTER V

The Cherokee Invasion

Henry Stuart says it was the receipt of a tart letter from the Committee of Safety of Fincastle County, Virginia,[1] that welded the Cherokees in favor of war. It was sent in by Isaac Thomas on his last trip into the Overhill towns as messenger. A tall tale, told them by Thomas, that there were "about six thousand men in arms on the frontiers of Virginia and North Carolina who intended to have gone to oppose the King's troops [on the seaboard] but had determined to stay and oppose the Indians," failed to intimidate or deter the Cherokees, who only awaited the announcement, by their war-lord, Oconostota, of the day for starting their march against the settlements. Significantly, yet another large quantity of ammunition (one hundred horse-loads) now reached the Overhills from the British, brought from Pensacola by James Colbert, a sub-agent in the Chickasaw nation.[2] Captain Nathaniel Gist, as seen, undertook the task of going to the Nolachucky settlement and enlisting the co-operation of the Tories there,[3] if he could only get four white traders and an Indian guide to accompany him. Rather than go on a mission so distasteful, most of the traders escaped and made their way to the white settlements.

Lieutenant John Sevier, in charge of the construction and gar-

---

[1] The Upper Holston Settlement, as seen, was yet treated as under the jurisdiction of Fincastle County.

[2] This speaks loudly against the contention that Superintendent John Stuart was averse to a redmens' campaign.

[3] William Tatham's writings reveal: "There were a number of people called Regulators [of North Carolina] who had fled to the extreme frontier for safety after their battle against Gov. Tryon at Alamance, and were actually about joining the Cherokees against the Americans." *Knoxville Gazette,* of April 6th, 1793. That the Regulators who remained in North Carolina were inclined to side with the royal cause is well known; but that the same thing was true of many Regulators in the West is not. Ramsey's was an overstatement:" Every settler at once became a determined Whig." (p. 150).

risoning of Fort Lee [4] on Limestone Creek of the Nolachucky, wrote a crisp note to the officers of Fincastle County, and hurried it forward by Isaac Thomas:

> Fort Lee, July 11, 1776.
> Dear Gentlemen:—Isaac Thomas, Wm. Falling, Jarot [Jarret] Williams, and one more [5] have this moment come in by making their escape from the Indians and say six hundred Indians and whites were to start for this fort, and intend to drive the country up to New River before they return.
> John Sevier.

This information had been secretly given to Thomas by Nancy Ward, a niece of Attakullakulla, who more than once in time of peril had shown his friendship for the white people.[6] Fort Lee

---

[4] Ramsey thought Fort Lee was on the Watauga, site of Fort Caswell.

[5] Seemingly John Bryant or Bryan.

[6] Nancy Ward was a character of such consequence as to deserve ampler treatment than she has so far received. The best account of her is that of A. V. Goodpasture in his *Indian War and Warriors*: "There lived in Chota a famous Indian woman, named Nancy Ward. She held the office of Beloved Woman, which not only gave her the right to speak in council, but conferred such great power that she might, by the wave of a swan's wing, deliver a prisoner condemned by the council, though already tied to the stake. She was of queenly and commanding presence and manners, and her house was furnished in a style suitable to her high dignity. Her father is said to have been a British officer, and her mother a sister of Attakullakulla. She had a son, Little Fellow, and a brother, Long Fellow (Tuskegetchee), who were influential chiefs. The latter boasted that he commanded seven towns, while thirteen others listened to his talks; and though he had once loved war and lived at Chickamauga, at the request of his nephew, General Martin, he had moved to Chestua, midway between Chota and Chickamauga, where he stood like a wall between bad people and his brothers, the Virginians. Like her distinguished uncle, Nancy Ward was a consistent advocate of peace, and constant in her good offices to both races."

Goodpasture cites Timberlake's *Memoirs;* Mooney's *Myths of the Cherokees;* Weeks' *General Joseph Martin; Publications of the Southern History Association,* and the *Calendar of Virginia State Papers.* Other authorities that might have been cited are: Haywood's *Natural and Aboriginal History of Tennessee,* 278; Starr, *History of the Cherokees,* and those below.

Starr, himself of Cherokee blood, says that another descendant of Nancy Ward, her daughter Nannie, married a descendant of Henry Timberlake of the *Memoirs,* seemingly Richard Timberlake. Influential descendants yet live in Oklahoma.

Another descendant, a granddaughter, married Michael Hilderbrand,

was located on the very fringe of settlement, and, before Sevier's little command had completed their fort, they received news of the invading host. "The inhabitants immediately took alarm, and, instead of flocking to the frontier barrier in strong and open ground and thereby serving their country, those of Nolachucky hastily fled, carrying off their livestock and provisions, leaving about fifteen of the volunteers at the frontier to make the best shift in their power." [7] As a result Fort Lee had to be abandoned and its garrison [8] was "joined by as many in the rear of this scamper as had not time to get safe off." They fell back on Fort Caswell (Watauga Fort) near Sycamore Shoals [9] before the Indians reached that place.

The number of the Indians on foray was about seven hundred, including, it seems, a few rampant Creeks. The plan of campaign was to divide this number into three separate commands,

---

whose name is preserved in "Hilderbrand Ford" of Ocoee River. Williams, *Early Travels in the Tennessee Country*, 460.

In confirmation of parts of the above, there is quoted from a letter written by Emmet Starr to the author before the death of the historian of the Cherokees, the following:

"I am quite certain that the family name of Timberlake derives from Lieut. Henry Timberlake. Levi Timberlake married Nannie Taylor a great granddaughter of Nancy Ward or "Granny" Ward, the Ghigan or Beloved Woman of the Cherokees. Allison Woodville Timberlake, their sole son and heir, was a graduate of the National Cherokee Male Seminary, and served four years in the Confederate army under Colonel and General Stand Watee. He married Margaret Lavinia Rogers, a paternal aunt of Will Rogers, the well known humorist. . . . Ex-United States Senator Robert L. Owen is a grand nephew of Oconostota." (January 16, 1928.)

The husband of Nancy Ward was Bryant Ward (not her father as stated by Goodpasture). This, on the authority of Gen. Joseph Martin whose Indian wife was Betsy, daughter of Nancy. *Calendar of Tennessee Papers*, (Draper Coll.), 81.

The remains of Nancy Ward were interred in Polk County, and at her grave the Daughters of the American Revolution have erected a marker. A chapter of that organization is named for her. She appears frequently in the pages which follow. The author may attempt a fuller sketch of her at some future time.

[7] Tatham in *Knoxville Gazette* of April 6, 1793.

[8] Of thirty volunteers in the fort "just above the mouth of Big Limestone where Mr. Gillespie lives" (1793). *Ib.*

[9] *Ib.* The last named fort was, according to Tatham, "on much weaker ground than was that which they had evacuated."

one under the irreconcilable Chief Dragging Canoe to attack those inhabiting near the Long Island, and beyond in Virginia; one under Chief Old Abram of Chilhowee to assail the settlements on the Nolachucky and the Watauga. These two forces were about equal in number. The third one was smaller and was under Chief The Raven. It was to destroy the then small settlement in Carter's Valley (now Hawkins County).[10] The command of The Raven deflected from the main body near the bend of the Nolachucky and followed the main Great War Trail across the Holston. Dragging Canoe and Old Abram proceeded up the Nolachucky valley.

The Battle of Island Flats: Finding Fort Lee abandoned, the Indians destroyed it and then made another division of their remaining force, one to go against the settlements north of the Holston, the other to advance against Fort Caswell on the Watauga. The first division of 170 to 200 warriors was under the whites-hating Dragging Canoe,[11] who had been the mainspring of this invasion.

Warned by Isaac Thomas, as we have seen, the militia of the region and of Virginia just above, gathered under six captains, the senior of whom, Capt. James Thompson, was in command. This force of militia was about equal in number to that of the oncoming Indians, and there resulted a battle of great significance, for two reasons: it was the first battle of the Revolution in the West, and the first fought by the Overhill Cherokees in open battle formation. The battle occurred on July 20, 1776. Fortunately, all of the captains promptly prepared a report and forwarded it to Colonel Wm. Preston, and it soon appeared in the *Virginia Gazette.* The report is a succinct and clear-cut outline of the occurrences:

[10] In 1776, "emigration had advanced over the Indian boundary as far as Big Creek on the north side of Holston . . . under the authority of no legal or efficient government." Tatham, in the *Knoxville Gazette* article.

[11] Their route is now unknown, but in likelihood it was up Limestone Creek, down Fall Branch and Horse Creeks to Long Island, thence across the island towards Eaton's Station. "The spies first discovered the Indians on the island." (Benj. Sharp). Captain James Thompson resided on the island, but he had gone to Eaton's Station with his family. Mrs. Thompson and her sister had returned home to get some household articles, and while there decided to bathe in the river. The Indians in crossing the Island wanted to kill them, but Dragging Canoe would not permit it. "They are only squaws," he said.

On the 19th our scouts returned and informed us that they had discovered where a great number of Indians were making into the settlements, upon which alarm the few men stationed at Eaton's completed a breast-work sufficiently strong, with the assistance of what men were there, to have repelled a considerable number; sent expresses to the different stations and collected all the forces in one body, and the morning after about one hundred and seventy turned out in search of the enemy. We marched in two divisions, with flankers on each side and scouts before. Our scouts discovered upwards of twenty meeting us, and fired on them. They returned the fire, but our men rushed on them with such violence that they were obliged to make a precipitate retreat. We took ten bundles and a good deal of plunder, and had great reason to think some of them were wounded. This small skirmish happened on ground very disadvantageous for our men to pursue, though it was with the greatest difficulty our officers could restrain their men. A council was held and it was thought advisable to return, as we imagined there was a large party not far off. We accordingly returned, and had not marched more than a mile when a number, not inferior to ours, attacked us in the rear. Our men sustained the attack with great bravery and intrepidty, immediately forming a line. The Indians endeavored to surround us, but were prevented by the uncommon fortitude and vigilance of Capt. James Shelby, who took possession of an eminence that prevented their design. Our line of battle extended about a quarter of a mile. We killed about thirteen on the spot, whom we found, and we have the greatest reason to believe that we could have found a great many more had we had time to search for them. There were streams of blood every way, and it was generally thought there was never so much execution done in so short a time on the frontiers. Never did troops fight with greater calmness than ours did. The Indians attacked us with the greatest fury imaginable, and made the most vigorous efforts to surround us. Our spies really deserve the greatest applause. We took a great deal of plunder and many guns, and had only four men greatly wounded. The rest of the troops are in high spirits and eager for another engagement. We have the greatest reason to believe they are pouring in great numbers on us, and beg the assistance of our friends.

> James Thompson,   John Campbell,
> James Shelby,   William Cocke,
> William Buchanan,   Thomas Madison.

The determination to march out of the rude fort at Amos Eaton's Station [12] was based, in part, on the fear that Indians

---

[12] Eaton (1725–1791) was born and reared in South Carolina; removed to Reedy Creek of Holston, near which the fort stood. He later moved to the Cumberland country where a fort near Nashville bore his name.

might pass by the station and in the rear destroy the houses, livestock and crops of many of the men met to give battle. Capt. Wm. Cocke led in advocacy of the plan not to wait for the Cherokees to attack the station.

Following, broadly speaking, the war trail the white forces reached the Island Flats, near the Long Island (in the environs of the present city of Kingsport). There an advance guard [13] saw about twenty Indians coming up the trail towards the station. The scouts fired, dispersing this squad of redmen. The main body of the militia then marched in "two divisions" (in two parallel lines) with scouts in front. Near the close of the day, a council of war was held in which Captain Cocke now favored a return to the station. Some of the men were dissatisfied with such a decision, and expressed themselves freely, commenting upon Cocke's change of front in the face of the foe. Cocke, always gifted with speech, harangued the troops in defense of himself. After a retreat in some confusion to higher ground, the line was reformed. One who had been reared in the immediate neighborhood [14] thus relates:

Our men, extending their lines to the right and the left, gave the enemy Indian-play by taking to the trees. It seems Captain Cocke, at the head of his company, aiming as he said to prevent being surrounded, extended his line until when he turned to see what had become of his men, behold they were not to be seen, he having run a little too fast for his men, or, what was thought more likely, ran farther than his own men chose to go, who had taken to trees and fought the battle out manfully; in which, however, their captain did not participate; he made for the fort. . . . He was ever afterwards considered a coward.[15]

---

[13] Of about a dozen, Alexander Moore, Robert Young, and Charles Young among them. (Draper MSS.)

[14] George Christian to Draper in 1842.

[15] Cocke was accused of cowardice and suspended from the office of captain. His reputation for martial valor had not gone without a blur during Lord Dunmore's War of 1774; though then a captain he managed not to go on the campaign to Pt. Pleasant. Thwaites and Kellogg, *Lord Dunmore's War, passim*. The double blot clouded Cocke's after-career; his enemies saw to that. Even the Indians joined in the criticism of Cocke. Chief Redbird paid for his communication to the *Kentucky Gazette* in which he said of Cocke, "the man who lives among the mulberry trees [the name of Cocke's home] talks very strong and runs very fast." H. Nicolay, *Our Nation in the Building*, 254.

The scouts reported, during the retreat, that the Indians were running up rapidly to attack in the rear. Their right line wheeled to the right, the left line to the left, thus forming a battle line of about a quarter of a mile in length. The Indian warriors when about three hundred yards away raised the war-whoop and rushed forward. While the battle line of the whites was forming some confusion resulted and the Indians sought to take advantage of it by a dash to outflank the militia. Dragging Canoe, leading and encouraging his warriors, lustily crying: "The Unakas [the whites] are running, come on and scalp them!" Roosevelt[16] says that the Indian front "was formed very curiously, their center being cone-shaped, while their wings were curved outward,"—a bracket reversed at the ends. The frontiersmen promptly re-extended their line so as to prevent being outflanked. The report of the captains credited this action to the initiative and "uncommon fortitude and vigilance of Captain James Shelby, who took charge of an eminence that prevented their design." No soldier in the history of Tennessee is more deserving of the descriptive "gallant" than James Shelby.[17]

At last ready for the attack with their long trusty rifles in skilled hands, the militia fired when the enemy had come within range. Many of the redmen fell, killed or wounded. Among the wounded was Dragging Canoe; his thigh was broken, seeing which the Indians fled in confusion, carrying their wounded from the field.[18] The fight was of short duration and at times at close quarters. The frontiersmen killed thirteen, not counting the wounded who may have died after being taken by their fellows from the field. They also took many guns and considerable plunder. Their own losses are set forth in the report of the battle.

An incident in the battle was a hand-to-hand struggle for life between Alexander Moore, of Shelby's company, and a retreating Cherokee warrior, both of whom were large and sinewy. Moore

[16] *Winning of the West* I, 289.

[17] His brother, Isaac, is by some historians credited with this achievement. Isaac was not in the battle. For James Shelby see pp. 97, and Williams, "Captain James Shelby" in *Filson Club Historical Quarterly,* a full length sketch.

[18] One of their leaders, Little Owl, advancing some thirty or forty paces ahead of the others, screaming encouragement to his band, "was soon shot down, with eleven bullet holes in his body." (Benj. Sharp).

shot and slightly wounded the brave in the knee. The Indian went into a shallow sink-hole to bind his wound. There Moore found him and renewed the contest. The brave drew his knife; Moore seized it by the blade which cut his thumb. The two men, evenly matched, then clinched. By his agility Moore was able to throw the Indian, who again tried to knife him. Moore knocked the weapon from his hand to the ground. Both yet clinched and now on the ground, the brave tried more than once to drag Moore towards the weapon which Moore, by a hasty kick, would move beyond his reach. The desperate struggle was kept up until a companion of Moore came up, shot and killed the Indian.[19]

This battle served to hearten the whites; it demonstrated their ability to meet and defeat Indian foes. The Cherokees were depressed; they never recovered full faith in their prowess against the whites. From that time forward that people gradually lost their old time confidence in their own valor.

Raid on Carter's Valley

The westernmost settlement, in Carter's Valley,[20] was inconsiderable and wholly inadequate to its own defense. The lands there were so fertile as to attract some of the hardier frontiersmen of Virginia, the names of some of whom are recoverable:

[19] Based on accounts given to Draper by Gen. Thomas Love and Col. George Wilson, and another by Benj. Sharp. This exploit was recounted at firesides on the frontier for generations and became something of a saga of the region. As is usual in such cases, different renditions arose, with the result that variant accounts are given by historians. Benj. Sharp in the *American Pioneer*, I, 333, names his own brother-in-law, William King, as the person who shot and killed the Indian. Taylor, in *Historic Sullivan*, 60, states it was private Handly, while the Draper Manuscripts names Charles Young, a fifteen year old brother of Robert Young. This writer believes that the experienced scout, Thomas Price, who lived not far from the Youngs, led the small party, and he named Charles Young. "Tom Price, an old Indian trader, told me so himself." (Gen. Thomas Love).

[20] A son of Robert Love wrote Draper that his father "was the first white man to plant corn in what is now Hawkins County." That statement can only be true if confined to the particular migration of 1775, since years before corn had been raised there, in Carter's Valley. Williams, *Dawn*, 349.

Samuel Love and sons, Robert and Thomas;[21] Rev. Jonathan Mulkey, the first preacher of the Baptist faith to appear in the Tennessee country; a Mr. Kinnard,[22] John Long; Moses Winters and Thomas Ownsby.

As the Indians approached the settlers fled in terror, most of the men towards the nearest fort at Eaton's across the North Fork of Holston, while women and children were conducted back as far as the present Wythe County, in Virginia. As Mulkey and a companion were trying to escape across the North Fork, Indians overtook them, knocked down, scalped and left for dead Mulkey's companion, while the young minister, himself slightly wounded by a bullet, leaped into the stream, swam across and made his way to Eaton's Station. Imagine his surprise when, on arriving there, he found his companion, thought to be dead, already in the station though scalpless. He had taken a shorter route to the station.[23]

The western contingent of Cherokees under Chief Raven probably did not exceed one hundred warriors. Finding little or no resistance, they moved rapidly, burning cabins and killing the livestock of the whites as they proceeded. Dispersing in small bands, they moved in fan shape, the westernmost flank harassing the settlements on Clinch River in Virginia while others bore down on neighborhoods near the Wolf Hills (Abingdon) and carried death and destruction as high up as Seven Mile Ford of Holston.[24]

In the autumn of 1776 some of the settlers of the previous year, named above, ventured back to Carter's Valley to repossess their

---

[21] These two brothers rose to distinction. See sketches in Williams, *History of the Lost State of Franklin*, and *Beginnings of West Tennessee*. The father had moved from Augusta County, Va., to the region after his stay for a time in the present Wythe County, Va.

[22] Probably John Kincaid of Kincade, of Fincastle County.

[23] Mulkey was the son of a Baptist preacher, the noted Philip Mulkey, mentioned later as being in the Cumberland Settlements. The son became an outstanding leader of his denomination. He served a long time as pastor of Buffalo Ridge church. His grave-stone near the site of the old church bears this inscription: "In memory of Jonathan Mulkey, Sen., born October 26, 1752; departed this life September 5, 1826, after having been a preacher of the Gospel of the Baptist order more than fifty years."

[24] For the Virginia angle, see Summers, *History of Southwest Virginia*, 229 *et seq.*

clearings; they thought that all was safe. But in January following the Indians raided the nearby Poor Valley and killed William Purviance and family. George Brooks escaped into Carter's Valley to the Love settlement and gave intelligence. Love "waited only long enough to catch horses to carry himself and sons away leaving other horses, cattle, etc., behind." They went back to Virginia and never returned.[25] Other families did the same.

Siege of Fort Caswell on the Watauga

The eastern division of the Cherokees, under Chief Old Abram of Chilhowee,[26] continued along the foot of the mountains [27] towards Fort Caswell with small squads deflecting to scout and pick up such whites as might be found. One such, Mrs. William Bean,[28] who was making her way from her home near the mouth of Boone's Creek toward Fort Caswell, was intercepted and taken prisoner to a camp of the Indians on the waters of the Nolachucky River. Ramsey says:

A white man was there also a prisoner. He told her she was to be killed, and a warrior stepped toward her and cocked his gun as if he intended to shoot her. The white man, at the instance of the chiefs, then began to ask Mrs. Bean some questions: How many forts have the white people? Where are the forts? Can they be starved out? Have they got any powder? She answered these questions so as to leave the impression that the settlements could protect themselves. After conferring a few minutes, the chief told the white man to say to Mrs. Bean that she would not be killed, but that she had to go with them to their towns and teach their women how to make butter and cheese.[29]

Taken into their country by the Indians, Mrs. Bean was condemned to death. Bound, she was taken to the top of one of the

---

[25] Gen. Thomas Love to Draper in Draper Note Book 30, pp 69 et seq. As to the David Crockett settlement, see p. ooo, post.

[26] Perhaps the least able of the three chiefs selected for command in this invasion. "Distinguished more for stratagem and cunning than for valor and enterprise." (Ramsey)

[27] Up Cherokee Creek (first called Indian Creek) under the Cherokee Mountains in the present county of Washington; in likelihood the creek and mountains were so named because of this march.

[28] Wife of Wm. Bean, Sr., or of his son, Wm. Bean, Jr; father and son lived on adjoining plantations.

[29] Annals, 157.

mounds to be burned. Nancy Ward, exercising the function of Ghigan, interposed and pronounced a pardon. For this act of grace the whites called her the Pocahontas of the West.

Fort Caswell was under the command of John Carter,[30] colonel; James Robertson, captain; and John Sevier lieutenant. The defending force of males, augmented by the arrival of the garrison of Fort Lee and of men driven out of the valley of the Nolachucky, numbered seventy-five.[31] The women-folk gave effective aid in many ways.

The red foe made a sudden and fierce assault in the early morning of July 21st, (the day following the battle of Island Flats) but it was repulsed by the rifle-fire of the defense, with a loss so considerable as to give the Indians pause. The fort was then invested and the siege lasted for about two weeks; the killed and wounded of the assailants were taken to their camp on the Nolachucky. Men were sent out as expresses to Virginia for succor. Colonel William Russell prepared to respond by sending rangers.[32] These did not arrive in time, and Colonel Evan Shelby, from Shelby's Fort [33] sent one hundred mounted men to aid those in the fort. Before their arrival the siege had been raised and the enemy had withdrawn.

During the siege James Cooper and a boy named Samuel Moore went out of the fort to get boards with which to cover a small cabin within the enclosure. Ramsey says of them, *Annals*, 158:

When near the mouth of Gap Creek, they were attacked by Indians; Cooper leaped into the river, and by diving hoped to escape their arrows and bullets, but the water became too shallow and he was killed by them and scalped. The firing by the

[30] According to one present, Wm. Tatham, though Carter is not mentioned as such by Haywood, Ramsey or Roosevelt.

[31] Haywood, followed by Ramsey, Roosevelt and Mooney and others gives this force as forty in number. Hamer in his *History of Tennessee*, I, 83, gives it as one hundred and fifty. The account of Wm. Tatham is here adopted, since he was one of the defenders and better qualified to speak to the point.

[32] "On their way the rangers fell in with a party of forty Cherokees fifty miles east of Long Island. Of these Col. Russell's men killed five, took one prisoner who had been mortally wounded, and also made prize of forty rifles belonging to the Indians." Ramsey, p. 158, quoting the *Maryland Gazette*.

[33] For a history of this fort: Williams, "Fort Shelby," in *East Tennessee Historical Soc. Pubs.*, VIII, pp. 28–38.

Indians and the screams of Cooper were heard in the fort, and lieutenant John Sevier attempted to go to his succor. Captain Robertson saw that the Indians were superior in force to that within the fort, and that it would require all the men he commanded to protect the women and children from massacre. The firing and screaming without he believed to be a feint on the part of the enemy to draw his men from the fortification, and he recalled Sevier and his party from the attempted rescue. Moore was carried prisoner to the Indian towns, and was tortured to death by burning. A few mornings after the battle, a man named Clouse was found in the thicket below the fort, killed and scalped. He had probably chosen the darkness of the night to reach the fort from some of the settlements, and had been intercepted and slain.

The besiegers kept up a desultory rifle-fire. A spent ball struck a man inside the fort without materially injuring him. Luke (Lew) Bowyer, Tennessee's first lawyer,[34] standing by, caught the bullet in his hand.[35]

The first approach and attack of the Indians was about daybreak and made stealthily. Some of the women and girls were up early and had gone out to milk cows. The first alarm to the defenders was the screaming of these women-folk in their flight to the fort, closely pursued by the savages. In this party of females was Miss Catherine ("Bonnie Kate") Sherrill, a tall and athletic young woman.[36] As the Indians blocked the direct path to the gate of the fort, she made a circuit to reach the enclosure on another side, resolved, as she afterwards said, to scale the palisades. "The bullets and arrows came like hail. It was now leap or die, for I would not live a captive." While she was scaling the stockade, the hand of a man reached down to aid her, and she fell into the arms of this man—John Sevier—whom she thus met for the first time. She was to become his second wife a little more than four years later.[37]

---

[34] For a sketch of Bowyer, see Williams, "Tennessee's First Lawyer" in *Tenn. Bar Asso. Proceedings for 1926*, pp. 116–122.

[35] Gen. Thomas Love to Draper, Note Book 30, p. 69 in Draper Collection.

[36] Daughter of Samuel Sherrill of the Nolachucky who with his family had been in the fort the day before.

[37] Roosevelt is in error in his statement that Sevier was at the time a young widower and soon after the siege married Miss Sherrill. The first wife, Sarah Hawkins, lived until 1780, after which Sevier's second marriage to Bonnie Kate occurred. The home of the Sherrill's was known

There was another and truer, though heretofore unheralded, heroine of the attack and siege, the young sister of James Robertson, Ann. A party of about twenty-five warriors during an attack on the fort reached the palisade and were making desperate efforts to set the fort on fire. The defenders could not reach them in firing their rifles. Ann was seized with an inspiration: it was wash-day in the fort; picking up a bucket of boiling water and bidding the women to supply more, she mounted the inner parapet amid a shower of bullets and poured a scalding stream on the attackers. Though wounded, she continued this until the enemy beat a retreat.[38]

During the siege, bands of the warriors made raids in other directions. One of these was against Womack's Fort, erected on the south side of Holston River, near the present village of Bluff City, by Captain Jacob Womack [39] and his neighbors.

Finally in discouragement the Indians withdrew from the immediate vicinity. They, however, hovered around the Nolachucky Settlements. There the company of rangers of Captain Evan Shelby, Jr.,[40] went to give aid and to frustrate any further raiding on the part of the Indians.

as "Daisy Fields" and was near where Sevier lived in 1780. Samuel Sherrill came to the West from the Yadkin Valley in North Carolina. Sketch of Catherine Sevier by the historian Putnam who married into the Sevier family, is in Ellet, *Pioneer Women of the West*, 29–42.

[38] Charlotte (Mrs. James) Robertson, quoted in Draper Manuscripts.

[39] For a short sketch of Womack: Williams, *Dawn*, 436.

[40] *Calendar of King's Mountain Papers* (Draper Collection) p. 160. Young Shelby was one of three sons of Evan Shelby, Sr., who were in the battle of King's Mountain. He was then a major. He later settled near Clarksville, Tenn.; he was killed by the Indians while returning from the Ohio with supplies.

CHAPTER VI

CHRISTIAN'S CAMPAIGN AGAINST THE CHEROKEES (1776)

Our historians have treated this campaign as one launched against the Cherokees in retaliation for the attacks made upon the whites in the valleys of the Holston and Watauga which resulted in the defeat of the Cherokees.

In fact, the authorities of Virginia, of Georgia and of the Carolinas before July, 1776, had anticipated and feared that the Cherokees, under the influence of John Stuart, his brother Henry, and Alexander Cameron, would co-operate with the British forces in the plan to subdue the Southern Colonies.

Weeks before the inhabitants of the Holston and Watauga were attacked, General Griffith Rutherford wrote (July 5, 1776) to the Council of Safety of North Carolina, stating that he, as brigadier-general of Salisbury District in command of all the western parts of his State, did not feel warranted in taking his troops out of his district in pursuit of the Cherokees of the Middle Towns who were then aroused and threatening action against the white people of his region; and he asked for instructions as to his course of action. He suggested that he should write to Virginia and South Carolina soliciting concerted movements against all of the Cherokees by the men of the frontiers of the four Provinces. General Rutherford assured the council that, if such co-operation should result, "I have no doubt of the final destruction of the Cherokee Nation." [1]

As soon as General Rutherford learned of the appointment of Colonel William Christian to lead the forces of Virginia against the Overhill Cherokees [2] he wrote to Christian promptly, and perhaps before he had heard of the raids of Cherokees on the white inhabitants of Watauga and Holston. In this letter Ruther-

---

[1] *N. C. Col. Recs.*, X, 651.

[2] William Christian had succeeded Patrick Henry, his brother-in-law, as colonel of the First Virginia Regiment, but had resigned to lead the expeditionary forces against the Cherokees.

48

ford asked to be informed by an express as to Colonel Christians's plans for marching adding that the information would be forwarded to South Carolina in order that "we may unite our strength, and as near as possible pursue the same measures in marching at once." [3]

The president of the Province of South Carolina was about the same time suggesting a plan for simultaneous attacks by the forces of the three Provinces. On July 7th, 1776, he wrote to the North Carolina revolutionary authorities, saying: "At the same time, or as soon as may be, the Overhills should be attacked from Virginia, from whence alone it can be done to advantage." He stated that General Charles Lee, still in command of the American forces in Charleston, was of the same opinion. General Lee also wrote the same day urging that the Cherokees should be treated as at war in aid of the British. Like communications were speeded from Charleston to John Page, president of the Convention of Virginia, and to the Continental Congress. The latter body on July 30th responded by passing a resolution recommending to Virginia, North Carolina and Georgia co-operation with South Carolina "in carrying on a war with all possible vigor against those savages." [4]

Virginia, already alert to the situation, was even more so when news reached Williamsburg that bands of the Cherokee warriors in the July raids had carried death and destruction far up her southwestern valleys. President Page made application to North Carolina for three hundred men to join the force to be led from Virginia by Colonel Christian, appointed for that purpose early in August. The Council of Safety of North Carolina promptly complied, and instructed General Rutherford to order out three hundred men from the Surry County regiment of militia. The rendezvous of these North Carolinians with the Virginians was to be at Stalnacker's on the Holston. [5] The need for this aid was thought to be the greater because of the report that had reached North Carolina that Cherokees east of the Alleghany Mountains

---

[3] *N. C. Col. Recs.*, X, 650.

[4] *Journal Continental Congress*, July 30, 1776; Burnett, *Letters of Members of Continental Congress*, II, 30. The news of the battle of Long Island Flats was not known in Charleston until late in August. *S. C. Gazette*, of August 21, 1776.

[5] *N. C. Col. Recs.*, XI, 333, 337.

had abandoned their settlements and fled to the Overhills. It seemed not improbable that it might become necessary for General Rutherford himself to march a part of his forces west of the mountains "to join the Virginians, as they will, if the above reports be true, have to encounter the whole force of the Cherokees." [6]

A battalion of the Surry regiment under Rutherford's orders was embodied under Lieutenant-Colonel Joseph Williams [7] and Major Joseph Winston [8] to respond to Virginia's call.

On August 1, 1776, the Virginia Council gave the following instruction to Colonel Christian, commander of the expedition, next to him in command being Colonel Charles Lewis, of the Second Battalion:

When your battalion and the battalion under Colonel Charles Lewis are completed, you are to march with them and the forces under the command of Colonel [William] Russell, and such others as may join you from North Carolina, into the Cherokee country; if these forces shall be judged sufficient for the purpose of severely chastising that cruel and perfidious nation, which you are to do in a manner most likely to put a stop to future insults and ravages and that may redound most to the honor of American arms. If the Indians should be reduced to the necessity of suing for peace, you must take care to demand of them a sufficient number of the chiefs and warriors as hostages for the performance of the conditions you may require of them. You must insist on their giving up all prisoners who may choose to leave them and on their giving up to justice all persons amongst them who have been concerned in bringing on the present war, particularly Stuart, Cameron and Gist, and all others who have committed murder or robberies on our frontiers. You may require any other terms which the situation of affairs may point out and you may judge necessary for the safety and honor of the Commonwealth. You must endeavor to communicate with the commanding officer of the Carolina forces and co-operate with him, making the attack as near the time of his as may be.

---

[6] *Ib.* 346, 352.

[7] Williams was the father of Col. John Williams, U. S. Senator from Tennessee, of Judge Thomas L. Williams, Supreme Court Judge and chancellor of Tennessee, of Lewis Williams, member of Congress from North Carolina, "father of the House of Representatives," and ancestor of Sen. John Sharp Williams. See also Draper, *Heroes of King's Mountain*, 433, and *Official Letters of Governors of Virginia*, I, 14 *et seq.*

[8] For a sketch of Winston, see Draper's *Heroes of King's Mountain*, 454. The city of Winston (now Winston-Salem) bears his name.

Lieutenant-Colonel William Russell was already at Long Island [9] and he thought it advisable to erect at that place a fort for the accommodation of the troops coming under Christian. This he did in September. He gave it the name of Fort Patrick Henry, in honor of the governor of Virginia. This fort was built on the north bank of the Holston about two hundred yards below the upper end of the island, where the river bank was high and the water four or five feet deep. The ground covered by the fort was about one hundred yards square. Only three sides were enclosed, since the bank of the river was well nigh impregnable. There were bastions at each corner. In the center stood the house for military stores and the home for the commander. Several small springs that bubbled out of the river's bank afforded water for drinking; the river afforded a supply for other purposes.[10]

Colonel Christian had fixed on September 20th for his arrival at Long Island. From Botetourt County he wrote Rutherford, August 15th and 18th, in the last letter saying; "Will it be possible for you to proceed to the Overhill towns after the drive off of the Valley people, or will the South Carolina army do it, or is it intended that either shall?"[11]

Christian on his march to Long Island found the people on Clinch River and Holston River from ten miles above Stalnacker's down to the island, in forts. He reported the number to be about three thousand. Great numbers were sick; many had died as a result of close confinement; all were in dire want. Colonel Christian distributed flour to the wives and widowed mothers of his troopers.

---

[9] From which he had marched just after the siege of Fort Caswell on the Watauga.

[10] "John Redd's Reminiscences," *Va. Mag. of History*, VII, 2. Redd was on the campaign.

[11] Rutherford, because of greater expedition and of proximity to the Cherokees of the Middle towns and the Valley, had, before the communication reached him, invaded the enemy's eastern territory. His main campaign was at an end before Christian crossed the French Broad. As Rutherford was returning home, he decided that it would be wise to send a small force back to the Cherokee country further to harass the Indians, perhaps in aid of Col. Christian across the Alleghanies. A force of one hundred under Capt. William Moore and Capt. Joseph Hardin harried the valleys occupied by the Cherokees in North Carolina. Hardin in after years moved to the Tennessee country where he was a leader in the affairs of the State of Franklin and of the Southwest Territory. Williams, *Lost State of Franklin*, 297; *N. C. Col. Recs.*, X, 895–898.

September 21st, the troops, including the Surry forces under Colonel Williams,[12] arrived at Fort Patrick Henry where they remained until October 1st, during which time a number of the Cherokees were skulking about the fort. They killed one soldier. Another, taken prisoner, escaped and gave information that the party of redmen were about twelve in number and were then making homeward. One countryman of the neighborhood was killed and others were wounded.[13] Another war party of Cherokees a few days later slipped past the fort, going to the settlements to the north, but on being pursued by a detachment of the militia, turned back to their towns.[14]

On the army's quitting the fort for the Cherokee towns a force of one hundred men under the command of Captain William Witcher, of Pittsylvania County, was left to guard the stores there.

The order of the commands on march was as follows: Colonel Christian in the center, Colonel Williams on the right, Colonel Charles Lewis on the left, Colonel William Russell in the advance guard, and Major Evan Shelby in the rear: "Along the route there was no road or path, not even the vestige of civilized man was to be seen." (Colonel Williams' Narrative.)

Christian's force crossed the river over Long Island, and marched the first day six miles up Horse Creek past the divide of its waters from those of Lick Creek and camped at Double Springs near the base of Chimney Top Mountain. Even up to this time Lieutenant-Colonel Haynes Morgan,[15] of Colonel

---

[12] The North Carolina battalion was without tents, had but few blankets, and some of the men were dressed in clothing made of rude materials derived from hemp, tow and wild nettle. Draper, *Heroes of King's Mountain*, 434. For Col. Williams "Narrative" of the campaign, see Williams, *"Col. Joseph Williams Battalion in Christian's Campaign,"* in *Tenn. Hist. Mag.*, IX, 102–116.

[13] Christian to Gov. Patrick Henry, *Va. Mag., Hist.* XVII, 52: *N. C. Col. Recs.*, X, 837.

[14] See *Am. Archives* (5th Series) II, 540, on occurrences of Sept. 26th and 29th.

[15] Some of the men under Morgan had seen service at Gwynne Island against the British under Lord Dunmore, and they had little regard for Morgan as a militia officer. On being ordered to muster for discharge at Long Island, they broke Morgan's sword near the hilt and shaved the mane and tail of his horse to show their dislike. McAllister, *Virginia Militia in the Revolution*, 89. Colonel, afterwards General, Daniel

Lewis's command, with one hundred and fifty officers and men, had not come up to join the main body. They, it seems, never did overtake the commander but on reaching it remained at Fort Patrick Henry until the campaign was over.

At Double Springs, or "6 Mile Camp," as Christian called it in his report to Governor Henry, the Watauga and Nolachucky troops, under Captains James Robertson and John Sevier, marching down Fall Branch, joined the main body. The companies of Captains Gilbert Christian, James Thompson and Daniel Smith, recruited in the neighborhood of Long Island, were already with Colonel Christian. These companies and those from the Watauga Settlements formed a battalion under Major Evan Shelby.

In the report of Christian, above referred to, he stated (October 6th):

> I shall march in less than an hour and take with me thirty days' flour and seventy days' beef. I hope to cross [French] Broad River the 15th inst., where it is most likely I shall be attacked or meet with proposals of peace. The men who have fled from the towns say the Indians will surely fight desperately; which they promised Stuart, the King's Superintendent, to do; and Cameron, his deputy, who remains amongst them is daily encouraging them to defend their country against a parcel of Rebels. I heartily wish that they may first attack me; and it is the wish of the army. Cameron, being an awful man, may invent measures to delay our march if the Indians will execute them with dexterity; but still I have no doubt of returning to the Island in five weeks from this time, six at fartherest.

The Reverend Charles Cummings, a Presbyterian minister from near Abingdon, and Rev. Joseph Ray [Rhea] accompanied the expedition as chaplains.[16]

From Double Springs, Colonel Christian sent forward four of his scouts toward the Cherokee towns for the purpose of lying in wait to capture a prisoner from whom it was hoped to learn the enemy's plans. The scouts were promised one hundred pounds, as rewards, in event of their success. Isaac Thomas, with

---

Morgan has, in error, been stated to be the officer who led these troops. *Va. Mag. Hist.*, XVII, 52, *et. seq.*

[16] Orderly book of Capt. Joseph Martin, Draper Coll. Patrick and Terry Vance were surgeons under Dr. Gay. Capt. Wm. Madison was chief of commissary, his assistant being Ephraim Dunlop, who was the second lawyer to locate in the Tennessee country.

intimate knowledge of the lay of the land and of the Indians' customs, was of the party and its pilot.[17]

The army of about 1800 men "well equipped and in high spirits," moved along one of the ancient Indian war-trails, down Lick Creek, but slowly since a road had to be cut and made wide enough for the passage of wagons loaded with supplies. The army was all infantry except one company of light-horse under the command of Captain John Sevier. Sixteen men of that company under Valentine Sevier, Jr.,[18] were selected to go forward as scouting spies to the intended crossing place on French Broad River. Cane-brakes and miry ground at the junction of Lick Creek with Nolachucky River impeded the army's progress.[19] Into the encampment at night Ellis Harlin, a white trader to the Cherokee towns, came in under a flag of truce and gave the commander information that seven or eight hundred men were lying on the south bank of the French Broad River to dispute a crossing.[20] At the bend of the Nolachucky abandoned camps of the Indians showed a very recent occupation by a large number of warriors.[21]

As the white forces had been moving forward, a sharp debate had gone on in the Cherokee towns. The chiefs were divided in regard to the course to be pursued. A trader of influence, Caleb Starr, addressed a red council urging that terms be made with

---

[17] Isaac Thomas served forty-six days as spy on the Cherokees under Christian, and was paid five shillings per day. Three others were Samuel Ewing, John Blankership and James McCall. They crossed the Little Tennessee and went to the home of one Davis who gave them intelligence of the designs of the redmen, which they on return to the column imparted to the commander. In later years these three were paid by the general assembly of Virginia the reward promised by Col. Christian. Summers, *History of Southwest Virginia*, 242–3. Capt. James McCall, from the neighborhood of Ninety-six, in South Carolina, had been taken prisoner on July 1st. He escaped on hearing of the approach of the expedition and joined Col. Christian who reported: "He has a wife and five children and wishes it to be published in the *Gazette* that he is here and well. By this means it will get into the Carolina papers and reach his family." The brave McCall made an enviable record during the war. Draper, *Heroes of King's Mountain*, 162.

[18] "Valentine Sevier, for 51 days as spy against the Cherokees at 5 s. 12 d." (Va. Records.)

[19] Ramsey's *Annals*, 166.

[20] Christian's Report to Governor Henry.

[21] Ramsey, 166.

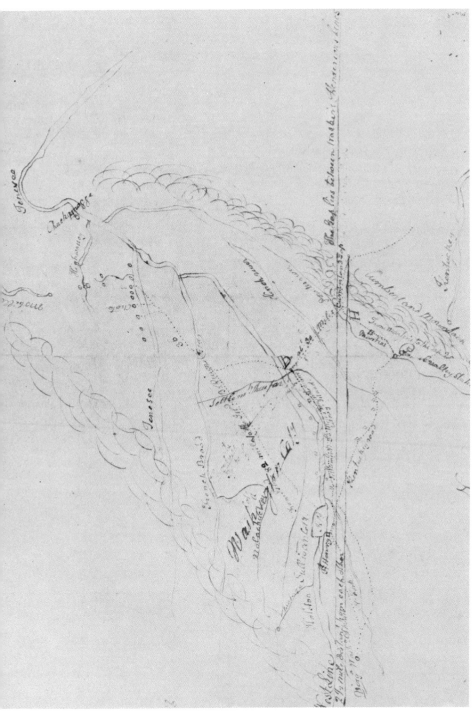

Colonel Christian's rough map of 1782, showing Henderson's and Walker's lines, and the trails to the Cherokee towns. Note that *north* is at the bottom. *Courtesy Virginia State Library.*

Christian; and The Raven and the other older chiefs were for appeasement. Dragging Canoe was strongly in opposition and Cameron stood firmly with him, contending that the towns on the Little Tennessee should be abandoned and the Indians withdrawn to the Hiwassee. The elders prevailed and Captain Nathaniel Gist was sent forward to treat with Christian.

The forces of Christian proceeded along the war-path up Long Creek to its source and down Dumplin Creek to a point a few miles from its mouth where the Great War Path struck across a small ridge to a ford of the French Broad near Buckingham's Island. Before the river was reached the army was met by Fallen, a trader, who bore a white flag on his rifle. The commander directed that no attention be paid to him. He soon left to inform the Indians of the large force they would have to confront.

On arriving at the French Broad the strategy of Christian was to leave the impression on the enemy that his army was encamped there to remain for some days. He ordered every mess to kindle a good fire and pitch tent; but at eight o'clock that night he took eleven hundred men and marched them about four miles below the island to a ford, which had been discovered by Sevier's scouts, and crossed over.[22] The night march in the forest was then continued in a flanking movement, the intention being, before rise of sun, to surprise from behind the large force of the enemy which was believed to be stationed on the south bank. To Christian's own surprise no redmen were to be found there. He then ordered the remainder of his forces to cross over.

Here reports from the scouts first sent out were received indicating that an attack might be expected in a day or so. Captain Nathaniel Gist, a Virginian who had been among the Cherokees for long periods intermittently through many years, came in to interview Colonel Christian, as spokesman for Chief The Raven. He interceded for the beloved town of Chota, and reported that the Indians had encamped about four miles south of the river, and that The Raven had used his influence to bring the Cherokees to yield to the superior force of the whites; that that Chief's party had already marched southward and other warriors at the

---

[22] "The ford was deep and the water so rapid as to require the men to march in platoons of four abreast, so as to brace each other against the impetuous stream." Ramsey, 167.

front had fallen back to the towns in order to move off their families and provisions. Gist said that Cameron's advice to the Indians was to burn their own towns and all stored crops, and to fall back to the Hiwassee River where a stand should be made; and that no general battle might be expected before that river was reached. According to Gist's account, the Valley and Lower Cherokees had swarmed over the mountain fleeing from General Rutherford's North Carolinians and Colonel Williamson's South Carolina forces as they had harried the eastern towns weeks before.

The course pursued by Captain Gist among the Cherokees had alienated his Virginia friends. Christian reported to Governor Patrick Henry respecting him:

I believe he is sorry for what he has done. I did intend to put him in irons but the manner of his coming, I believe, will prevent me. The officers tell me that the camp is in great confusion about him; some think there are many favorable circumstances attending him. And many are for killing him; of the last the greatest part. I spoke but little to him and don't know whether he wants to go back or not. He says the Creeks are expected soon. I believe I shall push for the island towns and those that bred the war and have thoughts of sparing Chota.[23]

John Redd in his account of the campaign says that the prejudice against Captain Gist "soon wore off and he became very popular." He went home to Virginia to serve with credit as a colonel under General Washington.[24]

Halting for a day in order to permit the men who had waded the lower ford to dry their clothing and baggage, the march was resumed. The route now was along the valley of Boyd's Creek and down Ellijay Creek to Little River; thence through the site of the present Maryville to the Little Tennessee. Approaching the latter stream, there seemed a probability of resistance by warriors of the towns on the south bank and the foot troops were ordered to go forward in a run. The river was crossed at Toqua Town without opposition October 18th, and camp was pitched at Tomotley. The next day the army passed through Tuskegee; then past the site of Old Fort Loudoun to the Great Island Town. Nowhere was there resistance. Colonel Christian made the last

---

[23] *Va. Hist. Mag.* VII. For a sketch of Gist, see Williams, "Nathaniel Gist, Father of Sequoah," in *E. T. Hist. Soc. Pubs.*, Vol. V, pp. 39–54.
[24] *Ib.*, 52 *et seq.*

named town his temporary headquarters. The Indians, in dismay, had beat a retreat so hurriedly, many in canoes down the river, that they left horses, cattle, hogs, and fowl, which, added to the large stores of corn, potatoes, and other provisions, gave variety to the dietary of the invaders. Christian in his report of October 23rd, reckoned that the Overhill towns contained forty to fifty thousand bushels of corn and ten to fifteen thousand bushels of potatoes.

Harlin, the first flag-bearer from the Indians, now told the Colonel that when he returned to the towns with news of the oncoming host, the Indians hurriedly packed what they could carry and fled precipitately, many towards the Hiwassee River: and that Cameron had tried to employ some of the Indians to kill him and Captain Gist "for their part in talking of peace." The commander sent two men to ask the chiefs to come into his camp. The Raven at this time was acting war-chief. The Cherokees were now in sad decadence. The great leaders of the olden time, Little Carpenter, Oconostota and Ostenaco (Judd's Friend) were yet alive but of advanced age and comparatively inactive. Colonel Christian wrote to the governor of Virginia:

I wrote The Raven that, as he wishes to speak to me, I was now here and found that his nation would not fight; that I was willing to hear him and the other chiefs; that I did not come to war with women and children but to fight with men; that his people had better be on their guard, because if they did not comply with my terms after seeing me I should see them safe from camp and then consider them as enemies. . . .

Tomorrow I expect The Raven, Oconostota, The Carpenter and many others of the Chiefs; and I suppose in three days I can open a treaty or begin to destroy the towns and pursue the Indians towards the Creeks. I know, sir, that I could kill and take hundreds of them and starve hundreds by destroying their corn, but it would be mostly the women and children, as the men could retreat faster than I can follow, and I am convinced that Virginia State would be better pleased to hear that I showed pity to the distressed and spared the suppliants rather than that I should commit one act of barbarity in destroying a whole nation of enemies. I believe that all the old warriors and all the women of the nation this side of the Hills [the Alleghanies] were averse to the war, and that the rest were led by Cameron, sometimes by bribing them and at others by threatening them.

In the conference with the chiefs Christian demanded that Cameron and Dragging Canoe be delivered up to him as the price of peace. It was explained that both had left the towns, going south. From Chickamauga Dragging Canoe wrote (November 14th) that he would never consent to make peace until Stuart and Cameron "agree to it and make it for us;" and that he would immediately set out to make war.

Colonel Christian reported that Chief Dragging Canoe, under Cameron's influence, had been the principal agency in urging on war against the Americans. Cameron, on Christian's command crossing the Little Tennessee, had hurried out of the nation towards the Alabama country.

Six or seven of the friendlier chiefs came to treat for peace. The difficulty was with those chiefs who were blood-guilty. The towns commanded by these were burned along with the provisions stored in them. Early and distinctly marked for retributive chastisement were two towns, the inhabitants of which had burned at the stake young Samuel Moore, who had been captured at the fort on Watauga in July and taken prisoner along with Mrs. Bean to their towns. Redd in his *Reminiscences* says that the troops found in the house of Dragging Canoe "seven scalps hanging up nicely painted, and just in front of the town a stake to which Dragging Canoe had a short time before bound a small boy [Moore] and burned him to death while a war-dance was held. Dragging Canoe sent in his agent and it was very well that he did not come in himself for the whites were so incensed with him on account of his many cruelties that he would have been murdered on his appearance." [25]

That chief continued to refuse to accept peace terms that were agreeable to the other chiefs, and in resentment he gathered the unruly of the nation and retired to Chickamauga Creek, where in course of time they were called "the Chickamaugas."

A preliminary treaty of truce was entered into which stipulated that the Cherokees should surrender their white prisoners and the horses they had taken and the following year send to Long Island a delegation authorized to treat formally for a boundary line that would give to white settlers the lands they then occupied as well as some additional territory. Colonel Christian did not follow his instructions in respect of demanding hostages.

The humanity and leniency thus shown by Christian did not please all of the leaders under him. Colonel Joseph Williams of

---

[25] *Ib.*, VII, 251.

the Surry County detachment, was among those who thought the truce-terms inadequate. He, on November 6th, wrote from "Citico Town" to the president of the North Carolina Provincial Congress that nothing had been done "except burning five of their towns and patched up a kind of peace. . . . I have this day obtained leave to return home with my battalion."[26]

November 12th, on the return march, Colonel Christian was at the home of Major Evans Shelby from which place he issued a proclamation forbidding the white inhabitants going, without express permission, into the Cherokee nation to get back their horses. A copy of the proclamation was speeded to Captain James Robertson, the fair inference being that the Wataugans were on the point of a self-enforcement of their rights.

It was apparent to both Christian and Williams that the expedition would result in a rush of new settlers into, and a rapid development of, the beautiful and fertile valleys their men had traversed. The average of the militiamen lusted for cheap and good land and had eyes open to the opportunities brought within reach by their own exertions. Both Christian and Williams were aware of what was to follow and each was jealous of the right of his own State to the lands opening, it seemed, to settlement. The boundary line between their States had not been extended and Virginia was still disposed to treat a large portion of the territory to be ceded by the Cherokees as being within her jurisdiction. Christian wrote home to Governor Henry: "If the people can settle in peace, I fear differences about land near the Carolina line will grow high if something is not done about it. . . . I like it [the country] better than the Virginia part of this side of Ohio [Kentucky]."

Colonel Williams, while among the Indians, had visited and spied out the beautiful site at the junction of the Holston and the Tennessee Rivers.[27]

Immediately upon the return of the army, we find William

---

[26] *N. C. Col. Recs.*, X, 892.

[27] *Ib.*, X, 912. Col. Williams in 1779 sought and obtained the command of the skeleton battalion which was ordered out as guard to the surveyors of the North Carolina-Virginia State line westward, thus demonstrating his interest in the Trans-Alleghany region, in the development of which three of his sons were to play leading parts. *N. C. State Recs.* XIV, 109, 177, 139, 144, 145.

Cocke asserting title to, and executing a deed for, the ancient treaty ground of the Cherokees, Long Island, in the instrument describing himself as "of Fincastle County, Virginia," though actually a resident south of the boundary line as later run.[28] Stronger proof of eager grasping it would be difficult to find.

Ramsey well describes the inflow of settlers that followed:

Each soldier upon his return home gave a glowing account of the adaptation of the country to all the purposes of agriculture. The story was repeated from one to another, till upon the Roanoke and the Yadkin the people spoke familiarly of the Holston, the Nollichucky, the French Broad, the Little River and the Tennessee. Particular places were selected, springs designated and points chosen as centres for future settlements. A flood of immigration followed to strengthen, build up and enlarge the little community already planted across the mountain.[29]

Roosevelt in concluding his account of the campaign, says, in the *Winning of the West*: "The war was thus another and important link in the chain of events by which the West was won; and had any link in the chain snapped during these early years, the peace of 1783 would probably have seen the Trans-Alleghany country in the hands of a non-American power."

It should be a matter of pride to Tennesseans more than one hundred and fifty years afterwards to know that so many inhabitants of the Tennessee country played important parts in this war, which was brought to a conclusion not less glorious by reason of the fact that a humane policy was adopted toward the redmen by one who deserves, in high degree, commemoration as the leader of the expeditionary forces—William Christian. It is sad to contemplate that this able and brave soldier lost his life at the hands of Indians. In 1786, while on an expedition against the Ohio tribes, he was captured and burned at the stake.

---

[28] *Ib.*, X, 911, deed dated Nov. 15th, 1776.
[29] *Annals of Tennessee*, 170.

CHAPTER VII

A YEAR BEGINNING IN TURMOIL, ENDING IN PEACE (1777)

The "peace" negotiated in the Cherokee country by Colonel Christian proved far from being anything but turmoil. Cameron, Dragging Canoe and some other chiefs saw to that. During the winter of 1776–1777 a fair portion of the warriors, especially the younger ones, followed Dragging Canoe as seceders from the nation. Dragging Canoe and his people settled on the site of an ancient town of the Creek Indians, on Chickamauga Creek.[1] His brother, Little Owl, settled further up that stream near the Georgia line, while those from Settico town on the Little Tennessee chose a home-site on the river and gave the village the name of the one from which they had migrated.[2] The old towns were left weakened in consequence but not to the point claimed by some.[3] It is true, however, that by reason of accessions from the malcontents and outlawed of other tribes and from renegade whites the Chickamaugas became numerically stronger than the Cherokees proper, and a source of grave concern to the whites within striking distance of them. The new tribe was given preferential treatment by Great Britain in the distribution of munitions. In consequence of these things animosity between the Cherokees and the Chickamaugas was kept alive and deepened. In ignorance of

---

[1] Chukko-mah-ko ("the dwelling place of the war chief"), according to Brown; but Tsi-ka-ma-gi, according to Mooney, who says the meaning has been lost.

[2] At the present time called Citico, within or near the corporate limits of the city of Chattanooga. The fullest treatment of this Chickamauga tribe is by Brown in his *Old Frontiers*, on which the author expended much research in archives. His work is somewhat marred, however, by over-straining to make a hero of Dragging Canoe who lacked much of the essential elements; also by errors.

[3] In *Old Frontiers* it is stated (p. 163) that the old towns of "Settico, Great Island, Tellico, Toqua and Chilhowee were depopulated." That this is an over-statement appears from Schneider's Report in Williams, *Early Travels in the Tennessee Country,* 254 *et. seq.* The loss was not so much in numbers as in virility and manpower for making war.

this, Governors Henry and Caswell, and Colonel John Carter were of opinion that all the Cherokees were bent on hostilities.

Dragging Canoe's threat to continue to make war was not an idle one. By January, 1777, Colonel Carter sent an express to General Rutherford giving an account of the unhappy situation in the West and soliciting aid from North Carolina in guarding the border.[4] One hundred men were ordered to go from the east side of the mountains to the assistance of Washington District.[5] The militia of Washington District was ordered to be embodied near Long Island. The people near the Island again took to forts.

In March Governor Henry thought it wise to speed up the negotiation of the treaty promised Colonel Christian by the Cherokees, and he wrote soliciting the co-operation of Governor Caswell in the appointment of commissioners. Four hundred of the militia of Virginia were ordered to be assembled by Major Evan Shelby for defense, though Governor Henry had in mind that another offensive expedition might be necessary.[6]

Raids by the Chickamaugas continued, and David Crockett, grandfather of the celebrated Davy Crockett, and some of his family, living on Crockett Creek and the site of the present-day Rogersville were killed. They had remained after the flight of most of the inhabitants of Carter's Valley.[7] Seemingly at the same time, about twenty-five of the followers of Dragging Canoe hovered in camp near the crossing place of the North Fork of Holston. From there they sallied forth burning and killing until spies discovered their hiding place, when the whites embodied and surrounded them. One of the whites prematurely fired into the redmen's camp, and most of the Indians plunged into the river which, being flush, proved to be a watery grave for several. About seven were killed in the skirmish.[8]

[4] Rutherford to Gov. Caswell, Feb. 1st, Robert Lynn being the express. *N. C. St. Recs.*, XI 372, and XXII, 903. The killing of a family within two miles of Long Island was, as reported by Carter, that of William Purviance of Poor Valley.

[5] *Ib.*, 393.

[6] *Ib.*, 428–9. "I heartily wish the people of your State would, in case of an expedition, lend us their aid; but an attack of Shelby might unite all the towns in the British King's interest." Shelby was yet treated as a Virginia officer, though residing below the true state line.

[7] *Ante*, p. 43.

[8] Taylor, *Historic Sullivan*, 62, and the Snodgrass MSS, in Draper Collection.

Governor Henry as early as January 24th named Colonel Christian, Colonel Shelby and Colonel William Preston "to negotiate with the Cherokees . . . for ratifying the late convention held at their towns." [9] Governor Caswell was slower in naming commissioners to act for North Carolina. [10] Nathaniel Gist on his return to Virginia (January 11th, 1777) was commissioned a colonel in the continental army on the recommendation of his old friend, General Washington. [11] Gist was then sent to the Tennessee country to use his influence with the Cherokees in bringing them and the seceding element into the promised treaty at Fort Patrick Henry (Long Island). He arrived at that post on March 27th and sent by an Indian messenger a talk to the chiefs. [12] A number of the chiefs of the upper towns did go to the Island to treat, The Tassel, Oconostota and Attakullakulla (Little Carpenter) among them. They met on March 20th at the Long Island the three Virginia commissioners only, none yet having been named on the part of North Carolina. [13] To conclude a treaty in this situation and especially without the presence and concurrence of Dragging Canoe was thought inadvisable. The sullen chief absented himself although a special and urgent invitation had been sent him by Colonel Gist. Colonel Christian persuaded Oconostota and some other chiefs to visit the governor at Williamsburg, [14] and suggested that there be an adjournment of further negotiation until June

---

[9] *Official Letters of Governors*, I, 94. In December Christian had sent two agents, Samuel Newell and Samuel Ewing, to induce The Tassel to meet the colonels at Long Island of Holston for a conference, but without success. In January, Newell returned on a like mission and lost his life at the hands of redmen on his way home.

[10] *N. C. St. Recs.*, XI, 447, 451. Early in April both governors thought that offensive operations might be necessary.

[11] Gist had accompanied Washington and his father, the famous Christopher Gist, on a tour to the Ohio River in 1751-2. Williams, "Nathaniel Gist, Father of Sequoyah," in *E. T. Hist. Soc. Pubs.* V, 39–54.

[12] This talk is preserved in the Manuscript Division of the Library of Congress. In it he reminded the chiefs that he, in the spring of 1776, had counseled against their beginning a war.

[13] However, Richard Henderson and Leonard Bullock turned up to protect their interests in the Transylvania Company, and "to raise men to go to Kentucky" to steady settlements there. Draper MSS 1 CC 226, letter of Henderson dated April 13th.

[14] General Washington had sent by Gist a letter to Oconostota, inviting some of the Indians to visit the General's camp.

26th. This was agreed to and the war-lord with Christian was off to see the governor. Gist on request of the commissioners journeyed to Chota and sent off a second message to Dragging Canoe.

The events of the immediate period were well summarized by Major Charles Robertson, whose command of Wataugans attended the conference in March—April as guards, in a letter to Governor Caswell, of which William Tatham was manifestly the penman: [15]

The many hostilities committed by the Cherokee and Creek Indians on this frontier since the departure of the Gent. Delegates from this County, merits your Excellency's consideration. I will give myself the pleasure to inform you of the particulars of this distressed place, and of our unhappy situation. There have been several late murders committed, and on the 10th of this instant one Frederick Calvatt was shot and scalped, but is yet living: and on the day following Capt. James Robertson pursued the enemy with nine men, killed one and retook ten horses, and on his return in the evening, was attacked by a party of Creeks and Cherokees, who wounded two of his men. Robertson returned the fire very bravely, but was obliged to retreat on account of their superior number; still, kept the horses, and brought them in. On the 27th of March last Col. Nathaniel Guess [Gist] brought letters from the Governor of Virginia, which letters were sent, by an Indian woman, to the Cherokee nation, soliciting them to come in, in eighteen days to treat for peace. Accordingly there came a party of about eighty-five fellows, (but none of the principal warriors that had first begun the war), and at their arrival, the commanding officers at Fort Patrick Henry sent for me to march some troops to that garrison, as a guard during the treaty. Accordingly I went, and on the 20th ulto. the Talks began, and the articles of the Treaty were as follows: first a copy of the Governor's letter was read to them, promising them protection, such as ammunition, provisions, and men to build forts, and guard and assist them against any nation, white or red; and in return the Commissioners required the same from them; to which the Indians replied they could not fight against their Father, King George, but insisted on Col. Christian's promise to them last fall, that if they would make a peace, they should lie neuter, and no assistance asked of them from the States. The Commissioners then asked some of them to go to Williamsburg, not as hostages, but to see their goods delivered, to obviate any suspicion of false reports. A number of about ten agreed to go. The Commission-

---

[15] *N. C. State Recs.*, XI, 458. Tatham was the only man on the Watauga who could have written in such phrasing and spelling.

ers then told them that Virginia and South Carolina gave them peace and protection, and North Carolina offered it; to which the Indians replied, they heard the talks from South Carolina, and they & the talks from Virginia were very good. The Indians then promised to try and bring in the Dragging Canoe, and his party (a party that lies out, and has refused to come in, but says they will hold fast Cameron's talks); they still made no doubt but they could prevail on him; and said that he had sent his Talk with them, and what they agreed to, he would abide by. But the Little Carpenter, in private conversation with Captain Thomas Price, contradicted it, and said that the Canoe and his party were fighting Capt. Robertson a few days before: and the last day of the Talks there arrived an express from Clinch river, informing us of two men being killed; to which the Indians replied to keep a sharp look out for there were a great many of their men out; & several of their women present declared that the talk was as before, the time to get guns and ammunition, and continue the war as formerly.

Accordingly they demanded them, which was the finishing of the Talks, and in sixty days they were to come in to treat and confirm the peace, and if they could not bring in the Dragging Canoe, they send word laying the blame of the late murder on the Creeks. This, Sir, is a true state of the whole proceedings, of which I have the honour to inform your Excellency, conscious you will take every prudent method for our security.

There has been to the number of about twelve persons killed since the Delegates departed [for the general assembly].

In the late spring of 1777 two companies of North Carolina's militia were sent to the western waters to succor the inhabitants on the Watauga and Nolachucky who were being harassed by the Chickamaugas and some of their sympathizers in the old towns of the Cherokees—young braves hard to be held in leash by the chiefs. One company under Captain Benjamin Cleveland [16] was stationed at Fort Caswell, sometimes spoken of as "Carter's Fort," Colonel John Carter being its commander. The other, seemingly, under Major Jesse Walton,[17] was on the Nolachucky. The fort on the latter stream was named Fort Williams.[18]

The general assembly of North Carolina on May 7th had pro-

---

[16] Later a colonel in the battle of King's Mountain. Andrew Greer was Carolina's agent to furnish supplies to the troops then in garrison. *N. C. St. Recs.*, XII, 37, 39.

[17] See below, p. 124.

[18] Doubtless, in honor of Lieutenant Col. Joseph Williams. Its exact location is not now known.

vided that four independent companies of rangers or scouts of fifty privates each, be raised west of the mountains and employed as General Rutherford should direct in building and garrisoning stockaded forts in Washington District.[19]   The people of the West, however, had already moved in the erection of stockades, as seen above.

On June 8th Dragging Canoe wrote a letter to Colonel Gist (produced later at the treaty) which shows that chief to have been a hero with much alloy.   In the letter he protested that his eyes had been opened to the lies told him by Cameron and Stuart; that the Virginians [20] were the greatest friends the Cherokees ever had.   "I am determined that I nor my people shall ever spoil their good talk. while I live. . . . If I should not come in [to the treaty] soon, pray excuse me to the beloved men." [21]

Dragging Canoe was far from being sincere.   He stayed away from the treaty ground.

The proceedings for a treaty were resumed on June 28th—two days late.   Four commissioners from North Carolina appeared on the 13th: Waightstill Avery, William Sharpe, Robert Lanier and Joseph Winston; [22] who now proceeded jointly with the Virginia Commissioners.   On the same day Oconostota and his party of forty-four arrived at the fort from Williamsburg,[23] accompanied by Colonel Christian.

An unfortunate occurrence on July 1st threatened the success

---

[19] One of the captains of rangers was James Stuart, later prominent in public life.   His party ranged from Greasy Cove (Unicoi County) to Dungan's Mill (Watauga Station on Southern Railway).

[20] The whites in Upper East Tennessee were nearly all considered Virginians by the Indians.

[21] Proceedings at Fort Patrick Henry are in *N. C. Hist. Review*, VIII, 64–65, edited by Archibald Henderson.

[22] These four came by Col. John Carter's and spent a night at his home (Elizabethton of this day).   They had been appointed on June 12th.   For a narrow escape of Avery and Sharpe from an Indian hunting party on Roaring Creek (North Carolina) as they passed, see *N. C. Col. Rec.*, 770.   Captains Thomas Madison and Isaac Shelby were commissary agents for Virginia, charged with supplying the attendants with food, etc.

[23] There Col. Christian and Dr. Thomas Walker were directed to provide for the Indians proper presents, and the governor met the chiefs and warriors from time to time.   An interesting scene: Patrick Henry in friendly chats with Oconostota.

of negotiations. A large number of warriors had followed their chiefs to the treaty ground. One of them, Big Bullet, had waded out to a small island in the Holston and was sitting on its bank mending his moccasins. A white man [24] crept within rifle-shot and killed him. The Indian camps were in turmoil. A reward was offered by the commissioners for the apprehension of the culprit but without success.

The next day Oconostota opened the proceedings by a reference to the killing of Big Bullet: "The white people have given the first stroke at the peace chain and tried to break it. . . . What they have done shall not spoil the good talks. . . . I shall think nothing of it. . . . Cameron and Stuart will hear of this accident and will laugh and be pleased at it; but I do not care for what they can say. I shall tell my own people not to mind Cameron and Stuart." [25] All the commissioners present joined in expressing regret and the hope that the occurrence "will not be a means of hindering the peace so happily begun."

On February 6th, 1777, Stuart had written Oconostota a biting letter, rebuking him for laying down the hatchet and "taking Virginians by the hand." [25a] The war-lord manifestly resented this.

The main complaint of the chiefs was that concerning white settlements on Nolachucky below Jacob Brown's and those on the Watauga near its mouth—seemingly Bean's and his neighbors'. The chiefs were much more amenable to the proposal of the Virginians than to those of the North Carolinians, due to the fact that the people on Watauga and Nolachucky were residents of North Carolina, and it was they who pressed hardest on the lands of the Cherokees. Avery was chief spokesman for his State and, being a fine lawyer, handled the case skillfully. Tassel (Old Tassel), really Corntassel, was the leading speaker for the Indians. Oconostota and Attakullakulla, now of advanced age, were spe-

---

[24] Later it was learned that this was Robert Young, who lived in the environs of the present Johnson City. See n. 40, p. 157, *post*.

[25] Henderson, "Treaty at Long Island," above cited, a full text of the proceedings and the treaty. See, also, Haywood, *Civil History of Tennessee*, Appendix. Tatham says that he "assisted the North Carolina commissioners in preparing the documents and conducting the conferences."

[25a] Papers of the Continental Congress (Library of Congress) 71, 2, p. 201.

cially honored by the commissioners: "after spreading three
match coats on two benches, seating Oconostota and Attakullakulla thereon."

Tatham left valuable pen pictures of the leading chiefs in attendance, and an outline of a speech of The Tassel, compact with
true pathos:

You say: Why do not the Indians till the ground and live as
we do? May we not, with equal propriety, ask, Why the white
people do not hunt and live as we do? You profess to think it
no injustice to warn us not to kill our deer and other game from
the mere love of waste; but it is very criminal in our young men
if they chance to kill a cow or a hog for their sustenance when
they happen to be in your lands. We wish, however, to be at
peace with you, and to do as we would be done by. We do not
quarrel with you for killing an occasional buffalo, bear, or deer
on our lands when you need one to eat; but you go much farther;
your people hunt to gain a livelihood by it; they kill all our game;
our young men resent the injury, and it is followed by bloodshed
and war.

This is not a mere affected injury; it is a grievance which we
equitably complain of and it demands a permanent redress.

The Great God of Nature has placed us in different situations.
It is true that he has endowed you with many superior advantages; but he has not created us to be your slaves. *We are a
separate people!* He has given each their lands, under distinct
considerations and circumstances; he has stocked yours with
cows, ours with buffaloe; yours with hog, ours with bear; yours
with sheep, ours with deer. He has indeed given you an advantage in this, that your cattle are tame and domestic while ours
are wild and demand not only a larger space for range, where we
are to hunt and kill them; they are, nevertheless, as much our
property as other animals are yours, and ought not to be taken
away without our consent, or for something equivalent.[26]

While treaty negotiations were in progress, Richard Henderson
for his land company, now at the Long Island for the second time,
presented a memorial regarding his purchases of lands from the
Cherokees at Sycamore Shoals of the Watauga in 1775.[27] It was
asked by him that "the commissioners will not proceed to run a

---

[26] Williams, *William Tatham, Wataugan,* 24–25. Tatham says that his
own account of this address is "bereaved of much of its native beauty by
the defects of interpretation; for the manly and dignified expressions of an
Indian orator lose nearly all force and energy in translation." Next to
Attakullakulla, The Tassel was the greatest Cherokee orator. See Appendix.

[27] On that treaty, see Williams, *Dawn,* ch. 32.

line through their purchases, or yield any part of the lands there to Indians." The negotiators proceeded in disregard.

Negotiations were concluded in a signed treaty [28] on June 20th. By it Virginia obtained a boundary line "to begin at the lower corner of Donelson's line [29] on the north side of River Holston and to run down that river and binding thereon, including the Great Island, at the mouth of Cloud's Creek; thence running a straight line to a high point on Cumberland Mountain between there and five miles below or westward of the Great Gap which leads to the settlements on the Kentucky; this last mentioned line is to be considered as the boundary between Virginia and the Cherokees." [30] North Carolina obtained a boundary line running from the mouth of Cloud's Creek, thence a right line to the mouth of Camp Creek, otherwise called McNamee's Creek, on the south bank of the Nolachucky; thence in a southward direction to the Alleghany Mountains.[31] No consideration passed from North Carolina, but it was agreed "that no white man on any pretense whatever shall build, plant, improve, settle, hunt or drive stock below the said boundary line on pain of being drove off by the Indians, and being further punished according to law." [32]

The line "between Virginia and the Cherokees" was run and marked by Wm. Campbell, of Washington County, Virginia, in the winter of 1777–78. No protest was made by the North Caro-

---

[28] Major Shelby did not sign the treaty. While present and active in the March phase, he attended few of the proceedings in June and July; evidently, he was detained much of the time at home by illness. He lived much nearer the site than any other commissioner.

[29] For which see, *Ib*. Chap. 29.

[30] Evidencing a persistence of Virginia's claim to jurisdiction over Pendleton District and Carter's Valley. "Two hundred cows and one hundred sheep, to be delivered at the Great Island when the said line shall be run" was the consideration and it was paid—to the ultimate benefit of North Carolina, as after-events demonstrated.

[31] North Carolina commissioners had asked for a line to strike the Nolachucky five miles below Camp Creek.

[32] How this pledge was kept may be seen in the fact that the whites continued to advance so fast that the site of Greeneville, which was left in the Indian country, in 1785 became the capital of the State of Franklin, after having become the seat of Greene County in 1783. In this connection note the remark of The Tassel in one of his speeches at Fort Patrick Henry: "It is a little surprising that when we enter into treaties with our brothers, the whites, their whole cry is for *more land*."

lina commissioners to this assertion of right on the part of Virginia.

The first fourth of July celebration on Tennessee soil and in all the West was at the fort during the treaty. Truly, it was a great occasion: four or five hundred Cherokees were there; many of the militia from Southwest Virginia and the District of Washington, also Captain Benjamin Cleveland's company from Surry County, North Carolina, were present. The minutes of the commissioners recite:

The anniversary of the Declaration of Independence was observed. The soldiers belonging to the garrison were paraded and fired two rounds; each in six platoons and for the thirteenth one general volley. The great guns were also fired.

The Indian Chiefs were acquainted with the festivity in the following speech, and had a present of whiskey delivered to them at the same time:

Brothers, Just one year ago the thirteen United States declared themselves free and independent, and that they would no longer be in subjection and slavery to the King of Great Britain. The Americans have now for one year since their freedom fought against their enemies that came in ships over the great water, and have beat them in many battles; have killed some thousands of them and taken many prisoners, and the Great Being above hath made them very prosperous. We hope, therefore, that this day every year hereafter will be a day of rejoicing and gladness. Brother, as this is a day of general rejoicing throughout the thirteen united colonies from Canada to the Floridas, we hope our brothers, the Cherokees, will now rejoice and be merry with us.

The young warriors then closed the entertainment with a dance.

The redmen whom the British had tried to incite against the Americans thus joined in a celebration of the freedom of the American people from British rule! No counterpart can be found in American history.

At treaty's close, the North Carolina commissioners employed James Robertson [33] as Indian commissioner to the Overhill Cherokees, and those of Virginia chose Joseph Martin to serve that State in the same capacity. The Cherokees evidenced their re-

---

[33] Robertson moved and made his home at the mouth of Big Creek (in present Hawkins County) where he constructed a small fort. The spot he selected is one of the most attractive in Upper East Tennessee. So it is that Robertson was not living on the Watauga when he left for the Cumberland country, in 1779. The Raven (on July 18th) proposed a line to begin "at the mouth of Big Creek just below Robertson's fort, etc."

gard for Colonel Gist by having made what was treated as a reservation in the treaty:

Memorandum before signing: that the Tassel yesterday objected against giving up the Great Island opposite Fort Henry to any person or country whatever, except Colo. Nathaniel Gist for whom and for themselves it was reserved by the Cherokees. The Raven did the same this day in behalf of the Indians and desired that Colo. Gist might sit down upon it when he pleased, as it belongs to him and them to hold good talks on.[34]

Colonel Gist, from the treaty ground, led seventeen warriors to the army of General Washington to serve as scouts.[35]

While treaty-making was yet in progress, a chapter in western history was being made—a chapter that up to the present has failed of being written in any history of Tennessee. Ramsey merely glimpsed it in a few lines.

In Filson's *Adventures of Daniel Boone* he wrote at Boone's dictation: "On the twenty-fifth of this month (July 1777) a reinforcement of forty-five men arrived from North Carolina, and about the twentieth of August following Col. Bowman arrived with one hundred men from Virginia. From now on we began to strengthen, and from thence for the space of six weeks we had skirmishes with Indians in one quarter or another almost every day."

Biographers of Boone have construed this to mean that the reinforcements "from North Carolina" went from Boone's old home on the Yadkin River. In fact, they were from Washington District where Boone had lived in 1772 [36] and where he had firmly-attached friends. Another Kentuckian, Captain William Bailey Smith,[37] had also lived among the Wataugans and served them in a post of honor. Smith turned up among his and Boone's old neighbors, reporting the dire straits of Boonesborough and other

---

[34] The Island for its fertility was envied by many throughout generations. It was finally formally ceded by the Cherokee nation in the treaty of January 7, 1806, at Washington. It was one of the last bits of land ceded by the nation. Royce, *Cherokee Nation*, 194.

[35] Led by The Pidgeon who went to London, England, with Henry Timberlake in 1761. Williams, *Memoirs of Lt. Timberlake, passim.*

[36] Williams, *Dawn*, passim.

[37] Smith was a skillful surveyor, and did much of the surveying for the Wataugans' land office. In 1778 he became a major in Kentucky. He finally settled on the Henderson consolation grant near Henderson, Ky.

settlements in the Kentucky country, then under attack by Indians. He appealed for aid. This people, some of whom had in 1774 gone to the Upper Ohio and fought at Point Pleasant, promptly answered this Macedonian call for aid from the western wilderness. A company under Captain Smith marched through Cumberland Gap to succor the hard-pressed settlers in the Kentucky country—with the result recorded by Filson. This, they felt, they could safely do, now that North Carolina had sent two companies to steady their own homeland. Surely, again the appellation of "the Volunteer State" was well earned long before the Mexican War. Its bestowal was merely belated.[38]

The Wataugans gave aid to Boonesborough and to Harrodsborough. The latter station was attacked by the Indians from the south, doubtless Chickamaugas incited by Cameron and, as related by a participant [39] a part of the troops, "marched to a place on the Cumberland to follow the Indians, which they did until

[38] "The year of the three sevens" (1777) was long known as "the bloody year" in the history of Kentucky, "the dark and bloody ground." Withers, *Border Warfare,* 217, 253n.

Two Kentucky residents kept diaries and recorded events of the year, 1777: George Rogers Clark and John Cowan. In sequence they are quoted here:

Clark, "May 23rd: A large party of Indians attacked Boonesborough Forts; kept a warm Fire until 11 o'clock at Night. Began it next Morning and kept a Warm Fire until Midnight, attempting several times to burn the Fort. 3 of our men were wounded, not mortally. The enemy suffered considerably.

"May 26. A party went out to hunt Indians; one wounded Squire Boone and escaped.

Cowan, "May 27. An alarm this morning . . . Boone's fort was attacked on Friday morning last and a brisk firing kept up until Sunday morning.

Clark "(July ?) 23rd. Express resive from Boone's and say that on the 13th Captain Smith arive with 48 men, 150 more on the March for this [place], also with an Ac't that General Washington had defeated Howe. Joyfull News, if true." Draper Manuscripts, 48 J 12; *Ill. Historical Collections,* VIII, 20–23. No muster roll of this company of Wataugans was kept, and the Wataugans, treating the "tour of duty" as a matter of course, left no record of it or its composition.

[39] James Patrick, Sr., in his pension statement of 1833: "He was at the time 103 years old and had served as a soldier under Gen. Braddock in 1755, as one of Washington's rangers in the Revolution under Lt. Adam Peck, from March 6, 1776. A. W. Burns, *Virginia Genealogies and County Records,* 86–87.

they passed the borders of Kentucky and got into Tennessee. "One hundred and fifty of us overtook the Indians at a place on the Cumberland called the French Lick, where the town of Nashville now stands, and succeeded in taking this place. This country then belonged to North Carolina. After destroying their corn and burning their towns,[40] the army returned to Boonesborough." It is highly probable that at least a few Wataugans were in this "army."

A degree of confirmation is found in the biographical sketch which was published just after the death of General Robertson in the Nashville *Clarion* of September 8, 1814:

About the year 1778, a few who had seen the Cumberland country returned to the Watauga frontier and gave such an account of the richness of the soil, the luxuriance of the growth, and the incredible quantity of game, as fired the desire of many to emigrate there. Time after time the people projected schemes for effecting their object; but they all failed until a company, mostly composed of those who had fought by the side of Capt. Robertson, made ready to start.

Ramsey is mistaken in attributing to Colonel John Bowman of Kentucky the embodying and leading of these troops into Kentucky. Bowman did go a little later to settlements in Virginia on the upper part of the Holston for succor, and a few men who lived just below the Virginia line may have gone with him.[41] The two occurrences, however, were distinct, as Boone related.[42]

---

[40] Not real towns but temporary camps erected in an effort to hold the region against all whites.

[41] See directions to Col. Arthur Campbell of Washington County, Va. *Executive Journal of Virginia* (for 1777) 306–7; and hold in mind that what is now Sullivan County, Tenn., was then treated as if under the jurisdiction of Virginia's county of Washington.

[42] The latest biographer of Boone, while stating that Capt. Smith led this company, like others failed to identify its members as Wataugans: "William Bailey Smith had gone back to North Carolina and on his own authority enlisted forty or fifty mounted riflemen, mostly former friends and neighbors of Boone. . . . Smith had his men open ranks as they marched into Boonesborough, with a distance of six feet, head-to-tail, between their horses. Watching Shawano scouts were thus deluded into reporting the arrival of two hundred men—four or five times their real number. Thus reinforced, the Kentuckians took the offensive and again went out looking for Indians. When cattle gave the alarm at a turnip patch near Harrodsburg, white men silently surrounded an ambush that

Colonel Christian in the fall issued orders that no white persons enter the Cherokee country without written leave.[43]   Attakulla-kulla with a band of warriors journeyed to Fort Patrick Henry and gave assurance of readiness to raise a large force of followers to fight with the Americans in the pending War for Independence. He and several other chiefs were named as delegates to go to the governors of Virginia and North Carolina in behalf of the nation. The Cherokees were in sore need of supplies and an opening of trade.

had been laid for them.   They drove off the Indians." Bakeless, *Daniel Boone*, 153–4.

[43] To Col. Wm. Russell, from the home of Evan Shelby, Nov. 12th, 1776.   Corbin's *Calendar of Manuscript Collections*, 35.

CHAPTER VIII

CIVIL AFFAIRS (1777)

Owing to the defensive and offensive military operations of 1777, the year passed with but few happenings in the civic life of the people on the western waters. All of their energy was taxed in combatting the Indians.

By an Ordinance appended to and made a part of the North Carolina Constitution, adopted in December, 1776, members of the court for Washington District had been named.[1] The district, treated as a county, with other counties comprised the District of Salisbury. However, the passage of an act by the general assembly establishing a court for it was thought necessary. Such an act was passed in the early part of 1777,[2] and under it the court was organized in August, with John Carter as chairman and Wm. Cocke as clerk. Until then the court of the Watauga Association functioned. The membership of the court varied somewhat from that which had been provided by the Constitution.[3] Its jurisdiction was comparatively broad, appeals being to the superior court at Salisbury. No records of the short-lived court survive.

Its members were: John Carter, chairman, Andrew Greer, John McNabb, William Clark, Joseph Wilson, Benjamin Gist, Thomas Houghton, Jacob Womack, John Chisholm, William Bean, George Russell, Charles Robertson, Zachariah Isbell and John McMahan.[4]

John Carter was in the Senate [5] and John Sevier in the House of Commons of the assembly from Washington "District." Two

---

[1] John Carter, John Sevier, Charles Robertson, Valentine Sevier, Robert Lucas, John Haile, Andrew Greer, Thomas Simpson, Jacob Womack, John Shelby, George Russell, Wm. Bean, Henry Clark, Zachariah Isbell, Aaron Pinson, John McNabb, Thomas Houghton, William Higgins, Isaac Johnston, Andrew Baker, jr., and William Clark. The omission of the name of James Robertson was doubtless due to his plan to remove to the mouth of Big Creek on the west side of the Holston; see note, *ante.*

[2] *N. C. St. Recs.*, XXV, 39, 64 and preceding note.

[3] *Ib.*, XXIII, 995 and the note above. Also, XII, 112–13.

[4] *Ib.*, XI, 653, compare with notes above.

[5] Carter thus was the first state senator in the Tennessee country.

sessions were held during 1777. At the April session an act was passed for the establishment of Washington "County" to succeed Washington District, except that the eastern boundary was made the Alleghany Mountains.[6] The area became that of the present State of Tennessee—the "Mother County" from which have sprung ninety-four other counties.

Following up the treaty at Fort Patrick Henry, another act was passed providing for the opening of an office for the entry of "lands which have accrued or which shall accrue to the State by treaty or conquest." John Carter was appointed entry-taker for Washington County. Lands were obtainable at the rate of forty shillings per hundred acres. An inadequate provision was made for the western folk in that each head of a family might take up a section; and in addition one hundred acres for his wife and the same quantity for each child. Further, such settlers should not be required to pay for the lands they occupied until January, 1779. Thus these lands on the Watauga and its waters had to be paid for twice. For any lands entered above the quantities above named, the purchasers should pay at the rate of five pounds per hundred acres. A prohibition was that no recognition should be given to occupant rights to lands lying south of the Indian boundary fixed in the July treaty.

On no American frontier was so much difficulty experienced as on our western waters in the procurement of clear titles to lands. The oldest claim was that of Lord Granville which covered the upper half, and more, below the Virginia line.[7] That incubus the general assembly of North Carolina was taking steps to remove by an act of confiscation.[8] The cloud of the Cherokee claim was ended for a part of the territory by the Cherokee treaty cession. But there was an uncertainty growing out of the contention on part of some of the landless States (those without colonial charter boundaries that reached beyond the Alleghany range) that the rights and jurisdiction of the British crown over the immense western country were dominant; and the lands in the West, therefore, had passed to the American nation and not to the claimant

---

[6] *N. C. St. Recs.*, XII, 238; XXIV, 43–48.

[7] For the Granville claim and Lord Granville's District, see Williams, *Dawn*, 311–316.

[8] A lawsuit resulted and was not finally settled, adversely to Lord Granville's heirs, until 1817.

States.[9] Did the power to grant such lands reside in the State of North Carolina?[10] Too, the North of Holston settlers were embarrassed, in this regard, by the uncertainty as to where the Virginia-North Carolina line would run upon being extended westward, and by the assertion and exercise of jurisdiction by Virginia over the region.

The settlers in Washington County availed of the opportunity to obtain grants from a government claiming sovereignty. Even those who had obtained grants or deeds from Charles Robertson, Trustee for the Wataugans, reinforced their titles by entries in John Carter's office, later followed by grants signed by governors of North Carolina.

A curious occurrence incident to Virginia's assertion of jurisdiction over North Carolina soil was this: In the spring of 1777 an election was held for members in the Virginia legislature from Washington County, Virginia. Arthur Campbell and William Edminston were opposed by Anthony Bledsoe and Wm. Cocke, both residing below the true state line. A hotly contested election resulted in favor of Bledsoe and Cocke, whose opponents filed a contest based on the ground that their opponents "received many votes given by persons who reside in North Carolina."[11]

In order to connect her own Washington County with North

---

[9] The rights of Virginia, North Carolina, and other States were assailed in the Continental Congress (1776) on the ground that the lands of the West had belonged to the king of Great Britain and, if and when wrested from him it would be by the joint efforts, the "blood and treasure" of all the States and should be the joint property of all as a nation. Virginia and North Carolina stood together in defending colonial charter rights, Thomas Jefferson taking the lead: "The limits of the Southern Colonies are fixed and Congress cannot lawfully meddle with them." Harrison, of Virginia: "Gentlemen shall not pare away the Colony of Virginia." The contention remained a live one for years. In the meantime, Virginia and North Carolina proceeded to sell and grant the lands west of the Alleghanies. Consult, *Journals of the Continental Congress* (Ford), VI, *passim;* and Williams, *History of the Lost State of Franklin, passim.*

[10] Williams, *Dawn,* 415, 430, 436.

[11] Summers, *History of Southwest Virginia,* 265; "East Tennesseans will find pride in the fact that they furnished Washington County, Virginia, her first representatives in the general assembly of the Commonwealth of Virginia." Virginia had collected taxes in the North of Holston region, and Bledsoe and Cocke were awarded their seats. Consistency demanded it.

Carolina east of the mountains, the general assembly of North Carolina appointed five commissioners [12] to lay out a road "by the nearest and best way from the house of Charles Robertson,[13] to the seat of Burke County." [14] The two counties named were authorized to construct the road. Virginia about the same time was ordering the survey and improvement of the road from Colonel Shelby's Sapling Grove southerly to Choate's Ford of Holston (site of Bluff City, Sullivan County) where it branched towards Colonel Carter's and towards the Nolachucky over what could only be described as horsepaths. In November a Virginia county (Washington) ordered the survey and construction of a road on Carolina soil, from North Fork of Holston "to Captain [James] Robertson's home at the mouth of Big Creek." [15]

In the fall (September) James Robertson was in the Overhill towns carrying on as North Carolina's Indian commissioner. On his return he reported, under date of October 17th, that while the upper towns appeared to be friendly, there was not a chance "of a lasting peace with them at Chuckemogo." The white traders who had shown friendship for the Americans in the latest war were leaving all the Indian towns under one pretense or another.[16] It was not improbable "that Cameron may have me taken prisoner, and any white people he knows to be friends to the American cause. I see no way to prevent it but by fixing a station either in the upper towns or in the Forks of the River,[17] that might enable

---

[12] The western commissioners were Jacob Womack and Ezekiel Smith. John Carter was first named but he, being in the senate, caused his name to be deleted and that of Smith substituted.

[13] Brother of James Robertson, and not the cousin, Charles, as is sometimes supposed. Williams, *Dawn*, 342, 345. The lands of the brother were on Buffalo and Sinking Creeks near Johnson City's site. He is referred to in local records as "Buffalo" Charles, the cousin as "Black" Charles.

[14] *N. C. St. Recs.*, XXIV, 135. The road followed the route of the present-day highway from Johnson City through Limestone Cove into North Carolina.

[15] Summers, *Annals of Southwest Virginia*, 1007. Elijah Robertson lived near his older brother, James. As to James' friend John Honeycutt, see Williams, *Dawn*, 340.

[16] Among them Ellis Harlin, Francis Budwine, John Benge and one, Hawkins. Fields, an armorer paid as such by Virginia, remained among the Cherokees to become progenitor of Cherokees of note.

[17] At the junction of the Little Tennessee and the Tennessee—as was advocated by Jefferson and Arthur Campbell in later years.

us to send a party down to the Chuckemogo and take that party of ministerial [British adherents] white people that is there. I understand there is about a dozen now, and Cameron is expected shortly. He has a house built now." Further, that Cameron had sent his agents to the Overhill towns with a report "that America in six weeks time would be in the hands of the English. All which I contradicted in my Talk [to the Indians] the 29th of September." [18]

The seeds of an outright war with the Chickamauga Indians were being sown thus early.

In the winter of 1777–78, as a result of the late Indian war, the treaty at Long Island, the opening of a land office, and the steps taken towards internal improvements, a strong current of migration set in towards all settlements in the Tennessee country. It never became less strong. Men who had heard much of the land as one of promise, sold out their possessions and took the roads leading towards it. Particularly did the Shenandoah, James and Upper Holston valleys in Virginia make contributions to the trek.[19] Not a few of the new comers preferred to purchase lands which had been improved by clearing, so that they might be able to use them at once in the raising of crops and grasses for cattle. More money was in circulation. There was a noticeable improvement of habitations; [20] cabins were enlarged and the modes of life kept pace.

A considerable number of the immigrants were poor young men

---

[18] Robertson to Commissioners Lanier and Winston. Draper Collection. It is evident that this letter was penned by Tatham at Col. Carter's home, to be carried by Carter as he journeyed to the November session of the general assembly. Robertson further reported that Oconostota, Attakullakulla and Willenawah had been delegated to pay a visit to the governor of North Carolina. These old chiefs were yet withstanding Cameron and Dragging Canoe. This letter is worthy of being termed historic, though heretofore overlooked too often. It appears in full, Appendix E.

[19] About this time there settled in the region Andrew Taylor, father of Gen. Nathaniel Taylor and founder of the Taylor family of Tennessee. Also so settling about the same time were Matthew Talbott, a Baptist minister, Rev. Samuel Doak, Maj. Jesse Walton, William, Pharaoh and Benjamin Cobb, Christopher Taylor, Thomas Amis, Daniel Kennedy and others, each of whom gave strength to his neighborhood.

[20] Ramsey (p. 176) notes that the first house covered with shingles, rather than clapboards, was erected in this year a few miles east of the site of Jonesborough, that town not as yet being established.

or couples who could only acquire homes as squatters by way of preemption rights. At that early period—long before laws providing for homesteads out of the public domain were thought of —no reproach attached to the word "squatter," or "occupant." Many of this class by dint of natural ability and energy became substantial and influential citizens; others merely held their status, or deteriorated to become progenitors of "poor whites."

Nor can the fact be blinked that there was an admixture of the criminal element which sought to hide behind the mountain walls. Nor that there were Tories, escaping from military service in their old homes. These two elements usually found homes on the outer fringe of settlement or in spots of isolation or near-isolation. How the purging process was begun and carried on against criminals and Tories is shown in a later chapter.

Foreign immigrants were very few, if indeed any; but some descendants of foreigners, Germans, Scotch-Irish and Irish in particular, appeared.

CHAPTER IX

A New Course Charted (1778)

At the opening of the year 1778 Patrick Henry, governor of Virginia, and George Rogers Clark[1] were formulating an ambitious plan for the capture, for their State, of the British fort at Kaskaskia in the faraway Illinois country, which plan Lieutenant-Colonel Clark was to execute as commander of seven companies of fifty men, each. These companies were to be raised in the West. It also was contemplated that a Virginian fort should be established "near the mouth of the Ohio. Cannon will be wanted to fortify it," and part of the great guns at Kaskaskia could be brought down to it. Clark in his first conference with Governor Henry gave the latter to understand that it was "expected to get men enough to complete the seven companies partly in Kentucky and partly *within the Carolina line.*"[2]

Captain William Bailey Smith, who had been so successful the preceding summer on the Watauga, "within the Carolina line," in getting volunteers to go and steady the Kentucky folk, was sent there by Clark to recruit a force, though by Henry's instructions he was "to take especial care to keep the true destination of your force secret. Success depends on this. Orders are therefore given Captain Smith, etc."[3] In fact, volunteers from Watauga and Holston were informed that they were to go again to succor the Kentuckians. Smith turned up in the Tennessee country, seemingly in the summer, when Colonel Evan Shelby approved of the plan to send "relief to Kentucky."[4] How many men were induced to go is not ascertainable, but probably not in excess of two companies of fifty, each. Clark in January had advanced Smith

---

[1] The plan originated with Clark. Jefferson in conference gave his approval. Bodley, *George Rogers Clark*, 45.

[2] *Official Letters of Governors of Virginia*, I, 235 (Henry to Clark, Jan'y 24, 1778).

[3] *Ib.*

[4] *Calendar of King's Mountain Papers*, 167.

one hundred and fifty pounds "to raise two hundred men and meet me at Kentucky in March." But Smith on his march through Kentucky from the Watauga and Holston was delayed through no fault of his. "All his men had been stopt by the incessant labours of the populace, except one company, . . . some on their march being threatened to be put in prison if they did not return." Clark had opposition from some of the inhabitants of Kentucky whose real wish was to have Smith's men remain in their region for its protection against Indians. Of Smith's force, collected in what is now Upper East Tennessee and Southwest Virginia, as it turned out, nearly all did remain there, replacing two companies which had gone forward from Kentucky towards the Illinois. To their captains only did Clark dare disclose the true destination and mission. Clark met with signal success in the capture of the Kaskaskia fort. That story is well known.

While Clark was on his way to the Illinois, Britain's Lieutenant-Governor, Henry Hamilton, at Detroit was planning to bring the Northwestern Indians and the Cherokees and Chickasaws into joint action in invading Kentucky and other frontier regions, "destroying the crops and habitations of all advanced settlers and driving them back upon their brethren of the Atlantic States, whom they would greatly distress by an additional consumption of goods and provisions." He proposed a meeting of the Southern and Northwestern tribes at the mouth of the Tennessee River to bring about their reconciliation and "to concert a general invasion."[5] He sent messengers southward to Superintendent John Stuart with letters asking him to further this plan. Stuart's own attitude is shown by his letter of February 4th to Sir William Howe of the British army, written after the visit of a delegation of ex-Cherokees (Chickamaugas): "The Cherokees were perfectly well affected, and, notwithstanding the severe chastisement they lately received, are ready to act when called upon. . . . They will be immediately followed home by Mr. Cameron who will hold them prepared for any service which may be re-

---

[5] *Manuscripts of Mrs. Spofford-Sackville*, II, 223. Later, in December, Hamilton reported that "belts have gone from the Cherokees and Chickasaws to the Shawnees and Delawares, requesting them to forget former quarrels and unite against western settlers; and that parties of the Cherokees and Chickasaws were being assembled at the mouth of the Tennessee." *Illinois Historical Collections*, I, 227–36. He referred to the seceders as Cherokees, not yet known to him as Chickamaugas.

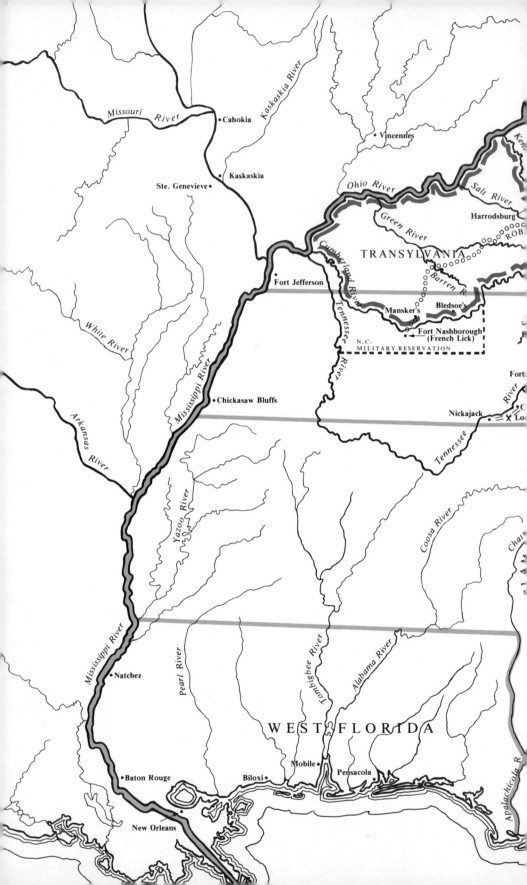

PENNSYLVANIA

MD

DEL

• Baltimore

Annapolis •

Point Pleasant

Winchester •

• Alexandria

Kanawha River

New R.

Staunton •

• Fredericksburg

• Charlottesville

VIRGINIA

Richmond •

Williamsburg •

Petersburg •

• Yorktown

Fincastle •

PROCLAMATION LINE OF 1763

GREAT TRADING PATH

Cumberland River

Powell River

Fort Chiswell

Island Flats

• Abingdon

Shelby's Fort

Ft.Patrick Henry

Long Island

Watauga

Sycamore Shoals

Nolichucky

Yadkin River

Edenton •

• Salem

• Hillsboro

✕ Guilford Court House

Fort Caswell (Watauga)
Jonesborough
Fort Lee

Salisbury •

NORTH CAROLINA

New Bern •

–Chilhowee
–Talasse

Broad River

Broad R.

• Charlotte

Cowpens ✕

Thicketty Fort ✕

Cedar Spring ✕

✕ Kings Mountain

• Camden

Cape Fear River

✕ Musgrove's Mill

Pee Dee River

Saluda River

Wilmington •

Ninety-Six •

SOUTH
CAROLINA

Augusta •

Savannah River

Fort Moultrie

Charles Town •

ATLANTIC OCEAN

GEORGIA

Savannah •

FLORIDA

• St. Augustine

THE SOUTHERN COLONIES
DURING THE REVOLUTIONARY WAR

quired of them. I have lately received assurances from those who live near and pretend to be in friendship with the rebels that they wish for an opportunity of acting which they will embrace whenever it offers."[6] Tories are here referred to.

With the pincers movement threatening from the north and from the south, the inhabitants of the Kentucky and Tennessee countries were in a perilous plight, along with other frontiersmen. The Wataugans were acting in a way to alienate and provoke the Cherokees of the old towns. In May Governor Henry wrote to Governor Caswell: "I beg leave to mention to your Excellency what the commissioners for this State on the Southern frontier have repeatedly informed me: It is that certain persons of your State have intruded on the Cherokees; entries for their lands are said to have been made even close to their towns, and some settlements are forming far over the line. I know your Excellency's supreme regard for justice and the public good, and that the good people of North Carolina will not advisably do anything that will embroil us with the Indians and thereby co-operate with the British emissaries."[7]

There was in this much truth but also a degree of exaggeration. There had been trespassing and a push of settlements slightly beyond the treaty line of 1777.[8] The pressure was more like that of a glacier than an avalanche, and it was by men of little principle and great ignorance. They did not wholly grasp the wide and disastrous effect of their actions. Indians of like type and propensities in some measure gave an excuse to the whites to retaliate, and retaliation took the form of raiding—but for land, as against raiding by the reds for horses and personal effects.

The year opened with the military department of Washington County manned as follows: John Carter, colonel; John Sevier,

[6] *Report on American Manuscripts in the Royal Institution,* I, 190. This sheds additional light on Stuart's attitude in preceding years. Gov. Patrick Tonyn of Florida was yet more rabid in his communications respecting the "rebels" on the western waters.

[7] *Official Letters of the Governors of Virginia,* I, 275, and *N. C. St. Recs.,* XIII, 128. Gov. Caswell replied that he had received similar complaints from the Cherokees and had issued a proclamation forbidding such settlements and trespasses. *Ib.,* 135.

[8] Probably not to or beyond the site of later Greeneville in May, 1778. The Cherokees failed to deliver up stolen horses as had been provided in the treaty of 1777. (James Robertson.)

lieutenant-colonel; Charles Robertson, first major, and Jacob Womack, second major. In the region north of the Holston commissions were yet held under the Virginia government by Evan Shelby, colonel; and captains in that region and in Pendleton District held like commissions: James Shelby, Gilbert Christian, John Duncan and John Anderson. In Carter's Valley "James Robertson, Watauga," held a captain's commission under Virginia.[9]

The county of Washington was represented in the general assembly of North Carolina this year by Charles Robertson, senator; Wm. Cocke and Luke (Lew) Bowyer in the lower house.

The civil government of the county was initiated by the opening of its first county court on February 23, 1778, the following being justices: John Carter, chairman; John Sevier, Jacob Womack, Robert Lucas, Andrew Greer, John Shelby, Jr., George Russell, William Bean, Zachariah Isbell, John McNabb, William McNabb, Thomas Houghton, William Clark, Charles Robertson, John McMahan, Benjamin Gist, John Chisholm, Joseph Willson, William Cobb, James Stuart, Michael Woods, Richard White, Jesse Walton, Benjamin Willson, Thomas Price, Valentine Sevier and James Robertson.[10]

John Sevier was chosen clerk, Valentine Sevier sheriff, James Stuart surveyor, John Carter entry-taker, John McMahan register of deeds, Jacob Womack stray-master and John McNabb coroner.

The court's sessions were according to the legislative act to be held at the home of Charles Robertson,[11] but some of them after the first were held at the home of Matthew Talbott.

Curiously enough, the first case tried before the court involved the younger brothers of two men who, then and ever afterwards during their lives, were premiers among the leaders of Tennessee:

---

[9] Summers, *History of Southwest Virginia*, 261. There was a James Robertson, militia officer, further up in Virginia; hence the descriptive, "Watauga."

[10] Washington County Court Records, yet extant in Tennessee Historical Society's Collection; reprinted for 1777–84 in *American Historical Magazine*. (Nashville) V, 343 *et seq*, though there are misprints and blanks that mar the same. James Robertson's name thus appears, but the records do not show that he sat on the bench. He had removed to Big Creek as above stated.

[11] Brother of James Robertson in the environs of the present Johnson City. The site should be marked by the Tennessee Bar Association.

"Elijah Robertson v. *Robert Sevier,* for an assault. Ordered that Robert Sevier be bound to his good behaviour and enter into Recognizance with two securities in the sum of Ten pounds himself (and five pounds each of the securities) for his good behaviour for the Term and Time of Twelve months."

The justices acted in a legislative capacity as a county court and in a judicial capacity as a court of common pleas. Each body was summary rather than deliberate in its actions and judgments —direct rather than technical in procedure. Thus—

Wm. Cocke by His Council Waightstill Avery Attorney moved to be Admitted to the Office of Clerk of the County of Washington—which motion was Rejected by the Court, knowing that John Sevier was Intitled to the Office.

Why should not this case be cited as authority that a court will take judicial knowledge as to who are its officers?

That the settlers were true Sons of Liberty had already been clearly evidenced. The court in truth may be said to have been a recruiting office for the continental army. The pages of the minute book of 1778 are studded with entries of which the following are examples:

State vs. Zekle Brown. Ordered that the defendant be committed to Gaol Immediately and be kept in custody until he can be conveniently delivered to a Continental Officer. . . .

Ordered that Zekle Brown be discharged by the Sheriff, the said Brown having enlisted in the Continental Service. . . .

State v. Moses Crawford.[12] The opinion of the Court is that the defendant be Imprisoned during the present War with Great Britain, and that the Sheriff take the whole of his Estate into Custody, and that the One-half of said estate Be kept by the Sheriff for the use of the State, and the Other Half remitted to the family of defendant. . . .

On motion of E. Dunlop, State Attorney, Ordered that John Holly for his Ill Practices in Harboring and Abetting Disorderly persons who are prejudicial and inimical to the Common Cause of Liberty and Frequently Disturbing our public Tranquility in General Be Imprisoned for the term and time of one year.

The Court further ordered that fifteen pounds due to Holly "for two negroes be retained as there is sufficient reason to believe

---

[12] The Crawfords were Tories, Samuel being a deserter from the overmountain Whigs as they were on the way to engage Ferguson; see p. 147. Grimes, another Tory on the border, met his fate after the battle at King's Mountain. *Ib.*

that said Holly's estate will be confiscated to the use of the State for his misdemeanors."

Ephraim Dunlop, the second lawyer to locate in the western country, appeared in this year along with the learned Avery of the bar east of the mountains and Luke Bowyer. The court at its November term fixed:

Tavern Rates for One Year [13]

Lodging—good bed and clean sheets	1 sh. 6 d.
Rum, wine and brandy, per gal.	3. 4. and 6.
Toddy per qt. & ½ pt of rum therein	8. 0
Corn or oats pr. gal.	4. 0
Stabledge, with hay or fodder, 24 hrs.	4. 0
Pasturage, 24 hrs.	2. 0
Cyder pr. Qt.	4. 0
Bear [beer] pr. Qt.	2. 0
Whiskey pr. Gal.	2. 0. 0.

The disparity in the prices to be charged for rum and whiskey was due to the fact that one was locally produced and the other was imported into the country and region, which meant heavy import and carriage charges. This was true also of carriage charges on all articles of merchandise. The result was a liberal use of homemade cloth, shoes, hats, etc.

The withdrawal, late in the preceding fall, by North Carolina of the militiamen sent to the West to garrison forts, was accompanied by the renewal of a provision for rangers, five in number, to act as warders of the border, the privates "to provide their own rations." This was a wholly inadequate step; it evidenced feebleness and parsimony on the part of the legislature of North Carolina. Too, news of all this must have trickled through to the Indians, Chickamaugas as well as Cherokees, through Tories who, in large part, lived on the Nolachucky and its waters. The Tories were emboldened to become active and a period of near-anarchy set in. The court entries above quoted show the conditions that prevailed, and Ramsey [14] well paints the picture:

---

[13] The high prices were due to the great depreciation in North Carolina's currency. By the court's May term, 1780, prices were increased, and fixed, now in dollars and cents, at: rye whiskey, $20.00 per quart; West India rum, $40.00; and, in 1781, such whiskey, $48.00, and W. I. rum, $120.00, per quart.

[14] *Annals*, 178–9.

The Tories from the disaffected counties of North Carolina[15] and other States had come in great numbers to the frontier, and there, combining with thieves and robbers, prowled about the feebler neighborhoods and for a time committed depredation and murder with impunity. Their number was considerable and they boasted that they were able to look down all opposition and defy all restraint. . . .

The law-abiding and honest people of the country took the affair into their own hands, appointing a committee[16] invested with unlimited power and authorized to adopt any measures to arrest the growing evil. The names of this committee of safety are not given, but it is known that under its direction and authority two companies of dragoons, numbering about thirty each, were immediately organized and equipped and directed to patrol the whole country, capture and punish with death all suspected persons who refused submission or failed to give good security for their appearance before the committee. Slighter offenses were atoned for by the infliction of corporal punishment; to this was superadded, in cases where the offender was able to pay it, a heavy fine in money. Leaders in crime expiated their guilt by their lives. Several of these were shot; some of these at their execution disclosed the names and hiding places of their accomplices. These in their turn were pursued, arrested and punished; and the country in less than two months was restored to a condition of safety and the disturbers of its quiet preserved their lives only by secrecy or flight.

Isam Yearly, a loyalist on Nollichucky, was driven out of the country by a company of whigs, of which Captain William Bean, Isaac Lane,[17] Sevier[18] and Robertson[19] were members. The same company afterwards pursued a party of tories, who under the lead of a Mr. [Henry] Grimes, on Watauga,[20] had killed Milli-

[15] Consult Ashe, *History of North Carolina*, I, 575–76: "Those who refused to take the oath of allegiance were ordered to depart the state within sixty days. . . . A great number determined to leave their homes and become wanderers on the face of the earth. (May 1777)." A number of these in counties west and south of Wake County (Raleigh) had been Regulators or sons of Regulators who were too incensed against leaders in the Revolution who had been active in defeating them in 1771—such men as Gov. Caswell—to follow them in 1776–77. It is not to be doubted that among the Tories coming to the Tennessee frontier in 1777–78 there were Regulators of 1771 (or their sons). Many were forced to leave and went on to Kentucky where they were not welcomed.

[16] Of the kind called "vigilance committees," in the Far West of later generations.

[17] Son of Rev. Tidence Lane.

[18] Younger brother of John Sevier.

[19] Younger brother of James Robertson.

[20] For Grimes see note preceding and Draper's *Heroes of King's Mountain*, 340.

can,[21] a whig, and attempted to kill Mr. [James] Roddy[21a] and Mr. Grubbs. The latter they had taken to a high pinnacle on the edge of the river and threatened to throw him off. He was respited under a promise that they should have all his property. These tories were concealed high up Watauga in the mountains, but Captain Bean and his whig comrades ferreted them out, fired upon and wounded their leader, and forced them to escape across the mountains.[22]

The court at its first term levied an ad valorem tax of two shillings, six pence, per hundred pounds on real estate for the building of a court house, prison and stocks, but construction awaited the selection of a county seat.[23] At the November term of court a report on the site was made. One hundred acres of land had been contracted for "the purpose of erecting a town thereon." There had been a contest for the location between the residents on the Nolachucky and its waters and those on the Watauga and its waters. Finally, the site chosen was within two miles or less of the dividing ridge or water-shed of the two rivers named—a sort of compromise, the deciding factor perhaps being the fact that the flow of population was distinctly to the westward of that watershed, though a large majority at the time lived on Watauga waters. The county seat was not named until the succeeding year.

Confiscations by the State of North Carolina of estates of Tories under legislative acts were made. Jesse Walton, John Sevier and Zachariah Isbell were appointed commissioners to administer such estates.

As the year drew to a close war-clouds appeared from the south;

---

[21] Milligan, of the family from which descended Samuel Milligan, who was a justice of the Supreme Court of Tennessee, and a judge of the Court of Claims at Washington.

[21a] For sketch, see Williams, *Lost State of Franklin*, 326.

[22] Among the other members of Bean's company mentioned by Ramsey were: Joseph Duncan, John Condley, Thomas Hardeman, Wm. Stone, Michael Massengill, John, George and Edmund Bean, James Roddy, Samuel and Robert Tate, Aquilla Lane; the last named also a son of Rev. Tidence Lane. Of these, Hardeman and Roddy became outstanding leaders in Tennessee.

[23] By Act of 1777, ch. 31, the tax had been so fixed. *N. C. St. Recs.*, XXIV, 141–2. The commissioners first named to choose the site, build a court house, and lay off the town into lots were: John Carter, Andrew Greer, Wm. Cobb, Jacob Womack, George Russell, John Sevier and James Stuart, "or a majority of them." Later on, changes were made in the commission's personnel.

the Chickamauga Indians continued pestiferous to the point of provoking retaliation on the part of Virginia and North Carolina. Cameron and an under-agent among those Indians, John McDonald,[24] were fomenting trouble on a large scale.[25] Joseph Martin, Virginia's agent to the Overhill Cherokees, turned up at Williamsburg and reported to Governor Henry that the Chickamaugas intended to make a vigorous attack on the frontiers in the approaching spring; that those Indians had sent three hundred horses to Pensacola to be loaded with supplies to be furnished by the British, and that they hoped to win over some of the Overhill Cherokees to the plan. Martin assured Henry that the Overhill people were by no means averse to seeing the Chickamaugas chastised. "He observed that the leading men of the Overhill are much exasperated at the conduct of the seceders who perpetually embroiled their public councils and, by repeated violence, instigated by British emissaries, tried to involve the nation at large in the suspicion of hostility and consequent war, which would evidently be destructive to them; and that numbers of those Indians have gone and are going to Chickamauga," notwithstanding their chiefs' remonstrances against it. Further, that those leaders had expressed great wrath and bitterness and the view that the headstrong and lawless warriors going over to the Chickamaugas might be obliged by a war to return to the old towns, which would prove highly acceptable. "Those of the men who may be slain will fall unlamented by their country." [26]

James Robertson, North Carolina's agent among the Overhills, reading the signs of the time and seeing the situation as did Martin, was preparing to leave Chota for his home to join his people in any war which might eventuate. He reported to his superior that The Raven thinks the white people justified in "warring against the rogues at Chuckemogo." [27]

In 1778 a strong Baptist preacher, Tidence Lane, removed from

---

[24] He lived in the environs of present day Chattanooga.

[25] Involving Georgia and the Carolinas as well as the western people.

[26] Gov. Henry to Gov. Caswell, *N. C. St. Recs.*, XIV, 343–6; also *Official Letters of Governors of Virginia*, I, 351–2.

[27] *N. C. St. Recs.*, XIII, 500. At the request of the Cherokees, Robertson named Ellis Harlin to substitute for himself. The Raven to Robertson: "I am very thankful to you for your many services, and in particular, in assisting in making strong our landmarks"—the boundary fixed at the treaty of 1777.

North Carolina and settled in Washington County. There in that year, as the writer believes, or in 1779, as Ramsey states, he established a church of his faith at Buffalo Ridge and became "Tennessee's first pastor," his congregation at that place being the first one of any denomination organized in the Tennessee country.[28] The Baptist soon grew to be the largest religious sect in the western country.

[28] For details, see Williams, "Tennessee's First Pastor, Tidence Lane" in *Tenn. Hist. Magazine.* The article was incorporated as a chapter in Tindell's *History of the Tennessee Baptists.*

CHAPTER X

Chastisement of the Chickamauga Indians, as has been seen, had been contemplated for several months before it was decided upon.[1] On January 8, 1779, Governor Henry wrote to Governor Caswell that he had given directions to Colonel Evan Shelby to raise three hundred men in his district to go at once to Chickamauga and "totally destroy that and every other settlement near it which the offending Indians occupy."[2] He asked the Carolina governor to increase that force to five hundred by ordering out two hundred men from Washington County, North Carolina, with a lieutenant-colonel in command under Shelby. The view was expressed that the men of Watauga and Nolachucky would serve with alacrity. A hint given to Caswell by James Robertson that such men would be willing to serve without compensation was further assurance to Caswell of a form of "alacrity" which would be of weight in reaching a decision on the part of North Carolina's general assembly. That body was in session at the time, and Washington County was represented in the senate by Major Charles Robertson and in the lower house by Major Jesse Walton. On January 21st it was resolved that the two hundred men asked for be sent under a lieutenant-colonel and four captains, the men to be "furnished from the militia of Washington County, formed

---

[1] General Rutherford in explanation of why he could not call out troops from Washington County to march to the aid of South Carolina, wrote (Nov. 15, 1778): "Their whole strength is employed in the suppression of the savages and other inhuman hostile wretches who have their livelihood from carnage and rapine," or Tories. *N. C. St. Recs.*, XIII, 282.

[2] *N. C. St. Recs.*, XIV, 343; also *Official Letters of Governors of Virginia*, 351. Under date of March 15th, Col. Arthur Campbell wrote Gov. Henry: "By Isaac Thomas lately from the nation I find that Cameron and his deputies are straining every nerve to engage the whole of the Cherokees to commence hostilities: however, by the apparent disposition of the Old Towns, I think he will fail." Further, that Cameron's scheme was to induce the Overhills to move to Chickamauga. He suggested the erection of a fort at the mouth of the Clinch.

by voluntary enlistments if they can be so procured." No draft was necessary—the men went as volunteers. Major Robertson was recommended to command such troops, and given the rank of lieutenant-colonel. Walton was appointed contractor or commissary. The general assembly gave words of admonition: that the women and children of the enemy be treated with tenderness, and that the friendly Cherokees be informed in advance of the beginning of hostilities and "treated with the utmost respect." [3]

Robertson and Walton promptly left the assembly for the West. The latter had been voted nine thousand pounds to be expended for supplies—a sum to be measured by the depreciation in the currency. However, a brief campaign was anticipated. Henry had written on that point:

I cannot help thinking no time should be lost in striking the blow that the militia may return in time to prepare their summer crops; and that for this purpose your orders will go to Holston without loss of time for the two hundred men to join Colonel Shelby who is getting ready to march immediately.

The rendezvous for the troops of Shelby and Robertson was fixed for April 1st at the mouth of Big Creek of Holston,[4] the home and fort of James Robertson. The troops seemingly had an advance rendezvous at the Long Island above. The captains and companies under Shelby from below the Virginia line were: Captain James Shelby, 43 men; Captain Aaron Lewis, 26 men; Captain Gilbert Christian,[5] 27 men; non-commissioned officers, three; John Rhea staff-officer and Isaac Shelby commissary.[6] No returns of the officers and men under Robertson have been preserved, since they expected no compensation. However, among his captains were William Bean, Thomas Vincent and George Russell.[7]

---

[3] Gov. Henry had given like instructions for the troops from his State.

[4] Roosevelt, in error, says "on Clinch River."

[5] His son said that Christian acted as major under Col. Shelby. Draper MSS. Capt. Joseph Martin was appointed major of a battalion for the campaign. *Calendar of Virginia State Papers*, I, 13.

[6] Return of April 6, 1779, in Draper Collection (not in print) and other data.

[7] According to Wm. Snodgrass. *Calendar of King's Mountain Papers*, 348. The name of the other captain has not been ascertained, but it is believed that Robert Sevier, son-in-law of Col. Robertson, was the fourth. James Robertson, for diplomatic reasons growing out of his being an

The expedition was two phased: first an attack on the Chickamaugas; then those under Colonel John Montgomery, and others volunteering, were to proceed down the Tennessee and up other rivers to join Colonel George Rogers Clark in the Northwest.

Virginia at the time was making a valiant effort to hold the Northwest from Great Britain. In that region Clark was displaying in her behalf an initiative and courage that gained for him immortality. A young Southwest Virginian, Captain John Montgomery, ordered to the West with Clark in 1778, had aided him in the capture of Kaskaskia, and been sent by Clark back to Virginia to recruit a military force to go to Clark's aid. This Montgomery did; and, as leader of the force, he was raised to the rank of lieutenant-colonel. It occurred to the Virginia authorities that it would be good strategy to combine the expeditions of Montgomery and Shelby in activities down to and around the Chickamauga towns. Without knowing of this arrangement Clark in the then Far West sensed its advisability. There, eagerly awaiting the coming of Montgomery, on April 29th he wrote to Thomas Jefferson after his signal exploit in the capture of Vincennes in the Indiana country. As already shown the British governor at Detroit, Hamilton, thought he had arranged for the support of the Southern tribes and had gone to Vincennes on the 15th of December. Clark wrote to Jefferson:

With these he [Hamilton] was to penetrate up the Ohio to Fort Pitt [Pittsburgh], sweeping Kentucky on his way, joined on his march by all Indians that could be got to him. He made no doubt he could force all West Augusta. The expedition was ordered by the commander-in-chief of Canada. . . . I am impatient for the arrival of Colonel Montgomery, but have heard nothing from him lately. . . . Many of the Cherokees, Chickasaws and their confederates are, I fear, ill disposed. It would be well if Colonel Montgomery should give them a good dressing as he comes down the Tennessee.

A good drubbing of the Chickamaugas was insured by the combination of the two forces. The instructions given by Governor Henry to Montgomery were:

Indian agent, seems not to have been on the expedition. Aaron Lewis and Gilbert Christian were captains of companies from the north of Holston and Pendleton Districts, respectively. Draper MSS, 16, D. D. 62.

You will cause the proper vessels for transporting the troops down the Cherokee [Tennessee] River to be built and ready. Let no time be lost in doing that. Captain Isaac Shelby, it is desired, may prepare the boats. But if he can't do it you must get some other person. . . .

I need not tell you how necessary the greatest possible dispatch is to the good of the service in which you are engaged. Our party at Illinois may be lost, together with the present favorable disposition of the French and Indians there, unless every movement is improved for their preservation; and no future opportunity, if the present is lost, can ever be expected so favorable to the interest of the Commonwealth. . . .

You receive 10,000 pounds, cash, for Colonel Clark's corps which you are to deliver him except 200 pounds for Captain Shelby to build the boats and whatever incidental expenses happen necessarily on your way.

Isaac Shelby in likelihood built some of the larger boats at the Long Island and others at the mouth of Big Creek. However, no fund was furnished him for the subsistence of the troops, as commissary. He had to purchase supplies on his own credit. The troops assembled at the mouth of Big Creek, more boats were built—pirogues and long canoes. Tall poplar trees were felled and by axe and adze made into such boats.[8]

On April 10th this unique flotilla of war set out for the country of the enemy, John Hudson acting as pilot. When the mouth of the Little Tennessee was reached, Hudson was dispatched by Colonel Shelby with a letter to Joseph Martin, then at Chota among the Overhill Cherokees, advising him to leave there for the Long Island, agreeable to instructions from Governor Henry. Hudson was drowned in the execution of the mission, and in requital his widow was later pensioned by the State of Virginia.

Pursuing the voyage and speeded by a current augmented by a spring freshet, at break of dawn in mid-April the expedition turned into Chickamauga Creek. Near the mouth an Indian, asleep near his fish-trap, was taken prisoner. With him as guide under compulsion, the troops waded through an inundated canebrake and entered Chickamauga, a town about one mile long. Dragging Canoe and Big Fool were its chiefs. The Indians, 500 in number, astonished at the sudden invasion of their country by an armed force by water, made no resistance and fled to the hills

---

[8] The militiamen had been ordered to bring along such implements.

and mountains. The town was burned. John McCrosky, later of
Sevier County, headed a party, followed the fleeing redmen and
dispersed a camp of them which he found on Laurel Creek. Another party took Little Owl's town and others were taken in like
manner; and all were burned. (Ramsey)

Haywood and Ramsey are not to be relied on in their estimates
of the number of militia out on this expedition and of the number
of Indians killed. They estimate that there were 1000 men in
the white army, but a truer estimate is about 600 men. No official report of Colonel Shelby has survived, and the most dependable account is that of Thomas Jefferson, based on a letter of
Shelby written at the time:

> I also enclose you a letter from Colonal Shelby stating the
> effect of his sucess against the seceding Cherokees and Chicka-
> mogga. The damage done them was killing half a dozen, burning
> eleven towns, 20,000 bushels of corn collected probably to forward
> expeditions which were to have been planned at the council which
> was to meet Governor Hamilton at the mouth of the Tennessee;
> and, also, taking as many goods as sold for 25,000 pounds. I
> hope that these two blows, coming together and depriving them of
> their head [Hamilton], will in some measure effect the quiet of
> our frontiers this summer.[9]

Among the booty taken was a large lot of valuable peltry collected, doubtless, at what is known at Ross' Landing by trader
John McDonald, grandfather of the later great Cherokee chief,
John Ross. Horses were captured and constituted perhaps the
most welcomed of all the booty, since they enabled many of the
militia to ride homeward. The animals were allotted to the officers and men by way of an auction sale.[10] A receipt was given to
Colonel Shelby for what must have been the best steed. It is interesting as disclosing the approximate date of the departure for
home and, also, to what extent the currency had depreciated:

Chickamauga Town, April 27, 1779.

This is to certify that Col. Evan Shelby Bou't a Black horse
Branded Thus L about six years old for 120 Pounds
Aaron Lewis,
William Parker.

---

[9] To Gen. Washington, June 23, 1779, *Jefferson's Works*, I, 163.
[10] Sale Creek in Hamilton County was the place of vendue and takes
its name from the fact.

Before beginning the return journey, overland, the boats which had been used in the descent were sunk, so as to be of no use to the Indians. In order to avoid ambush by the Chickamaugas and possible treachery on the part of some of the younger Cherokees, the men crossed the Tennessee in the boats before sinking them. The route on the return was up the west side of the river, passing a place later known as Post Oak Springs,[11] crossing the Clinch and Emory Rivers a little above their confluence, and the Holston some miles above its junction with the French Broad. Thus was disclosed to the marching soldiery the attractiveness of the region for settlement. As may be imagined, the return journey was one of hardships, particularly to those unmounted. For subsistence on the way through what was then a wilderness, reliance was on corn that had been seized and wild game brought down by trusty rifles. The only casualties of the campaign were the deaths of two men on the homeward march. Not many years were to pass until migrations began to the region traversed from Southwest Virginia and what is now Upper East Tennessee. The ancestry of many of our day might be traced to Shelby's and Robertson's men if fate had been kind enough to have preserved muster rolls of the expedition.

And what of Montgomery's men who assisted in the humiliation of the Chickamaugas? Roosevelt in his *Winning of the West* bluntly declares that some of his men were destined for Clark's assistance in his campaigning in the Northwest, "but were not sent him." The contrary is true, and Roosevelt's error can be fully attested. One hundred and fifty of those troops, using their boats, floated down the queenly Tennessee and joined Clark who was eagerly awaiting their coming. Montgomery was placed in command of Kaskaskia fort and district. During the winter of 1779–80 the British formulated a comprehensive plan for a recovery of the Northwest and, in particular, the Illinois forts. In May the attack came, but Montgomery, aided by forces from Clark, repulsed it. In other ways, also, Montgomery was a potent factor in holding secure the conquest of the Northwest, with the result that that imperial domain now represented by the States of

[11] At Post Oak Springs the troops encamped. Men of Capt. Wm. Bean's company turned out to hunt, and one of the Captain's sons brought in a fat bear on which the troops feasted. Rogers v. Burton, Peck's Reports (on Tenn.) 108.

Ohio, Indiana, Illinois, Michigan and Wisconsin, and a part of Minnesota, became America's possession, and not Britain's.

With Montgomery went to the Northwest Captain James Shelby, of the Tennessee country, with a skeleton company (seemingly sixteen men).[12] He became commander of Fort Patrick Henry at Vincennes, (thus going from Fort Patrick Henry on the Holston to Fort Patrick Henry on the Wabash). Shelby went forward to assist Clark in the latter's effort to capture the British post of St. Joseph's, as part of a campaign planned to be launched by Clark against the British at Detroit, not to mention his other activities. The services of young Shelby in the Northwest have gone without mention by historians; even his name has not been mentioned in accounts of Clark's conquest of that region, though materials disclosing his achievements were not lacking.[13]

The results of the Shelby-Robertson expedition was, on the

---

[12] The roll of Capt. James Shelby's company on the campaign against the Chickamaugas is an exception. The roster is preserved in the Draper Collection, and follows: Catel Litton, William Linn, Hans Ireland, David Hendrix, Andrew Linn, Benj. Sweet, Thos. Mauer, John Mauer, William Clem, William Harwood, Evan Shelby, Jr., Garrett Pendergrass, Alexander Caswell, Joseph Wells, John Harmison (or Harrison) John Fleming, Elias Dawson, Anthony Millon, Robert Chambers, John Brown, Thos. Applegate, Geo. Parker, John Shelby, Chas. Prather, Elisha Perkins, John Higgins, Robert Friggs, E. Bruster, Joseph Latman, Buch Nealley, John Pierce, Daniel Linn, Barrett Johnson, David Jennings, Richard Long, Samuel Price, Robert Blackburn, William Tom, Thos. Cheney, John Detgavoret, J. C. Friggs, William McSpadden, Isaac Morgan and Andrew Polson. A few troopers in other companies have their names in pension statements or elsewhere: John Sawyer, Francis Slaughter, Barney O'Gullion, William Snodgrass, George Turnley, Samuel Wear, James McElwee, James Houston and Isaac Ruddle. Being volunteers, few of the names of those who went to the Northwest are certainly to be recovered. Isaac Ruddle, who lived on the Holston, and one or more of the Linn brothers are believed to have gone on with their captain.

[13] For a full-length sketch of Capt. Shelby and an account of his services in the Northwest, see the author's "Military Career of Captain James Shelby," in *Filson Club History Quarterly*, XV, 227–238. See also, *Cohokia Records*, LXXVI; *Mich. Pioneer Coll.*, XIX; Wis. Hist. Coll., XVIII, 376, and Bodley's *George Rogers Clark*. In the last named work, "Shelby" is named but without any given name. Bodley evidently took it to be Isaac Shelby, since the index reference is to "Isaac Shelby." The career of the older brother did not need to have James deprived of honors his own.

whole, favorable to the white people. It showed the Chicka-maugas that in their location they were subject to attack by troops invading by the river route. It caused them to move far-ther down the Tennessee and establish new towns alongside and below "the breaks" of that river where it flowed through the Cum-berland Mountains. There was the Boiling Pot, Suck or Whirl so dangerous to all navigators. This was good strategy on the part of the Indians, as after-events proved.[14]

The whites of the region above, however, were disquieted until they could see whether the Indians would strike a counter-blow. One was to come, to be followed by a period of comparative peace. It fell on the inhabitants of the southern border, in what was to become Greene County. Ramsey says that it was incited by British agents, and thus describes it:

> The Indians invaded the country soon after and attacked Boil-ston's [15] house, on the frontier, with a loss to the assailants of four warriors killed and a number wounded. During the attack Wil-liams and Hardin [16] were killed. The enemy was driven off. They were pursued by George Dorherty, Joseph Boyd and others, but escaped.
> Other mischief was attempted, but the scouts and light-horse companies guarded the frontier so vigilantly that little injury was sustained by the settlers. The apprehension of danger kept up the military organization of the new country and made the inhabitants familiar with the duties of camp life.

Furthermore: the blow on the Chickamaugas by the forces un-der Shelby and Robertson came about the time of Clark's capture and imprisonment of Hamilton and the death of Superintendent

---

[14] The new towns, five in number, Steeoyee (or Lookout Mountain Town), Running Water, Nickojack, Long Island Town and Crow Town. Roosevelt, not grasping this fact, says that Shelby's men destroyed these towns, which in fact were then non-existent. Throughout the revolu-tionary period many families used the Tennessee River in going to the British possessions on the lower Mississippi. Few diaries or journals of such journeys were kept, but some brief accounts are to be found. Claiborne, *Mississippi, passim.*

[15] Really, William Boydston, from Bottetourt County, Va., and later of that part of Greene which became Cocke County.

[16] Likely a brother, or a son, of Joseph Hardin who became an adherent of the State of Franklin and whose name appears in that of Hardin County, Tennessee. See sketch in Williams, *Lost State of Franklin,* (2nd. ed.) 304.

Stuart in Florida.[17]   With those two master-manipulators removed, all the Southern Indian tribes were discouraged: the great
plan for a pincer movement from the north and south against
western frontiersmen faded out.   Cameron, though grown old in
age and service, was yet the chief dependence of the British in the
upper country.   Distraught, but still resolute, the old Scotchman
soon made another effort to rally his red adherents.   In July,
1779, from the Chickamaugas he dispatched a runner as far as to
the Middle Towns of the Cherokees, exhorting, cajoling and
threatening, in an effort to bring all branches of the Cherokees
into concerted action.[18]   Again is there demonstration that there
was throughout the struggle for American independence a "War
of the Revolution in the West," and that the campaign of the
spring of 1779 was not an insignificant part of it.   The tide was
running strong in favor of the British in Georgia and the Carolinas, and to the British it was imperative that all men on western
waters be held in check by the Indians and from sending manpower to assist the hard pressed Whigs east of the mountains.
This, in 1779–80 as well as in 1776–77, was the strategy of the
British.   As the eastern Patriots were growing groggy under repeated blows, scores of youngsters in the West were coming into
or toward lusty manhood, and ready, many of them eager, to
march across the mountain ranges and confront the enemy.   Cameron saw, but muffed, his chance.

---

[17] Stuart was succeeded early in May by Col. Thomas Brown, after
a short interim-service by John Graham.

[18] "Demanding them to join; if not they [Cameron, his Indian and
Tory followers] will come and destroy them [the Cherokees]" *N. C. St.
Recs.*, XIV, 162.   On July 12th a talk, evidently inspired by Cameron,
went to Northwestern Indians: "After we had lost some of our best
warriors, we were forced to leave our towns and corn to be burnt by
them, and we are now in the grass.   But we are not yet conquered, etc."
Haldiman MSS., quoted by Roosevelt (II, 238).   But about the same
time peace talks were sent to Col. Shelby, in June. *Ib.*

CHAPTER XI

EARLIER SETTLERS ON THE CUMBERLAND

Most historians of Tennessee and of Middle Tennessee have proceeded largely upon the assumption that James Robertson was the leader of the first group of white people to settle on the Cumberland in the revolutionary period; but that was an erroneous view. Prior to Robertson's arrival in 1779 there were numerous white families and individuals on that stream; indeed, so many as to attract the attention of British officials in the Northwest.

Timothe Demunbreun (real full name Jacques Timothe Boucher de Montbrun),[1] whose French ancestor was "the first man in Canada of the nobility," was at the French Lick when the Revolution broke out.[2] In February of 1777 he found six white men and one white woman on the Cumberland near what was later the village of Palmyra. In the fall of the same year he left for a visit to Vincennes on the Wabash, leaving his partner, another man of French descent, Le Fevre,[3] at the Lick but to join him at the mouth of the Cumberland. It was while at the Vincennes that Demunbreun came in contact with the British governor who persuaded him to act as a kind of reporting agent on the Cumberland. Since about 1776 the Tennessee country for British supervision had been under officials located in the Illinois country. It is from the agent's reports to Governor Baulon (at Vincennes) that the following facts are gathered:

In 1778 English-speaking Tories endeavored to form a colony

---

[1] For sketch and account of his ancestry: Williams, *Dawn*, 324–5.

[2] Arriving there about 1775. In the spring of 1776 he went down the Cumberland and other rivers to sell a boat-load of peltry and tallow and to visit his kinsman, Carlos de Grampre, later governor for Spain of Natchez and Baton Rouge. On his return trip he was robbed by Indians. (Haywood).

[3] He was later killed and scalped by Indians near a spring (said to be Wilson's spring) within the limits of present day Nashville. Evidently he was brother or father of Isaac Le Fevre mentioned by Haywood, p. 126.

on the Cumberland. About thirty such families were living there. One of these Tories appeared to be above the others in authority, and to him Demunbreun showed his letter of instructions from Baulon. The letter was read aloud by this leader to the others. All approved "and thanked the British governor for the kindness he had shown them and would propose to come and take shelter under the flag of his government." Two of the families had already embarked to take up lands above the Ohio. "Some other Englishmen there asked Sieur Demunbreun if he was willing to take them to the post, so as to protect them against any harm," but were answered that he could not consent, as Indians had recently killed three men on the Tennessee. Moreover, Indians [4] had already asked him to "pilot them in order that they might attack these very people, but he had refused to do so." The Tories added: "After leaving our properties to move elsewhere, we find it very hard to have some people incited to kill us under the flag of the King." They would send a messenger to those settled further up the river to let them know the good intentions of the governor. They asked Demunbreun to bring them powder, balls and needed supplies, but no promise to do so was made, as they might make a bad use of ammunition, but permission of the governor would be asked.[5]

The Tories were evidently those who had been forced into exile from North Carolina, east and west of the Alleghanies. We have a glimpse of such outcasts in the Kentucky country, collected in the stockade at Strode's Station:

Everybody coming to Kentucky could hardly get along the road for them; and all grand Tories, pretty nigh. All Tories from Carolina Had been treated so bad there they had to run off or do worse. . . . Our station never was strong after the first winter; heap of Tories settled there then but after that they went off.[6]

[4] Evidently those trading with Demunbreun at French Lick.

[5] Signed "Declaration" of the agent in *Haldimand* Papers (Canadian Archives) Vol. 122, p. 103. From Detroit Gov. Edward Abbott sent to Sir Guy Carleton at Quebec the "Declaration" with this comment: "You will plainly perceive that employing Indians on the Rebel frontiers has been a great hurt to the cause. . . . It is not people in arms that the Indians will ever daringly attack, but only poor inoffensive families who fly to the deserts to be out of trouble and are inhumanly butchered." A copy of this should have gone to Alexander Cameron—and as a rebuke.

[6] "Wm. Clinkenbeard's Account," to Rev. John D. Shane, the Kentucky antiquarian, in *Filson Club History Quarterly*, II, 95–128—a document

With Demunbreun, besides Le Fevre, were three other French Canadians; all five were encountered by James Robertson on his first trip to the Cumberland region. They were found hunting on Harpeth River.[7]

James Robertson, when he made this first trip to the French Lick in the winter of 1778–79 and as he and his companions floated down the Cumberland in small rude canoes, observed no human being until Jones' Bend about fifteen miles above the Lick was reached. There he saw a man by the name of Jones (whose name became the Bend's)[8] who had gone in earlier years from one of the seaboard States by the water route to the Illinois country.[9] Becoming dissatisfied there, he left and went by water to and past French Lick; he lived in the Bend for about nine months in a cabin; he cleared a spot of ground, planted corn and killed game. While out hunting he saw definite signs of the presence of Indians, and immediately packed his few personal effects and pushed his canoe far upstream and then traveled on foot to the Watauga where Robertson knew him. After a stay on the Watauga he returned to the Bend. The two men recognized one another on sight. Jones had described the country and his own location to Robertson while on the Watauga.

Too, Casper (or Gasper) Mansker[10] and Michael Stoner[11] were on the Cumberland and its waters before the advent of Robertson and his colony. Stoner, with an eye for good land, had blazed and partially cleared a homestead—the celebrated Clover

---

of great value on the manners and customs of the frontiersmen. William was a brother of John Clinkenbeard, a soldier in the Revolution, living on the Watauga.

[7] "Camped there for the purpose of killing game at a sulphur spring about a mile" from the place, later the home of Col. Benjamin Joslin. Draper MSS., 6XX50. This was on or near what later came to be known as the Natchez Trace.

[8] In which Gen. Andrew Jackson built his home in 1794.

[9] Thomas Jones in June, 1769, voyaged from the site of Pittsburgh by water to the Illinois country, and probably was the Jones, or the father of the Joneses, mentioned by Haywood. Alvord and Carter, *Trade and Politics*, 562–4 (Ill. Hist. Coll. XVI.)

[10] *Lord Dunsmore's War*, 51. The best accounts of Mansker are those by Haywood, Putnam and Roosevelt, particularly the last named whose fancy was evidently caught by Mansker.

[11] *Ib.* It is said that Daniel Boone accompanied Stoner on this trip to the Cumberland.

Bottom tract at the junction of Cumberland and Stone's Rivers. When Richard Henderson appeared on the scene in 1780, he cast longing glances at that beautiful and fertile bit of land and proceeded to make a deal with the German—a transaction that led to litigation in the courts of Kentucky, where Stoner removed.[12] Yet others were settled in the region before Robertson's arrival.[13]

---

[12] For data on and a transcript of this litigation the author is under obligation to his friend, the Kentucky historian, Samuel M. Wilson, of Lexington, Ky. Suit was brought in the court of Madison County, Ky., in September, 1794, by Stoner against the executors of the estate of Richard Henderson (Broomfield Ridley, John Williams, Robert Benton, Archibald and Pleasant Henderson). In plaintiff's pleading it was alleged that Henderson had agreed in writing, of date May 22, 1780, to convey to Stoner two tracts of land, totaling 1200 acres, one of which was the occupancy of Benj. Petit on the south side of Cumberland River, in exchange for the tract on which Stoner had previously settled; that Stoner conveyed his occupancy to Henderson but that Henderson had died without complying with the contract. Stoner was awarded a judgment, but a nulla bona returns of executions make it evident that he never was able to realize anything. The author has a photographic copy of the contract in Henderson's handwriting. It was witnessed by P. Henderson and Jonathan Anthony.

[13] Among them a German from Pennsylvania; Benjamin Petit, and James Shaw (Shor or Schor). To be remarked is the high percentage of foreign names; at no time in the after-history of Tennessee was there such a percentage of inhabitants of foreign birth or descent. Thomas Sharp Spenser was in the region but as a hunter and not a settler. For an account of him see Cisco's *Historic Sumner*.

CHAPTER XII

ROBERTSON'S CUMBERLAND COLONY (1779-80)

The genesis of the large group of people led to the French Lick on the Cumberland by James Robertson and John Donelson in 1779-80 was at the treaty of Long Island in 1777. The two and Richard Henderson met there, and, naturally, discussed the prospects of Henderson & Company's purchase from the Cherokees of a vast body of land within the limits of North Carolina—the Tennessee country. Donelson returned to his home in Pittsylvania County, Virginia, and soon began to shape his affairs for a removal to the West; in 1778 he was advocating the desirability of the region on the Cumberland for settlement. Henderson was an astute man and saw in Robertson and Donelson men of parts, well adapted to pioneering and colonizing. Robertson's appointment and service as North Carolina's commissioner to the Overhill Cherokees held up an immediate prosecution of any plans conceived at the treaty. A migration to the Cumberland earlier than in the fall of 1779 was contemplated by Robertson; he planned a push westward for the spring of that year,[1] but evidently the scheme was one of such magnitude that preparations caused a postponement until the fall. However, he did make his first trip farther to the westward in the winter of 1778-79, his party consisting of nine men.[2]

Leaving Robertson's home at the mouth of Big Creek of the Holston, they passed the Long Island, through Cumberland Gap

---

[1] "Daniel Boone having returned from one of his long hunting expeditions gave such a glowing description of the country on the Cumberland, etc., rivers that it induced Col. Robertson and nine others to go and explore the country:" Mrs. Lavinia (Robertson) Craighead, in Draper MSS., 6XX50. This daughter of Robertson says that the journey was begun in 1778. Putnam gives the date as February, 1779, which is the more probable one. *History of Middle Tennessee*, 64.

[2] George Freeland, William Neely, Edward Swanson, James Hanley, Mark Robertson, Zachariah Wells, William Overall and a negro slave of Robertson; all were sturdy woodsmen.

and then on westward through the trackless forests of the lower Kentucky country to a point on Cumberland River, below the Falls. There with axes and hatchets they constructed small canoes for a descent of the river. They carried seed-corn and as few articles as possible.[3] At French Lick they found the rude warehouse of Demunbreun, filled with peltry, tallow and smoked meats; but the proprietor was absent. When found, Demunbreun gave Robertson an account of the Illinois country and of the route to it. A party of Frenchmen out hunting with Demunbreun "had some handsomely made skiffs in which they had sailed from St. Louis.[4] Robertson gave them a guinea for one of them." After planting corn near the Lick, he with some of his party journeyed by water to the mouth of the Illinois River, where some of his men refused to go farther and left him. The others pushed on to the Oak Post, an Indian town and trading post. After they had remained there for a time to lay in supplies, the Indians began to suspect that Robertson was a spy. It was there that Robertson met Jean du Charleville and had from him a recital of his having been a young trader at French Lick in 1710–14.[5] This Frenchman aided in allaying the suspicions of the Indians respecting Robertson; he explained to them that Robertson's real mission was to purchase Spanish horses,[6] especially brood mares, to be taken south. The Indians then began to be friendly and assisted in the buying of horses. Robertson then turned to find Colonel George Rogers Clark to arrange for a purchase of "cabin

---

[3] Here see the incident at Jones' Bend before the French Lick was reached, in preceding chapter.

[4] See Williams, *Dawn.*

[5] *Ib.,* 75–6.

[6] Spanish horses were at this period in great demand. Gov. Patrick Henry wrote Col. George Rogers Clark to buy for him two stallions of truest blood, the best that the Spanish settlement, or the Indians, could furnish. "I would not have you value the cost of the horses." He also asked that brood-mares be purchased and sent to Hanover County. (Dec. 12, 1778). *Official Letters,* I, 340–342. Clark sent out an order for the purchase of two "blood-bays, five or six years old; that have covered none, and a few mares of "fine, delicate head, long necks, small ears, deep shoulders and chests, large arms, well legged, upright pasterns, clear of long hair, loins round and very wide, haunches to be as straight as possible, if small stars or blazes all the better." In view of the wide use of the horse on all borders, these specifications are, indeed, interesting. How nearly did Robertson and Clark agree on "points"?

rights" in a tract of 3000 acres at French Lick, claimed by the Colonel, he having purchased three years before a bonus entry from a Virginia military officer. The boundary line between North Carolina and Virginia had not been extended westward, and if Clark's tract was in Virginia, Henderson & Company could not support a claim to it. Robertson wisely desired to hedge by a purchase or lease from Clark. The two reached a tentative agreement.

It thus appears that Clark was three years ahead of Robertson in his effort to acquire lands at French Lick.[7] He had made considerable improvements on the tract, seemingly with a view to making his home there after his campaigns were ended. It is interesting to speculate on what would have been his career and influence in the development of the Tennessee country had this stalwart figure of a purposeful age settled on the Cumberland instead of remaining in Kentucky. He and James Robertson would have "made a team." Clark, as he feared, "in a manner lost his all" in losing the tract on which stands the capital city of Tennessee. He died a poor and distraught man.[8]

Robertson now turned towards his home, striking and traveling by the Boone trail. He gave attention to the forming of groups to emigrate to the Cumberland country. By an agreement between himself and Donelson the migration was to be two-phased: the former was to lead a party in a trek through the wilderness, taking along the horses and other livestock, their

---

[7] Among several entries on the Cumberland under Virginia authority was this Clark entry. Respecting it Clark wrote to Gov. Patrick Henry on March 9, 1779: "If I should be deprived of a certain tract of land on that [Cumberland] River, which I purchased three years ago, I shall in a manner lose my all. It is known by the name of the Great French Lick on the south or west side, containing 3,000 acres; if you can do anything for me in saving it, I shall forever remember it with gratitude." Williams, "Conquest of the Old Southwest," in *Tenn. Hist Mag.*, V, 214–15, quoting *Am. Hist. Review*, I, 94, where the letter was reprinted from the Canadian Archives, Series B, Vol. 122, p. 304. It would seem that the British intercepted the letter and that it did not reach Gov. Henry.

[8] Clark, it is said, in later years arrived at a "settlement" of his claim "under Judge Catron, of Nashville." *Calendar of King's Mountain Papers*, 345. This was John Catron who became chief justice of Tennessee, and associate justice of the U. S. Supreme Court. It is to be hoped that the old hero received a fair compensation for the improvements made by him, if not for the land.

route to be through the Kentucky country; the latter was to lead groups, many being women and children, down the Tennessee in boats, then up the Ohio and Cumberland to the French Lick. Robertson started first and, astride his horse, was in the van of his caravan. The order of march was: horses, including pack-horses and about thirty mares; next the cattle; then the hogs and last the sheep.[9] Most of the meat for food was wild game killed on the way.[10] The route towards the end was along the Kentucky-French Lick trace—hardly a road at that time.

Increased in numbers by a group under John Rains,[11] who originally had been destined for Harrodsburg but were persuaded by Robertson to join his party instead, the emigrants arrived at the Cumberland opposite French Lick as the year was closing. The weather was extraordinarily cold, the coldest it had been in a century,[12] and suffering was the keener because the cold spell

[9] The sheep were in charge of James Robertson's oldest son. An old unruly ram slowed down progress, to the boy's disgust; the ram butted him to the ground time and again!

[10] For a similar tour in 1784 along the same route see Williams, *Early Travels in the Tennessee Country*, 269–79. The route made a great bend through the Kentucky country. The main stations or localities it passed through were, after leaving Cumberland Gap: Whitley's Station on Dick's River, Carpenter's Station on Green River; thence along the north side of Green River to Robertson's Fork, down same to Pittsman's Station; then crossing and descending the stream on to Little Barren River, crossing same at Elk Lick; passing Blue Spring and Dripping Spring to Big Barren River; thence up Drake's Creek to a bituminous spring; thence to Red River; thence into Carolina, passing Mansker's Lick; then to French Lick.

[11] Rains was from the New River settlements in Virginia and had been a "long-hunter" on the Cumberland. Williams, *Dawn*, 328. Felix, son of James Robertson, says that Rains lived to a ripe old age and grew loquacious and vainglorious; and that Haywood in writing his history relied upon him too much, Haywood being "a most singularly credulous man." Draper MSS., 6XX50.

[12] Its intensity was thus described by a pioneer in the Kentucky region not far to the north: "You could go through the cane and see cattle laying with their heads on their sides, as if they were asleep, just literally froze to death; a great many lost their cattle. It was a great country for turkeys, and a heap! a heap! of them died." "Wm. Clinkenbeard's Interview," *Filson Hist. Qr.*, II, 112. A great sickness followed the freeze, and many people lost their lives when the thaw set in and the waters suddenly rose in flood. (Col. Wm. Fleming, then in Kentucky). Merenes, *Travels in American Colonies*, 626, et. seq.

had been preceded by spring-like weather.[13] They found the Cumberland frozen over and the livestock crossed on the ice in safety.

Others who in earlier years had hunted on the waters of the Cumberland and spied out good lands were also turning to the region to obtain possessions. Among those who accompanied the surveyors of the state line were the brothers, Major Anthony and Captain Isaac Bledsoe, the latter of whom served as pilot and woodsman.[14] Their choices of lands were at and near a lick afterwards known as Bledsoe's Lick, now Castilian Springs, in Sumner County. Ramsey, p. 193, misled by and following Timothy Flint, says that it was in 1778 that a settlement was formed at Bledsoe's Lick, thus making it the first permanent English-speaking settlement in Middle Tennessee. Records disprove that.[15] Later, in 1779, Major Bledsoe did head a number of emigrants to that Lick,[16] among them Shelby Blackman, Morgan Hall and Ephraim Peyton. Some South Carolinians on the move to the West overtook the Robertson party; and, being smaller in number and less encumbered, reached French Lick first, crossed the Cumberland on ice and began the building of cabins. The South Carolinians included: John Buchanan and his brother, Alexander; Daniel and Sampson Williams, brothers; James and John Mulherrin and Thomas Thompson.

The stout-hearted men and women who thus made their way to French Lick doubtless were aware that they were to found the first permanent white settlement, but none could foresee that

---

[13] Sampson Williams, an early pioneer, left a description of this or a somewhat later spell of weather in the same year: of a heavy fall of snow at a time when fruit trees were in bloom.

[14] Isaac had been a long-hunter. Williams, *Dawn*, 328, 330. See also "Journal of Daniel Smith," *supre*. It is altogether probable that the Bledsoes left the surveying party and with some members of the military guard deflected to the lick referred to, blazed the desired boundary and afterwards erected a stockaded station. Isaac settled there earlier than Anthony.

[15] The Bledsoes were yet in the eastern part of the country. *Summers, Annals of S. W. Virginia,* court entries for 1778. In Cisco's *Historic Sumner,* 1779 is named as the true date at p. 98.

[16] Guild in *Old Times in Tennessee* (p. 64) says that 6,280 acres were granted to Anthony Bledsoe by the State of North Carolina—for some of the best lands in the West. He did not remove from Sullivan County until 1781.

their little community would become the center from which would radiate other migrations that would materially aid in the foundation of civilization in West Tennessee, North Alabama, North Mississippi and Arkansas, not to mention again Robertson's Colony in far-away Texas.

CHAPTER XIII

DONELSON'S "ADVENTURE" AND FLOTILLA (1779–80)

At Fort Patrick Henry on the Holston [1] Colonel John Donelson constructed a large flatboat of the broadhorn type. It was named the "Adventure" and served in a sense as flagship of Donelson, the commander. Numerous other smaller craft, enlarged and partially covered pirogues, were also built at the same place. [2] At other points, Fort Blackmore on the Clinch (in the present Scott County, Virginia) and on the Watauga similar boats were built, each of size sufficient to accommodate a family, or more.

The flotilla from Fort Henry began its voyage which has always been reckoned the favorite saga of Tennesseans. A journal or log-book was kept by Donelson. [3] It has been printed in full by Ramsey and Putnam and by this author (with annotation) in his *Early Travels in the Tennessee Country*. Being so accessible to readers its contents will only be briefly summarized here.

The departure from the fort was on December 22, 1779; but, after proceeding nearly three miles, a stop was made at the mouth of Reedy Creek, due to "the fall of water and most accessive hard frost." The boats went no farther until past the middle of February, and on the 20th the mouth of Cloud's Creek was reached. There other vessels joined the flotilla. Three of the boats stuck on the Poor Valley shoals, causing another delay and much dis-

---

[1] At the present Kingsport, for long years the head of navigation on the Holston. The place was later called the "Boatyard" because of this fact. The fort was near the upper end of Long Island, as the water flows.

[2] This sort of craft was at times customarily one hundred feet in length and twenty feet in width; the hull built of hardwood squared, rising about two feet above the surface of the river, the sides often eight or ten inches thick so as to afford protection from rifle fire. A part was enclosed and roofed for sleeping quarters at one end, the opposite end being used for a pen for the poultry and live-stock. Steering was by means of two long sweeps, and the draft was about two feet of water when the boat was loaded.

[3] Now a priceless possession of the Tennessee Historical Society, in Nashville.

tress. A rainy season set in, and on March 2nd the mouth of the French Broad was reached, where, on striking a small island, the boat of Hugh Henry, Sr., was sunk, but the occupants of other boats lent asistance and she was raised and bailed out. There young Reuben Harrison [4] went out to hunt and was lost; many guns were fired to bring him in; this continued for two days "but all without success, to the great grief of his parents and fellow travelers." He was later found a considerable distance down stream [5] where Benjamin Belew took the youngster on his boat.

On March 4th the mouth of the Little Tennessee was passed and ten miles below a camp was struck (near the present town of Loudon). The high water enabled all to reach the mouth of the Clinch on the 5th, where a company in several boats from Fort Blackmore, under Captain John Blackmore, joined the little fleet. At the next day's end they camped on the north shore "where Captain Thomas Hutching's [6] negro man died, being much frosted in his feet and legs." On the 7th the old Chickamauga town was reached, but it was then evacuated.[7] At that place they camped and the wife of Ephraim Peyton (who had gone overland with Robertson) gave birth to a child. The voyagers moved down to the first new town of the Chickamauga Indians—and into trouble. The Indians invited the crews to come on shore, showing signs of friendliness; so much so that John Donelson, Jr., and John Caffrey entered a canoe and were crossing to accept the invitation, when Archy Coody,[8] a half-breed, came alongside and advised them to return to the "Adventure." This they did. Other Indians pulled up and were given some small presents. But soon other redmen were observed embarking in their canoes, armed and painted in war colors. Coody now falsely gave information that all the Indian towns had been passed. But in a short time another town was sighted opposite a small island. There another

---

[4] Of the Watauga group.

[5] Probably at or very near the site of Knoxville.

[6] Whose wife, Catherine, was a daughter of Col. Donelson; their son Capt. John Hutchins was in later years a business partner of Gen. Jackson who married Rachael Donelson. Early in the Revolution, Thomas Hutchings was a captain in the 6th Battalion of the 6th Regiment of regulars from Pittsylvania County, Va.

[7] The Chickamauga Indians thus early after Shelby's attack had abandoned it. See Chapter on Chickamauga Campaign.

[8] For Coody see Williams, *Early Travels in the Tennessee Country*, 235.

invitation to land was given. Young Payne, of the Blackmore
company, on approaching too near was shot from the Indian
shore. There the party from the Watauga under Thomas Stuart,
or Stewart, Sr., ran into serious trouble. In the boats from the
Watauga were twenty-eight men, women and children, whites and
blacks. Smallpox had broken out among them, and it had been
agreed that their boats should follow at such a distance as would
prevent the spreading of infection. Stuart was to be informed by
the blowing of a horn where those in advance had camped. After
the "Adventure" and other boats had passed the town, the Indians seeing the Wataugans far in the rear, intercepted them, killing or taking prisoners all of the occupants.[9] The crews of the
other boats were unable to give any relief to the Wataugans, being
alarmed for their own safety. As the flotilla approached the
gorge of the Cumberland Mountains (where was the perilous
Suck [10] or Boiling Pot (Untighni as the Indians called it), a large
number of Indians were seen following on the banks of the river.
John Cotton's boat, in order to run the rapids, had been tied to
the boat of Robert Cartwright. The latter's craft was overturned
and his goods plunged into the vortex. Seeing the plight of Cartwright, other crews rushed to the rescue. The Indians began firing on them, forcing a return to their own boats. The firing continued and in the confusion a young woman, Nancy Gower, took
the helm of her boat and steered it, the while exposed to the
enemy's fire; a ball penetrated her thigh. No word from her indicated that she had been wounded. However, the blood soon
showed through her clothing and her mother cleansed and dressed
the wound. All boats but one were steered past the Suck. That
of John Jennings ran against a large rock projecting above the

---

[9] See in confirmation, and identifying the groups as Wataugans, Mereness, *Early Travels*, 642. "Thomas Stuart, Jr., six years old, son of the
owner of the boat, was ransomed by the trader William Springstone and
turned over two years later to Col. Joseph Martin at Fort Patrick Henry.
"The Chickamaugas contracted smallpox from the captives, which caused
the death of several hundred Indians." (Brown, p. 182n.) The father
seems to have returned to the Watauga, where he participated in the
formation of the State of Franklin. Williams, *Lost State of Franklin*, 39.
Hugh Henry was also a Wataugan who had migrated from Pittsylvania
County—Col. Donelson's county.

[10] Earliest account of it was by De Soto's men. Williams, *Dawn*, 6,
33, *et seq*. The best description is that by Featherstonaugh, the scientist
and traveler.

river bed. The other voyagers, thinking Jennings and his people lost, passed along the gentle current west of the Suck ; and some days later were surprised to hear a cry for help. Jennings, seeing their camp-fires down the river, came up in a wretched condition and reported what had happened: he had ordered his people to throw overboard the contents of his boat ; and he, an expert rifle-man, returned the Indians' fire. In the terror, his son, another young man and one of his negro slaves jumped from the boat and swam for the shore opposite the redmen ; the negro was drowned, and the two white men were taken to one of the Indian towns where the young man was killed, young Jennings being saved by the intercession of John Rogers,[11] a white trader among the Chick-amaugas. Mrs. Jennings and a negro woman succeeded in un-loading and pushing off the rocks the boat in which was her daughter, Mrs. Ephraim Peyton, whose new-born babe was in some way killed in the midst of the turmoil. As Haywood says: the women of that day "possessed a firmness of soul and intrepid-ity in danger with other qualities," and esteemed only those men who possessed the same virtues.

On March 11th, after assigning members of the Jennings fam-ily to different boats the flotilla proceeded down stream, to be fired upon the next day by Indians from the bank. It came in sight of Muscle Shoals and the parties camped above. It had been arranged in advance that James Robertson, after arriving at French Lick, should come across country to the upper end of the Shoals and there leave a sign by which the voyagers might know that it was practicable for them to complete their journey by land from the Shoals. No sign was discovered, to their great disappointment. Nothing remained but to return to their boats and go forward through the dangerous Shoals, the noise of which resounded in their ears. All passed through unhurt, it taking three hours to do so. From there on the Tennessee's flow was gentle. They were fired upon but once more by Indians, five of the crews being injured, but not dangerously.

On March 15th the mouth of the Tennessee was reached. The water was high in the Ohio and their boats were ill-suited for stemming the swift current. Too, their provisions were about

---

[11] Ancestor of the late Will Rogers, the famed humorist: "Who paid the ransom price in goods." For data on John and his son James, see Brown, *Old Frontiers*, 183, 200, 452, 473, 498.

exhausted and the men worn down. Some of them decided not to attempt to pole the boats upstream and to go to the Natchez country. Among these was Captain Hutchings, with his wife whom her father was destined never to see again. So many men leaving, Ann, the sister of James Robertson, took a man's place on the "Adventure," and aided in steering the vessel upstream, as the men "poled." The "Adventure" was not constructed to breast a current, especially a swollen one. "Several boats will not attempt to ascend the rapid current." The "Adventure's" speed was slightly increased by raising a rude small square sail; and to prevent any ill effects from sudden gusts of wind "a man was stationed at each of the lower corners of the sheet, with directions to give way whenever it was necessary." In the scant twelve miles between the mouths of the Tennessee and the Cumberland the voyagers encamped on the Ohio's south bank to recuperate. At the Cumberland's mouth that stream appeared so narrow as to lead to some doubt of its identity; but all were gratified to see its current so gentle. Passing into that river it gradually widened and they felt more assured. With provisions exhausted, men of the group turned out and killed buffaloes and wild fowl for food, while the women gathered some herbs which some of the company called "Shawnee salad." [12]

On Friday, March 31st, this significant entry was made:

Set out this day and after running some distance met with Colo. Richard Henderson, who was running the line between Virginia and North Carolina. At this meeting we were much rejoiced. He gave us every information we wished, and further informed us that he had purchased a quantity of corn in Kentucky, to be shipped at the Falls of Ohio for the use of the Cumberland Settlement.[13] We are now without bread and are compelled to hunt the buffalo to preserve life.

---

[12] March 29th. These were, perhaps, dandelion greens, much needed to vary the dietary.

[13] The corn had been raised by Nathaniel Hart of the Henderson (Transylvania) Company at Boonsborough in 1779 and sent from there to the Falls (Louisville) in pirogues in charge of Maj. Wm. B. Smith, who continued with the cargo to French Lick in time to sign the Cumberland Compact of May 13, 1780. In the Draper Manuscripts is a letter of John Floyd, dated February 20, 1780, referring to this corn as about to be shipped by Col. Henderson to a settlement he was about to form. All this further indicates that Henderson was the mainspring of the Cumberland Settlement.

The next day the groups were at the mouth of a small river along which was a bottom of rich land. There was found a pair of hand mill-stones set for grinding, but the stones appeared "not to have been used for a great length of time."[14]   On April 12th the mouth of Red River[15] was reached and there the Moses Renfroe group[16] left the flotilla and ascended that stream to settle in the valley.   The current of the Cumberland increased in rapidity and the others proceeded so slowly that it was on April 23rd that they reached the settlement of Amos Eaton, called Eaton's Station, he having moved to that place from near Long Island of Holston.[17]

The closing entry was:

Monday, April 24th—This day we arrived at our journey's end at the Big Salt Lick, where we had the pleasure of meeting Capt. Robertson and his company.   It is a source of satisfaction to us to be able to restore to him and others their families and friends who were entrusted to our care, and who sometime since, perhaps, dispaired of ever meeting again.   Though our prospects at present are dreary, we have found a few log cabins built on a cedar bluff above the Lick by Captain Robertson and his company.

Colonel Donelson left a list of the heads of families and adult men on the voyage but it is incomplete.[18]

---

[14] By whom was this ancient mill built to serve a settlement?   It is the author's belief that the French built it in the period when they were active in trying to colonize the Mississippi Valley, (1744–51), and to hold it against any other European nation.   The French government was granting large boundaries of land and concessions to those who would form colonies and establish industries, such as tanneries, etc.

[15] Montgomery County, Tennessee.

[16] Including the families of Renfroe and of his sons, James and Joseph, also Solomon Turpin and family.   The Chickasaw Indians on whose soil they located resented this settlement and soon (1780) broke it up, killing Nathan Turpin, Joseph Renfroe and another man (Haywood, 127).

[17] See ante.

[18] John Donelson, Sr., Thomas Hutchings, John Caffery, John Donelson, Jr., James Robertson's lady and children, Mrs. Purnell, M. Rounsifer, James Cain, Isaac Neelly, Jonathan Jennings, Benjamin Belew, Wm. Crutchfield, Peter Looney, Capt. Jno. Blakemore, Moses Renfroe, Mr. ——— Johns, Hugh Henry, Sr., Mrs. Henry (widow) Thomas Henry, Frank Armstrong, Hugh Rogan, Daniel Chambers, Robert Cartwright, John Cotton, [Thomas] Stuart, David Guin, John Boyd, Reuben Harrison, Frank Haney, ——— Maxwell, John Montgomery, [John] Cockrill, John White, Solomon White and ——— Payne.   To which should be added, from other sources: Charles, the brother of James Robertson,

Rachel Donelson, who was then fifteen years old, was a passenger on the "Adventure," became the wife of General Andrew Jackson. Others of the Donelsons, destined to reach high station in later years, were Andrew Jackson Donelson, minister to Mexico and candidate for the vice-presidency, and General Daniel Smith Donelson, C.S.A., for whom Fort Donelson on the Cumberland was named. A daughter of Colonel Donelson was the wife of General John Coffee of the War of 1812–15. A descendant alike of Colonel Donelson and John Caffery, was a senator in Congress from Louisiana, and another is, in 1944, the ambassador to Brazil. Descendants of Jonathan Jennings were John S. Wise, congressman and author, and Jennings C. Wise; their mother, a Jennings, having married Governor Henry A. Wise of Virginia. Mrs. Ephraim Peyton was the mother of Balie Peyton, congressman, turfman and famed raconteur, and of Joseph H. Peyton, congressman. Wm. Gwin, a senator in Congress, was a descendant of David Gwin. Among descendants of Mrs. James Robertson were: Generals B. Frank Cheatham I and II; Joseph J. Cheatham, rear-admiral of the navy and E. Sterling Robertson, C.S.A.; the wife of Bishop Robert Paine of the Methodist Church, South; Edward White Robertson and his son, congressman Samuel M., of Louisiana. Among the descendants of John Cockrill and Ann Robertson were some of the outstanding men and women of Middle Tennessee; and most noted in public life was Sterling Robertson Cockrill of the Arkansas Supreme Court.

Had the flotilla of Colonel Donelson been lost, there is thus made evident what a loss it would have been to Tennessee, the South and the Nation.

Just before the Donelson parties landed at French Lick another smaller group of voyagers turned up there in even worse plight. In November preceding, another flotilla left Kaskaskia in the Illinois country for the Falls of the Ohio. It was led by Isaac Bowman, whose bateau carried seven or eight men and one family. All these were captured by the Chickasaws; but another large bateau containing twelve men and four families escaped and detouring up the Cumberland reached French Lick about the first of April in a pitiable plight.[19]

and their sister, Ann Robertson Johnson (or Johnston) and others named in the text.

[19] *Calendar Va. St. Papers*, I, 358.

CHAPTER XIV

EXTENSION OF THE VIRGINIA–NORTH CAROLINA LINE—1779

The survey by Jefferson and Fry in 1749 of the line between the Colonies of Virginia and North Carolina crossed the Alleghanies and stopped at Steep Rock Creek,[1] and not at "steep rock" of the Alleghany Mountains. There was, as seen, an unofficial experimental survey in 1771.

Seemingly, the earliest suggestion for the official extension was in 1776 by Colonel Joseph Williams, of North Carolina, after his campaign against the Overhill Cherokees. He tried unsuccessfully to prod his State to action:

I now send you a copy of a letter from Colonel Christian to Col. Russell, convincing proof to me that some of the Virginia Gentlemen are desirous of having the Cherokees under their protection, which I humbly conceive is not their right. . . . As our frontiers are Inhabited far beyond where the Colony line is Extended, in order to avoid further disputes, it would be well for Commissioners to be appointed from each Colony and have the line extended; otherwise by all probability there will be great contentions on our frontiers. One thing more I beg to mention: if North Carolina State would station a regiment at the mouth of Holston River it would be a means of breaking off communications between the Northward and Southward Tribes of Indians.[2]

Governor Caswell laid this communication before the General Assembly of 1777 but a resolution providing for a commission of surveyors to run the extension passed by the Senate was rejected in the lower house,[3] and a joint survey was postponed for two years.

The legislature of Virginia in 1778 provided for a joint survey

---

[1] Williams, *Dawn*, 120, with map. The creek is in Johnson Co., Tenn., and known as Laurel Creek, of the South Fork of Holston.

[2] *N. C. Co. Recs.*, X, 912, 951. Continuing: "I went and took a view of the place, and can venture to say I never saw any better formed by nature; provisions may be conveyed in five days from Big [Long] Island to the point in canoes or small boats." Not until the days of the Southwest Territory was a fort established there—Fort Grainger, at or near the present Lenoir City.

[3] *Ib.*, XII, 239, 432.

of the line westward from Steep Rock Creek. Curiously, the bill
was introduced by Anthony Bledsoe who lived on North Carolina
soil several miles south of the line, he being, as we have seen, notwithstanding, one of the members from Washington County, Virginia. He had run the experimental line in 1771. North Carolina's legislature acted favorably the next year.

The commissioners for Virginia were Dr. Thomas Walker and
Daniel Smith;[4] for North Carolina Richard Henderson, and
William Bailey Smith. A military guard was provided, of about
one hundred men, by each State. Colonel Joseph Williams was
in command of the North Carolina guards, and Samuel Henderson, younger brother of Richard, was commissary.

The two commissioners were to meet at Fort Chiswell in Virginia, but journeyed to a spot much nearer to the western terminus of the ancient line. There they met on September 1, 1779.
Two days before, search by a surveyor had been made along Steep
Rock Creek for the place where the old line had struck it; but
it could not be found, owing to so much marked timber having
died since 1749. It was determined to go to some mountain six
miles southwestwardly for their camp for better astronomical ob-
servations. There the degree of latitude was agreed upon, and
the survey proceeded due westward.[5] When Daniel Smith reached
the home of Evan Shelby, the latter accompanied him to Long
Island where the other commissioners were in conference with
Cherokee chiefs, in which The Tassel in a talk said that his
people claimed the land south of Cumberland River, "quite to the
mouth of it." "Carolina has gained a great deal of ground of us
for which we have never received any satisfaction, no, not even
so much as trade. The great men of Carolina seem to hold everything very fast in their hands; they are always getting what they
can and let nothing go, neither guns, goods or ammunition."
Colonel Henderson made a speech which "they (the Indians) did
not seem to like very well."[6]

---

[4] Later a citizen of Tennessee; secretary of the Southwest Territory
and United States Senator from Tennessee. Smith County, Tenn., bears
his name. Smith was appointed a commissioner in lieu of Rev. James
Madison, a professor in William and Mary College and cousin of Pres.
Madison.

[5] Sioussat, "Daniel Smith's Journal of the Survey," in *Tenn. Hist.
Mag.* II, 40–65.

[6] *Ib.* 51.

The survey proceeded across Carter's Valley, where a dispute arose between the two sets of commissioners, the North Carolinians contending that the line was two miles too far to the south.[7] One of the Virginia commissioners at first agreed with them, but later recanted. The two commissions then separated, running nearly parallel lines to Powell Mountain and on to Cumberland Gap. At the latter place Henderson and William B. Smith abandoned their survey after sending a letter of protest to the Virginia commissioners,[8] who continued on with their line to the Tennessee River, except that a gap was left unsurveyed from Deep Fork to the first crossing of Cumberland River, owing to the extreme roughness of the terrain, which was also almost barren. The detour made was northerly to the Kentucky road and down the north side of the Cumberland. Turkeys and buffaloes were killed for much needed food. On January 5, 1780, the weather was better and the Virginians lodged with Obediah Terrell[9] in his camp. They "were froze up for forty days on a river never known to be froze before."

When the main Cumberland River was first reached (February 25th) Dr. Walker took a canoe and went downstream to French Lick, "by which means a tolerable map of Cumberland River was taken." On March 23rd they were "joyfully surprised with the sight of the Tennessee." They turned back to the Cumberland, separated from the Tennessee by only nine and one fourth miles. Daniel Smith was also eager to visit the French Lick to view the region already well known in Virginia for its fertility. Smith followed the Cumberland road by way of Gasper's (Mansker's) Lick and passed the spot, or very near the spot, where he later entered lands and made his home. Walker, as seen, was already at French Lick,[10] as were also Henderson and Robertson. The fact that four such master spirits in Western history thus

---

[7] The dispute was set forth with the respective contentions by Walker and Daniel Smith in their report which appears in full in Haywood, *Civil and Political History of Tennessee*, appendix, and by Henderson, W. B. Smith and Williams in their report, in *N. C. St. Recs.*, XIV, 353–5.

[8] Sumners, *History of Southwest Virginia*, 299, and comments of Sioussat in *Tennessee Hist. Mag.*, 42.

[9] For whom Obey, or Obed, River was named.

[10] See *post.* The journalist, Daniel Smith, curiously does not mention James Robertson or any of his party at French Lick. They were "Henderson men."

met on a spot so remote fully proves that land-lust was rampant.

Smith in 1815 wrote: "On arrival at the French Lick, we received a letter from the Governor of Virginia, directing us, as the Spanish Governor Galvez was then conquering the Natchez country and adjacent parts from the British, to go to the Falls of the Ohio to Colonel Clark and apply to him for a guard, descend the Ohio and Mississippi Rivers to the proper latitude and there make marks and give all the publicity we could to the claim of Virginia that far south. This duty we performed and then returned home." Did Smith and his guard go as far as the strategic Lower Chickasaw Bluff which was in later years occupied by Spain?

The Virginians in their survey struck the Tennessee River at about 36 degrees 40 minutes, or more than twelve miles north of the true line. The surveyors, by reason of failing to make due allowance for a variation of the needle, had continuously deflected to the north. In consequence Virginia, and Kentucky as her successor, lost many hundreds of thousands of acres. This accounts for the off-set or jog in the line at the Tennessee River, so apparent on all maps.[11]

Colonel Henderson was in Kentucky when the line was being carried forward by the Virginians, buying corn for the infant settlement on the Cumberland in the Tennessee country, and was now on Cumberland River to see to its transportation to the French Lick. When he learned of the Virginians' point of terminus at the Tennessee he, doubtless, was elated.[12] The Virginians through their own mistake had given North Carolina jurisdiction over a long, wedgelike triangle of land to which that State was not entitled. The prime motive of Henderson in accepting the commission to run the line was the protection of the interests of his Transylvania Company in lands lying in North Carolina— the Tennessee country. By so far north as that line could be

---

[11] The survey of the line, in later years, from the Tennessee to the Mississippi was on the true line and this made the jog referred to.

[12] Long-headed Col. Arthur Campbell wrote the governor of Virginia: "When the Carolina commissioners found that the boundary run by Dr. Walker left the French Lick upwards of twenty miles to the south they seemed well satisfied, and it is generally thought that Dr. Walker's report would be agreed to by both parties," the two States concerned.

fixed his company stood to benefit. Virginia had already held void his company's purchase of the Cherokees at Sycamore Shoals of Watauga, so far as the Kentucky country was concerned, and this gave point to his efforts to have the line run as far to the north as possible.[13]

On the other hand, Dr. Walker was almost as much interested in conserving the interests of his Loyal Land Company, especially its claims to a large part of the Kentucky country.[14]

Not only was Walker disappointed in losing the lands on the Cumberland; the Commonwealth of Virginia received a blow. In December, 1778, her legislature had set apart a reservation for her soldiers. The survey showed a good portion of the reservation actually to be within the limits of North Carolina. To make good the loss, in November, 1782, another tract was opened to bounty claimants—that part of Kentucky between the Mississippi, Ohio and Tennessee Rivers.

North Carolina after some delay ratified the line run by the Virginia commissioners,[15] but the matter of its true location on the ground remained to vex the Virginians and Tennesseans throughout many generations.[16] Tennessee came out "first-best" in all later contentions and litigations, holding advantages which added considerably to her territory—indeed beyond her original

---

[13] See Williams, "Henderson and Co's, Purchase Within the Limits of Tennessee," in the *Tenn. Hist. Mag.* V, 5–27.

[14] From French Lick he wrote a letter to Col. William Preston regarding entries of land to be made in Virginia's western counties. Dr. Walker was tireless in the matter of acquiring land. Daniel Smith was at the time a sub-agent under Walker in the sale of lands claimed by the Loyal Land Company, while William Bailey Smith was interested with Henderson in Kentucky lands around the present Henderson, Ky. The survey, therefore, was in a sense one of the boundary between the lands claimed by the Loyal Land Company and those below claimed by the Henderson Company.

[15] *N. C. State Recs.*

[16] The history of the line from colonial days to 1890 appears in Garrett, "Northern Boundary of Tennessee," *Am. Hist. Mag.*, (Nashville) VI, 18–90. The best account of the victory of Tennessee over Virginia in the litigation settled by the decision of the United States Supreme court in *Virginia v. Tennessee* is to be found in Summer's *History of Southwest Virginia*, 725–746. For the legal phase of the Tenn-Ky part of the line see opinion by the writer as a justice of the Tennessee Supreme Court in the Tennessee Reports.

legal rights, had the same been seasonably and skilfully contested.[17]

Misunderstandings continued to arise along the boundary even after the survey was completed and ratified. One of these involved, the agile Wm. Cocke as precipitator. Having removed to the banks of the Holston (in what is now Hawkins County, Tennessee) Cocke encountered Virginia's tax collector busy there collecting taxes that had attached before the confirmatory acts were passed. Cocke challenged his authority, "asking what right he had to collect taxes there, as it was in Carolina and never was in Virginia; that the people were fools if they did pay him the public dues and that he [Cocke] dared him to serve any process whatever; . . . upon which sundry people refused to pay their tax and some that had paid wanted their money back." The arrest of Cocke was ordered if to be found in the country.[18] Cocke was not taken into custody and the matter was dropped by the Virginians who knew the weakness of their claim.

---

[17] The same thing might be said of the southern boundary line. Tennessee had a like advantage over Mississippi. North Carolina has had a better measure of success in contests over the eastern boundary line.

[18] Summers, *ib.* p. 299.

CHAPTER XV

CIVIL AFFAIRS (1779)

The year 1779 witnessed something like a migration in bulk to the Tennessee country, particularly from the Shenandoah Valley and the counties of Botetourt, Montgomery and Washington of Virginia. In large part, the immigrants were thrifty and inured to the hardships of frontier life. The inrush was such that no longer was there any real danger that the whites would be driven from the land by red foes at the south. That fact, itself, served to give a further impetus to the inflow of population.

Charles Robertson was senator and Jesse Walton and Henry Clark members of the lower house of the General Assembly of North Carolina. Walton introduced a bill, which was passed, to lay out the town of Jonesborough as the county seat of Washington County, the first town established in the Tennessee country. It was named in honor of Willie Jones,[1] a sagacious leader in North Carolina, who in 1776 advocated the recognition of the western people and had been their consistent friend. The honor was worthily and gracefully bestowed. New commissioners were named: Jesse Walton, John Woods, George Russell, James Stuart and Benjamin Clark. They were by the Act empowered to "lay out and direct the building of the said town . . . and to make or cause to be made a fair plan of said town and number the lots, and take subscriptions for said lots . . . and appoint a day for drawing same in a fair and open manner . . . the money arising from same shall be applied by the commissioners for the benefit of said town."[2]

---

[1] Pronounced Wylie. Jones was a son of Robin Jones, state attorney-general of North Carolina; the son was educated at Eaton in England; he threw his great influence in favor of the independence of this country. His official service included the presidency of the council of safety, 1776; membership in the House of Commons from the borough of Halifax, 1777 and 1778 and from Halifax County, 1779, 1780; state senator, 1782–1784, and in the convention of 1788 where he led the forces which defeated a ratification of the U. S. Constitution.

[2] Act of N. C. 1779, ch. 36. It was further provided: "Every grantee

The county records show that Walton was the leading spirit and active commissioner. He executed deeds and kept the accounts. He well deserves the title, "founder of Tennessee's first town, Jonesborough." [3] A list of the purchasers of lots, and the number of lots drawn, has been preserved.[4] The town had a slow growth in its early years.[5]

No description of the house first used for court sessions [6] has been preserved, but the one which succeeded it is thus described in records:

The court recommended that there be a court house built in the following manner; to wit: 24 feet square, diamond corners and hewed down after the same is built up, nine feet high between the two floors, and the body of the house four feet high above the upper floor, each floor to be neatly laid with plank. The roof to be of joint shingles neatly hung with pegs; a Justices' bench, a lawyers' and a clerk's table, also a sherriff's box to sit in.

The court ordered that Colo. Charles Robertson be allowed fifty pounds current money for building the court house in the Town of Jonesborough.[6]

---

of any lot shall within three years build on same one brick, stone or well-framed house, twenty feet long and sixteen feet wide, and at least ten feet in the pitch, with a brick or stone chimney. . . . If the owner shall fail to build and finish thereon as before described, then such lots shall be forfeited"—an early example of municipal building restrictions.

[3] At the town's sesqui-centennial celebration in 1929, such recognition was given. A monument to Walton was erected in front of the Washington County courthouse. For Walton's career: Williams "The Founder of Tennessee's First Town—Major Jesse Walton" in the *E. T. Hist. Soc. Pubs.* II, 70–80.

[4] "Robert Sevier, 1; Major Reynolds, 3; David Hughes, 2; Nathaniel Evans, 1; Martin Maney, 4; Jas. Allison, 8; Peter McClure, 2; John Allison, 2; Jesse Bounds, 2; Capt. Stephen Cole, 2; Capt. Charles Holliway, 2, since sold to Jesse Walton, now sold to Christopher Taylor May 2, 1785; Wm. Noddy [Snoddy] 1; James Ray, 1; Richard Minton, 2; Col. Andrew Belford [Balfour] 4; James Reese, 4; Spruce McCay, 2; John Gilliland, 2; James Lackey, 2; John Woods, 2; John Yancey, 1; James Stuart, 10; Jesse Walton, 9." *Am. Hist. Mag.* (Nashville), V, 224.

[5] Even county officials resided on their farms. John Sevier, clerk of the court, in 1778–1779 lived five miles west on Little Limestone Creek where he owned a water-mill (at Telford Station of Southern Railway, of the present day). The year following he removed to his estate on the south side of the Nolachucky.

[6] The first session on the site of Jonesborough was held May 24, 1779, "at the place appointed for the courthouse," indicating that a private home had been used, as was the fact.

There appeared (1779) in the West and was admitted to the bar, a young Carolinian, William Richardson Davie, who was to rise to high positions in North Carolina and the nation.[7] He came not merely as a lawyer but as a kind of liaison officer for the State with the Westerners, the Tories among whom he was to watch, and the Whigs among whom he was to cultivate as potential manpower in the Revolutionary War. William Sharpe, Waightstill Avery and Spruce McCay also rode across the mountains to practice at the bar.

The eyes of Carolinians were gradually opening to a realization of the advantages of the Tennessee Valley, and they began to enter and purchase lands—among them Avery, Sharpe and even Governor Richard Caswell.

One of the enigmas of western history is the supineness of North Carolina in regard to the exercise of jurisdiction by Virginia over a part of her territory—the North of Holston, Pendleton District and Carter's Valley, regions—with result that the former deprived herself of the considerable taxes collected there, as well as the control of the militia and the fort and trading post at Long Island of Holston. Each of these communities grew steadily and fast in population and wealth from the decades of their early settlements. The fertility of the soil and the other natural advantages almost compelled it.

That the line between the two Colonies, later States, on extension would include all these regions was made manifest by Anthony Bledsoe's experimental survey in 1771.[8] However, the people in those communities, being largely of Virginia origin, preferred to close their eyes and remain as Virginians as long as they could. Strangely enough, it was upon the invitation of Virginia that a step was taken which brought to an end her illegal assertion of jurisdiction, and North Carolina again acquiesced and followed suit—in the extension of the line westward.

---

[7] Brigadier General in the Revolution; governor of North Carolina; member of the Federal Constitutional Convention (1787), and minister to France. For sketches, see Ashe, *Biographical History of North Carolina,* VI, 188–197; Peele, *Lives of Distinguished North Carolinians,* 59–80; *James Sprunt Historical Monographs,* No. 7 (1907). Davie opposed the cession of the western country in 1783, but is said to have drafted the cession act of 1789, and to have been a most influential supporter of that measure.

[8] See in this connection the chapter on the Va.-N. C. State line.

At the fall session of the North Carolina general assembly an act was passed to establish a new county, carving it from Washington County. Sullivan County [9] thus became the first daughter of the "Mother County." The boundaries began at the Steep Rock Creek terminus of the colonial survey of 1751; [10] ran thence along "the dividing ridge that separates the waters of the Great Kanawha and the Tennessee," [11] to the head of Indian Creek; thence along the ridge that divides the waters of Holston and Watauga, to the mouth of the Watauga; thence in a direct line to the highest part of Chimney Top Mountain, at the Indian boundary." [12]   John Sevier, Isaac Shelby [13] and John Chisholm were named commissioners to run the line dividing the old and new counties. [14]   The first court was held at the home of Moses Looney. [15]   A commission was issued appointing the following first justices: Isaac Shelby, David Looney, Anthony Bledsoe, George Maxwell, John Anderson, Gilbert Christian, Joseph Martin, John Duncan, William Wallace, Henry Clark and Samuel Smith. John Rhea was elected clerk, Nathan Clark, sheriff, Ephraim Dunlop state's attorney, and John Adair entry-taker. Isaac Shelby was commissioned by the governor colonel-commandant of the county, Henry Clark lieutenant-colonel; David Looney first major, and John Shelby second major. [16]   The next session of the court was ordered to be held at the home of James Hollis. [17]

---

[9] Named in honor of Gen. John Sullivan of the continental army, who had conducted a campaign against the Northwestern Indians. See sketch in Taylor, *Historic Sullivan*, 85–88.

[10] This terminus was some miles south of the state line as it was finally established—well within Johnson County, Tennessee.

[11] A display of ignorance of geography.

[12] Acts of North Carolina 1779, ch. 29. There was lost to Washington County, Va., over one-third of the territory over which it had exercised jurisdiction. Summers, *History of Southwest Virginia*, 277.

[13] The Shelbys fell in Sullivan County.

[14] The same three, along with Charles McDowell, were directed to run the line between Washington and Burke Counties.

[15] It appears from records in the Draper Collection that the first or "Sullivan Old Court House" was not far from Eaton's Fort of 1776. Blountville was later made the county seat (1792).

[16] No Tennessee county has had an abler corps of first officials; a governor of Kentucky, a brigadier-general and a long-time congressman among them.

[17] *N. C. St. Recs.*, XIV, 136, 314.

Evan Shelby had just been appointed brigadier-general by the Virginia government, in recognition of his successful campaign against the Chickamauga Indians. Major Joseph Martin who lived at Long Island also fell into the new county.

The Virginia legislature of 1779 by a resolution proposed to North Carolina the recognition by the latter of the validity of the Virginia grants of lands below the state line, urging that the agreement with the Cherokees in the treaty of Lockabar (1771) had fixed the Holston River as the Indian boundary "sanctified" the settlement of the country north of that river "under Virginia jurisdiction." [18]

The year closed in some turmoil. Both Evan Shelby and Joseph Martin were notifying Governor Caswell that unruly whites were settled south of the boundary fixed by the treaty of 1777 which was deeply resented by the Cherokees who might give trouble. Particularly were those Indians incensed by the fact that Wm. Cocke had entered the Long Island reserved by them in the treaty of 1777. "He says he had a deed from the Indians which I can prove otherwise." (Martin).

Governor Thomas Jefferson coolly proposed to Governor Caswell that Virginia be given the control of Indian affairs so far as the Overhill towns were concerned, including trade relations with that part of the nation—a proposition which could not prove acceptable to the western folk or to North Carolina. [19]

---

[18] *Ib.*, 226, 234, 235.

[19] *Ib.*, 220–1: "They would be most convenient to us," Virginia becoming their "immediate patron and benefactor which will be a bond of peace and will lead to a separation of that powerful people." Somewhat later, Gov. Jefferson, quite as coolly, proposed that his State be permitted to continue to control and garrison Fort Patrick Henry, opposite the Long Island.

CHAPTER XVI

Over-mountain Men Early in the Carolinas (1780)

The next call upon the over-mountain men came in February, 1780, from the North Carolina council of state. It was to meet the menace to the Southern States involved in the threatened attack by a part of the British fleet on the South Atlantic coast, and the embarkation of land troops for the South at New York. It was evident that Charleston would have to be defended once more.[1] The governor of North Carolina was urged to embody two thousand militia "and to march them to the limits of this State, to be in readiness to act, offensively or defensively, . . . or to march to the aid of South Carolina."[2]

Orders were accordingly sent to all brigadier-generals, and General Griffith Rutherford of the Saulisbury District in turn sent orders for embodying one hundred men in each of the two western counties, Washington and Sullivan. In Washington County prompt action was taken as is shown by a record that came down to the historian, Ramsey.[3]

At a meeting of sundry of the Militia Officers of Washington County, this 19th day of March, 1780: Present John Sevier, Colonel, Jonathan Tipton, Major, Joseph Willson, John McNabb, Godfrey Isbell, William Trimble, James Stinson, Robert Sevier, Captains, and Landon Carter, Lieutenant, in the absence of Valentine Sevier, Captain.

In order to raise one hundred men, agreeable to command of the Hon. Brigadier-General Rutherford, to send to the aid of South Carolina.

It is the opinion of the officers, that each company in this county do furnish eight effective men, well equipped for war, except Samuel Williams' company, which is to furnish four men well equipt as aforesaid.

---

[1] For the first and successful defense and the part of Wataugans in the same: *ante.*

[2] *N. C. St. Recs.*, XXII, 967.

[3] *Annals*, 212.

John Sevier,	Jno. McNabb,
Joseph Willson	Jonathan Tipton,
Wm. Trimble,	Godfrey Isbell.
James Stinson,	

On the same page is a list of captains. They were Captains McNabb, Sevier, Hoskins, Bean, Brown, Isbell, Trimble, Willson, Gist, Stinson, Davis, Patterson and Williams.

The march of all troops was delayed on account of the absence of Colonel Isaac Shelby in Kentucky where he was surveying his claims to lands of the Transylvania Company. He was colonel commandant of Sullivan County. Intelligence of the crisis incident to the fall of Charleston (May 16th) was speeded to him and on June 16th he hastened home, as he himself wrote, "determined to enter the service of the Country, until her independence was secured."

Colonel Charles McDowell, of North Carolina, dispatched a messenger over the mountains to Colonels Shelby and Sevier urging that they bring to his aid all the riflemen they could spare, and as soon as possible; and stating that the British had overrun South Carolina and Colonel Patrick Ferguson was threatening an invasion of North Carolina from the south.

Not awaiting the equipment and readiness of the Sullivan troops, Sevier himself, unwilling to leave his county open to forays by the Chickamauga Indians,[4] responded by sending two hundred of his Washington County regiment under Major Charles Robertson. Later, about July 25th, Shelby leading two hundred mounted riflemen from Sullivan, joined McDowell at his camp near the Cherokee Ford of Broad River. Major Robertson's battalion had reached that camp some days earlier. Shelby, holding higher rank than Robertson, took command of their combined forces.

---

[4] Too, Sevier had recently lost his wife, Sarah Hawkins, and had a large family and many dependents. He married August 16, 1780, Catherine Sherrill (Bonnie Kate) while Robertson and his battalion were in South Carolina. Several historians state that Sevier headed the Washington County troops; among them, Phelan, Wheeler, Schenck, and Ashe, and even Ramsey following Haywood. The presence and activity of Capt. Valentine Sevier manifestly misled them. While Robertson was on this campaign in South Carolina, the Indians (seemingly Chickamaugas) in a small body raided the lower settlements but were met and driven back by Major Jonathan Tipton at the mouth of Flat Creek of the Nolachucky.

Capture of Thickety Fort

As Lord Cornwallis approached Camden, Tories embodied in Tryon County, North Carolina, under Colonel Patrick Moore and marched to join the British force moving northward. Moore took possession of a fort on Pacolet River (Thickety Fort) which had been erected by General Andrew Williamson in the campaign of 1776 against the Cherokees. It was surrounded by strong abattis, and had been put in repair. Colonel McDowell detached the troops of Shelby and Robertson along with a force under Colonel Elijah Clarke, of Georgia, to the aggregate number of six hundred men, to take this fort. These mounted riflemen took up a twenty miles march at sunset and by dawn of the following day had the fort surrounded. Shelby sent in Captain William Cocke,[5] a volunteer, to make a peremptory demand for surrender. Moore replied that he would defend the post to the last extremity. Shelby then drew in his lines to gunshot distance from the enemy, and more completely surrounded the fort. He was fully determined to make an assault.

Before doing so, he sent in a second demand for surrender. The "six hundred" grim riflemen made such a formidable appearance that Moore quailed and agreed to capitulate on condition that the garrison be paroled not to serve again during the war, unless exchanged. This was acceded to. Thus without firing a gun, ninety-three Loyalists, with a British sergeant-major stationed there to discipline the Tories, were surrendered. About two hundred stands of arms were taken, all loaded with ball or buckshot and so arranged at the portholes that the defenders could have successfully resisted twice their number.[6] The surrender was on Sunday morning, July 30, 1780.

---

[5] Later one of the first senators in Congress from Tennessee.

[6] The British charged cowardice on the part of Moore in the surrender. At King's Mountain there was found the fragment of a report, probably the original of a draft from Colonel Patrick Ferguson to Cornwallis: "The officer next in command, and all others, gave their opinion for defending it [the fort] and agree in their account that Patrick Moore, after proposing surrender, acquiesced in their opinion, and offered to go and signify as much to the Rebels; but returned with some Rebel officers whom he put in possession of the gate and place, who were instantly followed by their men, and the fort was full of Rebels to the surprise of the garrison. He pleaded cowardice, I understand." Ramsey, *Annals of Tennessee*, 215, to whose hands the document had come. Ferguson's disappointment was

Battle at Cedar Spring

After the return of the over-mountain men to McDowell's camp, without practically any rest they were ordered out again, along with troops of Colonel Clarke, to watch the movements of the enemy under Colonel Patrick Ferguson and to cut off parties foraging for Ferguson's command which included altogether about two thousand "American Volunteers" and Tories. Hearing of this adventure, Ferguson made attempts to surprise the Patriots. In the late afternoon of August 7th, Shelby's and Clarke's men halted to spend the night at Fairforest.[7] Before day they were warned of the approach of the enemy by the wife of a Patriot captain, and the command fell back toward Cedar Spring where suitable ground was chosen for a defense.

Major James Dunlap, who had much of the initiative and energy of his superior, Ferguson, attacked with a force of dragoons and mounted riflemen, but these troops recoiled at the first fire of the Americans. They were rallied to make another attack, led by Dunlap. A hand-to-hand conflict ensued, Dunlap being beaten back after the loss of about fifty men, including two officers. The enemy in rout was pursued for two miles when Ferguson came to Dunlap's assistance. The combined forces were too much for the Patriot force which made a hasty retreat. Ferguson was eager to retake all the prisoners; the Americans to retain them. To do this, they formed and fought rearguard skirmishes and so retarded Ferguson that the prisoners were placed beyond danger of being recaptured. Draper says: "When Ferguson and his men came in view, evincing a disinclination to pursue further, the Patriots from their vantage-ground, bantered and ridiculed them to their hearts' content. But Ferguson, having maintained the chase four or five miles, now abandoned it,

keener since he had sent a messenger from his camp to Moore with a note insisting that Moore "hold the fort to the last minute." Ferguson's plan was to attack the Americans while they were investing and attacking it. The fullest account of this feat at Thicketty Fort is that of Col. Shelby, followed by Haywood in his *Civil History of Tennessee,* 63–4. The names of two of the Captains under Robertson were given by John Clark, a private from Washington County, as Samuel Williams and Landon Carter. (Pension Statement) Another Captain was Valentine Sevier. His brother, Captain Robert, was along according to a statement of James Sevier, son of Colonel Sevier.

[7] Near Glendale Station of the Southern Railway.

with nothing to boast of save his superior numbers." Such a running fight in the forest was to the liking of the backwater men, enabling them to fight "Indian fashion." This was the first confrontation of Ferguson by the dare-devils of the western waters.

The loss of the Americans was four killed and twenty wounded; of the enemy, about thirty killed and wounded, and fifty captured.[8]

Battle of Musgrove's Mill

The term of enlistment of the over-mountain men being about to expire—short as it was from necessity and by custom—McDowell was solicitous to avail of their further active service before their departure. A body of them under Shelby, Captain Valentine Sevier, and other captains of Robertson's command, were sent on another raid which, next to King's Mountain, brought renown to the men of the Holston, Watauga and Nolachucky because of their accurate and deadly aim in bringing down officers of the enemy force.

McDowell, at his camp at Cherokee Ford, learned through his scouts that a large force of Provincials and Tories was posted at Musgrove's Mill on Enoree River, and of the arrival at Smith's Ford of the Broad, ten miles below his camp, of a Patriot force under Colonel James Williams. McDowell detached a part of his command to move under Shelby for a junction with Williams for a joint attack on the enemy at Musgrove's Mill. The success of the venture depended on celerity and secrecy of movement, since Colonel Ferguson with his command lay directly on the way and must be avoided.

A short time before sundown on August 17th about three hundred mounted riflemen proceeded from Smith's Ford toward Musgrove's. They traveled through the woods until nightfall, then turned into the main road and pushed on most of the time in a gallop and across several streams. However, they detoured so as to leave Ferguson about three miles on their left. Within a mile of a ford at Musgrove's Whig scouts discovered and opened fire upon a patrol of the enemy. This firing caused confusion in the camp of the Loyalists. Colonel Alexander Innis[9] in command of

---

[8] The fullest account of the running engagements at Cedar Springs is that of Bailey in *Some Heroes of the American Revolution*, 160–172.

[9] Draper in a note says: "Colonel Innis was a Scotchman. He was probably a protege of his countryman, Alexander Cameron, the British

the Provincials, called a council which decided to make an immediate attack, they having the superior force.

The Whigs and their horses, tired out by the night's hard ride, had no option but to fight. Securing their horses in the rear, their line was formed in a semi-circle on a ridge, both wings concealed and protected by woods. Old logs and brush were piled to serve as breastworks; so that within thirty minutes they were ready to receive the enemy. Shelby, in charge of the western men, occupied the right, Clarke the left, and Williams, as leader, the center. Back of each flank were parties of horsemen, shielded as much as possible from observation; in command of these on the right was Josiah Culbertson under Shelby.[10]

On his own initiative and suggestion, Captain Shadrack Inman [11] went forward with about twenty-five mounted riflemen to provoke the enemy to cross the river, his plan being to skirmish with them and withdraw so as to draw them on into a trap before they became aware of danger. The stratagem succeeded. Within two hundred yards of the Americans, the enemy tried hastily to form for battle. Orders were sent down the line of the Patriots not to fire until they could see the whites of the eyes of the enemy, and not then till orders to fire were given. The British and Tories advanced with blast of bugle, beat of drum and cries of "huzza for King George;" and when they reached a point about seventy yards from the Americans' line, they unexpectedly met a deadly fire, from which they at first recoiled. Innis and Major Fraser now formed the experienced Provincials and attacked the right wing. They drove Shelby's men at the point of the bayonet, bending back the line there, but not severing its connection with the center at the log barrier. Clarke's reserve was now rushed to support Shelby.

---

agent among the Cherokees; and was, it would appear, an assistant commissary at the Long Island of Holston, at one time; and in the fall of 1777, returned to the Cherokee nation, taking up his quarters with Cameron." *Heroes of K. M.*, 108. No doubt this was Long Island of the Tennessee near Bridgeport, Alabama, so as to be in touch with the Chickamaugas. In 1776–77 Ft. Patrick Henry at Long Island was garrisoned.

[10] A lieutenant on the campaign; removed from Washington to Lincoln County (Marshall part), Tennessee.

[11] A marker in honor of this admirable soldier has been erected on the spot. The Inmans in later years were a prominent family in Jefferson County, and Atlanta, Ga.

When the contest was at crisis the British leader was seriously wounded and fell from his horse, shot by William Smith, a Wataugan,[12] who, thinking he had killed Innis, exclaimed in exultation, "I've killed their commander!" Shelby's men then raised the Indian yell of the bordermen and rushed furiously on the enemy, forcing them back. Culbertson and his horsemen acted heroically in this onrush. Major Fraser, second in command, was wounded by Robert Bean of the Watauga, and was seen to reel from his horse. In this hot clash three other enemy officers were wounded and one captain was killed.

The British and Tories could but withdraw after such losses. Shelby's men, followed by Clarke's, pushed forward in pursuit, which became an enemy rout, the Patriots yelling, slashing and shooting on every hand. At this time the gallant Captain Inman fell, pierced in the forehead by a musket ball.

In full retreat the enemy hastened to recross the river still hotly pursued. American rifles and swords took heavy toll of them while in the river and even after they had crossed. Thomas Gillespie of the Nolachucky troops leveled his rifle and made one who had crossed over bite the dust. It was, truly, a day of feats for the sharpshooters of the Trans-Alleghany region.

The British loss was sixty-three killed, about ninety wounded and seventy taken prisoners. The American loss was four killed and eight or nine wounded. The battle lasted an hour and one-half; but it proved to be almost fruitless because of the disastrous defeat of General Gates at Camden. The disparity in losses was due, in part, to the fact that the Americans lay close behind their log breast-works and the enemy overshot them; but, in larger part, to the skill of the backwater men with the rifle.

Flushed with their victory, the three commanders of the American troops in consultation decided to move on weakened Ninety-Six, twenty-five miles away. Their horses, now rested, were ready for another surprise dash and attack. The officers had mounted their horses, to lead towards Colonel Cruger's force at Ninety-Six. Colonel Shelby in after years recorded: "At that moment an express came up from McDowell in great haste with a short letter in his hand from Governor Caswell, dated at the battle-ground, apprising McDowell of the defeat of the American

---

[12] Ramsey, *Annals*, 110. Later he was a justice of the peace in Washington County.

grand army under General Gates on the 16th near Camden, and advising him [McDowell] to get out of the way, as the enemy would, no doubt, endeavor to improve their victory to the greatest advantage by destroying all small corps of the American army.

"It was a fortunate circumstance that Colonel Shelby knew Governor Caswell's handwriting, and what reliance to place upon it."

Being questioned, the messenger said that McDowell was already moving towards Gilbert Town in North Carolina. Shelby and the Westerners could not retire to McDowell's Camp for his force was no longer there. It was, therefore, determined in a hasty council on horseback that the small command would deflect towards the mountains and make their way through the woods to an escape. Ferguson's men were in hot pursuit in an effort to retake the prisoners from the Americans.

Shelby in later years left an account of this pursuit:

It required all the vigilence and exertion which human nature was capable of to avoid being cut to pieces by Ferguson's light parties. . . . The enemy pursued as was expected fifty or sixty miles, until their horses broke down and they could follow no further. . . . The Americans never stopt to eat, but made use of peaches and green corn for their support. The excessive fateague to which they were subjected for two nights and days so effectively broke down every officer that their faces and eyes swelled and became so bloated in appearance, as scarcely to be able to see.[13]

The seventy prisoners were distributed one to every three of the Americans, who conveyed them alternately on horseback, each prisoner being required to carry his own gun, from which its flint had been taken.

Draper says in his *Heroes of King's Mountain*:

The Whig troopers, encumbered with their prisoners, now hurried rapidly away in a north-westerly direction, instead of a north-easterly one, towards their old encampment. They passed over a rough, broken country, crossing the forks of Tyger, leaving Ferguson on the right, and heading their course toward their own friendly mountains. As they expected, they were rapidly pursued by a strong detachment of Ferguson's men. Wearied as

[13] Consult on this campaign, Hamilton, "King's Mountain Letters of Col. Isaac Shelby," in *Journal of Southern History*, IV, 367–377, the extract being from Shelby's account to Col. Wm. Hill of South Carolina who was an active Patriot and fought at King's Mountain.

the mountaineers and their horses were, with scarcely any refreshment for either, yet Shelby's indomitable energy permitted them no rest while danger lurked in the way. Once or twice only they tarried a brief period to feed their faithful horses; relying, for their own sustenance, on peaches and green corn—the latter pulled from the stalks, and eaten in its raw state as they took their turn on horse-back, or trotted on foot along the trail, and which, in their hungry condition, they pronounced delicious. They were enabled now and then, to snatch a refreshing draught from the rocky streams which they forded.

Late in the evening of the eighteenth, Ferguson's party reached the spot where the Whigs had, less than thirty minutes before, fed their weary horses; but not knowing how long they had been gone, and their own detachment being exhausted, they relinquished further pursuit. Not aware of this, the Americans kept on their tedious retreat all night, and the following day, passing the North Tyger, and into the confines of North Carolina—sixty miles from the battlefield, and one hundred from Smith's Ford, from which they had started, without making a stop, save long enough to defeat the enemy at Musgrove's. It was a remarkable instance of unflagging endurance, in the heat of a southern summer, and encumbered, as they were, with seventy prisoners. No wonder, that after forty-eight hours of such excessive fatigue, nearly all the officers and soldiers became so exhausted, that their faces and eyes were swollen and bloated to that degree that they were scarcely able to see.

Colonel William Campbell's Campaign

A phase of the history made in the truly historic year 1780 that escaped the notice of Tennessee's historians was the campaign of Colonel William Campbell, of Virginia, against the Chickamauga Indians in midsummer. In June Thomas Jefferson, governor of Virginia, ordered Colonel Campbell, who had only recently succeeded Evan Shelby as colonel of Washington County, Virginia, to punish the Chickamaugas for continued and frequent murderous raids into Southwest Virginia, to raise 500 men from the counties of Washington and Montgomery and destroy the towns of those Indians. Jefferson's instructions were "to use utmost attention in distinguishing the friendly from the hostile Indians," —the Cherokees from the Chickamauga seceders; and "to spare no assurance and protection to the former."

It was left to Colonel Campbell to take his troops down the Holston and Tennessee or on horseback overland. He chose the latter course. Jefferson had been informed that North Carolina had a similar plan for a summer expedition from her western frontiers against the Chickamaugas and anticipated that Washington County, North Carolina, troops would join those under Campbell.[14] However, no such orders had gone out from the North Carolina authorities, and as Campbell passed southward he was not joined by any Carolinians of the western waters. They were away to the east under other orders, as we have seen.

On reaching the Nolachucky (at or near the Bend of Chucky) with about 400 men, Campbell was reinforced by two companies from Botetourt County, under Captains James Smith and James Barnett. These companies brought news of threats of Tory uprisings in Southwest Virginia, and doubtless rumors trickled through of Lord Cornwallis' march northward towards Western North Carolina and of the increasing danger to the American cause, soon to reach crisis in the disastrous battle of Camden in South Carolina, August 16th.[15]

A council of war was held on the Nolachucky and the decision was reached to go no farther. The entire command retraced its march; [16] and, after a very few days rest at home, Campbell and 300 of his men were at the Moravian Towns the latter part of August, to succor the Carolinians east of the mountains, who were flying in consternation before the advance of Cornwallis and Colonel Patrick Ferguson.

[14] *Cal. Preston Papers*, 129–3 and *N. C. St. Recs.*, XV, 47. "We instructed Col. Campbell to open a correspondence for the purpose of producing a cooperation."

[15] Letter of Arthur Campbell to Col. W. Campbell asking his return (Aug. 13th) *Cal. K. M. Papers*, 173; *Wis. Hist Coll.* XXIV, 244.

[16] Returning, Col. Campbell "discovered a disposition in the inhabitants of Washington County of your State [North Carolina] to bring on a war with the friendly Cherokees," if the Colonel's information was true. Governor Jefferson to Gov. Abner Nash, *N. C. State Recs.*, XV, 47. It seems that Col. Charles Robertson who was in the North Carolina senate in 1779, leaving for home in November, brought information to the effect that a campaign against these Cherokees would not be disfavored by the State of North Carolina. This conclusion of Robertson was given currency in his county—a ready currency since the Cherokees held lands for which they yearned. *N. C. St. Recs.*, XIV, 234. Too, before the year 1780 closed Col. Campbell was calling out militia for an expedition against the Cherokees, emboldened by what were conceived to be British successes.

CHAPTER XVII

THE KING'S MOUNTAIN CAMPAIGN *

A campaign that was to culminate in a battle of immediate and far reaching importance at King's Mountain in Upper South Carolina had its genesis within a few miles of the site of that battle a few weeks only before it was fought.

On their hurried retreat northward from Musgrove's Mill to overtake and join McDowell, Colonel Isaac Shelby suggested to Major Charles Robertson a plan to embody troops on the western waters to co-operate with North Carolina militia east of the Alleghanies in meeting the peril that all saw in the advance of Cornwallis and Ferguson into near-prostrate North Carolina. Robertson approved, and when a junction of the several small commands was made at Gilbert Town,[1] the plan was put before McDowell who readily gave concurrence. Then the over-mountain men returned home. Three young men, James, Jack and Archibald Neal (sometimes written Naile or Nail), sons of William Neal,[2] of Turkey Cove of the upper Catawba were ap-

---

* Conformably to the scope of this volume, this chapter is primarily concerned with the participation of the over-mountain forces. It must not be inferred that the contribution of the forces from east of the Alleghanies is depreciated.

[1] Three miles west of the present Rutherfordton, N. C.; and named for Wm. Gilbert who resided there. Draper says he was a Tory, but this seems to be incorrect. Rivers, "Two Carolina Pioneer," in *Am. Hist. Mag.* (Nashville) III, 259–267. Gilbert's widow moved to Maury County, Tenn., and settled on a 5,000 acre grant he had acquired. Maj. James Holland owned the Gilbert Town tract after Gilbert's death. Holland was his son-in-law. He, too, removed to Maury County. Holland was a member of Congress from North Carolina, 1795 to 1797, and from 1801 to 1811. He ran for Congress in Tennessee but was defeated by Francis Jones, of Winchester.

[2] Four or five miles southeast of and below Gillespie's Gap of the Blue Ridge. The cove is a large and beautiful one, to be seen from the Carolina, Clinchfield & Ohio Railway as it descends the Blue Ridge. The route taken by the messengers was evidently through Gillespie's and Carver's Gaps at the last of which the waters of the Watauga were reached.

pointed messengers to carry information to and from the commanders on the Watauga and Holston in relation to Ferguson's and their own movements. Other news-bearers from other colonels of the western counties of North Carolina were appointed. One of these colonels, Cleveland, named his brother, Robert, and Gideon Lewis to bear news to Colonels Shelby and Sevier. "Thus the news went the rounds as fast as horses could carry their riders." [4]

It was at first thought that Ferguson would exhaust the supplies laid in in Upper South Carolina and, for the sustenance of his command, would raid the upper reaches of Broad River for cattle and then pass over to the head of the Catawba. There he might be the more easily intercepted by the Whig forces and given battle. Ferguson did proceed to Gilbert Town which he made headquarters. McDowell continued northward to his own county, Burke, where he was followed by a detachment from Ferguson's command. McDowell laid an ambuscade on Craine Creek (in the southwestern part of the present McDowell County). A skirmish took place, so indecisive as to enable both sides to claim a victory.[5] The enemy force returned to Gilbert Town and McDowell and the major portion of his men, some with their families, in utter discouragement and fearing complete capture by a superior force, retreated across the Blue Ridge and Alleghanies to the Watauga. Leading one hundred and sixty men along Bright's trail through Carver's Gap,[6] McDowell marched down to the mouths of Gap and Buffalo Creeks, near Sycamore Shoals, where they constructed rude temporary camps and were succored by the people of the West, their late comrades in arms in South Carolina taking the lead, we may assume. The messengers from the east side of the mountains had now an added spur to activity.[7]

---

[4] David Vance's account. John Neal seemingly settled in Blount County, Tennessee, where is Naile's Creek, and was a pensioner there, on the rolls of 1832.

[5] The heartily detested British Maj. Dunlap was wounded in the action.

[6] The route later followed by them and the over-mountain men in going to seek Ferguson.

[7] There is no record to show, but it is altogether probable that news-bearers—"expresses"—were chosen on the west side of the mountains to speed from this camp news to Sevier on the Nolachucky and to Shelby at Sapling Grove.

Colonel McDowell and his men related to the western folk details of the high-handed methods of Ferguson and of his threat to subjugate and devastate their region. Indeed, as said by the historian Johnson, "the pursuit of the retiring Americans brought Ferguson so far to the left as to seem to threaten the inhabitants of the hardy race that lived beyond the mountains. He was approaching the lair of the lion, for many of the families of the persecuted Whigs had been deposited in this asylum."[8]

The refugees had been pursued by the British and Tories "to the mountains at the head of Catawba River, sending out detachments to scour the country and search the caves."[9] There hung on the rear of the Patriot scramblers westward spies of the enemy. Some of these were stationed at the two mountain gaps; others proceeded on to the westward settlements and contrived to send back reports of what was transpiring in the West.[10]

Theodore Roosevelt well describes the plight of the Southern States at this time:

Except for occasional small guerrilla parties there was not a single organized body of American troops left south of Gates' broken and dispirited army. All the southern lands lay at the feet of the conquerors. The British leaders, overbearing and arrogant, held almost unchecked sway throughout the Carolinas and Georgia; and looking northward they made ready for the conquest of Virginia. Their right flank was covered by the waters of the ocean, their left by the high mountain barrier-chains, beyond which stretched the intermidable forest; and they had as little thought of danger from one side as from the other.[11]

That this picture was not painted in too somber colors is shown by contemporary letters. Governor John Rutledge, compelled to conduct his government in North Carolina, far away from South Carolina, wrote from Hillsborough, September 20th:

---

[8] *Traditions of the Revolution.* The tale of McDowell's men "was a doleful one, and tended to excite the western militia who had an utter detestation of the tyranny of the British government." (Col. Arthur Campbell).

[9] "Capt. Alexander Chesney's Account" in Williams, "The Battle of King's Mountain, as Seen by British Officers," in *Tenn. Hist. Mag.* VII, 51–67.

[10] *Ib.*

[11] *Winning of the West*, II, 251–2. So desperate was the situation that some timid souls proposed to give up the Carolinas and Georgia to the British.

Not a man from Virginia is in this State, except about 250 Continentals under Beaufort [Buford], and about sixty of the militia who ran away from the action with Cornwallis and who have lately been brought to Hillsborough; nor can we hear of any being on the march from Virginia . . . Alas! When may we really and reasonably expect that all those things will come to pass.[12]

On October 4th the governor wrote of Cornwallis having taken possession of Charlotte: "When we shall receive enforcements, I know not. The present prospect is truly disagreeable, for everything goes on slowly." In a postscript he added that Ferguson was in Burke County.[13]

Ferguson determined to send a message to Shelby. A distant kinsman and a near neighbor of the latter, by name Samuel Phillips, had gone with Shelby as a trooper across the mountains into South Carolina and been made a prisoner at the battle of Musgrove Mill. Now in Ferguson's hands at Gilbert Town, he was paroled with the understanding and pledge that he would bear to Shelby a message to the effect that, if he and the other backwater officers "did not desist from their opposition to the British arms, he would march his army over the mountains, hang their leaders and lay their country waste with fire and sword."[14] Ferguson mistook the man Shelby. Phillips went directly to Shelby and delivered the message, and, also, much information about the locality and strength of the enemy.

Of the Loyalists composing a part of Ferguson's command, some had previously been west of the two mountain chains and knew the passes through which the western settlements were reached. One of them had been subjected, during the summer just past, to the indignity of a coat of tar and feathers by the light-horsemen of Captain Robert Sevier on the Nolachucky; and, in deep resentment, this Tory proposed to serve Ferguson as pilot through the mountains.[15]

Provoked and stung by Ferguson's brazen and taunting mes-

[12] Correspondence of Gov. Rutledge in *S. C. Mag. of Hist. and Biography*.

[13] For conditions in Upper South Carolina, see, also, S. C. Williams, "Gen. Richard Winn's Notes—1780," in *S. C. Mag. of Hist. and Biography*, XLIII, 201–212, and XLIV, 1–11.

[14] Shelby's account in his Pamphlet of 1823, reproduced by Draper, 560, *et. seq.*

[15] Ramsey, *Annals*, 223.

sage, Shelby at Sapling Grove promptly mounted his horse and rode about forty miles to the home of Colonel John Sevier, south of the Nolachucky. There he found Sevier in the midst of festivities—a horse-race and barbecue—to which crowds had come. From Shelby's stern countenance it was evident that something portentous was brewing. Drawing Sevier aside, the insolent message of Ferguson was disclosed to him, along with the other information that Phillips had imparted.

For two days plans were discussed by the two leaders. Both were firm believers in the strategy of defending by attack, particularly a surprise attack, and that, too, before the enemy could invade their territory. No other plan was considered; rather how to collect and combine forces adequate to cope with Ferguson whose force had been augmented since the major disaster to the Whigs at Camden.[16] It was agreed that it was advisable to ask for the co-operation of the militia of Washington County, Virginia, then under the command of Colonel William Campbell. As that county adjoined Shelby's county of Sullivan on the north, he undertook to bring Campbell into the campaign.[17] In his pamphlet of 1823 Shelby wrote:

Having made the arrangements with Sevier, I returned home immediately, and devoted myself to all the necessary operations for our intended enterprise. I wrote to Col. Campbell, informing him what Sevier and I had agreed upon, and urged him to join us with all the men he could raise. This letter I sent express to him at his own house, forty miles distant, by my brother, Moses Shelby. Col. Campbell wrote me for answer, that he had determined to raise what men he could, and march down by Flower Gap, to the southern borders of Virginia, to oppose Lord Cornwallis when he approached that State; that he still preferred this course to the one proposed by Sevier and myself, and therefore declined agreeing to meet us. Of this I notified Col. Sevier by an express on the next day, and immediately issued an order calling upon *all* the militia of the County to hold themselves in readiness to march at the time appointed. I felt, however, some disappointment at the reply of Colonel Campbell. The Cherokee towns were not more than eighty or one hundred miles from the frontiers of my County, and we had received information that these Indians were preparing a formidable attack upon us in the

---

[16] "At this period the North Carolina men joined us fast" (Chesney's Account). The reference was to Tories in North Carolina.

[17] Shelby used John Adair as a messenger to Campbell, as well as his brother, Moses.

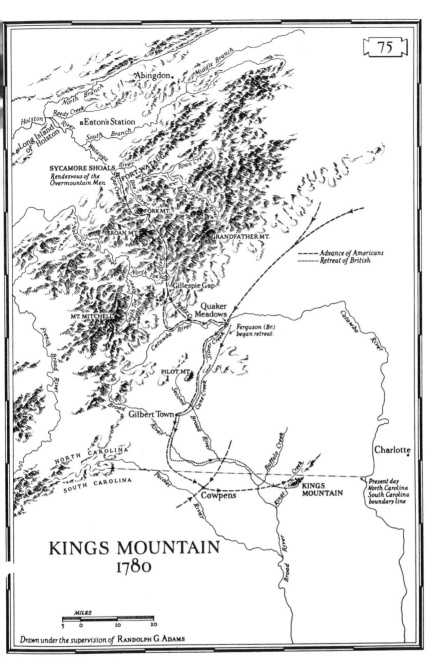

Abingdon

Middle Branch

North Branch

Reedy Creek

Eaton's Station

Holston

Long Island of Holston

Holston River

South Branch

Watauga River

SYCAMORE SHOALS
Rendezvous of the
Overmountain Men

FORT WATAUGA

Roan Creek

FORK MT.

ROAN MT.

GRANDFATHER MT.

Unaka

- - - - - Advance of Americans
. . . . Retreat of British

North Toe

Gillespie Gap

MT. MITCHELL

Quaker
Meadows

Ferguson (Br.)
began retreat.

Catawba River

Catawba River

Silver Creek

PILOT MT.

Cane Creek

French Broad River

Broad River

Gilbert Town

Jacobs Creek

Charlotte

NORTH CAROLINA

SOUTH CAROLINA

Pacolet

Buffalo Creek

KINGS
MOUNTAIN

Present day
North Carolina
South Carolina
boundary line

Cowpens

River

KINGS MOUNTAIN
1780

Broad River

MILES

5   0   10   20

Drawn under the supervision of RANDOLPH G. ADAMS

The map of Kings Mountain is reprinted with the permission of Charles
Scribner's Sons from ATLAS OF AMERICAN HISTORY, edited by James Trus-
low Adams, Copyright, 1943, by Charles Scribner's Sons.

course of a few weeks; I was, therefore, unwilling that we should take away the whole disposable force of our Counties at such a time; and, without the aid of the militia under Colonel Campbell's command, I feared that we could not otherwise have a sufficient force to meet Ferguson. I, therefore wrote a second letter to Col. Campbell, and sent the same messenger back with it immediately, to whom I communicated at large our views and intentions, and directed him to urge them on Col. Campbell. This letter and messenger produced the desired effect, and Campbell wrote me that he would meet us at a time and place appointed.

The facts appear to be: shortly after his return to his home from South Carolina, Shelby had written Campbell soliciting cooperation. At the time, (August 22–29th) Campbell was, under orders, preparing his command to march "with all possible expedition" to aid against the Tories of Surry and Wilkes Counties. He could but refuse, at that time, to change his plans. Upon his return from his tour of duty into those upper counties of North Carolina, Campbell readily acceded to Shelby's later request, and must have used utmost diligence and speed in preparing his command to march towards the place of rendezvous to join Shelby and Sevier.

Sevier took it upon himself to keep Colonels McDowell and Hampton [18] and the refugees under them informed and to have them equipped and supplied for the campaign.

From a grist mill near Matthew Talbot's home at the rendezvous came meal for breadmaking; and on what has ever since been known as Powder Branch of Buffalo Creek Mary Patton superintended a small powder mill which supplied, at least in part, the needs of the western riflemen. Lead for balls was mined in the mountains in the rear of John Sevier's home.[19] Intense activity was in evidence at each of these places in the production of essential supplies and munitions.

For the purchase of supplies and meeting the expenses of the expedition, Sevier and Shelby were in hard lines. There was very little currency and less coin to be found in the West; and what little the people had been able to procure had been paid to the entry-taker in the purchase of North Carolina public lands. The

---

[18] Col. Andrew Hampton, of what is now Rutherford County, N. C., was a refugee with a small number of his men.

[19] Bumpass Cove, where in later years iron and zinc deposits also were found and developed on a fairly large scale.

entry-taker for Sullivan County was John Adair.[20] Sevier, perhaps accompanied by Shelby, went to see him and proposed that the public funds in his hands be advanced to meet the exigencies. He replied: "Colonel Sevier, I have no authority by law to make that disposition of this money; it belongs to the impoverished treasury of North Carolina, and I dare not appropriate a cent of it to any other purpose; but if the country is overrun by the British our liberty is gone. Let the money go too. Take it. If the enemy, by its use, is driven from the country, I can trust that country to justify and vindicate my conduct—so take it." [21] For its return, if demanded by the Sate of North Carolina, the two colonels gave their personal pledges.[22]

The rendezvous for all commands was fixed at Sycamore Shoals of Watauga, a spot already made famous by the Transylvania treaty of 1775, where already lay McDowell and the North Carolina refugees.[23] The 25th day of September, about ten days away, was the day named. In Washington Counties, Virginia and North Carolina, and in Sullivan County, there was unprecedented excitement and bustle. Beeves were being rounded up and assembled at the Shoals; family ovens were kept hot, and the women early and late plied their needles in making their militiamen comfortable and presentable. Catherine Sherrill Sevier, the Colonel's recently wedded wife, spent a part of the honeymoon in making and mending clothes for her husband and three of his sons who ranged in age between sixteen and twenty-one.[24]

The men who were to stay and defend the homes on Nolachucky and Watauga against any Indians on foray, gave to those who were to march all needed aid, whether in horses, cattle or

---

[20] Later of Knox County, Tenn., (Caswell Station). He was one of ten nominated for membership in the council of state of the Southwest Territory, five to be chosen; member of Tennessee Constitutional Convention of 1796; a first justice of the peace for Knox County; a first trustee of Blount College (University of Tennessee). He died in Grassy Valley at the age of ninety-five. See also Kate White, *"John Adair, the Entry Taker* in *Tenn. Hist. Mag.,* XIII, 112–118.

[21] Ramsey, *Annals,* 226.

[22] In 1782 an acquittance or receipt was given Adair. *Ib.*

[23] "The whole met at Col. McDowell's encampment on Watauga." (Arthur Campbell).

[24] Years afterwards Mrs. Sevier said: "Had the Colonel's ten children been sons and large enough to serve in that expedition, I could have fitted them out."

equipment, regretful only that they were denied the privilege of active participation in the fatigue and hazards of the expedition. "A spirit of congenial heroism brought to the standard, in a few days, more men than it was thought either prudent or safe to withdraw from the settlements, the whole military force of which was estimated at considerably less than a thousand men [in Sevier's county]. Fully one-half of that number was necessary to man the forts and stations and keep up scouting parties on the extreme frontier." [25]   Left in command of forces remaining in Sullivan was Colonel Anthony Bledsoe; in Washington Major Charles Robertson. The test for selection, generally speaking, was age; [26] but there were exceptions, notably in the case of experienced captains.

When September 25th arrived, the valleys, large and small, almost emptied themselves of inhabitants. All were eager to see the clans gather and march away to battle, and to bid farewells.

There were selected at Sycamore Shoals two hundred and forty men under Shelby, the same number under Sevier, and about two hundred under Campbell. Colonel Arthur Campbell, also of Washington County, Virginia, fearing that all there from his county did not constitute a force sufficiently strong to cope with the enemy, arrived on the ground with more militia of his county, thus raising their aggregate to about four hundred riflemen under Campbell and the total to nearly nine hundred, and above if there be included the refugees. Arthur Campbell returned home to direct the protection of the frontiers of his county against the Indians and the almost as troublesome Tories. Bivouacking for the night, early on the morning of the 26th, the officers ordered their men to assemble for a brief religious service. Rev. Samuel Doak, who had spent some time in Sullivan County, but had recently moved to Little Limestone Creek of the Nolachucky, was present and led the devotions in a fervid invocation for Divine blessing upon the expedition, praying that the men might smite the foe, closing with an Old Testament phrase: "The sword of the Lord and of Gideon."

---

[25] Ramsey, *Annals*, 225.

[26] Young boys insisted upon going. "Here" pointing to Sevier's sixteen year old son, said Mrs. Sevier to his father, "is another of our boys who wants to go with his father and brothers to war; but we have no horse for him, and, poor fellow, it is a great distance to walk." A horse was provided and the boy went.

Hearts were thrilled by these words; and then farewells were waved as the riflemen mounted horses to commence a toilsome advance up Gap Creek from which they crossed to the waters of Doe River. There at the Shelving Rock they encamped for the night. There John Miller,[27] a blacksmith, lived who shod several of the horses of the men.

On the morning of the 27th it was decided that the cattle, following in the rear, would impede the advance, and it was determined to have some of them driven back towards the settlements while others were slaughtered, the meat cooked and carried along for subsistence. This caused a considerable delay. The march was resumed, climbing towards Carver's Gap which was reached near nightfall. They turned aside and camped on top of Roan[28] Mountain, a beautiful tableland, or "bald" from which "a spring issued, ran through it and over into Watauga," through the Doe.

On the bald of the Roan, the troops were paraded, though "the sides and top of the mountain were covered with snow, shoe-mouth deep." During the parade rifles were ordered discharged, but such was the rarity of the atmosphere that there was scarcely heard any report. Let one, in imagination, review these parading mounted riflemen of the West: Some few of them had been in the battle of Point Pleasant on the Ohio in 1774, and the tribute paid to the soldiery of their region on that earlier expedition may be aptly applied to them in 1780: "Although without experience of drill it may be doubted if a braver or physically finer set of men were ever got together on this continent." [29] No beat of drum or martial music served to inspire; yet the spirit of battle stirred their souls. They were clad in fringed hunting shirts, and their long Deckard rifles gleamed in the sun. "A shot-pouch, a

---

[27] See Williams, *Early Travels in the Tennessee Country*, 332. This was about one mile up Doe River from Roan Mountain Station of the E. T. & W. N. C. Railway, and not as Draper states one mile from Crab Orchard.

[28] In accounts left by men of the expedition and given by Draper the mountain was called the "Yellow Mountain," as it was known in 1780. The distinctive name of "Roan" was later given. On the adjoining Yellow Mountain of today there is no spring which could flow into the Watauga. The spring is the one which supplied Cloudland Hotel on the Roan.

[29] *Winning of the West*, I, 222.

tomahawk, a knife, a knapsack and a blanket, completed the soldier's outfit." Officers and men turned towards the east and Ferguson, with a grim resolution to conquer.

There also took place on "the Bald" a discussion by the colonels in regard to the choice of a chief commander.[30] Any determination reached was probably tentative, awaiting confirmation by at least some of the colonels east of the mountains.

There was an incident on "the Bald" which might well have brought the expedition to defeat. Two men of the Nolachucky Settlement, under Colonel Sevier, Samuel Chambers and James Crawford, Tories at heart and probably having already served the British as spies,[31] escaped under cover of darkness to make their way to Ferguson's headquarters with news of the approach of the Westerners. At roll-call at the noonday meal, these desertions were discovered. The colonels were put on guard and ordered the troopers to turn sharply to the left of the usual and better road, and cross a divide to Roaring Creek, down which they continued to its mouth at the North Fork of Toe River. This place was on what was known as "Bright's Trail." They encamped at Bright's Spring branch of Roaring Creek, having made slow progress during the day. The next day, passing Bright's Place [32] proper, they followed, broadly speaking, Toe River to the mouth of Grassy Creek (two miles beyond the present town of Spruce Pine), where they camped for the night. Six or seven miles farther Gillespie's Gap of the Blue Ridge was reached. Emerging from the Gap, the beautiful coves and valleys of the Upper Catawba were disclosed to view. There lay the outer fringes of settlements east of the mountains. As a precaution against ambuscade, the commands were divided and the

[30] Draper, p. 178n. says, in respect to what occurred at the place: "No account other than Capt. Christopher Taylor's confirms this." In this he was mistaken. Confirmation comes from one of Col. McDowell's men, David Vance, whose account reads: "When the officers met at the spring on Yellow [Roan] Mountain, it was quickly agreed that they would send Col. Charles McDowell to General Gates, etc."

[31] A Loyalist wrote: "Our spies from Holston, as well as some left at the Gap of the mountains, brought us word that the rebel force amounted to 3,000 men, on which unexpected news we retreated, etc." (Chesney Account), *ante.*

[32] Where Captain Robert Sevier died, of a wound in battle, and was buried on the return trip. See p. 156n. Bright's settlement was about one mile below the mouth of Roaring Creek.

men directed to move along two separate routes down the mountain slope, one heading for Turkey Cove and the other for a cove which gave the name to North Cove Creek. The two divisions came together again at Quaker Meadows (site of Morganton), the home of the McDowells, where, also, a junction was made with the forces from Wilkes and Surry Counties under Colonels Cleveland and Winston. These added three hundred and fifty men to the pursuers of Ferguson.

On October 4th the patriot army was near the mouth of Cane Creek in what became Rutherford County. A council of the colonels was held in a gap at South Mountain when what had been previously discussed was matured into action: Colonel McDowell was dispatched to General Gates for a commanding officer, but with the hope expressed that the one sent should not be a martinet:

We have now collected at this place about 1500 good men, drawn from the counties of Surry, Wilkes, Burke, Washington and Sullivan in this State, and Washington County in Virginia, and expect to be joined in a few days by Colonel Clarke of Georgia and Colonel Williams of South Carolina, with about 1000 more. As we have at this time called out our Militia without the orders of the Executives of our different States, and with a view of expelling the enemy out of this part of the Country, we think such a body of men worthy of your attention, and would request you to send us a General Officer to take command of such Troops as may embody in this quarter. Our Troops being all Militia, and but little acquainted with discipline, we could wish him to be a gentleman of address, and able to keep up a proper discipline, without disgusting the soldiery. Every assistance in our power shall be given the Officer you may think proper to take command of us. It is the wish of such of us as are acquainted with General Davidson and Col. Morgan (if in service) that one of these gentlemen may be appointed to this command.[33]

This action was advocated by Shelby and based, doubtless, on his observation of the senior colonel, McDowell, in the earlier campaign in South Carolina—that he lacked an essential element of a military leader, having shown lack of initiative, slowness and a disposition to send rather than lead into battle those under him.

Not willing to await the arrival of an officer under orders from

[33] Reproduced from the Gates Papers by Archibald Henderson in his "*Isaac Shelby*" in *N. C. Booklet*, XVIII, 7; also in *N. C. St. Recs*, XIV, 663-4.

headquarters, Shelby urged: "I suggested these things to the council and then observed to the officers that we were all North Carolinians except Colonel Campbell who was from Virginia; . . . that he commanded the largest regiment; and that, if they concurred with me, until a general officer [34] should arrive from headquarters, appointing him to command us, we march immediately against the enemy." Campbell assumed the chief command, and his choice was fully vindicated by the event. However, the colonels were to meet in council each night to decide themselves upon the next day's action, Campbell to execute their plans.[35]

Where to find Ferguson was a perplexing problem. They learned that he had retreated from Gilbert Town toward South Carolina. They were the more puzzled by conflicting bits of news gathered from Tory sympathizers who lived along the line, of their march southward and from Whig adherents. Yet more baffling proved to be the fact, unknown to them, that the British leader had divided his horsemen into three parts: two to deflect to the west in an effort to intercept Colonel Elijah Clarke's force.

After the battle of Musgrove Mill Clarke was encouraged to believe that he could capture the town of Augusta in his home State and he hurried south to make the attempt,[36] and was believed by the British to be now making his escape past Ferguson's left—between him and the line of the Middle Town Cherokees. One party of the horsemen was sent under Captain Alexander

---

[34] Gen. Wm. Lee Davidson was, as successor of Gen. Rutherford, commander of Salisbury District which included Washington and Sullivan Counties. See Williams, "Generals Francis Nash and William Lee Davidson," in *Tenn. Hist. Quarterly*, I, 250, *et seq.*

[35] Shelby's Statement, Draper, *King's Mountain*, 564; also his account in the *Journal of Southern History*, above referred to. Archibald Henderson in his *Shelby* says: "During the progress of the conference Campbell took Shelby aside and requested that his name be withdrawn and that Shelby himself take the command. To this Shelby very correctly replied that he was the youngest colonel present, and that McDowell under whom he had previously served would resent his elevation to the chief command. The selection of Campbell was undoubtedly a temporary expedient, a tactful mode of bridging an awkward situation."

[36] The attempt was nearly successful, and would have been entirely so, but for a body of Cherokees then going to Augusta for presents and to trade. They gave aid to British Lieut. Col. Brown until the latter was relieved by Col. Cruger.

Chesney with orders to proceed along the Indian line until he could discover Clarke's route, and join Captain John Taylor (of the New Jersey Volunteers) at Earl's Fort. Chesney learned that Clarke was proceeding up the Brushy Fork of the Saluda. "I took six of the best mounted men and got on his track until I overtook the main body and made one of the enemy a prisoner within view of it, whom I carried to Col. Ferguson who thus obtained the information required."[37] Clarke, yet bearing to the west, escaped. Ferguson himself on September 30th was in rapid retreat along the north side of Broad River, his wagons going, for safety, on the south side as far as the Cherokee Ford, where they were to rejoin the troops. On October 1st, Ferguson was at Denard's Ford of the Broad, having started at five o'clock in the morning and marched twenty miles to reach there. The devious marching of Ferguson before he ascended King's Mountain has been baffling to historians. A diary kept by one of his men has recently come to light, and the entries measurably solve the doubts.[38] The day before he had received news of the oncoming mountaineers. His trepidation was manifested in a proclamation he now issued, casting unwarranted slurs at the "invaders" and descending to obscenity, all calculated to inflame those appealed to:

---

[37] Chesney Account, *ante*.

[38] The writer has been privileged to examine this diary, and without doubt it is authentic. It has been edited by Mary H. McCown and published in *E. T. Hist. Soc. Publications*, No. XIV, pp. 102–5. The diary was apparently that of an "American Volunteer" from one of the Eastern States. Copying entries beginning with—

"Oct. 1. We continued at Camp: about noon Col. Ferguson Marched into Camp.

"Oct. 2. About half an hour by Sun in the afternoon we marched Across Broad River, and marched in the night Eastward to Barnet Kings' (?) And Camped.

"Oct. 3. We marched off Very Early in the morning and Crossed Second Broad at the high Shoals and Camped on the West of first Broad River.

"Oct. 4. We continued our march to the southeast and Incamped on the east side of Buffalo.

"Oct. 5. We Continued to Camp.

"Oct. 6. We marched off towards Tryon old Courthouse, and near King's Mountain. From thence we marched to the high Pinnacle of K. M. where we thought we would camp But Adverse fortune Confused our Imaginations, for on the 7th of October the cursed rebels came upon us and killed and Took us every Soul."

Denard's Ford, Broad River
Tryon County, October 1, 1780

Gentlemen: Unless you wish to be eat up by an inundation of barbarians, who have begun by murdering an unarmed son before his aged father and afterward lopped off his arms, and who by their shocking cruelties and irregularities, give the best proof of their cowardice and want of discipline; I say if you want to be pinioned, robbed and murdered, and see your wives and daughters, in four days, abused by the dregs of mankind—in short if you wish or deserve to live, and bear the name of men grasp your arms in a moment and run to camp.

The Back Water men have crossed the mountains; McDowell, Hampton, Shelby and Cleveland are at their head, so that you know what you have to depend upon. If you choose to be p—d upon by a set of mongrels, say so at once, and let your women turn their backs upon you and look out for real men to protect them.

Pat. Ferguson,
Major 71st Regiment.[39]

Before leaving the camp on Cane Creek the Whig troops were addressed by Colonels Cleveland and Shelby. The former told them that "the time was at hand to grapple with the enemy, but if any of you shrink from sharing in the battle and the glory, you can now have the opportunity of backing out, and leaving." Shelby then spoke: "You who desire to decline, when the word is given march three steps to the rear." Not a man stepped backward. "I am heartily glad," continued Shelby, "to see you to a man resolved to meet and fight your country's foes. When we encounter the enemy, don't wait for the word of command. Let each one of you be his own officer, taking every care you can of yourselves, and availing yourselves of every advantage that chance may throw in your way. If in the woods, shelter yourselves and give them Indian play! advance from tree to tree, pressing the enemy and killing and disabling all you can." [40]

On reaching a ford of Green River it was determined in a council of the American colonels to select mounted riflemen who could speed up the pursuit. "Accordingly the officers were engaged all night in selecting the best men, the best horses and the best rifles,

---

[39] Henderson's *Shelby*, 10–11. Ramsey, in his *Annals*, expurgated by moderating the obscenity; and, without referring to the document, others have followed his rendition.

[40] Draper, *op cit*, 196.

and at dawn of day [October 6th] took up Ferguson's trail and pursued him." [41] During the thirty-six hours following they alighted from their horses only once, then for an hour to refresh at the Cowpens, where they were joined by Colonel James Williams with about 400 men. There was then made a second selection of the fittest and 910 horsemen were chosen to make the push, about 85 foot-soldiers to follow, starting on the night of the 6th. The night was dark and rainy; and there was a downpour the next morning. Three of the colonels urged a halt to rest the jaded men and beasts; but the indomitable Shelby replied: "I will not stop until night, if I follow Ferguson into Cornwallis' camp," which was at Charlotte. Shelby with a small party pushed on and surprised and took the enemy's picket. This was hailed by all as a good omen. It was thus made certain that Ferguson was on King's Mountain. The hunters and the hunted were soon to meet. After hesitating as to his course, Ferguson chose at last to make a stand and put to hazard his fortunes.

The movements of Ferguson from Wednesday, 4th, to Friday, 6th, and his reasons, have never been fully explained. On September 30th he had written for reinforcements to Lt. Col. Cruger at Ninety-Six, but without avail. At the same time messengers were speeded to Lord Cornwallis at Charlotte, and later was sent this message: "My Lord: I am marching towards you by a road leading from Cherokee Ford, north of King's Mountain. Three hundred good soldiers, part dragoons, would finish the business! *Something must be done soon.* This is their last push in this quarter. (Signed) Patrick Ferguson."

By this Ferguson intended to convey the ideas that he would move past the mountain towards Cornwallis as far as he safely could, in order to form a junction with the detachment of three hundred he had requested be sent to succor him, but that he preferred to make a stand and give battle.

Major Robert Timpany, with his Third Battalion of New Jersey Volunteers and Tories, was at the time nearby at Saluda, and "would have gone to reinforce Ferguson had he not been ordered to halt." [42] Manifestly Ferguson had appealed to Tim-

[41] Shelby's "Autobiography" in the Durrett Collection, University of Chicago.

[42] Sabine, *Biographical Sketches of the Loyalists.*

pany for aid, who, apparently, was disposed to give it. From King's Mountain, on October 6th, Ferguson wrote the Major:

I am sorry to hear of your sickness . . . Between you and I, there has been an inundation of Barbarians, rather larger than expected, to be joined (by repeated intelligence) to Sumpter, Macdowal, Hampton, Cleveland, Brevard and Graham. They give themselves out for 3800 men. In fact, they are not above half that number, but as to quality—but we must not praise ourselves. I did not think it necessary to stake our young Militia to an over-match without Orders; but, with the advantages of Arms, our people and the four from Cruger, I should (not?) have thought myself justifiable in committing myself, had I not expected re-inforcements. The word is said—presto, you will hear of a scramble till when you need not bring forward your commoditys.

Yours most sincerely,
Pat Ferguson.

By way of postscript there was added:

Here we are Kings of King's Mountain—although there is another throne or ridge opposite to us where Gen'l Sumpter with your humble servant may, like the two kings of Brentwood, reign vis-a-vis in day Light—but at night war shines.[43]

"The 'two Kings of Brentwood' were characters in George Villiers' 'The Rehearsal' on the boards in London when Ferguson was last in that city." (Archibald Henderson)

Of course Ferguson was mistaken in thinking that he would confront Sumter as commander of the Whig forces. His readiness to do so may be inferred.

The real motive appears to have been: Ferguson was a Scot and felt that he had not been advanced equally with English officers or in accordance with his skill and experience as a soldier. In the earlier part of 1780 he thought to quit the service. Germain wrote to Clinton, July 5th: "Maj. Ferguson is to be dissuaded from quitting the army." [44] He was advanced in rank to

---

[43] In W. L. Clement Collection, Ann Arbor, Mich. "Presto" well describes the sudden change not to march on past the mountains to Cherokee Ford. A British officer, a critic of Ferguson, in later years wrote: "After retreating 60 miles he loitered away two days most unaccountably at King's Mountain, and thereby gave time for the rebel militia under Gen'l Williams to come up with him, etc." This officer estimated the troops under Ferguson at 630, of whom 60 were "regulars" and 600 militia— misinformation, truly.

[44] *Report on American Manuscripts in the Royal Institution*, II, 152.

a lieutenant-colonelcy of militia a small regiment of which, on his own proposal, was to be raised by him. When danger now confronted him in the sudden appearance of the mountaineers, he, in pride, preferred to fight rather than to go to Cornwallis at Charlotte only to confess defeat of his cherished plan.

It was unfortunate for the British cause that Ferguson did not take his position on the mountain earlier so that he could have had trees felled for breastworks and abattis.

The mountain was scarcely deserving of the name. At its top, sixty feet above the plain, was a plateau about six hundred yards long and of about two hundred and fifty acres. It was located in York County, South Carolina, about one and one-half miles south of the North Carolina line. "Its shape was that of an Indian paddle, varying from one hundred and twenty yards at the blade to sixty yards at the handle, in width. Outcropping boulders upon the outer edge of the plateau afforded some slight shelter for Ferguson's force. On the summit Ferguson pitched his camp, "boasting that only the Almighty could take it from him." [45]

The approaches were through forests. At the mountain base, the Patriots tied their horses and small groups were detailed to guard the animals. Guns were dried and freshly primed, and the riflemen were ready for action. The rain had ceased and the sun was shining. The colonels' plan of battle was to surround the mountain so as to hem the enemy on its top. The center to the northeast was held by Cleveland, Winston and Chronicle, leading most of the North Carolinians; at the south were Campbell, Sevier and Major Joseph McDowell succeeding to Colonel McDowell's command; and on the north were stationed Shelby and South Carolinians under Williams and Lacey. The counter-

---

[45] In Ferguson's force were New Jersey and New York Volunteers, King's Rangers and Queen's Rangers, numbering in all above one hundred, the remainder being Tories from the Carolinas, many of whom had been drilled and armed with Ferguson's repeating rifles by Ferguson himself. Practically all were well armed and disciplined in the use of firearms, swords and bayonets—the latter to be freely used. "There were, undoubtedly, one or two British regular officers present . . . and there may have been individual regular soldiers incorporated for their proficiency as marksmen," admits Gen. J. W. DePeyster, writing in later years, largely from the British standpoint.

sign of the day was "Buford," the name of the colonel whose troops Tarleton had recently defeated and butchered.

The Americans moved up the ravines between small rocky knobs; their orders were not to fire until the signal, an Indian yell of battle, was given. The battle now began, and was of nearly an hour's duration [46]—a battle that was ferocious and an hour that truly made history. The opening fire was by the British about three o'clock in the afternoon of October 7th, and on Shelby's men. They begged leave to return the enemy's fire but the Colonel replied: "Press on to your places and your fire will not be lost." Onward they went amid whistling bullets till they reached their places. Then Shelby shouted, "Here they are boys! Shoot like hell and fight like devils." Campbell pulled off his coat and the yell of battle was sounded by the Virginians and taken up by the other mountaineers. DePeyster, second in command, turned to Ferguson and remarked, "There are the same yelling devils that were at Musgrove Mill."

Shelby's men were charged by bayonets and retreated down the slope, until cover was reached. Then, their rifles reloaded, the riflemen returned to the attack. In the meantime, Campbell, after a little delay caused by a marshy place that had to be crossed, came up in the rear of Ferguson and his men poured in a withering fire, causing the enemy to face about, only to have bullets rain in from the men of Shelby. The firing now became general. The circle was drawing in on Ferguson from every direction. Sally after sally with bayonets were led by the well-trained Provincials in Ferguson's ranks; the Americans receded again to sheltering trees only to reload and return—Indian fashion. Captain Chesney well described the dilemma of his fellows: "By this time the other Americans who had been repulsed had regained their former stations, and, sheltered behind trees, poured in an irregular, destructive fire. In this manner the engagement was maintained for nearly an hour, the mountaineers flying when there was danger of being charged by the bayonet, and returning again so soon as the British detachment had faced about to repel another of their parties." In the precipitate onrush men of one Whig command became mingled with another and took orders

---

[46] Some accounts by participants say forty minutes, others an hour and five minutes; still others, more exactly, forty-seven minutes.

from a commander other than their own. The smoke of battle was so great as to obscure vision at times. "It was almost equal to storming a battery; in most places we could not see till we were within twenty yards of the enemy; they repulsed us three times with charged bayonets; but being determined to conquer or die, we came up the fourth time and fairly got possession of the eminence." (Shelby, on Oct. 10th). When the conflict was at peak, Sevier threw his men against the British center and was countercharged stubbornly. His charge tightened the deadly coil and enabled Shelby and Campbell to reach and with him hold the eminence after a desperate struggle. Shelby and Sevier then met for the first time since the battle began. Sevier, as he scanned his fellow officer's face, exclaimed, "They have singed off your hair!"

It was probably in this charge that Captain Robert Sevier received the wound from which he shortly afterwards died.[47] Stooping to pick up his ramrod, he received a wound from a buckshot which lodged near one of his kidneys.

With cool courage, Ferguson passed down his lines, blowing his large silver whistle to call troops to him at some weak spot. His North Carolina Tory militia broke under the impact and were in great disorder, which communicated itself to other troops. Twice, without official authority, a white flag was raised in the ranks of the enemy only to be cut down by the sword of Ferguson. Later this sword was found on the field, broken at the hilt. Two horses were killed under the recklessly brave British commander. Sensing disaster, Ferguson was urged by some of his officers to surrender but he refused. He did later endeavor to make his escape, accompanied by two of his officers. They chose for this

---

[47] The over-mountain men had no surgeon with them. A British surgeon, Dr. Uzal Johnson, dressed the wound and found the shot near the kidney. He advised that if the young captain would remain quiet the ball could be extracted and that he would probably recover. Young Sevier insisted on being conveyed home by his men. His kidney became inflamed and about the ninth day after being wounded he died on the way home at Bright's Trace. His body, wrapped in a blanket was buried at the base of a mountain oak tree near the summit of the Trace. Robert was a younger brother of Col. John Sevier, and married Keziah, daughter of Maj. Charles Robertson. One of their sons, Major Charles Robertson Sevier, distinguished himself under Jackson in the Creek War. Other descendants of note are, Revs. Drs. James I. Vance and Joseph A. Vance, of the Presbyterian ministry.

purpose that part of the line held by Sevier which had now about reached the crest of the hill. As soon as they reached that sector, all three British officers fell.

One of Sevier's men, John Gilliland,[48] who had received several wounds and was almost exhausted, tried to shoot Ferguson, but his gun merely snapped. Then he called to his companion, Robert Young,[49] "There's Ferguson,—Shoot him!" "I'll try and see what Sweet Lips[50] can do," replied Young as he drew a sharp bead, discharging his rifle, and Ferguson fell from his horse and his associates[51] were killed while fleeing. The British commander after the battle was found to have several bullets in his body. It staggers credence to believe that four or five balls struck Ferguson while in his saddle. When he reeled from his saddle, a foot caught in a stirrup, and the riderless horse galloped around the encircling lines of the American troops, dragging the body. No doubt some of the bullets were from rifles then fired.

The feeling of desperation which seized the British troops is shown by the closing lines hurriedly penned on the battlefield by the unknown diarist above referred to: "My Dear friends, I bid you farewell for I am starting to the warm Country."

The command of the Royalists passed to Captain Abraham de Peyster, a New Yorker of the King's American Regiment. He continued the contest with spirit,[52] "disputing the ground as long as possible," but finally sent out a flag of truce. In the smoke and commotion it could not be seen by many Americans; but on its being given to a soldier on horseback the emblem became more

---

[48] Gilliland migrated from Virginia to the Tennessee country. A typical frontiersman, he moved on to the mouth of Pigeon River about 1783, and became one of the first settlers of Cocke County. He was one of the members of the Constitutional Conventions of the State of Franklin.

[49] See p. 67. He was evidently of Capt. Valentine Sevier's company, the two being related by marriage. At his grave is a marker placed by John Sevier Chapter, D.A.R., of Johnson City.

[50] Named for Young's wife who in later years when asked about the incident said she was glad not to know of a certainty that her "cold-steel" namesake had killed Ferguson.

[51] Draper, 275, with whom Schenck agrees. *North Carolina, 1780–81,* 170. Draper says the two associates, Col. Vezey Husband and Maj. Daniel Plummer were killed.

[52] The Loyalists in numbers took refuge behind their supply wagons and kept up the combat, but were soon driven into a ravine nearby and there they were more successfully attacked.

visible. In the meantime, the carnage continued. Those who had seen white handkerchiefs as emblems lifted earlier, and cut down by the dauntless Ferguson, may have doubted whether a genuine surrender was now proposed. Others of the Whigs, more unrelenting, remembered the fate of the American Colonel Buford's men who were denied quarter by Tarleton who cut them down mercilessly. Now was heard the vengeful yell: "Give them Buford's play. Buford! Tarleton's quarters! Tarleton's quarters!" And not a few gave the quarters which had been meted out by the brutal and hated Tarleton.[53] Young James Sevier heard that his father, the Colonel, had been killed; and would not be restrained. "Standing erect, with deliberate aim he would bring down a Tory," to avenge the blood of a Sevier. It was afterwards learned that it was his uncle, Captain Robert, who had fallen wounded. Young Major Evan Shelby, brother of the Colonel, shouted to the victims, "Throw down your arms." It was instantly done, but not before De Peyster had ridden up to an American commander and rightly said: "This is unfair," whereupon DePeyster was ordered to dismount, and an American command rang out, "Officers, go to yourselves; prisoners take off your hats and sit down." When this was done the Whigs were "drawn up around them in a continuous circle; the enemy was under double guards; and finally the guards were four deep." Noise of an approaching force was then heard and was thought by some Americans to be Tarleton, in which event they feared the surrender would prove illusory. This, no doubt led to some further slaughter of the trapped enemy. It turned out to be a body of footmen, left behind by the Whig horsemen, coming up after the battle had closed. "After the surrender of the enemy, our men spontaneously gave three long and loud shouts . . . The sword of the British commanding officer, De Peyster, was received, not by me, but by my brother, Major Evan Shelby." (Shelby)

The numbers engaged on each side have long been a matter of dispute. Figures have been juggled in estimates made to show a disparity on the one side or the other. Two British historians fairly treat of the point: Trevelyan[54] says: "It was a decisive

---

[53] The British in the attack on Charleston in May had also given them a precedent. "The rebels sent out a flag soon after; our firing continued without taking any notice of the flag." (Allaires' Diary.)

[54] *George III*, 120.

trial of strength under equal conditions of numbers and leader-ship;" and Fortesque [55] says the number under Ferguson was eleven hundred, which certainly was not exceeded by the Americans. The entire British force was captured save a few who escaped in the turmoil by putting in their hats pieces of paper, in imitation of the Whigs' emblem for identification. The British losses in killed far exceeded those of the American forces.[56] Fifteen hundred stands of arms were taken along with munitions and stores, but the baggage wagons and many of the supplies were consumed in a bonfire. The wagons were hauled over replenished camp fires and went up in flames. The most reliable estimates by the American colonels of their entire force were those made at the time: "Agreeable to their daily returns for rations, 1187." (Lenoir). "Colonel Ferguson had about fourteen hundred men, of whom one hundred fifty fell and eight hundred and ten were made prisoners." (General Davidson, Oct. 10th, on information from an officer who had been in battle).

The Whigs camped for the night on the battleground, and the next day, after burying their dead, marched into North Carolina. Their prisoners were required to carry captured guns; many to bear two, each. About sunset they met some of the other footmen who had been left behind and "who had prepared a plenty of rations, for the want of which the Whigs who had fought in the battle were almost famished."

At Biggerstaff's in Rutherford County, after a march which had been slowed down by litters carrying their own wounded men and was marked by biting hunger,[57] a court-martial was urged by the colonels from the Carolinas to try Tories who in the past had been guilty of great outrages on the Whigs and their families. Campbell called such a court which condemned thirty-odd Tories to death. A long line of atrocities on Whig prisoners and their de-

---

[55] *History of the British Army*, III, 323.

[56] Of the three commands from west of the Alleghanies, these losses were: Campbell, 33; Sevier, 12; and Shelby, probably 15. Tabulation is in Roosevelt, *Winning of the West*, II, 285. Even the wounding and death of Capt. Robert Sevier is not therein included, and other inaccuracies there must be.

[57] The troops ate, principally, of pumpkins sliced and fried. One of them later wrote: "I thought it about the sweetest eating I had ever had in all my life."

fenseless families was at the base of this demand for retaliation,[58] else there would be repetitions, it was thought. The accounts given by Major Wm. Candler [59] of the outrages on the Georgians following the retreat from Augusta did not serve to abate the desire for revenge.

When nine of those condemned had been executed, Sevier and Shelby interceded and saved the others.[60]

The over-mountain men turned homeward, traveling their out-

---

[58] Cornwallis had set the example of ordering all men found in the rebel ranks, after having sworn allegiance to the King, to be hung, and the Americans of course retaliated. Ferguson's troops themselves had hung some of their prisoners." Roosevelt, *op. cit.*, 292, citing Allaire's Diary, entries of Aug. 2nd and 20th.

[59] *South Carolina in the Revolution.* See, also, McCall, *History of Georgia*, II, 336; Candler, *William Candler* 29, 35, 47, 63; Draper, *op. cit.*, 214. It is interesting to note that two descendants of Sevier and Candler who were then linked together by ties of hospitality and comradeship in battle, in the third generation following became close friends and confreres as bishops of the Southern Methodist Church—E. E. Hoss and Warren A. Candler. The plight of the refugees was in part described by Col. Clarke: "Col. Cruger, from Ninety-Six, with a body of Tories and Indians, followed us into the upper settlements of Georgia; and, finding us out of reach, fell on our sick and wounded, together with old men, women and children of the families of those that adhered to or retreated with me. . . . Lads were obliged to dance naked between two large fires until they were scorched to death; men were stripped, dismembered and scalped, afterwards hung up. It is too painful for me to dwell on this subject." *Virginia Magazine of History*, XXVII, 315. For the outrages, near Augusta, on the Whigs captured, see, Bailey, *Some Heroes of the American Revolution*, 175. For a more detailed account of Clarke and the refugees on the western waters, see this writer's "Colonel Elijah Clarke in the Tennessee Country," in *Georgia Hist. Quarterly*, XXV, 151–158.

[60] Shelby MSS in University of Chicago Library. See p. 147 *ante*. Col. Sevier, now as ever generous, intervened in behalf of James Crawford and Samuel Chambers who had secretly left the army on the Bald of the Roan to give information to the British. Some of the other officers demurred on the ground that the two were traitorous informers; but they were more disposed to clemency for Chambers who was a callow youth, easily misled. As to Crawford they stood out until Sevier demanded that Crawford, as originally one of his command, be left to his, Sevier's, own disposal. He was granted a pardon on condition that he would thereafter serve the American cause. Crawford redeemed his promise when, in the next year, he marched under Maj. Charles Robertson and fought bravely in the battle of Guilford Court House. He later removed to Georgia. It is said that the noted Col. Grimes, a troublesome Tory on the western waters, was one of the nine executed.

bound route. Along with them was a group of Georgians who had fought in the battle at King's Mountain under Major Candler. As Colonel Elijah Clarke was escaping from the pursuing British and their Indians after his repulse at Augusta, he was met by Captain Edward Hampton who gave information that the over-mountain forces were on the march to attack Ferguson. Candler and Captain Johnson filed off, joined those forces at Gilbert's Town and took part in the battle. Clarke and others of his command moved on, making an eleven days' march of about two hundred miles through the wilderness, at the head of a helpless multitude (400) of women and children to the settlements on Watauga and Nolachucky Rivers. They arrived in a deplorable condition, nearly starved. Many of the adults had gone without food, except nuts gathered in the forests, for several days. During the last two days even the children were compelled to live on the same kind of food. Colonel Clarke and his family were received as guests in the home of Colonel Sevier, and other families were distributed to homes of comparative peace and plenty, and remained until the coming of peace among the hospitable people on the western waters. McCrady, the South Carolina historian, said of these refugees: "Supplies of clothing, substenance and shelter were in no instance withheld from them, nor were these gratuities momentary; they ceased only with the demands on their bounty, which the occasion called for."

The soldiery, when they reached their valley homes, were joy-fully welcomed by the refugees and their own families. Few of them could have realized the full meaning of the victory to which they had contributed. Lord Cornwallis was forced to beat a retreat back into South Carolina.[61] Both the British and American writers are in accord in the view that the battle on King's Mountain turned the tide of the Revolution in the South, and was a material factor in the surrender of Cornwallis at Yorktown the next year. What Thomas Jefferson wrote was justified: "That memorable victory was the joyful annunciation of that turn in the tide of success which terminated the Revolutionary War with the seal of independence."[62]

---

[61] From Ninety-Six Col. Cruger reported that the Tories of that region were so discouraged and intimidated by the defeat of Ferguson that no further aid from them could be counted on.

[62] Fortesque in his *History of the British Army*, (III, 323): "This un-

expected blow shattered Cornwallis' whole plan of campaign at a stroke."

Trevelyan: "The battle of King's Mountain has justly been regarded as the turning point in the war in the Southern States. After the catastrophe the loyalist party was so cowed and prostrate that military men serving with Lord Cornwallis began to doubt whether such a party any longer existed." *George III*, 129.

Roosevelt: "The victory was of far-reaching importance, and ranks among the decisive battles of the Revolution. It was the first great success of the Americans in the South, the turning point in the Southern campaign, and it brought cheer to patriots throughout the Union." *Winning of the West*, II, 286.

Van Tyne: In speaking of "the brilliant victory of the backwoodsmen," he says: "From that position on the mountain, with characteristic Tory sentiment, Ferguson challenged 'all the rebels outside of hell to dislodge him.'" It seems that most of them were there when the attack began, October 7, coming from behind every tree on the mountain-side. No human heart could stand the steady, ruthless advance of those Indian hunters." *American Revolution*, 302.

Greene: "In the southern campaign of 1780 the men of the western waters were brought into closer touch with the main operations of the war. In the early autumn of that year these sturdy pioneers were able to strike a blow which, coming as it did after the disaster at Camden, proved to be a kind of turning point in the whole history of the war in the South." *Fundamentals of American Nationality*, 500.

Nevins: "Fortunately, North Carolina had better soldiers than lawmakers. The far-reaching victory of King's Mountain not only freed the upper country of North Carolina from the threat of the Tory force raised there but halted the British invasion of the State. Most important of all, the battle checked the well-laid schemes of Cornwallis and the Tory leaders for a general uprising. This Province is most exceedingly disaffected! Cornwallis wrote to a fellow-officer." *The American States During and After the Revolution*, 380.

Paxson: The advance of Cornwallis in the autumn of 1780, called the frontier riflemen from their cabins. They came from South Carolina and Virginia, as well as from Tennessee. John Sevier was there, and Isaac Shelby, but it is hard to tell who devised their tactics. . . . Each little group fought by itself with a minimum of direction. King's Mountain turned the southern invasion towards its ultimate defeat. *History of the American Frontier*, 40.

Bancroft: The appearance of a numerous enemy from the settlements beyond the mountains, whose names had been unknown to the British, took Cornwallis by surprise, and their success was fatal to his intended expedition. He had hoped to step with ease from one Carolina to another, and from those to the conquest of Virginia; and now he had no choice but to retreat. *History of the United States*, X, 340.

Washington Irving and John Marshall in their biographies of Washington are in accord, the latter saying: "It was a sharp action gained by the victorious mountaineers." The great Chief Justice summed the result in a few apt words.

CHAPTER XVIII

CIVIL AFFAIRS (1780)

The year 1780 was, in large part, given over to the making of war. However, some progress was made in civil life, and, too, in ways which proved to be highly significant and influential in the civilization of the Western country.

Rev. Samuel Doak, a young Presbyterian minister and graduate of Nassau Hall (Princeton College), came to the Tennessee country and preached in 1778 and 1779 in the Fork Country in Sullivan County. Noting that the drift of population was westward, he moved in early 1780 to the western part of Washington County. Tradition that is dependable relates the following circumstances which led him to locate on Hominy Branch of Little Limestone Creek:

As he was riding through a wood which then covered that vicinity he came unexpectedly upon some settlers who were felling trees. Learning that he was a minister, they requested him to preach to so many of them as could be assembled immediately. He complied, using his horse for a pulpit and the shady grove for a sanctuary. They were pleased with the sermon, and entreated the preacher to tarry longer with them. He yielded to this entreaty and this led to his permanent settlement among them.[1]

Soon by the help of the settlers there arose, on a farm acquired by Doak, three log buildings, one to shelter his family, another for use as Salem Church and the third for an academy.[2]

Doak's classical school prospered and became of great historic import as the first institution of higher learning west of the Alle-

---

[1] MSS of Col. G. W. Telford, quoted in Alexander and Mathes, *History of Washington College*, 3. Col. Telford, a man of great intelligence, was for many years a resident of the vicinity. The nearby village of Telford was named for him.

[2] "The structures for the church and the school stood on rising ground shadowed by grand old trees, quite near each other and only a few yards west of the present (1890) Salem Church. A small monumental ridge of earth marks sites of the historic church and school." Alexander and Mathes, *op. cit.*, 4.

ghanies,[3] and later to become Washington College.[4]

This institution was established and carried forward under conditions of real peril—from the Indians.[5]

As a result of the Walker-Henderson survey of the state line westward, many efforts were made to procure North Carolina entries and grants covering lands which previously had been granted by Virginia south of the line and which were in the actual possession of the grantees. To prevent injustice to such possessors, the North Carolina legislature in September, 1780, by an act [6] provided that all entries made in Washington and Sullivan counties of such lands be suspended, and entry-takers and surveyors prohibited from taking any further proceedings in relation to such lands. By legislation in a later year such Virginia grantees were declared entitled to their holdings.

---

[3] So considered by Roosevelt in his *Winning of the West*, II, 223. That author, misled by the writings of John Allison, gives the date of the founding of the school as 1777.

[4] The development of the academy may be outlined as follows: In 1782 it was chartered by the North Carolina legislature as Martin's Academy, the name bestowed in honor of Alexander Martin, at the time governor of North Carolina. The first legislature of the State of Franklin in 1785 re-incorporated the institution as Martin's Academy. In 1794 the legislature of the Southwest Territory (1795) granted a charter to the school, by an act introduced by John Sevier, but the name was changed to Washington College. Undoubtedly this college was the first to operate as such in the Tennessee country. Its first graduates were given A.B. diplomas at the first commencement, August 15, 1796. They were John Whitfield Doak, son of the president, and James Witherspoon, perhaps a relative of the president of Nassau Hall (now Princeton University). The two must have advanced in their studies at the Academy so far as to be able to complete the collegiate course in the first year of the existence of the college as a chartered institution.

[5] "Soon after the settlement at Salem, Mr. Doak had occasion to go some thirty miles towards Abingdon for family supplies. His wife, seeing some Cherokee warriors approaching, snatched up her infant son, John Whitfield, and fled to a place of concealment, from which she saw them plundering and burning the cabin. Had the child wakened and cried, both it and the mother would have been captured or killed; but she escaped in the night to a blockhouse where she met her husband on his return." Alexander and Mathes, *op. cit.*, 7, quoting MSS of Rev. W. S. Doak. "On another occasion while he was preaching at Salem, a man rode up in full gallop, exclaiming, 'Indians! Indians! Ragdale's family are all murdered.' Mr. Doak immediately closed his discourse, snatched up his rifle and led in pursuit of the savages." *Ib.*

[6] *N. C. St. Recs.*, XXIV, 353, Acts 1780 (second session) Ch. 7.

In January, 1780, about sixty Delaware Indians passed through the Cumberland country on their way to settle on Bear Creek of Tennessee River where they established a foothold to the annoyance of the Chickasaws who owned the region. The Delawares, in passing through, observed the defenceless situation of the infant Cumberland settlement; and in the fall they returned to pillage and murder.[7]

In the North Carolina legislature of 1780, the two western counties were represented by the following: Washington County in the senate, Charles Robertson; in the lower house, Charles Allison and Henry Clark; Sullivan County, in the lower house, David Looney.

The State was already suffering from inflation and a depreciated currency, but the assembly passed an act authorizing the emission of an additional 1,240,000 pounds in paper money, with power in the governor to issue more in case of an emergency. All prices of commodities went skyward. In Washington County, the county court fixed the following prices to be charged by tavern keepers:

For good West India Rum, the quart,	40 Dollars
For good Rye Whiskey,	20 ditto
For good peach or apple brandy,	30 ditto
For Continental Rum,	30 ditto
For Strong Beer,	5 ditto
For a Hott Diatt,	12 ditto
For breakfast or supper,	8 ditto [8]

In the year before, because of the enormous issue of paper money in the same county, the prices had been fixed: for rum, wine, or brandy, 3 pounds, four shillings, per quart; beer 2 shillings per quart; whiskey 2 pounds, per gallon, and a diet 8 shillings.

The effect of this inflation and the war was deadening on trade to the Carolinas where surpluses of horses and cattle had been disposed of previously. The only bright side of the picture was that, out of their mounting surpluses, the western folk were enabled to equip and feed the large number of troops they were called upon to send in the same year and in 1781 into the Carolinas to confront the British.

Added to difficulties of North Carolinians, east and west of the

[7] Haywood, op. cit., 125.
[8] Washington County Records, in Am. Hist. Mag., IV, 61.

mountains, was the counterfeiting of currency issued from printing presses. "The greater part of which counterfeiting is done
with such exactness as to deceive the most skillful observers."
The legislature passed another act requiring all county courts to
appoint three or more inspectors with direction "to write COUN-
TERFEIT in large letters on the face of such bills as they adjudge
bad." [9]

Promptly the court of Washington County appointed John
Sevier, Wm. Cobb, Thomas Houghton and Andrew Greer "to be
the viewers and judges of all such monies." [10]

One cannot scan the record books of county courts without being impressed by the large increase in the permits granted for the
building and operation of grist mills in this year. The operation
of such mills and the taking of toll were franchises, affecting the
public's interest. In instances, not a few, distilleries were operated by millers, but that feature did not require a franchise.
Roads also received much more attention than in former years.

The flagrancy of war prevented much activity in civil life in
what is now Upper East Tennessee. The chief event of that kind
was on the Cumberland—the establishment there of civil government—an event which deserves full treatment in another chapter.

---

[9] N. C. Act of 1780, Ch. 11, *N. C. State Recs.*, XXIV, 328.

[10] Washington County Records, August, 1780, in *Am. Hist. Mag.*,
IV, 67.

CHAPTER XIX

The Cumberland Compact

Henderson's arrival at the French Lick was on April 24, 1780. He at once turned his attention to the organization of a government for the infant colony. A "Compact of Government" was prepared in the handwriting and phraseology of Henderson who devoted the larger part of the document to defining the rights of his Transylvania Company, the terms and conditions of entering the company's lands; rights of priority in land claims—matters which lost any considerable historical interest when the claims of Henderson and his associates under their purchase of the Cherokee Indians of Sycamore Shoals in March, 1775, were in 1783 refused recognition by North Carolina and the company accepted in lieu from that State a consolation grant of 200,000 acres of land in Powell's Valley.[1] The document, it may be fairly assumed, was the joint production of Henderson, Robertson and Donelson. Its frame of government was quite like that of the Watauga Association, with which Robertson was most familiar. They realized that the government of North Carolina was conducted so far away as to be unable to stretch forth a protecting arm and that they, as had the Wataugans, must rely upon self-help and a voluntary association for the protection of their property and lives. The situation called for decisive measures and a form of government that would prove to be simple and understandable, and would command the support of all the settlers.

A meeting was held at Nashborough (later Nashville) May 1, 1780, and a Compact, reduced to writing, was agreed upon. The settlers then adjourned to meet May 13th, at which time additional articles were adopted and the entire document signed by the white adult male settlers. Two hundred and fifty-six names were then or later signed, a few in German script. While only

---

[1] Williams, "Henderson and Company's Purchase Within the Limits of Tennessee," in *Tenn. Hist. Mag.*, V, 5–27.

one signed by mark, it staggers credence to assume that only one man of the great number was unable to write his name. Many had received no school advantages, and many names must have been written by others.

A single copy of the Compact has come down to us, and it in a mutilated form.[2] It was reproduced by Putnam in his *History of Middle Tennessee.* This little constitution provided for the establishment of a tribunal of twelve members, with certain defined judicial, legislative, and executive functions. It distributed the membership of that body between the eight then existing stations, or sub-settlements: Nashborough, three; Gasper Mansker's (Mansker's Lick) two; Bledsoe's (later Castalian Springs) one; Asher's (Station Camp Creek) one; Stone's River (Donelson's Station or Clover Bottom) one; Freeland's (one half mile northwest of French Lick) one; Eaton's (East Nashville, west part) two, and Fort Union (later Haysboro) one.

The elective franchise was conferred on all free men over the age of twenty-one; provisions were made for descent of lands; for the administration of justice in courts, of first instance and appeal, in civil and criminal cases. It bound all signers to abide by decisions of the courts and to renounce all right of appeal to the courts of North Carolina. It subjected all males over sixteen years of age to military service, but in reciprocal consideration conferred on them the right to hold lands. Each station was empowered to elect its own officers of the militia, who might enforce discipline and impress horses for military service. The judges were termed "Judges, Triers or General Arbitrators," and were subject to recall. It was stipulated that "such court do not proceed with execution so far as to affect life or members." In such cases, the accused was to be safely bound and sent under strong guard to a place where a more strictly legal trial could be had.

Like the older government of Watauga, the one on the Cumberland was denominated an "Association." In broad outline the two constituting instruments were no doubt quite similar. The spirit of both breathed in the closing paragraph of the younger Articles:

---

[2] This was found by the historian, A. W. Putnam, in 1846 in an old trunk of one of the judges of the Association, Barton. The first page was destroyed, the second torn, but the remainder was in fair condition and legible. Putnam, *History of Middle Tennessee,* 84–103.

That the well-being of this country entirely depends, under Divine Providence, on unanimity of sentiment and concurrence in measures, and as clashing interests and opinions, without being under some restraint, will most certainly produce confusion, discord and almost certain ruin, so we think it our duty to associate, and hereby form ourselves into one society for the benefit of present and future settlers, and until the full and proper exercise of of the laws of our country can be in use, and the powers of government exerted among us: *we do most solemnly and sacredly declare and promise each other,* that we will faithfully and punctually adhere to, perform, and abide by this our Association, and at all times, if need be, compel by our united force a due obedience to these our rules and regulations. . . .

It is lastly agreed and firmly resolved that a dutiful and humble address or petition be presented, by some person or persons to be chosen by the inhabitants, to the General Assembly, giving the fullest assurance of the fidelity and attachment to the interest of our country, and obedience to the laws and Constitution thereof. Setting forth that we are confident our settlement is not within the boundaries of any nation or tribe of Indians, as some of us know and all believe that they have fairly sold and received satisfaction for the land or territories whereon we reside; and therefore we hope we may not be considered as acting against the laws of our country or the mandates of government.

That we do not desire to be exempt from the ratable share of the public expense of the present war, or other contingent charges of government. That we are, from our remote situation, utterly destitute of the benefit of the laws of our country, and exposed to the depredations of the Indians, without any justifiable or effectual means of embodying our militia, or defending ourselves against the hostile attempts of our enemy; praying and imploring the immediate aid and protection of government, by erecting a county to include our settlements, appointing proper officers for the discharge of public duty, taking into consideration our distressed situation with respect to the Indians, and granting such relief and assistance as in wisdom, justice, and humanity may be thought reasonable. Nashborough 13th May, 1780.

Two brothers of Colonel Henderson were at Nashborough and signed: Pleasant Henderson and Nathaniel Henderson. The latter was appointed entry-taker for the lands of the Transylvania Company.

To Richard Henderson, draftsman of the Compact, must be attributed the naming of Nashborough—in honor of General Francis Nash of Hillsboro, North Carolina, who was killed in action in the battle of Germantown in 1777. Nash had served as clerk of the court over which Henderson presided as judge. Two or three members of the Transylvania Company were also residents of Hillsboro,[3] and more than willing to have the honor bestowed on a former friend.[4]

---

[3] Williams, "Generals Francis Nash and William Lee Davidson" in *Tennessee Historical Quarterly,* I, 250–268.

[4] For an analysis of the Compact by Joshua W. Caldwell, see his *Constitutional History of Tennessee,* 32, *et seq.*

CHAPTER XX

Indians Seek to Destroy Cumberland Settlements

The building of a fort (Fort Jefferson) under orders of Governor Thomas Jefferson, of Virginia, in the spring of 1780, at the Iron Banks on the east bank of the Mississippi about four miles below the mouth of the Ohio, had a serious repercussion on the Cumberland settlement just as it was in the embryonic stage. That fort was within the domain of the Chickasaw Indians and its construction was in callous disregard of their rights and of their claims on the American people for favorable consideration.[1] Their permission was not even asked. This was an affront that could not be borne by the most valiant of all the Southern tribes, greatly reduced in numbers as it was. Under Chief James Colbert,[2] the Chickasaws invested Fort Jefferson and recurrent attacks continued for six days and nights. These were met by the small garrison with a courage born of desperation, since sickness and hunger were rapidly reducing their power of resistance. Colbert, bearing a demand for surrender, was seriously wounded as he approached the fort. The Indians, infuriated by this, made a mass attack at night and were driven off by the firing of swivel guns in the fort. But the fate of Fort Jefferson was sealed: shortly

---

[1] The very important part played by the Chickasaws in winning the Mississippi Valley east of that river from the French is set forth in Williams, *Dawn, passim.* Gov. Jefferson was in ignorance of the ownership of Western Kentucky by the Chickasaws; he thought the Cherokees owned it. His attitude towards the Chickasaws is shown by his instructions to George Rogers Clark, January 29, 1780: "Against those who are our enemies let loose the friendly tribes. The Kickapoos should be encouraged against the hostile Chickasaws. Ammunition should be furnished gratis to those warriors who go actually on expeditions against the hostile tribes." Draper MSS.

[2] Half-breed son of an old Scotch trader of the same name among the Chickasaws at an early day. The Colberts were to figure in the later history of their tribe and of Tennessee. In 1779 he served as deputy under Alexander Cameron, assistant superintendent of British Indian affairs.

the emaciated survivors of the garrison were taken by water to the Falls of the Ohio, led by Colonel John Montgomery.

The Chickasaws now turned to the "Long Knife" which was being unsheathed at the French Lick and below on the Cumberland. The settlers there, also were, without leave asked, building homes and stockaded forts in the domain which the Chickasaws had taken from the Shawnees in 1710–1714.

The first attack the Indians made was on the westernmost settlement, but recently made by Renfroe and his company on Red River, a tributary of the Cumberland. Renfroe and fellow settlers, as we have seen, had accompanied Colonel John Donelson on the voyage of the flotilla from Fort Patrick Henry on the Holston, and left the other voyagers when the mouth of Red River was reached.[3]

This settlement was small, weak and the most exposed to attack. Prudence was thrown aside when the attempt was made to found it. When it was learned through reports that Indians were out in bands, it was decided to abandon the place temporarily and go to the stations around French Lick, traveling by land through the thick and tangled forests. Around the campfire on the first night in the woods, several of the women reproached the men for having left behind too much movable property in their hasty flight. A group turned back to recover what they could; others moved on to the stronger stations and reached them in safety. Those who had returned to their homes, after turning eastward the second time, were attacked in their first night's encampment; about twenty were killed, Joseph Renfroe, Mr. Johns and all his family, save his wife, among them. The wife was the only one of the party to escape and tell the sad story to the settlers farther up the Cumberland. "Her clothes were nearly in shreds as she ran through the bushes for twenty miles." [4]

The stream on which this slaughter occurred was in after

---

[3] "Donelson's Journal of the Voyage of 1779–80" under date of April 12th refers to this happening. Renfroe or Red River settlement was near the site of the later town of Palmyra. It is highly probable that one of the Renfroes, who knew the name of the stream, had been in that region as a long-hunter in 1770–71. The Renfroe family was from Southwest Virginia where they had lived near the Bledsoes and Neelys. Williams, *Dawn.*

[4] Putnam, *History of Middle Tennessee*, 100.

years known as Battle Creek. There was, however, no semblance of a battle; the name should have been Massacre Creek.

Under the cumulating blows, one man demonstrated anew the qualities he had displayed on the Watauga and the Holston. James Robertson, an innate leader of great resolution and boldness, stepped forward to stay the panic and cope with the crisis. He had lost a son, John Randolph Robertson, a young man of promise, in a red foray. This fact added force to his words, which alone carried great weight even with distraught men and women. Without minimizing the dangers that confronted all, he pointed out the perils incident to a trek through the wilderness to the older settlements; they were in a fair and fertile land which was certain to be conquered and held by civilized men at no distant date. Why yield it to other comers and lose it, with the improvements made, to their own children? The testing time had come, and as for himself there would be no turning back. His words and conduct gave new courage to the remaining settlers. Another year's trial should be given by the colonists. Arms were bared for countering the blows of adversity. Men ventured into the woods as far as Caney Fork River where buffalo, bear and deer were killed for meat; and the forests yielded quantities of nuts and berries. The colony remained—to make history on a larger scale in Robertson's Second Land of Promise.[5]

At French Lick and its environs, bread, bullets, and powder were failing. Robertson met the emergency: he was off to Kentucky through the barrens and the Indian-infested forests to procure these necessities.[6] The stationers grimly carried on; and in doing so, without knowing it, earned again this encomium from a historian of the West: "They were the advance guard of civilization, on the fartherest border yet pushed out into the western wilderness."

While Robertson was away, the Chickasaws not discouraged to do so by British agents among them, went on another hostile incursion. On January 11, 1781, Robertson returned, reaching

---

[5] The Watauga Valley was the first. Williams, *Dawn, passim.*

[6] While in Kentucky Robertson heard of a body of emigrants coming down the Ohio in search of places for settlement. He went to the Falls (present Louisville) to persuade them to go to the Cumberland, only to find that the rumor was baseless.

Freeland's station [7] in the evening, to be joyfully received. The adults sat up late listening to Robertson's recital of the incidents of his journey. Feeling comparatively secure against a raid in the depth of midwinter, all slept soundly except Robertson whose wife had that day given birth to a son,[8] and had much to relate of happenings during his absence. About the hour of midnight the alert ear of Colonel Robertson heard a movement at the gate that aroused his suspicion. He raised himself up, seized his rifle, and gave the alarm, "Indians!"

A large party of Chickasaws, having found means to unfasten the gate, were now entering the stockade. In an instant every man in the fort—eleven in number—was in motion. Major Robert Lucas, who occupied a house that was untenantable because the cracks between the logs had not yet been chinked and daubed, rushed out into the open, and was shot down, mortally wounded. A negro man of Colonel Robertson's, who was in the house with Major Lucas, was also killed. These were the only fatalities, though the death of Major Lucas alone was a serious loss to the colony. He had been a leading pioneer on the Watauga, as he was on the Cumberland. He was a party to the treaty on Sycamore Shoals, and in connection with Colonel John Carter, had received from the Cherokees a deed to a part of Carter's Valley. On his removal to Cumberland, he was elected major in the first military organization of the district.

Hundreds of shots had been fired into the houses; and so great was the uproar from the firing, and the whooping and yelling of the Indians, that the stationers at Eaton's and the Bluffs (Fort Nashborough) were aroused and the sound of the small cannon at the latter place gave notice that relief was at hand. The Indians then withdrew. They had lost one killed, whose body was found, and the traces of blood indicated that others had been wounded.[9]

This was the last attack launched on the settlements by the Chickasaws. Soon afterwards Colonel Robertson held a conference with their chief, Piomingo, and entered into a compact

---

[7] Where the Robertson family was staying.

[8] Dr. Felix Robertson, the first white male born in the limits of the city of Nashville. A child of Timothe Demunbreun was born earlier but outside the town. Felix Robertson became an outstanding figure in Middle Tennessee.

[9] Goodpasture in *Tenn. Hist. Mag.*, IV, 48. Lucas' estate was on Brush Creek of Watauga—the site of the city of Johnson City. He also owned lands on Knob Creek just north of that city. He migrated from Virginia and was of a family of note.

by which that tribe was won over from the British. They were ever afterwards the faithful friends of the colonists on the Cumberland.

A respite followed, but only a brief one. The Chickamaugas were now as ever the implacable foes of the whites of all the border. A band of that tribe, for such it had become, invaded the settlements in November, 1780.

Colonel John Donelson, leader of the flotilla from Long Island of Holston, in the spring of that year, planted crops of corn and cotton at Clover Bottom near the mouth of Stone's River. He erected there a "half-faced" stockaded camp. Near him, Colonel Richard Henderson had erected the same sort of camp on an adjoining tract he had acquired from Michael Stoner,[10] and redmen had killed a white servant and a slave of Henderson. Donelson at once retired with his family to Mansker's Station. In November he set out to gather the crops on his Stone River plantation. Fearing an Indian attack he employed men at Fort Nashborough to go and aid his own force of slaves and workmen. Donelson's boat was in charge of his son, Captain John Donelson, and another boat from Fort Nashborough was commanded by Captain Abel Gower,[11] whose two crews consisted of seven or eight men, whites and slaves. The men engaged in gathering and loading corn for several days. Early one morning young Captain Donelson poled his boat across Stone River and began to gather cotton.[12] The Gower party moved into and down the Cumberland where a band of Chickamaugas from the cover of a canebrake poured in a deadly fire. Captain Gower, his son Abel, Jr., and James Randolph Robertson, the eldest son of Colonel Robertson, were killed. Captain Donelson, hearing the fusillade, rushed for his rifle and fired at the Indians. The boat of the Gower party floated on down stream and was recovered at Fort Nashborough with the dead and wounded still on board. This attack and the killing of such prominent settlers created

---

[10] See note *ante*.

[11] Gower was a relative, probably brother, of the mother of James Robertson, Mary (Gower) Robertson. The Gowers were an English family (Gloucestershire) of some prominence; lived in Brunswick County, Va., after having lived in Henrico County. Abel Gower was with Col. Donelson on the water journey from Ft. Patrick Henry and father of the heroic Nancy who was wounded by the Indians at the Suck.

[12] Probably the first raised in Tennessee.

consternation. Colonel Donelson withdrew with his family to a more secure station in the Kentucky country—a loss, truly, to the colony in its infancy, and one that must have been felt by Robertson, the more sorely because Donelson was followed by others who had come out with him.[13]

In the fall of 1780, Mansker's Station suffered from Indian depredations. William Neely, one of the long-hunters, companion of Mansker, had undertaken to make salt at Neely's Lick, assisted by some of the stationers from Mansker's. His daughter, sixteen years old, went along to do the cooking. One day after a hunt Neely brought in a deer, and sank down to rest. Suddenly the crack of a rifle was heard. Neely, trying to raise himself up, groaned and fell back dead. The daughter was made a prisoner and taken into the Indian country where she remained in captivity for some years. When the men returned to camp for supper and found Neely dead and his daughter gone, they rushed to Mansker's Station, which in the excitement was promptly abandoned in favor of a more central one.[14] However, two young men, David Gower and Patrick Quigley, remained another night; the Indians crept up, shot through the portholes and killed both.

The year 1782 opened with renewed attacks by Indians on the settlers, who were so harassed that it was dangerous to plant crops or hunt for game. Many horses had been lost to the Indians; and, what touched the women and children more keenly, milk cows were killed by red raiders without any thought of making use of their flesh for food. Many more now moved for security to the Kentucky country. Other stout-hearted men quailed when they faced the future, especially when their women-folk pleaded with them to leave the country. A mass movement was in agitation. Penned up in their stockades much of the time, conditions became more and more intolerable. Hunger gnawed and women and children suffered.[15]

---

[13] Donelson did not find immunity from the Indian in Kentucky; he was killed by Indians in 1785.

[14] "All who could get horses went to Kentucky. That brave Irishman, Hugh Rogan, took charge of the widow Neely and her family and conducted them in safety to Kentucky." Carr, *Early Times in Middle Tennessee*, 20.

[15] John Cockrill, who had come out from Virginia in the fall of 1779, perhaps with the Bledsoes, and married Ann Robertson Johnston. Ann had three children by her first husband, all girls; and she and Cockrill

The additional year of trial pleaded for by Robertson proved to be enough to tide the little colony through to happier days. It may be doubted that any other colony in all the history of the West suffered as much from death, wounds, and privation as did the one founded around the site of Nashville through the efforts of Henderson and Robertson.

The Campbell-Sevier expedition left the Chickamaugas unscathed. Those Indians felt the freer to engage in war against the whites, though as seen they chose to strike the weak Cumberland settlement, rather than to provoke the people of the Holston and Watauga to play a return engagement. Towards the last of March, 1781, they sallied in large numbers from their towns for the Cumberland where on April 1st the fort on the Bluff (site of Nashville) was invested.[16] It was the home of Colonel James Robertson. If it fell the fate of the colony would be sealed—the last white man expelled from the Cumberland, since the two weaker forts yet remaining could not survive.

Chief Dragging Canoe seemingly led the Indians, whose plans were skillfully laid. They approached under the cover of night. One party took its stand on a branch about half a mile from the fort and the palisade. No one of the garrison suspected the pres-

---

became progenitors of a number of distinguished Tennesseans and Arkansans. Cockrill left an account that is revealing: "It had been three days [in the fall of 1780] that we had very little to eat. . . . As it was, the children were following their mother about the cabin and saying, 'Mother I'm hungry.' I said, 'I can't stand that; I must have meat or die.' So I took my gun and started. My wife said, 'You better come back; you'll never see the fort again.' I said, 'The children are starving; I must go. I can see as good as the Indians and I will not follow any path; so they can't waylay me.' I went out and killed a bear and cut off his skin and, with most of his meat wrapped up in the skin, took it on my back and carried it home. The children came around as my wife was helping to cut it up. They said, 'Give me a little; I've had nothing for three or four days;' and others said, 'Divide it out; only save some for to-morrow.' Others [neighbors] said, 'My children are starving.' I said, 'I will go out again tomorrow. Divide it out.'" Matthews, *James Robertson*, 221.

[16] Frequently called Nashborough Fort, on the river at the foot of Church Street. It was the strongest of the forts in the settlements. In it were cabins of two stories, with port-holes and look-out stations. In the enclosure was a spring. On the west side there was a large gate. On the east side the precipitous bank of the river afforded protection. In recent years the fort has been reproduced by the Nashborough Chapter of the Daughters of the American Revolution.

ence of an enemy in such force, though caution was known to be necessary,[17] and a sentinel, James Menifee, did discover an Indian scout prowling near the fort and fired at him in the darkness. On the morning of April 2nd, about daylight, three warriors approached the stockade, fired and fell back out of range of the stationers' rifle fire. Colonel Robertson at the head of about twenty mounted men started in pursuit, unaware of an ambuscade prepared for them. The whites followed the three Indians up the river and passed those lying concealed between a branch and the fort. Immediately from the places of concealment issued a murderous fire. Robertson and his men dismounted to give battle; the fire was returned with effectiveness. At this time the other party of Indians emerged from cover and extended their lines to the river to cut off a retreat of the stationers to the fort. The peril to the whites was apparent, but the horses became panicy and dashed through the Indians' rear line, and ran towards the French Lick. The redmen could not resist the temptation to capture the horses and in pursuing the animals [18] left a gap in their ranks. The excitement incident to the horse-Indian race was seen from the fort, and Mrs. James Robertson quick-wittedly ordered the gate of the fort opened and let loose a large pack of dogs already infurated by the scent of Indians. Trained to trail and fight redmen, the dogs now gave battle in a fierce onset which busied the Indians in taking care of themselves.

While this tragi-comedy was in progress on the upland, the sortie was being repulsed by overwhelming numbers in the bottom. Already Peter Gill, Alexander Buchanan, George Kennedy, Zachariah White, and James Leiper lay dead on the field, and James Menifee and Joseph Moonshaw were disabled by wounds. Seeing a chance to pass through the breach made by the horses and dogs in the Indian line that intervened between them and the fort, the whites determined to retreat; and, taking their wounded with them, started on a run, hotly pursued by the enemy. After they had passed the Indian line and approached the fort, Isaac Lucas was shot and fell with a broken thigh, but his comrades could not stop to assist him. He hastily primed his gun, which he had charged as he ran, and shot dead the foremost of his pursuers. A daring Indian overtook Edward Swan-

[17] About the last of March, Samuel Barton, a leader in the settlements, while riding out in search of cattle, was fired on and wounded.

[18] Some of the horses were captured by the Indians, and with them some bridles and saddles—a grievous loss to the stationers.

son within thirty yards of the gate, and struck him on the shoulder, causing him to drop his gun. Swanson turned and seized the gun of his antagonist, but the Indian wrenched it from him, and knocked him to his knees. Before he could pursue his advantage further, the elder John Buchanan reached the fort, and, seeing Swanson's danger, fired and killed his antagonist. The Indians, seeing that the whites had reached the stockade, and were maintaining a brisk fire from its gate, halted before they reached Lucas, who had crept within range of their guns. He and Swanson were both brought into the fort. The Indians then withdrew. They reappeared at night, but a single discharge from the old swivel, loaded with broken stone and scraps of iron, and an answering boom from the small piece at Eaton's dispersed them, and they abandoned the conflict; though the garrison, reinforced by a relief party from Eaton's kept watch until daylight next morning.

The settlers firmly believed that the frightened horses and infuriated dogs saved them from destruction in this, the most formidable invasion ever, before or later, undertaken against them. "Thank God," they must have thought, "that he gave Indians a fear of dogs and a love of horses." [19]

New courage came for a time to the Cumberlanders; if they could hold out until other settlers in number came among them, they in combination might yet come to possess the whole of the rich Cumberland Valley.

---

[19] In addition to the authorities cited above, the following were consulted on the "Battle of the Bluffs:" Haywood, Ramsey and Clayton's *History of Davidson County*, 24–30.

CHAPTER XXI

DOUBLE CALL TO ACTION—1780–1781

Scarcely had the Wataugans returned from King's Mountain to their homes before they had a double call to action: one by way of encore—to return to the stage east of the Alleghanies; the other to defend their own homes against the Cherokee and Chickamauga Indians who were threatening from the south.

We have seen that the first choice of the western soldiery of a leader in the battle of King's Mountain had been General William Davidson;[1] and now from him came a call to return east to aid him directly against Lord Cornwallis.

That British general was beating a slow retreat from Charlotte southward to Winnsborough, in South Carolina. A rainy season had set in and his army was suffering severely from sickness, while he himself became so ill that he relinquished the active command to Lord Rawdon. The Americans followed and harassed the crest-fallen British. The Tories of Surry County, N. C., in an endeavor to aid Cornwallis, embodied to the number of three hundred under the pestiferous Colonel Gideon Wright, and were marching in the direction of his lordship, plundering, disarming and punishing Whigs as they went. They were intercepted at the Shallow Ford of the Yadkin and defeated with such a considerable loss as to cause them to hasten homeward, pursued by two hundred Whig horsemen.

A plan was now conceived[2] by Generals Davidson and Smallwood: to call on the western militia, to serve under Davidson in delivering a final blow to Cornwallis. A message went by grapevine telegraph to the West. The request was not thought to be unreasonable, even in the situation that confronted the western

---

[1] The favor in which Davidson was held by the Trans-Alleghany people was shown in the naming (1783) of the County of Davidson, whose seat became the capital city of Tennessee. See note on p. 233.

[2] *N. C. St. Recs.* XIV, 704, Oct. 20.

folk. It was promptly responded to by the Wataugans: On November 20, 1780, a meeting of the officers was held at Jonesborough over which "Colonel Sevier presided, present Majors Charles Robertson and Jonathan Tipton; Captains John McNabb, Joseph Willson, Jacob Brown, Samuel Williams, Wm. Trimble, James Patterson and Robert Bean.[3] It was ordered that Captains Luke Bowyer, James Gibson and James Stinson, with their respective companies, rendezvous the 30th inst., and march to join General Davidson." [4]

Doubtless a like request went to Sullivan County, but Colonel Shelby was absent as an adviser to General Daniel Morgan east of the mountains.[5] General Davidson understood that any force from the Trans-Alleghany region would come only on a definite call and for a quick blow and a hasty return home, where was a constant red menace.[6]

In the confusion incident to the change in the chief command in the South, from Gates to Greene, the plan of Davidson could not be brought to consummation; and the privilege was denied the western riflemen of participating in the signal American victory under General Morgan at the Cowpens on January 17, 1781. The failure was due to no fault of theirs.[7]

---

[3] Draper's Note Book, 325, 201, with a bracketed statement by Draper after the name of Robert Bean "(afterwards major and settled Bean's Station)." He was son of Wm. Bean, Sr.

[4] Records of Washington County.

[5] Morgan to Gen. Gates Nov. 23, 1780: "Col. Shelby has been in camp for some time, waiting to lend his aid; but, apprehending not much will be done this winter, and his domestic business calling him, and he, having no command, is now on his way home." N. C. St. Recs., XIV, 749.

[6] Davidson's plan was thus outlined by himself: to raise 1000 volunteer militia, "which I can raise in twenty days," to be joined with Morgan's troops "and a forced march made against Ninety-Six. . . . I think the scheme practicable and certain of success unless the enemy be reinforced." Ib. 759-60. We may assume that this was the plan he sent across the mountains.

[7] Moses Shelby, of the Sullivan troops, certainly, and perhaps others of the over-mountain men, wounded in the battle of King's Mountain, did participate in the Cowpens victory. "Moses Shelby, after lying on his back for nearly three months" was only able to ride out a few days before General Morgan came into the district of Ninety-Six. He joined Morgan at the Cowpens and was wounded more severely than at the Mountain." (Isaac Shelby.)

An Indian Campaign

While the King's Mountain campaign was in inception and progress, Virginia's agent to the Cherokees, Major Joseph Martin, had the delicate task of holding in leash the Cherokees, the Overhills as well as the Chickamauga seceders. It was his duty to mediate between the Indians and the whites who were fast passing south of the treaty line,[8] and making settlements. This naturally gave umbrage even to the friendlier part of the Cherokees. Quite as delicate and more serious was the counteracting influence of the British over the Indians.

The dependence of the Overhills for goods and ammunition had long been on South Carolina and Virginia, but now neither State was in a position to carry on a trade with them. The exigencies of war rendered it impracticable.

After the British had captured Savannah and Augusta in Georgia, it was in their power to send the Indians much needed aid of this kind by way of the Savannah River and Augusta, at which town a large depot was established. The Overhills and Chickamaugas resorted there in large numbers.[9] Governor Jefferson fairly stated the situation to General Washington early in 1781: "The distress of the Cherokees had too much ripened their alienation from us, and gathered to a head." Here was offered to the British an opportunity which they were not slow in improving. A treaty with the Indians was held in Georgia. The Cherokees were promised a return of their hunting grounds which had been lost to the white people. The redmen were to make war not only on that people, but also on the Carolinas and Virginia; a part of the American traders in their towns were to be put to death, the others made prisoners and sent into Georgia. As Colonel William Campbell reported to his superior, Colonel Wm. Preston, as early as December 12, 1780: "In the treaty held there [Georgia] this country was given to that tribe if they would conquer it." [10]

The decision of the Indians to act in concert with the British

---

[8] Of 1777.

[9] Even after the campaign, now being treated of, had ended, Col. Arthur Campbell wrote to Gov. Jefferson (Apr. 25, 1781), that "he had no hopes the Cherokees would sue for peace, as long as Augusta is in the hands of the British who promise them all the supplies they need." *Cal. Va. St. Papers*, II, 72.

[10] "Preston Papers" in *Va. Mag. of History*, XXVII, 315.

was made in the fall of 1780, before the battle of King's Mountain, or at least before the result of that battle was known. That battle was to prove that decision one pregnant with adversity for them.

Agents, principally one, Scott, were sent up by Colonel Brown from Georgia to the Chickamauga towns under the Dragging Canoe, where they were a constant threat to the peace of the white people. John McDonald [11] a British factor among the Chickamaugas appeared in the Overhill towns and at Chota attempted to seize and make a prisoner of Major Martin. Chiefs Oconostota and Hanging Maw protected Martin and expelled McDonald. Other chiefs were more pliant, with the result that they cast their people's fate with that of the British. Hostilities on the part of the Indians were inspired by orders from Lord Cornwallis, as he confessed in a letter that was a tribute to the prowess of the "back-mountain men." [12] This direct interposition of Cornwallis distinctly marks the campaign that followed another of the "Revolution in the West."

Major Martin, finding that he could with difficulty, if at all, stay the rising tide, had hurried a messenger to the governor of Virginia, Thomas Jefferson, for a letter of friendship and medals to the chiefs. The governor dispatched these; they arrived before December 12th, but too late to defeat the manipulation of the British agents. War was soon flagrant; the chiefs and warriors

---

[11] Reporting to Lord Cornwallis from Augusta, Brown wrote: "In consequence of letters sent to the Cherokee Nation, the Indians have agreed to attack rebel plunderers who have taken possession of their hunting grounds on Watauga, etc. Chiefs of 2500 Cherokees promise to continue the war during the winter if they were provided with arms and ammunition, and their families with clothing. White men have been sent with them to prevent outrages. Have adjusted the quarrels between the Creeks and Cherokees and the former have promised to assist. In consequence of the encouraging letters, I have given directions to the Abenahkies to keep out parties on the Ohio to obstruct navigation, etc." *Report on American MSS. in the Royal Institution of Great Britain,* II, 221.

[12] Lord Cornwallis to Gen. Henry Clinton, from Winnsborough, S. C.: "When the numerous and formidable bodies of back mountain-men came down to attack Maj. Ferguson, and showed themselves to be our inveterate enemies, I directed Lt. Colonel Brown to encourage the Indians to attack the settlements of Wataga, Holstein, Caentuck and Nolachuckie. . . . A large body of the mountaineers were soon obliged to oppose the incursions of the Indians," etc. *Ib.,* 225.

of the old towns finally were persuaded to join the Chickamaugas.

Sensing danger from that direction to the homes of his men, Sevier [13] a few days after the battle of King's Mountain had detached Captain George Russell and his company to make a forced march homeward. Two traders, Isaac Thomas and Ellis Harlin, were on the Watauga, sent from the Cherokee towns by Nancy Ward to give warning that a large body of the Indians was about to march against the white inhabitants.[14]

Captain Russell kept his company in readiness until Sevier's return. When the latter reached home he was allowed scarcely a day's rest before setting on foot an expedition to repel the savage invaders. Messengers hastened from company to company to give orders to prepare to march. Some Washington County officers were asked to repair to the home of Martin near the Long Island (Kingsport) for a consultation with Colonel Arthur Campbell, who now as leader alternated in campaigning with his kinsman, Colonel William Campbell. A North Carolina colonel was to lead the forces to be sent from the upper counties.[15]

Sevier's strategy in Indian warfare was based on the idea that the best defense is to attack. His county was nearest the redmen. To wait in stockaded forts would leave the enemy to burn homes, destroy crops, and seize horses and cattle of the people on the border below. While Campbell consulted, Sevier was in the saddle and away at the head of a small advance force, consisting of Russell's company, joined by that of Captain Thomas Gist as he marched southwestward. Other volunteers [16] were being

---

[13] John Carter was yet colonel of the western forces, but he was now old and feeble. He passed away in 1781 while his regiment was on this campaign. During his life in the region he had been ranked first in leadership and regard. Not so dashing as Sevier and not so picturesque as James Robertson, both of whom were his subordinates, John Carter's part in the founding of the West has never been adequately appreciated. Consult this author's *Dawn, passim*.

[14] Another trader, Wm. Springstone, deflected and, by way of the Long Island, hurried to Washington County, Va., and gave a like warning. *Cal. of Preston Papers*, 137.

[15] *Cal. Tennessee Papers*, (Draper Collection) 15. This was about December 15th. Col. Wm. Campbell from his home was issuing orders for his militia to turn out. *Cal. Preston Papers*, 137.

[16] "Every man was punctual; there was no dodging in those days." James Sevier to Draper, in Manuscripts, 32, S. 140. This was his father's first campaign against the Indians as leader of all forces.

equipped and soon followed rapidly. The rendezvous was to be at Swan Pond of Lick Creek. The main force of the enemy must at all hazards be held back before crossing the French Broad. The second night out, Sevier's party camped on Long Creek of Nolachucky. Captain Gist was sent forward with a few men to reconnoitre, and from a small hill discovered a body of Indians about forty yards away. They fired from horses, wheeled and galloped back to the camp of Sevier, who now prepared against a night attack. Before day Captain Wm. Pruett and his company of about seventy rode into the camp, soon followed by other companies. The advance was now pressed vigorously by the troops, who crossed the French Broad at the Big Island (later Sevier's Island).[17] Early in the morning of the next day, an advance guard under Captain James Stinson, after going about three miles saw fires of the Indians' camps yet burning. These were discovered by Scouts Joseph Dunham and Joseph Gist. Seeing a halt of the advance guard, Sevier rode forward, and, scanning the surroundings, located Indians in a half-moon shape, ambuscading in the grass. He ordered up reinforcements while the guard went forward under directions that, when they should come up with the enemy, they were to fire and retreat, thus drawing the Indians into a counter ambuscade.

Three-quarters of a mile from their camp, the enemy fired upon the advance from an ambuscade. It returned the fire and retreated, and, as had been anticipated, was pursued by the enemy till it joined the main body. This was formed into three divisions: the center commanded by Colonel John Sevier, the right wing by Major Jesse Walton, and the left by Major Jonathan Tipton. Orders were given that as soon as the enemy should approach the front, the right wing should wheel to the left, and the left wing to the right, and thus enclose them. In this order were the troops arranged when they met the Indians at the Cedar Spring, who rushed forward after the guard with great rapidity, till checked by the opposition of the main body. Major Walton with the right wing wheeled briskly to the left, and performed the order which he was to execute with precise accuracy. But the left wing moved to the right with less celerity, and when the centre fired upon the Indians, doing immense execution, the latter retreated through the unoccupied space left open between the

---

[17] In 1778, Sevier and Gov. Richard Caswell entered, and received a grant covering this island which ever after was called "Sevier's Island." Greene County Records.

extremities of the right and left wings, and running into a swamp, escaped the destruction which otherwise seemed ready to involve them. The victory was decisive. The loss of the enemy amounted to twenty-eight killed on the ground, and very many wounded, who got off without being taken. On the side of Sevier's troops not a man was even wounded. . . .

Another narrative of this engagement gives further details:

Lieutenant Isaac Lane and John Ward had dismounted for the fight, when Sevier, having noticed the semi-circular position of the Indians, ordered a halt, with the purpose of engaging the two extremes of the Indian line, and keeping up the action until the other part of his troops could come up. Lane and his comrade, Ward, remounted and fell back upon Sevier without being hurt, though fired at by several warriors near them. A brisk fire was, for a short time, kept up by Sevier's party and the nearest Indians. The troops behind, hearing the first fire, had quickened their pace and were coming in sight. James Roddy, with about twenty men, quickly came up, and soon after the main body of the troops. The Indians noticed this reinforcement and closed their lines. Sevier immediately ordered the charge, which would have been still more fatal, but that the pursuit led through a swampy branch, which impeded the progress of the horsemen. In the charge, Sevier was in close pursuit of a warrior, who, finding that he would be overtaken, turned and fired at him. The bullet cut the hair of his temple without doing further injury. Sevier then spurred his horse forward and attempted to kill the Indian with his sword, having emptied his pistols in the first moment of the charge. The warrior parried the licks from the sword with his empty gun. The conflict was becoming doubtful between the two combatants thus engaged, when one of the soldiers,[18] rather ungallantly, came, shot the warrior, and decided the combat in favor of his commander. The horse of Adam Sherrill threw his rider, and, in the fall, some of his ribs were broken. An Indian sprang upon him with his tomahawk drawn. When in the act of striking, a ball from a comrade's rifle brought him to the ground, and Sherrill escaped. After a short pursuit, the Indians dispersed into the adjoining highlands and knolls, where the cavalry could not pursue them.[19]

Major Jonathan Tipton evidently misunderstood the orders for his wing. Some of his men tried to explain to him that this

[18] By another account, Joseph Dunham was with Sevier at the time, and mistook the falling lock of hair for the brains of his commander and was in the act of firing on the Indian when, to his surprise, the redman drew his knife and plunged it into his own throat and died immediately.

[19] Ramsey, *Annals*, 262–3. Ramsey's best bit of work as an annalist is his treatment of this battle. His home was not far from the scene of action.

was the case, but he gruffly replied, "Mind your own business and be damned. I know my orders." Had he executed the order few of the redmen would have escaped death or capture.

Some other details of this engagement, known as the Battle of Boyd's Creek [20] have been preserved.[21]

Only three of Sevier's men were wounded in the action—Major Tipton among them. A brother of Chief John Watts was slain. It was Sevier's first offensive engagement with Indians, and the only battle in which he was scathed, ever so slightly. As Ramsey truly says: "This battle has always been considered one of the best fought battles in border wars in Tennessee." [22] It was fought on December 16, 1780.

Just after the battle two messengers rode up with a letter to Sevier from Colonel Campbell stating that he would arrive with his forces within a week and asked that Sevier await his coming before moving on the Indian towns. Sevier fell back and camped on the Big Island. Campbell not appearing within the week, the troops were again marched to Boyd's Creek where it was thought a wider field for hunting game could be had. In this they were disappointed, though experienced hunters, led by Wm. Bean and Isaac Thomas, ranged far into the woods for game. Before Campbell and Martin of Sullivan County arrived the men were reduced to living on haws, grapes, nuts, even parched acorns.

---

[20] The name of this creek was that of Alexander Boyd, killed there and his body thrown into the water by the Indians in 1766. Williams, *Dawn of Tennessee Valley and Tennessee History*, 291.

[21] Ramsey, *op. cit.*, 263–4. "Among the booty taken by Sevier were some of Gen. Clinton's proclamations and other documents."

[22] Notwithstanding, Sevier was criticised for bringing it on, particularly by Col. Arthur Campbell who was noted for the gentle art of seldom being agreeable. The son of Major (afterwards General) Joseph Martin, in later years wrote to Draper: "Col. Sevier of Washington went on, of his own accord, with some three or four hundred men several days before the army—had a little fight—killed a few, and retired some distance waiting for the main army. This was complained of at the time not only as an unauthorized move, but as apprising the Indians of their approach before the army was in the situation to act efficiently. It was thought that the motive of Sevier was to get glory for himself." Draper MSS., 3XX4. See *Calendar of Va. St. Papers*, I, 434. Of Campbell Draper gave this estimate: "His character was of the haughty, austere cast, little disposed to make compromise and often getting into trifling quarrels."

Finally a stray cow and her calf were found and their meat added variety to their diet.[23]

Campbell arrived December 22nd, having 100 Virginia militia; Major Martin brought 300 Sullivan County troops which, added to Sevier's force, made about 700 to 750 for the push. With Sevier was Colonel Elijah Clarke of Georgia who insisted upon joining his host on the campaign. Campbell, colonel-commandant of his county, was senior in years and service, and nominally the chief command was yielded to him. In fact, the superior forces of Sevier and Martin each operated quite as independent commands. The combined troops made a forced march the next day, Campbell having supplied Sevier's troops from his stock of provisions. It was learned en route that the Indians had obstructed the usual fording places over Little Tennessee River, and would in force there oppose a crossing. On the 24th a feint was made to cross to the town of Maliquo (the island town); the crossing was attempted and made to Tommotley on the river above. Major Martin came near drowning in attempting to swim his horse over. Such Indians as were seen appeared "to be flying in consternation." At Tommotley the force was divided, a part going against the towns below while the other marched toward Chota. Indians were observed between Toqua and Chota, stretched out along the hills, with design apparently to attack the van. Seeing the mounted riflemen in such numbers, the Indians let them pass, only firing a few scattering shots at those in the rear. Chota was reached on Christmas Day which was one of real cheer—there was found "a welcome supply of provisions." Sentries were kept out and at daybreak of the following day John Bean was sent out with five scouts to trace the route taken by the Indians now in flight. Martin led other scouts, killed one warrior and took seventeen horses loaded with clothing and skins, and making towards the town of Tellico. Major Tipton with a detachment of horsemen was ordered to recross the river and go against the only town on the north side of the river, Tellassee;[24] while Major Gilbert Christian with 150 footmen attacked Chilhowee on the south side.

---

[23] "Hungry Camp" on Boyd's Creek, as the spot was called for many years following.

[24] The report of the campaign states: "The officer of the horse, by unmilitary behavior, failed to cross the river."

The famous Indian woman, Nancy Ward, came to camp; she gave us various intelligence and made an overture in behalf of some of the chiefs for peace, to which I avoided giving an explicit answer, as I wished first to visit the vindictive part of the nation, mostly settled at Hiwassee and Chestowee, and to distress the whole as much as possible by destroying their habitations and provisions. (Campbell).

It was at Chota, too, that Nancy Ward ordered a small herd of cattle driven in to be slaughtered to feed the troops. Colonel Clarke, of Sevier's command, in passing met the escort driving the cattle and ordered some of the hungry men to begin the slaughter. They had been in the wilderness nearly a fortnight longer than their fellows from upcountry. When Major Martin heard of this he became wrathy, since he had reason to believe it was his influence with the Beloved Woman [25] that had largely induced her gift. Martin drew his sword, called his men to follow and took away the beef, then quartered and hung up. On Clarke's return he and Martin, after hot words, engaged in person combat —a fisticuff between two pugnacious stalwarts.[26] This incident widened the rift between the Washington troops, on the one side, and the Sullivan and Virginia men on the other. Jealousy of Sevier had already developed as the result of his advance. Too, of the three commanders Sevier was the only one who had King's Mountain laurels. Martin's treatment of a guest of Sevier and his men touched them keenly.[27]

The fact that Clarke had scarcely recovered from the disability due to battle-wounds added to the resentment, and the resulting coolness between Sevier and Martin and their men, lasted for years. From every standpoint this clash was unfortunate.

On the 28th, fire was set to Chota, Tellico and Little Tuskegee,[28] and the army moved to Kai-a-tee, on the Tellico River. In

---

[25] While agent of Virginia among the Overhill Cherokees, Martin had taken to wife Betsy, daughter of Nancy Ward and grandniece of the great Chief Attakullakulla. Williams, *Early Travels*, 490. Evidently Clarke was not aware of all the facts.

[26] Martin was fully six feet high and weighed about 200 pounds. Clarke was fully as tall and had time and again proven his prowess, earning the title, "Backwoods Titan."

[27] This episode is given in more detail in Williams, "Col. Elijah Clarke in the Tennessee Country," *Georgia Historical Quarterly*, XXV, 151–159.

[28] The last-named village was the home of the Indian boy, Sequoyah, then about eight years old; later to become inventor of the Cherokee

the afternoon, Martin on returning from a patrol, attacked a party of Indians, killed two and drove several into the river. Captain James Elliott,[29] a gallant officer of Martin's command, was killed in a skirmish.

Leaving Major Gilbert Christian at Kai-a-tee with 150 men to fort and thereby secure a possible retreat, and to lay in provisions, the troops moved on Hiwassee town, which they found abandoned, and this they destroyed. Captain Landon Carter with fifty men out on scout failed to locate any body of redmen. Some of the Wataugans now turned back. A move was made by the other troops against Chestowee (Chestuee) twelve miles farther, which also had been abandoned. It was put to the torch. It had been learned that McDonald, the British emissary, with some Tories and Indians would confront them there. It was expected that a stubborn defense would be made at Chestowee since it had been a stronghold of the Chickamaugas in 1779. "Our troops becoming impatient and no other object of importance being in view, it was resolved to turn homeward," on New Year's Day, 1781.[30]

As Kai-a-tee was approached on the way back, it was learned from warriors taken prisoners by Martin that a group of the chiefs had been in council to discuss means of making peace. A talk was prepared, and sent in by one of the prisoners.

At Chota there was found "in Oconostota's baggage, which he left behind in his flight, various manuscripts and other archives of the nation, some of which showed the double game that his people have been carrying on during the present war."[31]

The returns made to the commanders showed twenty-nine Indians killed, and many wounded but taken off the field by the

syllabary and achieve fame. Williams, "Father of Sequoyah" in *E. T. Hist. Soc. Pub.*, V, 39–55.

[29] Father of Isabelle Elliott to whom Gen. Evan Shelby was married, second wife, 1787. Capt. Elliott was buried beneath an Indian hut which was burned to prevent desecration of his remains.

[30] Ramsey, following Haywood, extends the expedition as far south as Coosa River, with details and incidents that really pertain to Sevier's campaign of the year 1782, and against the Chickamaugas. Some other writers follow Ramsey.

[31] This is demonstrated to be true in many ways. The Cherokees felt warranted in playing one side against the other, but their hearts were with the British against the encroaching white settlers ever eager for more and more of their land.

other warriors and not counted. Only seventeen prisoners were taken, mostly women and children, who were taken to the Long Island and left in charge of Martin. "Besides these, we brought in the family of Nancy Ward, whom, for their good offices, we considered in another light." [32]

The expedition was successful in that it materially weakened the Overhill Cherokees' power and almost their will to further resist the whites. The entire nation, not including the Chickamaugas, had been decadent since 1776 and now it became more so.[33]

The better to conserve the results of the expedition and defend against British machinations among the Southern Indians, Colonel Arthur Campbell immediately on his return home opened a correspondence with Governor Jefferson and others. He urged the advisability of a fort at the confluence of the Holston and Tennessee (site of Lenoir City).[34] Jefferson concurred, though he was of opinion it was a matter which "we must refer to Congress." [35] Nothing was done by the do-nothing Continental Congress; though Campbell, under Jefferson's authority, in the same year constructed a fort at Cumberland Gap to safeguard those going to and from Kentucky.

---

[32] Jefferson wrote: "Nancy Ward seems rather to have taken refuge with you. In this case, her inclination ought to be followed as to what is done with her." (Feb. 17, 1781) *Writings of Jefferson*, I, 295.

[33] For evidences of this decadence, see accounts of travelers among them, 1784–1800, in Williams, *Early Travels in the Tennessee Country*.

[34] At the junction of the Holston and Tennessee there did rise, in the period of Southwest Territory, Fort Grainger. Campbell argued thus in favor of an immediate construction: "There a good stockade with some outworks can be conveniently built, and effectually supplied and supported from the country above on the Holstein. Part of the garrison ought to be regular souldiers, and the officer that commands the whole ought to be an active and intrepid man who would keep up an exact discipline. My experience of Major Joseph Martin and his acquaintance in that country, makes him the most proper man I know of. The utility of the post would be such that it would be giving us certain possession of the Cherokee Country now conquered, or may [be] ceded to us; will keep that nation always at our mercy and prevent our enemies from sending emissaries among them; be a terror to the British . . . whilst, in the Southern States, open a communication with the Chickasaws (a friendly disposed people) and our posts on the Mississippi; and be a security to the South Western frontier."

[35] *Writings of Jefferson*, I, 295.

While the troops were on campaign, bands of the Chickamaugas were out on foray in Powell's Valley and beyond. Major Martin on his return sent out scouts and a few weeks later, having been made a lieutenant-colonel of Sullivan, headed sixty-five militia, and tracked the Indians towards the mouth of Powell's River thirty miles below Cumberland Gap. The band was there surprised and surrounded but the cane was too thick for successful attack by the mounted riflemen. The pursuit continued a distance of about seventy miles to quite near the Chickamauga towns before Martin, unwillingly, but persuaded by his men, stopped and returned by way of the Holston valley. Settlements on the Holston were also invaded by bands of Shawnees; one carried off a son of Captain Isaac Bledsoe. Another invasion was threatened by the Creeks as well as by the nearer tribes, all under British incitement.

CHAPTER XXII

AGAIN IN THE SADDLE (1781)

On the 3rd of February, 1781, Sevier was commissioned by Governor Abner Nash as full colonel of Washington County, in place of John Carter, deceased; but the fact that he had been appointed had not reached the West before Sevier was again in the saddle, this time on an expedition against the Middle Towns of the Cherokees. These were located east of the Alleghanies and were difficult of access from the west. Raids on the white settlements on the Nolachucky Sevier attributed to warriors from these towns, and he determined to stop further forays by punishing their inhabitants. He had for guide through the treacherous wilderness the old and reliable Indian trader, Isaac Thomas. The invading force was collected early in March, 1781, in Greasy Cove (now in Unicoi County). It was about the same size as the battalion which was away at the time under Robertson at Guilford Court House—three companies aggregating 130 men, under Captains Valentine Sevier, James Stinson and David McNabb, the major being Jonathan Tipton.[1] The march was through Coxe's Cove Gap of the Bald Mountains (Alleghany range) to and up Cane River, down the Ivy, and on to the Tuckasegee [2] where was the enemy town of the same name. That town was surprised and taken; fifty warriors were slain, and as many women and children taken prisoners.[3] About fifteen other small

---

[1] See note, p. 198.

[2] The route, part of the way, was along an ancient war-trail of the Middle Town Cherokees, used in going to war against Northern tribes, and by the latter in attacks on these Cherokees and the Catawbas. Passage over the dividing mountains, from the head of one creek to that of another, was very difficult. Capt. James Stinson's arm was injured in a fall at such a place, on the outbound trip. Maj. Jonathan Tipton was ordered to accompany him homeward over the roughest part of the trail, then to return to the party under Sevier. Instead, Tipton continued on to his own home, for which Sevier had his commission revoked.

[3] Ten of these were chosen by Col. Sevier and taken as hostages to his home. A few escaped; others lived on his estate for about three years and were then exchanged through Martin, as agent to the Cherokees.

towns were destroyed together with all the granaries or cribs of corn that could be found.

At Cowee,[4] contrary to the orders of the colonel, Valentine Sevier, Nathaniel Davis and John Bond swam the Little Tennessee River on horseback to sack and burn some Indian cabins, when a band of warriors rushed from hiding between the three men and the river, killed Bond, and wounded Davis who was taken by Valentine Sevier, yet mounted on his horse, and the animal swam the river carrying both men to safety. Colonel Sevier with fifty men rushed into the river to rescue the imperilled men; but, before they had crossed, the red men had decamped. Davis died of his wounds on the way home. These two were the only men lost by Sevier on the expedition. The return trip, it is believed, was through Indian Gap in the present Great Smoky Mountain National Park, thence by the war fords of the Big Pigeon and French Broad (near Newport). The campaign disabused the minds of the Middle Town Cherokees of the notion that the Alleghanies guaranteed immunity from invasion from the West and convinced them that for further murderous and thieving forays in the Nolachucky valley they could be punished, and too, severely.

The hardihood and daring required for such an expedition is almost beyond conception. It was, on the whole, Sevier's most arduous campaign against Indians, minor as it was.[5]

The expedition was intended, also, to influence the Overhill Cherokees, ripening them for terms favorable to the whites at a peace treaty then on foot.

In the meantime, the flow of white settlers into the region, later Greene County, went on at an accelerated pace.

---

[4] Near the headwaters of the Little Tennessee. For an entrancing description of "the vale of Cowee," see Bartram's *Travels in North America,* 345–48.

[5] It appears from a statement of a son of Col. Sevier, James, that there had been an earlier attempt (in August) to organize a campaign against the Middle Towns. The men were assembling on Indian Creek of the Nolachucky when one, "Hill went into the nearby mountains to hunt and was shot at by an Indian who missed," whereupon Hill killed his assailant. This made the men fearful that their families would be attacked if the expedition were undertaken. "The campaign fell through." (James Sevier pension statement of 1838.)

CHAPTER XXIII

ANOTHER CALL TO CONFRONT CORNWALLIS

After General Gates had been succeeded by General Nathanael Greene, Lord Cornwallis, yet at Winnsborough in South Carolina, determined on another campaign into North Carolina in order to assuage the sting of two defeats: at King's Mountain and at the Cowpens. Greene, knowing that the British commander headed strong combined forces in which regulars predominated, delayed coming to grips until he could summon to his standard additional aid. A call went from him to Colonel Isaac Shelby,[1] but as that officer found it impracticable to embody a command, a message from Greene was sent to Sevier. Just returned from one Indian campaign, Sevier was about to enter on another, and, therefore, delegated to Major Charles Robertson the leadership of a battalion to go to the aid of Greene, again alternating with Sevier in leading the Wataugans eastward over the mountain ranges. Major Robertson hurriedly chose three small companies under as many captains to take up the long march. The force numbered between one hundred and one hundred and thirty men, but the names of all the captains are not certainly known, and the names of the soldiers, save a few, are also unrecorded.[2] No annalist accompanied the battalion and no muster roll was preserved, if ever made out. It is manifest that the march was begun about the last of February, 1781, and continued until Greene's army was reached about March 6th, that army being then encamped near the site of the battle of the Alamance (1771).

---

[1] The legislature of North Carolina on Feb. 13th passed a resolution, expressing deep appreciation of what had been done by the militia of the two counties in the West and urging Cols. Shelby and Sevier to "press a continuance of the same active exertions," to save the gravely imperilled Commonwealth. Ramsey's *Annals*, 250.

[2] No doubt the men were not those who had just gone on the Indian campaign under Col. Sevier, and certainly not those who were to march in a few days against the Middle Town Cherokees.

Among Robertson's men there may have been a few, very few, who had participated in that earlier struggle.

A like call had gone to Colonel William Campbell of lower Southwest Virginia, who fully expected to take 1000 men. He was humiliated to turn up on March 2nd, bringing to Greene only sixty riflemen. He must have asked that the other over-mountain men from the Watauga be placed under him, and every indication is that this was done. Robertson did not operate independently and his natural alignment was with and under Campbell, the leader of all men from the western waters at King's Mountain.[3] Historical datum is scant. Ramsey in his *Annals*, (page 251) devotes only four or five lines to this battalion, not even naming Robertson as commander. The forces under Campbell took part in preliminary skirmishes as the two commanding generals converged towards what became the main battlefield.[4] On March 15, 1781, the two armies met near Guilford Courthouse and there was begun a battle described by Lord Cornwallis as "one of the bloodiest of the war." In no other battle of the Revolution was there such a contrast in the two contending armies. Cornwallis was outnumbered, but he had under him an army largely composed of regulars. With him were Major-General Leslie, Brigadier-Generals O'Hara and Howard, a Hessian regiment under Major Du Buy, Lieutenant-Colonel Tarleton with his famous cavalry and the gallant Lieutenant-Colonel Webster. In the line of battle Campbell's riflemen were on the American's left flank opposite General Leslie with a battalion of the Queen's Guard, and the Hessians.

The battle opened at 1:30 in the afternoon and lasted for an hour and a half. Campbell's men fought in King's Mountain fashion, as Cornwallis in his report said: "The excessive thickness of the woods rendered our bayonets of little use, and enabled the broken enemy to make frequent stands, with an irregular fire, which occasioned some loss and to several of the corps

[3] Lee stated that "Campbell's men were part of the conquerors of Ferguson."

[4] Lee, in command of Lee's Legion, selected twenty-five of the riflemen for a certain task, and wrote in that connection: "It was no uncommon amusement among them to put an apple on the point of a ramrod; and, holding the rod in the hand with the arm extended, permit their comrades, known to be experts, to fire at it, when many balls would pass through the apple." *Memoirs*, I, 326n.

great delay, particularly on our right"—the Americans' left.

The militia of North Carolina from east of the mountains and battleground were placed in the center with orders to fire twice and retreat; they fired twice and retreated, but from the battle-field, thus allowing the British to break the American army into two parts; and against Campbell they poured in increasing numbers until his riflemen were driven back to a range of wooded hills. There they began to gain a decided advantage, until Cornwallis in person went to the rescue and Tarleton's cavalry rushed in through the smoke, driving them farther back. The contest with Campbell was so spirited that the British regiment "found men behind trees on all sides of them," and Tarleton's account was that "when he made his charge, he found officers and men of both corps in the possession of the enemy." Colonel Campbell, with his Virginia and North Carolina riflemen, was "the last to fire a gun on this bloody field, and was still firing when Greene sounded the retreat."

Cornwallis, while he held the field and may for that reason be accorded the victory, suffered casualties nearly equal in number to one-third of his army, far above Greene's 320 killed and wounded. The British general remained in the vicinity of the battleground from Thursday until Sunday, when he started a retrograde movement to Wilmington—no longer towards Virginia, his planned destination. At Wilmington he was south of Winnsborough, the point from which he started. In effect, Greene's was the victory. The great Charles J. Fox in the British parliament soon afterward fairly summed it up: "If the British army had been vanquished, they could only have left the field and fled to the coast, precisely the measure Cornwallis was compelled to adopt. . . . Another such victory would destroy the British army!" Pitt regarded the result as "the percursor of ruin to British supremacy in the South." [5]

Campbell's men were not only the last to retire from the field; they were the first to engage, and above any other command bore the brunt of battle. General Greene from his headquarters addressed a letter to Campbell thanking him for his faithful serv-

---

[5] Stedman, the British historian, wrote: "The victory at the expense at which it was obtained rendered it of no utility." Sir Henry Clinton, Lord Cornwallis' superior, was caustic in his comments on Cornwallis' retreating to Wilmington.

ices. "It would be ungenerous not to acknowledge my entire approbation of your entire conduct, and the spirited and manly behavior of the officers and men under you. Sensible of your merit, I feel a pleasure in doing justice to it. Most of the riflemen having gone home, you have my permission to return home to your friends." [6]

The route of the Wataugans, both ways, was doubtless along the line of the federal highway which now runs from Elizabethton through Boone, and it is probable that some of Campbell's sixty from Washington County, Virginia, accompanied them homeward, all conscious of duty done.[7]

It must always be a matter for regret that Greene was deprived of the services of General William L. Davidson in this battle. Just after a consultation between the two as to the conduct of the campaign against Cornwallis, Davidson was killed at Cowan's Ford—"like a summer-dried fountain when need was the sorest." Had he lived, in likelihood, he would have commanded the Watauga and Nolachucky troops, he being brigadier-general of Salisbury District which embraced all of the "back-water men."

---

[6] Lt. Col. Lee also felt impelled to write Campbell: "The bravery of your battalion displayed in the action of the 15th is particularly noticed by the General. It is much to be lamented that a failure took place in the line which lost the day . . . I hope that your men are safe and that the scattered will collect again. Henry Lee, Jr."

Campbell felt that Lee's Legion, in the center, was not blameless for the break in the line there, and was openly resentful. See App. G.

[7] Customarily, the companies of the western militia were, for a campaign, built up by "eights" and it is this writer's estimate that each company under Major Robertson had forty privates and that, officers added, the battalion was at least one hundred and thirty strong.

Materials for this chapter (other than the authorities cited) were drawn, in large part, from: *The Clinton-Cornwallis Controversy*, I; Summers, *History of Southwest Virginia;* the Draper Manuscripts, and Schenck, *North Carolina, 1870–81*, the last named being a close, but not always an impartial, study. He places the Robertson battalion as 100 strong at Guilford Courthouse, and labors unsuccessfully to show that the Eastern North Carolina troops have by other writers been erroneously charged with responsibility for the disastrous break in the battle line.

CHAPTER XXIV

TREATY AND TURMOIL (1781)

A main object sought to be attained by the settlers in the counties of Washington and Sullivan was to keep the old Overhill towns and those of the Chickamaugas from combining against them. Colonel Martin used diplomacy to the utmost to prevent such a coalescence. His influence was by far greater with the older chiefs. He wrote in February, 1781, that Chief Hanging Maw was opposed to war and had threatened to leave the Indians and take up his residence among the whites, and that chief ruled towns which contained four hundred souls. The British agents among the Indians were as alert as Martin, but not as astute. The War of the Revolution was at crisis and the services of Martin as Virginia's agent, while not spectacular, were of utmost value to his State, the Carolinas and the cause of Independence.[1]

As seen, Campbell, Sevier and Martin at the close of their expedition in January, had warned the Overhills to repair to the Long Island of Holston for a treaty if they really wanted peace. General Greene from his "Camp in Caswell County, North Carolina" on February 16, 1781, addressed to William Christian, Wm. Preston, Arthur Campbell and Joseph Martin, of Virginia, and to Robert Sevier,[2] Evan Shelby, Joseph Williams, and John Sevier, of North Carolina, a commission empowering them to treat with the Indians[3] for peace, an exchange of prisoners and an adjustment of boundaries. Any five of the commissioners were au-

---

[1] This is the thesis of Stephen B. Weeks in his General Joseph Martin, *Am. Hist. Asso. Rep, for 1893*, pp. 403–477.

[2] So written at two places in General Greene's commission. Haywood gives Robert Lanier, but Greene wrote the names of both Seviers "Severe" not knowing of the death of the younger of the brothers, Robert. Lanier had been a commissioner in the treaty at Long Island in 1777 and Haywood may have been influenced by that fact. *The North Carolina State Records*, give no hint of Lanier having been named in 1781.

[3] The Chickasaws were also to be brought into the treaty.

thorized to act, though any treaty negotiated was to be subject to the action of the Continental Congress. The commissioners were also instructed to call on the Indians to appoint delegates to go to Congress "for obtaining such enlargements or confirmation of their treaties as may appear to them requisite." [4]

The last clause did not sound assuring to the Westerners, we may be sure. Any "enlargements" they felt should be in their favor. Their lust for land was almost insatiable. Sevier and the Shelbys could not have been enthusiastic over that part of the commission's contents, and less so with another feature: "You are hereby charged to call on the commanding officers of the adjacent counties for force and assistance to prevent any further encroachment of the subjects of the United States on the lands of the tribes, or Nations of Indians."

A treaty meeting was appointed for July 20, 1781, at the Long Island of Holston; [5] but proceedings did not get under way for nearly a week thereafter. The Tassel was the principal spokesman for the Indians. He attributed his peoples' plight to the bad advice of Colonel Brown, the British superintendent at Augusta. Addressing himself to Colonel Sevier, he said: "I know that you are a man and a warrior. I have heard different talks by different people quite different from what I expected. I fear you must have been angry and that it was caused by some evil persons. . . . You have risen up from a warrior to be a Beloved Man. I hope your speech will be good." [6]

Sevier replied that he had never hated the Cherokees, but had fought them for the safety of his people.

At this point there was an occurrence that is without parallel in the history of the West. An Indian woman spoke in treaty negotiations with the whites; no ordinary squaw, but a woman whose status might well be described by a now coined word "chieftainess." Nancy Ward [7] arose, left the group of women and thus addressed the commissioners:

---

[4] Col. Arthur Campbell had suggested the appointment of a commission, but it may be doubted that he was father of the "enlargements" feature.

[5] *Calendar of Virginia State Papers*, II, 199.

[6] From the Gen. Greene Papers in Manuscript Division of the Library of Congress, See also *Calendar of Tennessee Papers*, 15–18. The full proceedings have never been published.

[7] See a full note, *post*.

You know that women are always looked upon as nothing; but we are your mothers; you are our sons. Our cry is all for peace; let it continue. This peace must last forever. Let your women's sons be ours; our sons be yours. Let your women hear our words.

Delivered with something of the grace of her famous uncle, these words reached the hearts of her hearers. They knew that her repeated acts of friendship towards the white people added weight to her appeal. Colonel William Christian was chosen to make answer:

Mothers: We have listened well to your talk; it is humane . . . No man can hear it without being moved by it. Such words and thoughts show the world that human nature is the same everywhere. Our women shall hear your words, and we know how they will feel and think of them. We are all descendants of the same woman. We will not quarrel with you, because you are our mothers. We will not meddle with your people if they will be still and quiet at home and let us live in peace.[8]

Chivalry mounted to a control over cupidity in the hearts and minds of the bordermen. The negotiations were concluded without any demand for a cession of territory on the part of the people of the "Pocahontas of the West."

Another unique expedition was launched in the meanwhile. The leonine Colonel Clarke had won the high regard of the people of the Nolachucky and Watauga; his strong character and soldierly qualities appealed to them. Admiration was mutual. He had begun early to plan to take a force from the western waters to aid his Georgians in their struggles which were growing bitterer instead of ameliorating.

Just after the close of the Sevier-Campbell campaign, Clarke marched southward (probably from Chota) with a "number of our best men"—probably a battalion of 130 men.[9] To all seeming, at their head was Major Jesse Walton,[10] but as to who were

---

[8] Greene Papers.

[9] Ramsey (p. 210) under a wrong date, says Robert Bean, was with Clarke. This indicates that Wm. Bean's company, or a part, was also. Two sons of Matthew Talbott, Thomas and Matthew, Jr., were at the fall of Augusta, the latter being wounded. In later life he became governor of Georgia.

[10] Walton was a near neighbor of Col. Sevier on the Nolachucky; and Clarke making his home with Sevier evidently came in close touch with Walton who had relatives in Georgia. A few years after this expedition Walton removed to the upper part of Wilkes County, Ga., as it then stood,

the captains we, too, can only surmise. Again no muster rolls survive, if kept. Among those so marching must have been some men of Georgia yet sojourning in the western valleys.

Colonel Clarke turned up in time to take part in the later stages of the successful siege of Augusta; yet later in the battles of Long Cane, and at Beattie's Mill where Major James Dunlap was attacked. That leader on being surprised retired into the mill and determined to sell his life dearly. He resisted until finally he and thirty of his officers and men were killed. The prisoners taken were forty-two in number. Draper says that but for the surrender all would have been picked off by the unerring riflemen, and that the prisoners were sent to the Watauga Settlement for safe keeping.[11] Truly, the people of the Watauga and Nolachucky, in their secure stronghold, were a main reliance of the hard-pressed Southerners. At the same time they were entertaining many refugees, but their abundance was thought equal to the care of these prisoners of war. The captives were, doubtless, conducted to the West by the over-mountain soldiers. How long they were kept, no record shows.

There now journeyed to these settlements one of North Carolina's greatest leaders,[12] taking his family to an asylum and leaving them there. This was ex-Governor and now General Richard Caswell. His home was in Eastern North Carolina where in 1781 a state of near-anarchy existed. Bitterness and retaliation prevailed to a degree that in our day staggers belief. Life, for Whig or Tory, was at constant hazard. In May and June the British, operating from Wilmington as base, held the upper hand; and the conditions were such as to lead Caswell, a man of undaunted courage, to seek a temporary retreat for his family. The party journeyed through Southwest Virginia. A troop of horsemen set out on June 6th to escort the group into Abingdon. A team was sent forward to assist them over a piece

the county also of Col. Clarke. For a sketch of Walton, see Williams, "Founder of Tennessee's First Town: Major Jesse Walton," in *E. T. Hist. Soc. Pub.* II, 70–81.

[11] *Heroes of King's Mountain*, 163.

[12] "Caswell's character and his career, more than any other of North Carolina's revolutionary worthies, resembles that of the Father of his Country . . . If Virginia is proud of Washington, North Carolina may justly be proud of her Caswell." Wheeler's *History of North Carolina*, I, 90.

of bad road. The General was invited to be guest of honor at a
dinner at that place; and he, his family, and retainers were urged
to be Colonel Arthur Campbell's guests as they passed "Goodwood." "There are some public matters under consideration
which concern the western frontier of both States; your advice
will be highly acceptable to all." [13]

Caswell and Isaac Shelby were intimate friends and a stop was
made at Sapling Grove. There Caswell depicted "the melancholy
circumstances of North Carolina" and urged Shelby to turn to
her relief.

There can be little doubt that Sevier's home became that, temporarily, of the Caswells.[14] The graciousness and the managerial
skill of the mistress of spacious "Mount Pleasant," Bonnie Kate,
were taxed but not overstrained. It takes no stretch of the im-
magination to see the leaders of the two valleys coming in to
interview Caswell. He was the most noted visitor the region
had ever entertained. High cheer must have marked the inter-
course of the Easterner with the Westerners as they sat viewing
the broad level lands of Sevier which extended in long reaches up
and down the Nolachucky, beneath eminences, on one of which
stood the Sevier home.[15] Ever given to abounding hospitality, it
is no wonder that like Jefferson Sevier died comparatively poor
in worldly goods.

Archibald Henderson in his biography of Isaac Shelby [16] says:
"No account with any pretensions, either to accuracy or consecu-
tiveness, has ever been given of the relation of Shelby, Sevier and
the Western leaders to the cause of the Revolution subsequent to
the battle of King's Mountain. The histories teem with inaccuracies and inexplicable confusions of names and dates."

---

[13] Campbell to Caswell from "Goodwood," June 7, 1781. Tannehill's
Portfolio, I, 219.

[14] The two leaders had been friends from 1776, and after 1781 they remained such, acquiring lands jointly. Caswell in later years contemplated
a removal to the West and members of his family did do so. Consult,
Williams, *Lost State of Franklin, passim.*

[15] Few scenes in the region exceed in beauty the Sevier plantation which
was later owned by Samuel D. Jackson, formerly a Philadelphia merchant,
and is yet in the possession of his heirs, the Fuller brothers of Nashville.

[16] Henderson gave much and valuable research in bringing order out of
the chaos he describes, but even he overlooked some noteworthy materials which support his statements and conclusions.

In writing to General Greene on November 3rd, General Daniel Morgan said:

I have been speaking to him [Shelby] to raise about three hundred good riflemen this winter for the campaign, and join me in the spring. He says he would willingly undertake it, provided he had a sanction for it. How far the Assembly of North Carolina would be disposed to counsel such a thing I don't know, but I assure you that a number of such men would be a valuable Corps when annexed to the Light Infantry, which must be made equal if not superior to Tarleton's Legion before this country can be defended. If you think proper to countenance a matter of this kind, you'll be kind enough to signify your approbation to Colo. Shelby and point out the mode.

On December 30, 1780, South Carolina's Governor John Rutledge in writing from the Pee Dee, looked longingly for a return of the backwater men; but also noted "the fact that the Cherokees have lately killed some people on the frontiers of North Carolina which will prevent them from turning out in the remote country." As early as November he had tried to persuade "Colonel Cleveland and other mountain men to assist us for a short time." [18]

On February 23, 1781, the general assembly of North Carolina took this action in respect of the services of Shelby and Sevier: "Feeling impressed with the very generous and patriotic services rendered by the Inhabitants of said Counties [Washington and Sullivan] to which their influence had in great degree contributed, we earnestly urge that they would press a continuance of the same active exertion; that the State of the Country is such as to call forth the utmost powers immediately in order to preserve its freedom and Independence." The resolution ended with a like appeal to Southwest Virginians.[18]

---

[18] Letters of John Rutledge in *South Carolina Historical and Genelogical Magazine*, XVII, 131 *et seq.*

[18] *Civil and Political History of Tennessee*, (2nd. ed.) 114, and *Ramsey's Annals*, 251.

CHAPTER XXV

Sevier's Indian Campaigning—1782

As was not unexpected, when preparations of the troops of Sevier and Shelby were on foot, news of it leaked by subterranean channels to the British agents among the Chickamaugas near the site of present Chattanooga. Tories at heart were yet to be found, though comparatively few in number, on the Nolachucky ready to earn favors or financial rewards for their espionage. To aid John McDonald in managing the Indians, Colonel Thomas Brown, superintendent for the British in the South, sent up a deputy by the name of Scott who resided a short distance below the site of Chattanooga. John Watts, a half-breed chief under the influence of Dragging Canoe, spent a good part of his time among the Overhills on the Little Tennessee in order to report any news of import to the Chickamaugas and to combat the efforts of the older chiefs for peace with the whites.

In the spring of 1782, a committee of the North Carolina legislature, headed by Willie Jones, reported that there was "little or no probability of peace during the ensuing summer. The Indians under Dragging Canoe and the other chiefs averse to peace are pushing the war and almost daily perpetrating acts of cruelty and murder." The committee recommended that independent military companies be raised immediately, four in Washington District, and "employed in building and garrisoning forts and scouting and on ranging service and other public service that shall most conduce to the safety of the inhabitants."[1] This

---

[1] *N. C. St. Recs.*, XIX, 897. The committee also recommended it to be expedient to place 500 pounds of gunpowder, 1000 pounds of lead and a quantity of salt at Carter's, west of the mountains. It was the intention that Col. Isaac Shelby should go on the campaign, and as the senior officer be the commander. In September (no day given) Gov. Alexander Martin wrote to McDowell that a place should be named for a rendezvous of all forces, "five hundred volunteer horsemen." Instructions were given to destroy "the Chickammoggy Town, with such Indian Males as you shall find therein. You will preserve all female prisoners and children, for

squinted at offensive action by the troops.

From his home near Long Island of Holston, Colonel Martin was not uninformed of the danger that was brewing.[2] Writing to Colonel Arthur Campbell, September 20th, he disclosed:

Scott, the present English agent, is very industrious in stirring up the Indians to war. Oconostota insisted hard on my going to attack him; he promised all the assistance I would ask; he told me I could march on horseback from Chota to where he resided in two days without being discovered. Scott keeps a few armed white men around and the Indians who live with him are chiefly employed in stealing horses on the frontier.[3]

Martin declared that with fifty well equipped men, aided by a detachment of Overhill warriors, the Chickamaugas could be put down. After the return of Shelby from South Carolina, Martin had written to him making much the same suggestion, adding, "I should think myself happy to be one of the number" to march against Scott and the Tories who surrounded him. Scott's strength was in his control of supplies from Augusta, much needed by the Indians. Campbell thought to parry by having Martin conduct two of the principal chiefs of the Overhills to Washington's headquarters, "that they might see with their own eyes the

whom you will negotiate exchanges for our prisoners in Captivity with their people." Thomas Amis, as superintendent commissary for Washington and Sullivan Counties, was to have charge of supplying the troops. Of Shelby's part, Draper said, somewhat obscurely: "Shelby was engaged during the spring [really late summer] in preparing for an expedition against the Chickamauga band of Cherokees, . . . in which enterprise he was to have been joined by two hundred men from Washington County, Virginia; but on account of the poverty of that State the authorities discouraged the scheme; and, reaching Big Creek, thirty miles below Long Island of Holston, the expedition was relinquished." Consult *Heroes of King's Mountain* and *N. C. St. Recs.*, XVI, 696–98. Did Shelby discover when he reached Big Creek that there was a hang-over of the bitterness engendered between the Washington and the Sullivan troops in the campaign of 1781? Was the attitude of the Virginia government influenced by Martin, yet motivated in part by that bitterness, and by the fact that Shelby and not he was to lead the Sullivan troops? Certain it is, the greatest State in the South was not so poor as to be unable to support its part of such an expedition.

[2] Oct. 26th, Col. Arthur Campbell wrote Gen. Washington that "intrigues by Tory emissaries had created a defection." Washington kept an eye on the people of the border.

[3] Draper Manuscripts, quoted in Weeks, *General Martin*, 433.

power of America and hear from your [his] own mouth the fate of their nation." Martin also was solicitous that this be done, as some of the Overhill towns were friendly [4] and their young warriors might no longer continue to desert to the Chickamaugas, if supplies of necessities could be assured their people.

No persuasion could avail with the outbreaking Chickamaugas; and, soon after his return from the South Carolina campaign, Sevier had his cloth cut out for sewing.[5] He appointed a rendezvous at the Big Island of the French Broad, where 250 men assembled, and from there they rode southward on September 20, 1782. On reaching Chota John Watts (later a noted chief) [6] offered his service as guide, intending to steer the detachment away from the principal Chickamauga towns. His offer was accepted. Chief Hanging Maw (Squallacutta) gave assurance of the friendly attitude of the towns of Tellico and Hiwassee, and they were spared. Passing southwestward along Chestuee Creek, Sevier proceeded to the Chickamauga [7] where several

[4] March 22, 1782, deputies of the Cherokees, proper, were at Kaskaskia in the Illinois country, appearing before Timothe Demunbreun, temporary commander there, to beseech that peace be maintained with the whites, and to solicit the good offices of the commandant to that end. They were given presents and returned home. Demunbreun was serving in lieu of Col. John Todd, and no doubt personally knew some of the delegates. Mason, *Some Chapters in Illinois History*, 274.

[5] Gov. Martin had appointed and instructed Col. Charles McDowell, of Burke County, to lead the expedition, but he failed to do so. As matters shaped, Sevier was left to lead and see the campaign through at the head of the troops from his own county.

[6] Kunoskeskie, son of John Watts, Sr. The father had been among the Overhill Cherokees from a date considerably before 1763 (perhaps of the Fort Loudoun garrison, 1758–1761), since he had become familiar enough with the Indians' language to be able to act as interpreter at the treaty of Augusta, in 1763. The younger Watts was also a nephew of Chief The Tassel, and a cousin of the great Sequoyah.

[7] Scene of the battle in 1779. While camping at Bull Town, at the junction of Chickamauga Creek and Tennessee River, a white girl, Jane Iredell, who had been captured by the Indians on a raid into what is now Johnson County, Tennessee, was brought to Col. Sevier who doubtless saw to her being returned to her family. Other incidents, drawn from the Draper Manuscripts, may be found in Brown's *Old Frontiers*, 199–200. See, also, Armstrong, *History of Hamilton County*, I, 519. Patrick Clements, a Tory ex-sergeant, was captured on the Coosa, where he was living with a half-breed sister of Archy Coody. In an effort to escape, Thomas shot him down.

towns were destroyed; then the volunteers crossed the river and had a skirmish with the Indians. The fighting was hot but lasted only a short while, ending in a defeat of the Chickamaugas —the first battle fought on Lookout Mountain. The white force moved to Coosa River in Georgia, the towns on which were destroyed, Spring Fog Town, Ustinaula, Ellijay, and Coosawatie. The inhabitants, as usual, fled before the invaders.

Then Sevier turned back to Chota where a friendly conference was held with Oconostota, The Tassel and Hanging Maw. On the campaign were Majors Valentine Sevier and James Hubbard; Captains Wm. Bean, Samuel Wear, Alexander Moore, George Russell, Neely [Cornelius] McGuire and William Smith. James Sevier, the Colonel's son was on the campaign, as were, also, Bean's sons: William, Robert, John, Jesse, and Edmund—the Beans were always to the front when an expedition was on foot. Isaac Thomas was along. Sevier and his men reached home early in November. A beneficial effect of the campaign was the lifting of the pressure, temporarily, on the Cumberland settlements. But in the long run it operated to their detriment. The Chickamaugas had been taught to fear the soldiery of Washington and Sullivan, and turned upon the Cumberlanders as weaker foes. This was the last campaign of the War of the Revolution in the West, incited too, as had been the earlier ones, by British agents among the Indians.

Sevier received what he deserved, the seal of official approval of his initiative. Governor Martin, in writing later to the State's delegates in the Continental Congress, said that Sevier had been given specific instructions to join General McDowell in what was a necessary campaign, and: "The expenses of this campaign, as you so justly observe, hath equal claim to Continental Credit as others of a similar nature." [8] If McDowell failed to turn his steps towards the West, bring with him troops as ordered and take command of the expedition, Sevier did not hesitate. He, as with a flaming sword, pointed the way to his soldiers in an effort to bring to an end the travail of his countrymen.

The white settlements progressed down the East Tennessee Valley. Official pressure was brought by the British to induce the Overhill Cherokees to move south. Towards the end of 1782, Colonel Brown reporting to London said: "As the towns of the

[8] N. C. St. Recs., XXVI, 449.

Cherokees are too much exposed to the incursions of the rebels from the frontiers of Virginia and Carolina, I have prevailed on the headmen of the Cherokees to move their towns this winter to that part of the country between the heads of the Coosa, Chatahauchie, and the Tanassie River where it empties itself into the Ohio, that, in case rebels presume to disturb them, they may be in a capacity of intercepting the rebel and Spanish boats navigating the Mississippi and Ohio." [9]   The Cherokees were to be made subservient to Britain's policy in holding the lower Mississippi Valley, if possible.

Disintegration and decay of the once powerful Cherokee nation had kept pace with the feebleness from age or from the death of their great chiefs. Attakullakulla (Little Carpenter) their greatest leader had recently passed to rest with his fathers.[10]   His diplomacy had been their main reliance in dealing with American officials.[11]   Now their war-lord, Oconostota, was ripening for the sickle of the grim reaper, and more and more coming to Attakullakulla's views and policies.   In July, 1782, planning for his demise he resigned as war-lord in favor of his son, Tuckasee (Terrapin) and begged Martin to use his influence to obtain recognition of his son, as successor, by the government.[12]   Oconostota managed to make the trip, by canoe up stream perhaps, to Martin's home near Long Island, in the fall of 1782. He spent the winter there. Martin's son, William, many years later wrote Draper his reminiscences of the stay. With the coming of spring, the great warrior felt his strength to be ebbing, and his wish was to die in the beloved town of all the Overhill Cherokees. "He was very lean, stooped and emaciated."   Martin accompanied him home by canoe, and remained with him till death came as a release. "My brother," he said to Martin, "I want to be buried and I want my body to face the Long Knife." [13]   The wish was

[9] Jan. 12, 1783, in *Report on American Manuscripts in the Royal Institution*, III, 325.

[10] Probably in 1780, at an age above ninety years.   (Felix Walker).

[11] His niece, Nancy Ward, tried to carry on in his tradition.   His uncle was Old Hop (Connecorte).

[12] This display of nepotism was in sharp contrast with the action of Old Hop in like circumstances. Williams, *Dawn*, 189. For the resignation of Oconostota, see *Southern Historical Association Publications*, VIII, 448—Martin to Arthur Campbell.

[13] Our Westerners were so called by the Indians, the name being given because of the long knives carried by the frontiersmen.

granted; the body was placed in a canoe and interred after the manner of Christians.[14]

The son of Oconostota had to give way to the able Tassel, and figured inconspicuously in later years.

A majority of the Cherokees moved south. However, a considerable remnant clung to their old towns on the Little Tennessee, but they were the less virile. There they underwent stagnation and decay—objects of contempt by the nearby whites and objects of near-pity by their fellows who moved down-country.

The Chickamaugas were far from being conquered. Their strategy now, doubtless dictated by Dragging Canoe, was not to rebuild the few towns the second time destroyed on Chickamauga Creek, but to fall back and consolidate all his tribesmen in what were called their Five Lower Towns: Running Water and Nickajack, towns in the Tennessee country; Crow and Long Island towns in the Alabama region and Lookout Mountain town in Georgia. There they had a wellnigh impregnable stronghold as against the riflemen coming from Washington and Sullivan Counties to attack. On the river below the Suck (Whirl or Boiling Pot) where the Tennessee flows through the gorge in the Cumberland Mountains so narrow that the water rushes rapidly and strikes the cliffs, a swirl or vortex being made. Navigation was dangerous; and the stream left little room for a path along the river. Nature had made the spot one for defense by way of

---

[14] Wm. Martin, son of the General, in his voluminous correspondence with Draper, left an account of the personal appearance of the two greatest of Cherokee chiefs; as did also other pioneers named below. From these sources composite pen-portraits may be drawn: Attakullakulla (Little Carpenter) was small of stature, slender and even of delicate frame, "so light habited that I scarcely believe that he would have exceeded in weight more than a pound to each year of his life," estimated to be nearly ninety years at the time. He was a fluent orator, and "the Solon of his day." In personal appearance, Oconostota was in marked contrast. "He had a powerful frame, and in his prime must have weighed over two hundred pounds, having a head of enormous size." His countenance was heavy and to some forbidding. His face was pock-marked. In mental makeup, the two chiefs differed. Oconostota's mind was slow, in comparison; he had no powers of oratory, and avoided speaking in public when he could do so. He put forward as spokesmen for the tribe, Attakullakulla, and later The Tassel. (Wm. Tatham, Felix Walker, Pleasant Henderson, Thomas Love and Wm. Martin). No other Southern tribe had as able a pair of leaders, serving as contemporaries.

ambuscades. Too, their five towns were located near the Creek path which crossed the Tennessee near the Long Island (at Bridgeport, Alabama). This made easy co-operation with the powerful Creek nation in warring against the white people of the Cumberland and other settlements. In consequence, the more lawless and refractory Creeks, as well as Overhill Cherokees, in increasing numbers joined the Chickamauga tribe raising it to about one thousand warriors, and making it powerful and dangerous. Any suggestion that this augmenting tribe would suffer absorption or incorporation into the decadent Overhill Cherokee remnant was now at an end.

The followers of the surly and indomnitable Dragging Canoe were soon to demonstrate their inveteracy by forays up Clinch River, killing three whites and causing widespread dismay; [15] and, in the early spring, ravagings were repeated.[16]

Just before this expedition was begun and while it was in progress, Colonel Martin was among the Overhills using his influence in keeping them consolidated for peace, and arranging the preliminaries of a treaty.[16] To Martin the Old Tassel gave a pathetic talk for delivery to the governor of North Carolina:

Brother: I am now going to speak to you. I hope you will listen to me. A string. I intended to come this fall to see you, but there was such confusion in our country, I thought it best for me to stay at home and send my Talks by our friend Colonel Martin, who promised to deliver them safe to you. We are a poor, distressed people, that is in great trouble, and we hope our elder brother will take pity on us and do us justice. Your people from Nolachucky are daily pushing us out of our lands. We have no place to hunt on. Your people have built houses in one day's walk of our towns. We don't want to quarrel with our elder brother; we, therefore, hope our elder brother will not take our lands from us, that the Great Man above gave us. He made you and he made us; we are all children, and we hope our elder brother will take pity on us, and not take our lands from us,

---

[15] *Cal. Va. St. Papers*, III, 424.

By Dragging Canoe, for whose earlier career, see Williams, *Dawn*, 407, 410, 426. He died in March, 1792, though his death had been often rumored prior to that year; and the rumors were gladly believed to be true by the whites of the border.

[16] Elsewhere shown never to have been held. Any stiffening of the Indian policy of North Carolina is believed to have been due to Caswell who while visiting in the West had learned much from the Shelbys, Sevier and other leaders as to the true conditions.

because he is stronger than we are. We are the first people that ever lived on this land; it is ours, and why will our elder brother take it from us? It is true, some time past, the people over the great water persuaded some of our young men to do some mischief to our elder brother, which our principal men were sorry for. But you our elder brothers come to our towns and took satisfaction, and then sent for us to come and treat with you, which we did. Then our elder brother promised to have a line run between us agreeable to the first treaty, and all that should be found over the line should be moved off. But it is not done yet. We have done nothing to offend our elder brother since the last treaty, and why should our elder brother want to quarrel with us? We have sent to the Governor of Virginia a talk on the same subject. We hope that, between you both, you will take pity on your younger brother, and send Col. Sevier, who is a good man, to have all your people moved off our land. I should say a great deal more, but our friend, Colonel Martin, knows all our grievances, and he can inform you. A string.[17]

---

[17] As edited by Roosevelt. In his *Winning of the West,* II, 317–18, Roosevelt again tripped and stumbled when he referred to the engagement near the base of Lookout Mountain as "mythical" and "pure invention." He had made inadequate research and should have hesitated before speaking so baldly. Besides printed sources, we here quote from the pension statement of Abram Sevier, a brother of Colonel Sevier: "In 1782, I was four months in Captains George North's and James Richardson's companies, under Colonel John Sevier, . . . and in the engagement on Lookout Mountain."

CHAPTER XXVI

LAND BOUNTIES TO SOLDIERS

The State of North Carolina, having a depleted treasury and being hard pressed by the Continental Congress to cede to the national government her Trans-Alleghany lands, as preliminary to such a cession, in her general assembly took under consideration the rewarding of the officers and soldiers of her Continental Line—not her militia—for their patriotic services in the Revolutionary War.

Colonel (later General) Wm. Russell, of Southwest Virginia, thought that the people of his own State and of North Carolina should move on parallel lines in reserving western lands for soldiers of the line, and exert influence on their respective legislative bodies accordingly. In a letter of April 9, 1782, to General Sumner of North Carolina he urged that, as a preliminary, there should be ascertained the true location of the state line in the western country before reservations were defined. As a necessity for prompt action: "particularly it will prevent lawless intrusions, which, from the nature of things at present, the officers and soldiers of Virginia and North Carolina have too great reason to expect." [1] In short, the land-grabbing squatter and preemptor must be watched.

By the act of 1782, the Carolina general assembly made provision for those then "in service and shall continue in service to the end of the war" (with provision also for those disabled by infirmities). A military reservation was established in the West,[2] in which there was awardable to each private 640 acres of land; to each non-commissioned officer 1,000 acres; to each subaltern 2,560 acres; to each captain 3,840 acres; to each major 4,800; to a lieutenant-colonel 7,200 acres; to a brigadier-general 12,000 acres; to a chaplain 7,200 acres, etc.

Under a previous act (1780) a military reservation for the con-

---

[1] *N. C. St. Recs.*, XVI, 587.
[2] *Ib.*, XXIV, 420.

tinentals had been indicated: one along the Virginia line between the Holston and the Tennessee Rivers, as far up as the mouth of the French Broad River, thence by a direct course to the mouth of Powell's River, thence to Cumberland Gap, thence to the beginning. No machinery was then set up for carrying the act into effect; and the later act of 1782 superseded it.

Absolom Tatum, Isaac Shelby, and Anthony Bledsoe were appointed commissioners to survey and mark the boundaries of the reservation. Each commissioner was to receive 5,000 acres for his services.[3]

The reservation finally created was farther to the west and had the following boundaries: Beginning on the Virginia line where Cumberland River intersects the same, thence south fifty miles, thence west to the Tennessee River, thence down the Tennessee to the Virginia line, thence with that line to the beginning. It was provided that soldiers of the line, who had rights of preemption by reason of settlements made prior the summer of 1780, should have priority to grants thereto for a period of three years. Colonel Martin Armstrong of North Carolina was appointed surveyor to locate the claims of the individual soldiers. Too, there now appeared the first member of the noted Polk family in the West. Colonel Wm. Polk was appointed by the legislature in 1783 as surveyor-general for the region now known as part of Middle Tennessee. He arrived in December, 1783, and fixed his office "at the French Lick Fort, the site on which Nashville stands. Here he remained until 1786 during which time he was twice elected a member of the House of Commons of North Carolina from Davidson County."[4] The Colonel came with a batch of soldiers' land warrants, some of friends, and others which he had acquired in George Washington fashion. He accompanied the surveyors who ran the south line of the reservation with a view to choosing good lands for himself and his father, General Thomas Polk. Coming with or soon following the Colonel into the Tennessee country was Ezekiel Polk, grandfather of President Polk, who also followed the survey.[5] The surveyors began at

---

[3] Provisions were also made in lands to surveyors, chain-carriers, hunters and guards. Elijah Robertson acted as chief of the commissary.

[4] Polk's "Autobiography," in Hoyt, *Murphey Papers*, II, 408.

[5] With them was Henry Rutherford, a surveyor, son of Gen. Rutherford. Wm. and Ezekiel Polk and Rutherford each kept a journal of the streams

Mount Pisgah (Murray County) near the middle of the south line. Dividing there, one party went east and the other west, marking a tree at the end of every mile. "The creeks crossed were generally named in honor of the oldest man in the party"— one after another in the order of their ages.

The official survey was made in February, 1784, though an earlier experimental survey had been made for the commissioners by Daniel Smith.[6] That month was chosen because the forest foliage had not come out to obstruct the work of the surveyors.

By the same act the legislature directed that a grant for 25,000 acres of land be issued to General Nathanael Greene, "as a mark of the high sense of his extraordinary services in the War of the Revolution." This was a graceful action, though the lands were laid off on Duck River, in the present county of Maury, where the Indian title (Cherokee or Chickasaw) had not been removed.[7] The grant was the first one recorded in the registry of Greene County,[8] in the bounds of which it was laid.

The opening of the military reservation, along with the establishment in the same year of the land-office of John Armstrong for the issuance of land grants to non-soldier settlers and purchasers, caused a pronounced emigration into the middle portion of the Tennessee country. A large portion came to the reservation from

---

crossed in running the line. *Boyd v. Trimble,* Cooke's Tenn. Reports, 281. Others along were Ephraim McClain, John Hardin, and John Hibbett whose name appears in that of the late Judge John Hibbett DeWitt, the historian. A long list of the men of Cumberland who were along on the two surveys is given by Spence, *History of Hickman County,* 22–24.

[6] Smith's survey was made in 1783. Gen. Griffith Rutherford supervised that made in 1784. Rutherford's was adjudged to be the true line. *Polk's Lessee v. Gentry,* I Overton, 270. The eastern line was not run and marked until 1807 and then by Wm. Christmas, surveyor of the first district of Tennessee. Seemingly it was thought that the Cumberland range rendered an earlier marking unessential.

[7] It seems that the defect pointed out—land lying in a region not cleared of the Indian title—was cured by a reissue Nov. 28th, 1807, after the treaty of 1805 by which the Indian claim was removed. The Greene tract was entirely west of the road between Columbia and Mt. Pleasant. The heirs of General Greene sold off the land in tracts. A grant of Gen. Rutherford conflicted with the Greene grant but the latter prevailed in a suit which went to the U. S. Supreme Court. Rutherford's grant was "removed" and laid elsewhere, in consequence.

[8] Greene County registry.

North Carolina, many of them ex-soldiers of the line, but more who were not. Such others purchased land warrants from men of the line who were unable or indisposed to make the long and difficult trek into the new country. Some of North Carolina's strong men came out then, or a little later, to settle on lands granted to them. The most notable of them was General Griffith Rutherford. Also came families from which derived President Polk, Thomas Hart Benton, ("Old Bullion"), John Bell, John Catron, Matthew F. Maury, and General Nathan Bedford Forrest, to mention only a few.

There appeared, too, on the Cumberland in 1782–3, a rather remarkable group from Natchez, where they had joined General Phineas Lyman in the English rebellion against Spain, which power held that place. When that movement failed, they had to flee. Some of them had been Regulators in North Carolina, others "akin to the Regulators," and had friends in the Cumberland settlements. Among the number were: Philip Alston, John Turnbull, Thomas W. Alston, James Cole, Philip Mulkey,[9] Thomas Hines.[10]

A number of these "refugees" returned south after the peace of 1783, and there went with them others whom the Cumberland settlements could ill afford to lose: Turpins, Freelands, Shaws and Greens.[11]

---

[9] Father of Jonathan Mulkey, the first Baptist preacher in the Tennessee country. The remarkable career of the father in the Southern Colonies and in the Mississippi and Tennessee countries may be traced in Paschal, *North Carolina Baptists*, and Benedict, *History of the Baptists*.

[10] Hines returned to Mississippi, where he, or his son, became a general and served as such (commanding the light-horse) in the battle of New Orleans, 1815.

[11] Green figured in the marriage of Andrew Jackson to Rachel Donelson Robards at Natchez, Rachel then being a visitor in the Green home.

CHAPTER XXVII

The Closing Scenes of War in the East

After the battle of Guilford Courthouse General Greene turned his attention to Georgia and South Carolina and the reduction of British forts there.[1]

Following the fall of Augusta, in Georgia, on June 25th, 1781, only one British fort remained to be taken in Upper South Carolina, at Ninety-Six, which the Americans had failed to take in an attempt on June 18th–19th, as was explained in an appeal for aid then made by Greene in a letter of June 22nd to Shelby:

We have been on the eve of reducing all the enemies' interior posts in South Carolina and Georgia. Ninety-six was the last and four days more would have completed its reduction, when, unfortunately, we were compelled to raise the siege, the enemy having been reinforced at Charlestown. Lord Rawdon marched out in force and is now in our neighborhood. To secure the advantages of our past success it is necessary we should drive the enemy into the lower country. To enable us to effect this I beg you to march to our assistance a thousand good riflemen, well armed and equipped fit for action. If you can join us in a few days with such a force you will render an important service to the public in general, to the State of South Carolina in particular, and lay me under very particular obligations. I feel myself deeply interested in this application.[2]

Shelby had written Greene, explaining the situation on the border west of the mountains.

At the time of the receipt of Greene's appeal, treaty negotiations with the Indians were in progress at the Long Island, Shelby being in attendance. Shelby went to Sevier's county for an interview. From there he wrote the following:

Camp on Wattauga, Washington County,
North Carolina 3d August 1781.

Hond. Sir: In answer to your request of the 22nd June last I wrote you by the Express, that I should march by the 15th July

[1] See Chapter, *ante.*
[2] Henderson's *Isaac Shelby,* 44.

with what force cou'd be raised in this quarter, but the Cherokee Treaty not being over found it impracticable to draw any force from here untill that important Business (to this frontier) was finally ratified, which was done the 29th July, and immediately every step taken to reinforce you; about 700 good riflemen well mounted were now in motion toward you & should have been down in as short a time as possible but an Express arrived in camp last night from General Pickens that informed us of the enemys retreat to Orangeburg and perhaps to Charles Town; that distance being so very great for us, the warm season of the year & the men not prepared for so long a Tower, had induced Colonel Sevier of this county and myself from proceeding on our march, until we hear further accounts from that quarter tho the men are ordered to hold themselves in readiness to march on the shortest notice, and as our country is now in a state of peace and tranquility, have no doubt we can furnish you with a large proportion of good men from here whenever you may find necessary to require us.[3]

The distressed Greene expected and eagerly awaited succor from the two western counties, and throughout July he was heard to exclaim, "What can detain Shelby and Sevier?"[4]

Writing to Lighthorse Harry Lee from Camden, August 25th, Greene said: "Colonel Shelby, I believe, has gone back, if he ever set out which I much doubt. . . . Not more than one half of the Militia from North Carolina are arrived. . . . You know that I never despair nor shrink at difficulties, but our prospects are not flattering."

It cannot be disguised that the Westerners, particularly those on the southern fringe of settlement, yet felt a degree of umbrage toward General Greene because of his attitude toward "encroachment on the lands of the Indians." The General had been reared a Quaker. There was nothing of Quakerism in the make-up of the men of the border. They believed that, when they opposed the Indians, they were fighting allies of the British (and who moved as) incited by British agents; and that conquest of such an enemy earned them a reward in lands they conquered; such should be held as where whites subdued whites. To distinguish in favor of red "savages" was beyond them. Sevier had to contend against this attitude of some of his followers.

General Greene was compelled to rely upon reinforcements

[3] *Ib.*
[4] Johnson's *Greene*, II, 210.

from the over-mountain riflemen. After his victory at Eutaw Springs, on September 8th, he wrote again to Shelby in the "back parts of North Carolina:"

> Head Quarters,
> High Hills of Santee
> Sept. 16, 1781.
>
> Dear Sir:
> I have the pleasure to inform you that we had an action with the British Army on the 8th in which we were victorious. We took 500 prisoners in and killed and wounded a much greater number. We also took nearly 1000 stand of arms, and have driven the enemy near the gates of Charleston. I have also the pleasure to inform you that a large French fleet of nearly thirty sail of the line, has arrived in the Chessepeak bay, with a considerable number of land forces; all of which are to be employed against Lord Cornwallis, who it is suspected will endeavor to make good his retreat through North Carolina to Charleston. To prevent which I beg you to bring out as many riflemen as you can, and as soon as possible. You will march them to Charlotte, and inform me the moment you set out, and of your arrival.
> If we can intercept his lordship it will put a finishing stroke to the war in the Southern states.
> Should I get any intelligence which may change the face of matters I will advise you. I am with esteem and regard, your most obedient and humble servant.[5]

Promptly on the receipt of this letter, Shelby again consulted with Sevier. In enlisting volunteers, the two Colonels gave the men the assurance that they should be absent not above sixty days. In his *Autobiography*, Shelby outlined what followed:

> I made great exertions, and collected the men in a few days thereafter, many of them had not received more than 24 hours notice and lived more than 100 miles from the place of rendevous —but were willing to go as the call was made for a special purpose—to wit, to intercept Lord Cornwallis who it was suspected would endeavor to make good his retreat through N. Carolina to Charleston and Gen. Greene thought and so did I that if we could intercept him, it would put an end to the war in the S. states. To effect this important object, the people on the western waters were induced to volunteer their services—it was for this purpose that they were prevailed upon to leave their homes 500 miles from the scene of operations to defend a Maritime district of country surrounded with a dense population and in comparative quiet, while their own fire-sides were daily menaced by the

---

[5] Henderson, *ib.*, 46.

Chickamauga Indians, who as you know had declared perpetual war against the whites and could never be induced to make peace. I was far advanced on my road when I received vague information of the surrender of Cornwallis in Virginia and hesitated whether to proceed. But as the men appeared to be willing to serve out a tour of duty which at the time of entering the service I repeatedly assured them should not exceed 60 days absence from their homes, I proceeded on more leisurely to Green, who observed to me that such a body of horse could not remain in the vicinity of his camp on account of the scarcity of forage and requested me to serve out the tour with Marion, to which I consented, however, with some reluctance as the men would be drawn 70 or 80 miles further from their homes.

The rumor of the surrender of Lord Cornwallis at Yorktown in Virginia was heard as the two commands passed through North Carolina.

Shelby had about four hundred mounted riflemen and Sevier, for reasons above stated, only two hundred. On their incorporation under Marion it was with the admonition that, if he would keep them he must keep them busy—truly a wise and fitting observation.[6]

Since the war was continued in the Far South after the surrender at Yorktown, the services of the over-mountain men in South Carolina deserve a fairly detailed account. Isaac Shelby left such an one in his *Autobiography,* and it follows, with slight changes in the spelling of proper names:

The enemies main Southern army, it was said, lay at that time near a place called Fergusson's Swamp on the great road bearing directly to Charleston. General Marion received information several weaks after our arrival at his camp that several hundred Hessians, at a British Post near Monk's Corner, eight or ten miles below the enemies main army, were in a state of mutiny, and would surrender to any considerable American force that might appear before it; and consulted his principal officers on the propriety of surprising it, which was soon determined on and Shelby and Sevier solicited a command in it. Marion accordingly moved down eight or ten miles, and crossed over to the South side of the Santee River, from whence he made a detachment of five or six hundred men to surprise the post, the command of which was given to Colonel Mayham. The detachment consisted of Shelby's mounted riflemen with Mayham's Dragoons, about one

---

[6] This assignment to serve under "The Swamp Fox," Marion, was not to Shelby's liking. Late in life in conversation with his son-in-law, Chas. S. Todd, he explained why.

hundred and eighty, and about twenty or thirty lowland mounted militia, the command of the whole was given to Colonel Mayham. They took up their march early in the morning, and traveled fast through the woods until late in the evening of the second day, when they struck the great road leading to Charleston, about two miles below the enemies post, which they intended to surprise. They lay upon their arms all night across the road with a design to intercept the Hessians in case the enemy had got notice of our approach and had ordered them down to Charleston before morning. In the course of the night which was dark as pitch an orderly Sergeant rode into the line amongst us, and was taken prisoner. No material papers were found upon him before he made his escape except a pocket book which contained the strength of the enemy's main army and their number then on the sick list, which was very great.

As soon as daylight appeared, we advanced to the British Post, and arrived there before sunrise. Colonel Mayham sent in one of his confidential officers with peremptory demand for a surrender of the garrison, who in a few minutes returned and reported that the officer commanding was determined to defend the post to the last extremity. Col. Shelby then proposed that he would go in himself and make another effort to obtain a surrender, which Mayham readily consented to. Upon his approach he discovered a gap in the Abbaties, through which he rode up close to the building, when an officer opened one leaf of a long folding door. Col. Shelby addressed him in these words: "Will you be so mad as to suffer us to storm your works; if you do, rest assured that every soul of you will be put to the sword, for there was several hundred men at hand that would soon be in with their tomahawks upon them"; he then inquired if they had any artillery. Shelby replied, "that they had guns that would blow them to pieces in a minute." Upon which the officer replied, "I suppose I must give up." Mayham seeing the door thrown wide open, and Shelby ascending the high steps to the door, immediately advanced with his dragoons and formed on the right. It was not until this moment we discovered another strong British Fort that stood five or six hundred yards to the East, and this is the first knowledge we had of that post, the garrison of which immediately marched out, about one hundred infantry and forty or fifty cavalry came around the North Angle of the fort all apparently with a design to attack us; they however soon halted as we stood firm and prepared to meet them. We took a hundred and fifty prisoners, all of them able to have fought from the windows of the house, or from behind Abbaties. Ninety of them were able to stand a march to Marion's camp that day which was near sixty miles; and we paroled the remainder most of whom appeared to have been sick and unable to stand so hard a march. Information soon reached Marion's camp that the Post had been burnt down immediately on our leaving it; but it was always the opinion of Col. Shelby that the enemy had abandoned it, and burnt it themselves, for Mayham and Shelby were the two last men that left the place, and at that time there was not the least sign of fire or smoke about it. This it is most probable they would do, as they had previously destroyed and burned down almost every building in that part of the country. This post was an immense brick building, calculated to hold a thousand men, and said to have been built by Sir John Colleton a century before that period as well for defense as comfort; and was well enclosed by a strong abbaties. In it were found, besides the prisoners, three or four hundred stand of arms, and as many new blankets. The American detachment left this post between nine and ten o'clock of the same day, and arrived at Marion's camp the night following at three o'clock. Gen. Stewart who commanded the Enemy's main army, eight or ten miles above, made great efforts to intercept us on our return. And it was announced to Marion about sunrise next morning that the whole British army was in the old field about three miles off at the outer end of the causeway that led into his camp. Shelby was immediately ordered out with the mountain men to meet him at the edge of the swamp, to attack the enemy if he attempted to advance, and retreat at his own discretion, to where Marion would have his whole force drawn up to sustain him at an old field. Shortly after his arrival at the edge of the open plain, he observed two British officers ride up to a house equidistant between the lines; after they retired he rode to the house to know what inquiries they had made; a man told him that they had asked him when the Americans detachment had got in, what was their force, and of what troops it was composed; he replied that the detachment had come in just before day, that he had supposed as they went out they were six or eight hundred strong, and were composed chiefly of Shelby's and Sevier's mounted men, with Mayham's mounted Dragoons. The enemy, then being in the edge of the woods, slightly withdrawn out of sight, retreated back in the utmost disorder and confusion A small party, sent out to reconnoiter the enemy, reported that many of them had thrown away their napsacks, guns and canteens. A few days afterwards Gen'l Marion received intelligence that the British commander had retreated with his whole force to Charleston. Marion's sole design in moving from the camp when the mountain men first joined him, and crossing the Santee River below, was to get within striking distance of the before mentioned post, to make [safe] the said detachment, and be able to protect and support them on their retreat if hard pushed by the enemy. After this the enemy kept so within their lines that little or no blood was spilt; and all active movements appearing to be at an end, Shelby made application to Gen'l Marion for leave of absence to go to the Assembly of North Carolina, of which he was a member, and which was to meet about that time at Salem, and where he had private business of his own of the first importance. The mountain men had then but a day or two to stay, to complete their tour of duty, of sixty days, and he verily believes that they did serve it out, as he never heard to the contrary.[7]

The mountaineers did remain until their time expired and some days afterwards, since Sevier, for the time leading all of them, did not arrive at home until early in January, 1782.[8] Of them Shelby said:

These mountaineers were poor men who lived by keeping stock on the range beyond the mountains; they were volunteers and neither expected or received any compensation except liquidated certificates worth two shillings in the pound. General Greene had no right nor ought to have expected to command their services. For myself, for the whole services of 1780 and 1781, both in camp and in the General Assembly, I received a liquidation certificate which my good agent in that county [Sullivan], after my removal to Kentucky, sold for six yards of middling broadcloth, and gave one coat made of it to the person who brought it out to me. Indeed I was proud of receiving that.[9]

Could any words speak louder? If so they are added by Haywood in an encomium: "To the honor of the troops under Sevier and Shelby, no such captive negroes or property came with them into the counties of their residence; their integrity was as little impeached as their valor." [10]

The Wataugans had sent a platoon to Charleston to take part in the opening battle of the Revolution in the South, early in May, 1776, and now the over-mountain men, seven hundred strong, were again in the South hurling the British back to their picket lines around Charleston—a coincidence that should be a matter of pride for all time to natives of the "Volunteer State." In truth, thus was given a further example for the tradition that,

[7] Greene MSS, cited in *Greene's Life of Gen. Greene*, III, 419; Henderson, "Isaac Shelby" in *N. C. Booklet*, XVI, 109, XVIII, 3–56, a study based on much research.

[8] Haywood's *Civil History of Tennessee*, 105.

[9] To C. S. Todd.

[10] Haywood, *op. cit.*, 105, after recounting the looting practiced by some other troops and by the Tories, particularly the stealing of negroes who were stealthily taken to other parts for sale into slavery.

as time ran, gave the Commonwealth that title, than which no sister State has a prouder.

In the meantime, and afterwards until peace was declared (1783), as we shall see, these same hardy backwoodsmen continued the War of the Revolution in the West against the Indians and the Tories who had taken shelter among the redmen, their superiors from almost all angles.

The settlements as high up as those North of the Holston suffered from raids by Indians, perhaps Chickamauga bands who were out on the chase and deflected to strike quick blows on the whites. Captain Moses Looney, of Sullivan County, and brother of Major David Looney, was captured and taken to their towns where he remained until August, 1782. He was then allowed to return home where he informed the authorities of the Indians being willing to make peace—that they were assembling at Chota for exchange, whites who had been made captives. These numbered about fifty to be offered in exchange for Indian captives, in a treaty which the Indians were willing to negotiate. The sobering news that their British allies had lost the war had reached the towns of the Chickamaugas and prepared that tribe for peace.

In the North Carolina general assembly of 1781, Washington County had only one representative, Charles Allison, and Sullivan County one, Evan Shelby in the senate. This small representation was due to absorption in war. The same reason accounts for the fact that there were few occurrences in the civil life of the people worthy of being noted.

CHAPTER XXVIII

LAND LUST RAMPANT—1782–1783

In order to determine the amount due to its militia and to others whose properties had been impressed by the State for military uses, the North Carolina general assembly appointed in each district a board of auditors to adjust and settle claims against the State. The members of the board named for Washington and Sullivan Counties by the legislature were: Anthony Bledsoe,[1] of Sullivan, Edmund Williams[2] and Landon Carter, of Washington. John Sevier was chosen as clerk by this board.[3]

Richard Henderson and his Transylvania associates by petition brought before the general assembly in 1782 their purchase from the Cherokees at Sycamore Shoals in 1775 of large boundaries of land on rivers Powell and Cumberland. On May 13th a committee of the assembly reported that the purchase was illegal but "may save the State some expense in attaining peaceable possession of the lands from the Indians." In other words, the Indian grants were void as to Henderson and his associates, but had some validity as against the Cherokees. That theory prevailed in later actual procedure. North Carolina never offered to pay that tribe a penny for the immense boundary in the Cumberland Valley, but treated it as her own, to dispose of at will.[4]

---

[1] Bledsoe had previously served on the board for Salisbury District, under the Act of 1781. He was then the only auditor who lived in the West.

[2] Born in Wales; came to Massachusetts where he married Lucretia Adams, said to be of the noted Adams family of that State; removed to the Watauga before 1778; died in 1795; his home fell into Carter County on its creation in 1796.

[3] The results of the board's labors are set out in Allen, *Tennessee Soldiers of the Revolution.*

[4] When a few years later the United States government assumed to itself the function of negotiating treaties with the Indian tribes, it also availed of the benefit of Henderson's purchase. At the Treaty of Hopewell (1785) the Cherokees made a claim to the region granted to Henderson; a commissioner quieted them by saying: "Henderson's purchase

The legislature then proceeded to compensate the Henderson group by way of a 200,000-acre consolation grant of western lands, for which the Commonwealth never paid anything. By Act of 1783, Chap. 38, it was provided:

That two hundred thousand acres be and are hereby granted to the said Richard Henderson, Thomas Hart, John Williams, William Johnston, James Hogg, David Hart, and Leonard Henly Bullock, the heirs and assigns, or devisees, of Nathaniel Hart, deceased, and the heirs and assigns, or devisees, of John Luttrel, deceased, to Landon Carter, heir of John Carter, deceased, his heirs and assigns forever, and to the heirs and devisees of Robert Lucas; the said two hundred thousand acres to be laid out in one survey, and within the following boundaries, to-wit: Beginning at the old Indian town in Powell's Valley, and running down Powell's river not less than four miles in width on one or both sides thereof to the junction of Powell's and Clinch river, then down Clinch river on one or both sides, not less than twelve miles in width, for the aforesaid complement of two hundred thousand acres.

As this act indicates, there had been sales of interests and parts of interests of the copartners intermediate the date of the deeds of 1775 and the year 1783. There were at the outset eight full shares, Henderson, Williams, Johnston, Hogg, Thomas Hart, Luttrell and Nathaniel Hart taking full shares. It would appear therefore that Robert Lucas, an early Wataugan and with Henderson a signer of the Cumberland compact, had purchased the shares of Williams and Johnston, and assigned a portion of his holdings to John Carter, for whose son, Landon, Carter County, Tennessee, was named—the county of his residence.

The State of North Carolina issued a grant in accord with this act; and the grantees proceeded to have the lands surveyed and platted by Stockley Donelson, surveyor.[5] The boundary was divided into lots, "A," "B," etc., beginning at the extreme northwest or at Old Town Creek in later Claiborne County, Tennessee. The eastern boundary of the granted tract begins about five miles (direct line) from Cumberland Gap, and the western boundary caused it to run off at an acute angle from the northeastern boundary (patently contrary to the spirit of the legislative act and the grant), the evident purpose being to leave out of the

---

must not be disputed," and in the treaty its boundaries followed those of Henderson's grant from the Cherokees.

[5] Son of Col. John Donelson and brother of Mrs. Andrew Jackson.

grant to Henderson and associates a very fine body of agricultural land between the southwestern boundary and a line that, very nearly, is represented by the present line of the Knoxville and Ohio branch of the Southern Railway at Careyville, Tennessee. The tradition is that Donelson, who was acutely affected by land lust, and who was to become perhaps the largest owner of acreage in the West, so ran the lines that he might acquire, under a later grant to himself, the tempting lands in this angle. This he proceeded to do; and the tradition further runs that Donelson's action in this matter led to a breach between him and Henderson.

It is observed that there had been a transfer of the interest of Robert Lucas' heirs to Landon Carter, whose father, John Carter, had had an interest since 1775. Interpartes deeds passed in accordance with the partition.

The boundaries of the whole covered lands that lie in the present counties of Claiborne, Union, Campbell, Anderson and Knox; and an interesting fact is that Norris Lake, where the Tennessee Valley Authority erected a dam in Clinch River, covers much of the land that passed under the consolation grant. Equally interesting is the fact that the grant was so laid as to include much of the fine bottoms of Powell's and Clinch Rivers, leaving out the Cumberland Mountains, little dreaming that they were thus purposely excluding a section that was to become of great value because of its seams of coal.[6]

The Henderson group were not the only North Carolinians who were intent on procuring holdings on the western waters. Caswell, through Joseph Martin and Colonel John Donelson, was reaching out for lands on the French Broad, and he and William Blount and General Griffith Rutherford were associates of Martin and Donelson in efforts to acquire an immense boundary in the Bend of the Tennessee River, in the North Alabama region. It took a large grant to "console" the governor of North Carolina, Alexander Martin. Colonel William Polk turned up at French Lick to remain quite a while rounding up claims for choice boundaries,[7] and to serve there as surveyor-general of North

---

[6] Further details of the survey and later transactions may be found in Williams, "Henderson and Company's Purchase in Tennessee," in *Tenn. Hist. Mag.*, V, 5–28.

[7] Hoyt, *Murphey Papers*, II, 405–8. Polk later wrote that "he took up his residence and fixed his office at French Lick Fort the site on which

Carolina for the district which is now known as Middle Tennessee. Nor was the fever affecting only the leaders of the Old North State. In Virginia, ex-Governor Patrick Henry had Martin locating for him lands on the Holston, and Thomas Jefferson suffered a seizure. In 1782, before North Carolina declared void the Henderson grant of lands within her limits, he joined Henderson and his friends in a project concerning those lands. As he himself wrote from Paris, France, November 11th, 1784:

In 1781 I joined some gentlemen in a project to obtain some lands in the western part of North Carolina. But in the winter of 1782–83, while I was in expectation of going to Europe, and that the title of western lands might possibly come under discussion of the ministers [concerning the peace treaty] I withdrew myself from the company.[8]

The thrust of migration was distinctly Tennesseeward, and for reasons set forth by the level-headed Colonel William Christian, who in 1782, wrote that trouble from the Indians in the Kentucky country "tends to turn the tide of immigration into Carolina towards the Cherokees, where they may live in safety." [9] To another he wrote: "In order to give you a better idea of the country, I have scratched down a rough map of that part of the country in question. The [Long] Island is in North Carolina about ten miles; and in my opinion it is not very agreeable to the North Carolinians to have a trade and agency in that State, although they do not complain much about it." [10]

Many of those moving into the region preferred to buy lands and make homes in the older settlements. This afforded opportunities for residents there to dispose of their holdings and move

Nashville stands." Here he remained until 1786 "and was twice elected a member of the House of Commons of Davidson County." *Ib.*

[8] *Writings of Jefferson,* (Ford ed.) IV, 368. For confirmation that "the company" was Henderson's Company in Tennessee, see Draper MSS., 2 CC 34. Jefferson further wrote: "I am further assured that the members never prosecuted their views," which evidently refers to their designs concerning the Cumberland country. That feature was defeated when the associates accepted the consolation grant of 200,000 acres of land in East Tennessee.

[9] To Gov. Harrison, September 28, 1782. *Cal. Va. St. Papers,* III, 331.

[10] To Sampson Matthews, member of the Virginia Council of State, Dec. 30, 1782. The reference is to the agency of Martin, near the Long Island. Col. Joseph Williams had complained to the authorities of his State of North Carolina, in 1776. See p. 50 *et seq.*

down the valleys where they could obtain larger boundaries, even if in doing so they ran risks at the hands of affronted redmen. There was a distinct movement of population down the Nolachucky after the campaign of 1780–81 and particularly in 1782. This led to complaints by the chiefs of the Overhill Cherokees, which brought to Sevier from the governor of North Carolina the following:

Danbury, Feb. 11, 1782.

"Sir: I am distressed with the repeated complaints of the Indians respecting the daily intrusions of our people on their lands beyond the French Broad River. I beg you, sir, to prevent the injuries these savages justly complain of, who are constantly imploring the protection of the State and appealing to its justice in vain. By interposing your influence on these, our unruly citizens, I think will have sufficient weight, without going into extremities disgraceful to them and disagreeable to the State. You will, therefore, please to warn these intruders off the lands reserved for the Indians by the late Act of the Assembly, that they remove immediately, at least by the middle of March, otherwise they will be drove off. If you find them still refractory at the above time, you will draw forth a body of your militia on horseback, and pull down their cabins, and drive them off, laying aside every consideration of their entreaties to the contrary. You will please to give me the earliest information of your proceedings. The Indian goods are not yet arrived from Philadelphia, through the inclemency of the late season; as soon as they will be in the State, I shall send them to the Great [Long] Island and hold a treaty with the Cherokees.

The Cherokees renewed their remonstrances against the tide of population which continued to flow towards their towns on the Little Tennessee.

A matter of great import at the time, and one which grew in importance as time ran, was this: The general assembly of North Carolina in 1783 [11] authorized a treaty to be held at Long Island at which there might be ceded to the State more lands of the Overhill Cherokees, and it appropriated monies to be expended by the governor in the purchase of goods to be passed to the Indians as consideration. In May following Governor Alexander Martin notified the Cherokees of his authority to lay in goods "to buy your lands as far south as French Broad River," for

---

[11] Act 1782, Ch. 21; *N. C. St. Recs.*, XXIV, 509. The State was following Virginia which also provided for a treaty at Long Island.

settlement by whites; "that stream we propose to be the boundary line between you and us." [12]

Before any goods were even purchased, not to say delivered to the Indians, the general assembly opened the lands south of the treaty line of 1777 down to the French Broad to entry and grant,[13] and North Carolina received the purchase money as if the Indian title had been satisfied and removed. By February, 1784, "the Indian goods are not arrived from Philadelphia. As soon as they arrive I will give you notice and fix the time of holding the treaty." [14] The goods were never sent west; no treaty was ever held. Lands of the Cherokees were taken without any sort of compensation, though compensation had been promised by the State of North Carolina.

The Cherokee tribe justly resented such treatment, but the western people bore the brunt of their umbrage and attacks.[15] Sevier held that this course of action was a poor requital of what the western soldiery had done in defense of North Carolina and the Confederation of States from May, 1776, until the end of 1781—and history can but pronounce his contention valid. The matter furnished a major argument against the parent State by John Sevier and his followers in the State of Franklin movement.[16]

This looting of the Trans-Alleghany region was facilitated by the opening of a land office for grants in the fall of 1783, and its closing by legislative act only a few months later, after the leaders in the eastern part of the State had rushed the land office and

---

[12] N. C. State Recs., XVI, 810.

[13] N. C. Act of 1781, also letter of Caswell, N. C. St. Recs., XVI, 958, in which he shows his plans to have Col. John Donelson appointed surveyor of Greene County, and obtain lands for himself on the north of the French Broad.

[14] Governor Martin to Joseph Martin, Indian Agent, Feb. 11, 1784. N. C. St. Recs., XVII, 15.

[15] It is believed that the State of North Carolina never paid the Indians anything for the several cessions from which that Commonwealth benefited; and in the above instance a cession was not even treated for.

[16] It is one of the mysteries of North Carolina history: were the goods ever purchased? What became of them? Did Wm. Blount divert and use them in furtherance of his scheme for the acquisition of a principality in the Great Bend of the Tennessee? See Calendar of Tennessee Papers, (Draper), 25, and Lost State of Franklin, 62, 64, 72, 74 et seq.

procured for themselves the choicest of the western lands.[17]

The results of this work of those few months has told heavily against the State of Tennessee in all succeeding generations—particularly in the matter of her educational activities. Only the shell of a public domain was left out of which she could establish common schools, a college or university.

Ramsey (p. 273) has preserved this bit of pioneer history of this year which is revealing on more than one phase:

During the infancy of the settlements on Nollichucky, corn became scarce and, availing themselves of a short suspension of hostilities, Jeremiah Jack [18] and William Rankin [19] descended the river in a canoe to barter with the Indians for corn. They reached Coiatee [Kaia-a-tee] without interruption. The warriors of that place refused to exchange or sell the corn, and manifested other signs of suspicion, if not of open enmity. They entered the canoe and lifted up some wearing apparel lying in it and which covered some rifles. This discovery increased the unwillingness of the Indians to trade, and they began to show a disposition to offer violence to their visitants. The Beloved Woman, Nancy Ward, happily was present, and was able by her commanding influence to appease their wrath and to bring about a friendlier feeling between the parties. Little Indians were soon clad in home-made vestments brought by the traders. The canoe was filled with corn, and the white men started on their return voyage well pleased with the exchange they had made, and especially with the kind offices of the Beloved Woman.

On their return, the white men landed and camped one night one mile above the mouth of French Broad, on the north bank. Mr. Jack was so well pleased with the place that he afterwards selected it as the site of future home, and actually settled and improved it on his emigration to the present Knox County in 1787.

[17] The land office had been located at far-away Hillsborough, accessible to Easterners but not to the men of the western waters.

[18] Jeremiah Jack was a son of Patrick Jack; and as to the father's transactions with the Cherokees, see Williams, *Dawn*, 316.

[19] Wm. Rankin was a soldier of the Revolution, and a member of the first Constitutional Convention of Tennessee from Greene County, and figured in the State of Franklin movement. He was ancestor of a number of men of ability and influence. Rankin is listed as a participant in the battle of King's Mountain. White, *King's Mountain Men*, 219.

CHAPTER XXIX

CIVIL AFFAIRS (1782–1783)

A new governmental district was created by the North Carolina general assembly of 1782; Morgan District was struck off from the Salisbury District, with Washington and Sullivan Counties as parts of the new district; and for those two westernmost counties a court of oyer and terminer was provided, to be held for both at Jonesborough, this, because of "the extensive mountains that lie desolate between the inhabited parts of Washington and the inhabited parts of Burke Counties."[1] The jurisdiction of the court included the trial of criminal cases and of appeals from the county courts of the two counties.

The first session was held August 15th, 1782, Judge Spruce McCay presiding. Waightstill Avery, Esq., of Morganton, was appointed prosecuting attorney for the State, and John Sevier served as the court's clerk. Before 1782, felonies were triable across the mountains, with much inconvenience and at great expense to the western people.

The process of progressive settlement continued beyond the Cherokee line fixed by the treaty of 1777. Though settlements to the south of the line were unlawful, many hardy men staked out claims, cleared lands and built cabin homes in reliance that, finally, rights of preemption would be recognized—after the Indian line should be shifted farther south. The North Carolina legislature of that year divided Washington County by creating the county of Greene, so named in honor of General Nathanael Greene.[2] Thus Greene County became in size the premier county

---

[1] Acts of 1782, ch. 22; also in *N. C. St. Recs.*, XXIV, 450.

[2] The dividing line was thus described: "Beginning at William Williams' in the Fork of Horse Creek at the foot of the Iron Mountain, thence a direct course to George Gillespie's house at or near the mouth of Big Limestone; thence a north course to the line which divides the counties of Washington and Sullivan, thence from said line to the Chimney Top Mountain, thence a direct course to the mouth of Cloud's Creek in Holston River; and all that part of Washington County westward of the said

of the West, ousting Washington County from the place of honor. Jurisdiction over all the Tennessee country outside of the boundaries of the counties of Washington and Sullivan passed to the fledgeling county for a time.

Before this, a blockhouse for protection against raiding Indians had been erected in the limits of the county now created, on the plantation of James English. A bold spring on the site of present-day Greeneville indicated where should be the seat of government. There were already located on the site the home and tavern of John Kerr (or Carr) and the first courts were held in his tavern, by the justices first in commission. These were: Joseph Hardin,[3] John Newman, George Doherty, James Houston, Amos Bird and Asahel Rawlings. Daniel Kennedy [4] was clerk. It is noteworthy that the only justice who resided north of Greeneville was Hardin. Some of the settlers were living just north of the French Broad River.[5]

Greene County itself was soon to submit to the legislative carving knife. At its fall session in 1783 (October) the general assembly of North Carolina created on the Cumberland another county with boundaries so ample that it, too, was soon to have another new county (Sumner) carved out of it. The new county was named Davidson in honor of General William Lee Davidson.[6]

---

line is declared to be a distinct county by the name of Greene." *N. C. Act 1783*, Ch. 2.

[3] Sketch in Williams, *History of the Lost State of Franklin* (Revised ed.) 304.

[4] Sketch *Ib.*, 307.

[5] Among the prominent settlers in 1783 were, besides the above: Henry Earnest, Anthony Moore, James Penny, Felix Earnest, Robert Hood, David Harrison, Wm. Dunwoody, Richard Wood and Capt. James Stinson who had led a company under Sevier at King's Mountain. Mill construction permits were granted in that year to Charles Lowery on Little Chucky, George Doherty on Flower's Creek, Thos. Jarnagin on Long Creek, Stephen Copeland on Sinking Creek, Thos. Buckingham on Holly Creek, and Thos. Stockton at Christian's Ford of the French Broad River.

[6] Gen. Davidson, as we have already noted, was a favorite of the western people. He had been killed in action at Cowan's Ford of the Catawba, Feb. 1, 1781, while resisting the advance of Lord Cornwallis against Gen. Greene. "He was a trained continental officer, courageous, enterprising and efficient and greatly esteemed throughout his State. His death was a great loss to the American cause and was widely lamented. The Continental Congress ordered that a monument be erected as a memorial of his distinguished worth." Ashe, *History of North Carolina*, 651–2. His

Nashborough was the new county's seat (the name not being changed to Nashville until the following year) [7] "in memory of the brave and patriotic General [Francis] Nash." [8]

Winsor [9] states that the legislature of North Carolina first officially pushed her jurisdiction to the Mississippi River by an act passed in May, 1783.[10] But this overlooks the fact that in the creation of Washington County in 1777 its western boundary was that river. However, the passage of the act in 1783 was an additional warning to Spain that the claim of that power to any part of the territory east of the great river would be seriously contested.

By another act of 1783 (Chapter 2) the legislature undertook to make the Indian line run with "the middle of the Tenasee and Holston to the middle of French Broad, thence up the middle of French Broad River (which lines are not to include any island or islands in the said river) to the mouth of Big Pidgeon River, thence up the same to the head thereof, etc." All lands north of that line were opened to entry and grant. A fertile and inviting part was below the French Broad. The shift was made without the consent of the Overhill Cherokees, the rightful owners. As is elsewhere shown, the Cherokees never received any sort of compensation, while North Carolina granted the lands at the usual price.

The legislative act reserved for the Cherokees that territory which is now known as lower East Tennessee, prohibited entries of land and settlements by whites in that reservation. Significantly, no such reservation was made in behalf of the Chickasaws

widow and several of her children moved out to the new county and settled a few miles north of Nashville. See n.   p.   *ante.*

[7] For both Davidson and Nash, see sketch in *Tennessee Historical Quarterly,* I, 250–268.

Perhaps in no other county in the Union have two generals of the Revolutionary War been recognized as were Davidson and Nash in having their names given to a county and to its seat, respectively.

[8] N. C. Act of 1784, ch. 47. Sam'l Barton, Thos. Mulloy, James Shaw, Daniel Smith and Isaac Lindsay were named to lay out the town and sell lots, the first named being treasurer.

[9] *The Westward Movement,* 327. Winsor, in referring to the Cumberland settlements, estimated the population in 1783 at 3500. He and the present writer are in agreement that that people sprang "from the loins of Watauga."

[10] N. C. Acts of 1783, ch. 2; also in *N. C. St. Recs.,* XXIV, 478.

who owned what is now West Tennessee, and this opened that region to entry and settlement, notwithstanding the fact that the Chickasaws had been less hostile to the Americans throughout the war than any other Indian tribe. This, in callous disregard of the unquestionable rights of that gallant tribe. Soon surveyors swarmed into the land of the Chickasaws to locate entries, largely for residents of North Carolina.[11]

This year witnessed the appearance of the first circuit rider of the Methodists in the Tennessee country, Jeremiah Lambert, who traveled the Holston circuit as a missionary under appointment. At the end of the year 1783 he reported sixty members. In the following year Henry Willis rode that circuit and at year's end returned seventy-six members—hardly indicative that Methodism would grow by leaps and bounds and become one of the two largest and most influential denominations in Tennessee.

That other denomination was the Baptist, churches of which were built on Sinking Creek, a few miles from the site of Johnson City (about 1782), and on Cherokee Creek in Washington County, and elsewhere within the period being treated of.

The Presbyterians were also expanding by the formation of congregations and the building of edifices: Weaver's, and at New Bethel, in the "Fork country," between the Watauga and the Holston; in Greene County and, perhaps, at other points. No student can review our period without agreeing with us that this denomination was far in advance of the others in the matters of a trained ministry and the education of the young. He could, in fairness, say no less.

It cannot truthfully be said that religion was yet a primary concern of the people of the frontier. Pressure from other directions diverted attention from matters spiritual, and educational as well.

---

[11] The shabby story is told in the *Beginnings of West Tennessee.*

CHAPTER XXX

Chickasaw Treaty at Nashborough—1783

About a year after the attack by the Chickasaw Indians on Fort Jefferson a strange thing happened. Captain Robert George [1] who had commanded the garrison during the siege was in the late summer of 1782 in the Chickasaw country fraternizing with the chiefs and warriors of that tribe.[2] He seems to have been adopted, in a way, into the tribe and to have led its warriors in battle in years subsequent to 1782. He went among those Indians at first under orders of Colonel George Rogers Clark to prepare the way for a treaty of peace; and he used his influence to bring the Chickasaws into amicable relations with the Americans. In September two Chickasaw warriors accompanied by a white man, Simon Burney, made their way to the Kentucky country with a written message signed by the chiefs. This gave assurance of their desire to live in peace with all settlers south of the Ohio, and explained why they had laid siege to Fort Jefferson and attacked the Cumberland stations. They stated that these movements had been incited by other tribes in the British interest.[3]

Colonel Donelson, now in the Kentucky country, wrote Governor Benjamin Harrison of Virginia urging the advisability of

---

[1] For a brief sketch of this officer, see *Ill. Hist. Coll.*, II, No. 1. For some account of him see Mereness, *Travels in Am. Colonies*, 665, 666, 668.

[2] The Chickasaws differed much from the other Southern Indians. Valiant themselves, they appreciated valor even in enemies. This visit of George is mentioned in a letter of Wm. Fleming to Gov. Harrison, of Virginia, of date November, 1782.

[3] *Cal. Tenn. Papers*, 19. In this they referred to a communication they had received from the Illinois region which expressed a desire for peace. This was signed by Col. John Montgomery, at the time commandant in Illinois under Clark. Doubtless the Chickasaws had been influenced to make war upon the Cumberland people by John Douglas, deputy agent among the Chickasaws at the time; he served under Lt. Col. John Graham of the British army, who was superintendent.

holding a treaty with the Chickasaws at French Lick. Donelson, Joseph Martin and Isaac Shelby were appointed Virginia commissioners to treat; and goods for the Indians were sent out from Richmond to Long Island of Holston, thence to French Lick. The primary objective was the acquisition of the tract of land between the Tennessee, Ohio and Mississippi Rivers, north of the Virginia-Carolina line.[4]   The commissioners were also to hold treaties with the Chickamaugas and Overhill Cherokees at the Long Island.   Shelby ordered John Hall, one of his captains, to hurry sixty bushels of corn down from Shoate's Ford[5] of the Holston, by flat boats, to the Island.[6]

Governor Harrison sent out young Major John Reid[7] to make preparations for the treaties.   Reid journeyed to the home of Martin near the Long Island where he delivered the governor's instructions, then passed through Cumberland Gap into Kentucky and arrived at French Lick (Nashborough) on May 2nd.   Colonel Robertson personally was opposed to the assembling of the Indians at Nashborough, and as an official of North Carolina he forbade Reid going on to the Chickasaw towns until he had taken the votes of the Cumberland stationers to be affected.   To avoid complications, the Cumberland court had but recently ordered that no settler trade with the Indians below the ridge dividing the Cumberland and Tennessee waters.

The action respecting a treaty taken by the court, sitting as a committee, was entered of record:

State of North Carolina, Cumberland District, June 3, 1783
    The committee met according to adjournment; members present, Col. James Robertson, Geo. Freeland, Thos. Malloy, Ebenezer Titus, Sam'l Barton, James Shaw, Isaac Bledsoe, David Rounsevall, Heydon Wells.

---

[4] Later known as "Jackson's Purchase" because the treaty with the Chickasaws in 1818, was negotiated by Jackson along with Isaac Shelby.

[5] Site of Bluff City.

[6] Shelby also feared the coming to Nashborough of a great number of the Chickasaws: "the only method to avoid approaching evil is to send off all Indians who are not of weight in treaty."

[7] A gallant and intelligent man; in later years he settled on the Cumberland waters, at Franklin, and became Gen. Andrew Jackson's private secretary in the Creek War, and at New Orleans.   He was one of the authors of *Reid and Eaton's Life of Jackson*, the first biography of Jackson.   He was ancestor of a notable Tennessee family.

When, on motion made by Major John Reed, relative to assembling of the Southern Tribes of Indians at the French Lick, on Cumberland River, for holding a treaty with the commissioners appointed by the State of Virginia; when the committee, considering how difficult it will be for a handful of people reduced to poverty and distress by a continued scene of Indian barbarity, to furnish any large body of Indians with provisions, and how prejudicial it may be to our infant settlement should they not be furnished with provisions, or otherwise disaffected with the terms of the treaty; on which considerations the committee refer it to unanimous suffrages of the people of this settlement whether the treaty shall be held here with their consent or no; and that the suffrages of the several stations be delivered to the clerk of committee by Thursday evening, the 5th inst., at which time the suffrages of Freeland's Station, Heatonsburg and Nashborough were given in, and are as follows:

Freeland's Station, no treaty here, votes 32.

Heatonsburg [Eaton's] treaty here, votes 54; no treaty, 1.

Nashborough, no treaty here, votes 26; for a treaty here, votes 30.

The other stations of Gasper Mansco and Maulings failing to return their votes.

"For the treaty" carried by totals of 84 ayes to 54 nays. Mauldin's Station appears in the returns for the first time.

The Chickasaws named the time for the treaty; and were on hand promptly, but ten days in advance of the arrival of commissioners Martin and Donelson. Shelby was unable to attend, due to the recent killing of his brother, Captain James, in Kentucky by Indians.[8] The treaty was held away from Nashborough, at a sulphur spring about four miles northwest.[9] A large number of the Chickasaws were present, led by Mingo-homa, (the Red King), Piomingo (the Mountain Leader) and other chiefs. A band of Delaware Indians had squatted within the Chickasaw domain, below the Muscle Shoals, and that they should be expelled was stipulated.[10] The Chickasaws ceded a large boundary

---

[8] *Cal. Va. State Papers*, III, 533. See also the case of Shelby's Heirs v. Shelby, Cooke's Rep. (3 Tennessee), 179.

[9] Where Gov. James Robertson in later years built his home.

[10] "Some traders from the Spanish dominion on the Mississippi have came up the Tennessee as far as the mouth of Bear Creek, and are making houses for the reception of their goods, and are using all such prevailing arguments with the Indians against the interest of the United States." (Martin to Gov. Harrison.)

of land on the south side of Cumberland River—extending to the water shed—a cession they confirmed in the treaty of Hopewell in South Carolina, 1786.[11]

For once Robertson erred in judgment. However, his own station had voted with him unanimously against the holding of the treaty. The affair went off without mishap, and the Indians turned homeward firm friends of Robertson and his people—a friendship which was to bring forth fruit in the years to come.[12]

The treaty concluded in June, 1783, was a most remarkable one: It was held by Virginia's commissioners on North Carolina soil, and Virginia's money was spent in negotiating it. It did not accomplish the acquisition of Western Kentucky, but it did result in the clearing of the Chickasaw claim from a boundary of very fertile land, south to the Tennessee River ridge, for North Carolinians. The sour grimaces of Governor Harrison as he read the treaty may easily be imagined. For their part, leading North Carolinians east of the mountains were at that time working strenuously in parcelling out a part of the domain of the Chickasaws (the present West Tennessee) to "insiders," and, too, without even leave asked of the Chickasaws.

The three commissioners (Shelby being now with his fellows) held a quasi-treaty at the Long Island of Holston with a part of the Chickamauga tribe, on July 9, 1783.[13] No lands were acquired. Indeed, this lawless aggregation of redmen owned as of right no domain as against the Cherokees from whom they had seceded. No State, therefore, could afford to treat with them for a cession of lands.

In the spring of 1783 it seems that another call for military aid from the Tennessee country came from Kentucky. The Indians from north of the Ohio were crossing the river and raiding settlements, attacking forts and killing men, women and children. Among those killed was an influential leader of that people, Colo-

---

[11] For the story of Piomingo, the greatest of the Chickasaw chiefs of his period, see Malone, *The Chickasaw Nation, passim;* Williams, *Beginnings of West Tennessee,* 39, 59.

[12] See p. *ante.*

[13] "The chiefs of Chota and other peaceable towns, did assist to make themselves responsible. The Creeks did not appear according to expectation and we fear are for war." (Martin to Gov. Harrison.)   Presents to the Chickamaugas were of ruffled and plain shirts; of red and blue cloth for match coats, also of powder and lead sent by wagons from Richmond.

nel John Floyd.[14] In January Lieutenant-Colonel Thomas Brown, superintendent of Southern Indian affairs, reported from St. Augustine, Florida, that a combination of Northern and some Southern tribes was forming: "A deputation from the Northward Indians, with 1200 Cherokees, arrived at St. Augustine lately to establish a league and confederacy among the different tribes. . . . The Cherokees contain 3,000 gunmen."[15] In July, of the same year, Brigadier-General Archibald McArthur reported to General Sir Guy Carleton: "Mr. [John] McDonald, commissary to the Upper Cherokees, arrived here yesterday. He says a Col. Christie [Christian] with 800 and a Col. [Evan] Shelby with 400 men had marched from Powell's Valley and Holstein and expected to be reinforced by a considerable body of rebels from Caintuck [Kentucky] against the Shawnees and Delawares. About 150 Cherokees and some Creeks have set out to assist the Northwards."[16]

Evidently the Indian coalition failed for some reason. Kentucky quieted down and Colonels Christian and Shelby did not march into Kentucky, though ready to do so on further call.

---

[14] A son and a grandson of Floyd became governors of Virginia.

[15] Including all branches and the Chickamaugas, obviously. The letter is in *Report of American Manuscripts in the Royal Institution of Great Britain,* III, 325.

[16] *Ib.,* IV, 202; the letter was dated July 5th.

CHAPTER XXXI

IN WEST TENNESSEE

While there were no permanent white settlers in the region between the Tennessee and Mississippi Rivers—now known as West Tennessee—to take part in the War for Independence, the banks of the Mississippi, nevertheless, became the theater of strife. The Chickasaw tribe owned the region and occupied, on occasion, the Bluffs that bore their name. Of the proven valor of that tribe the British purposed to make use when opportunity should offer. For many years the Chickasaws had been under the tactful superintendence of John Stuart, and at the outbreak of hostilities the tribe was under the immediate charge of his brothers, Charles Stuart, assistant superintendent of Southern Indians, and Henry Stuart. All activities in the region were incidental to the navigation of the Mississippi.

In 1778 Spain through her port of New Orleans was prepared to give aid to the Americans in a way much needed, supplies; and a committee of the Continental Congress authorized the sending of a party down the Ohio and Mississippi to secure and transport such supplies upstream. Placed in command of this party was the bold and enterprising Captain James Willing.[1] Instructions had been issued by John Stuart to incite the Chickasaws to resist the party as it passed the Bluffs, and to Henry Stuart was entrusted the handling of the Indians. The Willing party slipped past the Upper Bluffs, but at the Lower Bluff (site of Memphis) young Stuart organized a slight resistance, and a small skirmish resulted.[2] A sharper clash occurred below at the Walnut Hills (site of Vicksburg).

---

[1] Of the influential Philadelphia family of Willing. The young captain had been a merchant at Natchez from 1774 to 1777 and knew the country from the mouth of the Ohio southward. The Willing party left Fort Pitt (Pittsburgh) on January 11, 1778, in the "Rattletrap," twenty-seven strong. En route adventurers swelled the number to about one hundred.

[2] "Henry Stuart undertook to revive the flagging devotion of the Indians," with the results indicated. Gov. Peter Chester to Germain, March 25, 1778, C. O. folio 341, No. 41.

While Spain co-operated with France she was unwilling to enter into an outright alliance with America, at the same time pursuing a policy of seizing strategic points (then under British control) on the east side of the Mississippi above New Orleans. In 1779 Galvez, the ablest soldier and commander Spain ever had in Louisiana, captured several of these British forts, among them the one at Natchez. In April, 1781, the Tories in and around Natchez, thinking that Britain was about to be successful in regaining these posts, rose against the Spaniards and by ruse recaptured Fort Panmure at Natchez, only to yield it and scatter in dismay upon the return of Galvez from his recent triumph over the British at Pensacola. Some fled to the Chickasaws, among them John Turner.[3]

James Colbert, a Chickasaw leader, who had aided the British in attempting to hold Pensacola, now planned to harass the Spaniards by raids on their commerce on the river between Natchez and St. Louis. Turner joined Colbert in carrying on a sort of guerilla warfare along the river and chose the Lower Chickasaw Bluff as base of operations. Rude buildings were erected there, the approximate location of which may be ascertained at this day, it is said.

Colbert's gang was particularly active in 1782–1783. On the 19th of March of the first named year, a party led by Turner sallied from their stronghold and captured a large barge on its way to the Illinois country,[4] and a few days later a boat of Don Balthasar de Villars, commandant at the Arkansas, was captured along with ten men and a cargo of corn and flour bound from St. Louis.

On April 2nd there was an important sortie, the details of which have been preserved. It was made from the mouth of Wolf River and resulted in the capture of an upbound flotilla under the command of Don l'Abide. In one of the boats were Madame Cruzat, wife of the Spanish commandant at St. Louis, and her two sons on their way to join Cruzat. There suddenly rushed from hiding in the bushes at the mouth of the Wolf canoes and pirogues

---

[3] Who turned up for a short stay on the Cumberland.

[4] "They took all the arms without leaving even a knife." A return attack was made by the Spaniards four hours later, resulting "in the capture and killing with the oars and throwing into the river of six Englishmen and two negroes of Turner. Turner escaped to one of his pirogues."

manned by thirty white men and one mestizo, all armed with carbines, daggers and clubs. The occupants of the boats of the flotilla were seized, tied and then taken up the Wolf "a quarter of a league" to a rude prison "situated on a decline of the Barrancas at the right hand of the river which empties through them into the Mississippi." This prison was of two stories, constructed of unhewn logs, with a bark roof. One large and two small log cabins sheltered members of the gang, composed of three hundred, whites and blacks, divided into two separate encampments, one of which was on the Mississippi on another on the Chickasaw Bluffs "called Dumilien, ten leagues above the encampment at Margot [Wolf] River." Madame Cruzat in an account left says that during this sortie but two Chickasaws were seen, but that eight or nine days after her capture about two hundred of that tribe appeared, until which time a distribution of the spoils was not made.

The loot taken in these and later raids accumulated fast and was of considerable value. It was divided in this manner: Six thousand pesos, belonging to the King of Spain, and the guns and clothing were evenly divided among the captors. Slaves and tableware were sold by auction to the highest bidder, and only powder, bullets and brandy were distributed to Chickasaws who had not been actual participants in the raiding and were only visitors to the encampments.[5]

Colonel John Montgomery, after his campaigning in the Northwest under George Rogers Clark, settled in the Tennessee country on the Cumberland below the site of Nashville. He at once took rank as a leading citizen and in 1783 was elected sheriff of the district. He gave little personal attention to the duties of the office and engaged in exploring the country farther down the Cumberland. Rumors became current that he was connected with "Colbert's gang" in its raids against the Spaniards. The Davidson County court ordered that Montgomery be held to security for his appearance to answer at its next term as to his being an abettor of Colbert. The governor of North Carolina also issued a proclamation charging Montgomery with such complicity and ordering his arrest. How far, if at all, he had gone towards or into guilt will never be known. At a later term of the

---

[5] For other details of these activities and supporting references, see Williams, *Beginnings of West Tennessee*, 32–40.

court there was an entry which recited that "the said proclamation being afterwards countermanded, the court considers that said recognizance of course had become void." This gallant officer who had served his country in a signal manner was no longer held in reproach by his fellow-citizens or the State. This is amply evidenced by the fact that in 1796 the county of Montgomery was established and named in his honor.[6]

The inhabitants on the Cumberland were concerned to keep the Chickasaws friendly and to prevent the occupation of the Chickasaw Bluffs by any European nation. To compass the first and obviate the latter, Colonel James Robertson in December, 1782, established at the Lower Bluff a depot to which supplies for the Chickasaws were to be sent. In later years Robertson was the chief factor in maintaining friendly relations between the general government, the people of the Cumberland and that Indian nation.[7]

---

[6] Montgomery and Col. Martin Armstrong in 1784 laid out a town on the north bank of the Cumberland just above the mouth of Red River, to which the name of Montgomery's commander in the conquest of the Northwest was given. Thus the chief's name is borne by the city of Clarksville and his subordinate's by the county. Montgomery was first named in the commission for the establishment of the town, and its name was doubtless proposed by him.

[7] For further light on West Tennessee, see the chapter "The Tennessee Country in Diplomacy."

CHAPTER XXXII

THE TENNESSEE COUNTRY IN DIPLOMACY

In a volume published earlier than this one,[1] the author attempted to show that in colonial times France came dangerously near to prevailing over Great Britain in the contest for the Tennessee country as a part of the Mississippi Valley. In the period of the War of the Revolution, it was another European power, Spain, which sought, time and again, to wrest that country from the Americans. Spain was not bound to the United States by a treaty of alliance; she became so bound to France against Great Britain after France had entered into a treaty to come to the aid of the Americans. In this attitude, Spain was left freer to move in her own interest and against the United States in the matter of territorial gains should the struggle go against Great Britain. Three nations were playing a game of chess against Great Britain, but the spoils of war, in the form of territory, primarily concerned the United States and Spain. Spain feared this country would we become her neighbor. She believed herself now to be in a position to apply the stiletto to the young republic.

During the half-decade before the outbreak of the war, the Spaniards at New Orleans were strengthening their posts along the west bank of the Mississippi, and when the struggle began the claims of the United States and of Spain to the territory south of the Ohio River made impracticable an alliance between those two powers. The two Bourbon courts were as one in their mistrust and hatred of the common enemy, Britain. Both began early and secretly to furnish supplies to the young republic, New Orleans being the common depot. The chief players in the diplomatic game were Vergennes, France's minister of foreign affairs, and his assistant, Rayneval; Florida Blanca, chief minister of state of Spain, and Oranda, Spanish minister to the court of Versailles. By the summer of 1778 Florida Blanca had reached the

---

[1] *Dawn of Tennessee Valley and Tennessee History, passim.*

determination to drive both the British and the Americans from the Mississippi Valley and he began bringing unsuccessful pressure on France to that end. Spaniards feared, in particular, the growing settlements of Americans on the waters of the Mississippi as the Indians were being driven farther south and west by settlers.

It was after the formal alliance of France and the United States in 1778 that the former power began to look for an open ally in Spain; and, in order to bring that power into the war, she was willing to put a degree of pressure on the United States in Spain's behalf.

Gerard, the French representative in this country, began to argue with members of the Continental Congress that the rightful western boundary of their country was the proclamation line of 1763—the base of the Blue Ridge. He met with able opposition led by a member of a great family of Virginia, Richard Henry Lee. Spain and France entered into a treaty in the summer of 1779, and Spain actively engaged in the war; but not, as seen, as a formal ally of the United States. Vergennes knew that Spain had no regard for the territorial rights or claims of the infant republic, and felt that France's two allies were in danger of clashing. When the year 1780 was reached, the Spaniards began to formulate claims (to be advanced in any peace parleys) under the international rule of law—*uti possidetis*, (as you possess by force at the time).[2] Galvez, the enterprising Spanish governor at New Orleans, attacked and took from the British the fortified town of Natchez on the Mississippi, and his country could then urge that this gave Spain a right to the Great Valley east of the Mississippi, at least that part below the Ohio. Americans were willing to concede that it gave Spain a title up to latitude 31 degrees. The application of the same principle would give to Britain Georgia and South Carolina and a claim to a part of North Carolina. Hence, there was given greater significance to the battles in which the over-mountain men fought and were to fight in those States. Luzerne, the new French minister (November,

---

[2] This rule was back of steps taken by Virginia to secure possession of the Great Valley above the Ohio; and it may have been back of James Robertson's establishing a depot on the Lower Chickasaw Bluff in 1782. Haywood in this matter thought Robertson went there "to make a treaty with the Chickasaws."

1779) advanced the argument of the non-right of the United States to lands west of the Blue Ridge, only to raise the ire and indignation of members of Congress from the South. Burke, of North Carolina, was in eruption: "I know the force and the extent of our charters and of our rights, and if those of my constituents in the territories in question [Wataugans and Cumberlanders] are not clear and certain, our rights on the Atlantic coast are equally obscure and doubtful, for they emanate from the same source." [3] Luzerne admitted that actual possession of what was later called West Tennessee would sustain America's claims, but he denied that there was such possession. (Hence the significance of the Holston, Watauga, and Nolachucky settlements, and that of Robertson's advance to the Cumberland). Spain, encouraged by France's stiffened attitude, now demanded that the States with charter claims running to the Mississippi refrain from permitting any further settling of the western country, and cease efforts at further conquests, though she looked to Galvez to carry his conquests farther up the great river. The stiletto was now out of its sheath. Luzerne in an attempt to aid his European ally sought to parry this country's claim to priority under *uti possidetis* by urging that any settlements founded in the West by Americans were made by authority of the British crown, and as such they were still subject to conquest by Spain. He was ignorant of the facts that the Watauga country had been settled in disregard of Britain against whom war was flagrant only after the move into the region began. The French minister proposed to the minister of Spain that they, in combination, force the issue on the Americans whose fate was at the time truly trembling in the balance (1780). Fortunately, Vergennes did not back his minister, and thought the Americans had a right to be indignant over the proposal to deprive them of the fruits of their efforts in settling the West.

The boldest and most vehement opponent in Congress of Luzerne's proposals was Burke, as is shown by the former's report:

---

[3] The French minister wrote home to Vergennes, June 24, 1780, that the British were trying to persuade the people of South Carolina that their sister States had abandoned them; also, that it was the plan of Great Britain to form a new colonial dependency out of the two Carolinas, Georgia and the Bahamas. Phillips, *The West in the Diplomacy of the Revolution,* 156.

Mr. Burke, a man of violent emotions and obstinate temper, though otherwise an excellent citizen, looks upon the projects of Spain as unjust, contrary to the rights of the Thirteen States and prejudicial to their welfare and to their peace; and, if the representations of Mr. Jay induce Congress to make any change in its decision, I fear the full wrath of this representative.

Luzerne now urged Spain to proceed to conquer the West.[4] Some members of Congress weakened and proposed a compromise: a cession to Spain of the country between the Mississippi and the right bank of the Appalachicola, as far north as the Tennessee River. This met with the violent opposition of Southern members.

Another compromise was suggested: An offer to Spain, as a price of her further aid, of a corridor of "one hundred miles of land on the left bank of the Mississippi." Had this been consummated nearly all of the present West Tennessee would have been yielded to the Dons.

With Congress so distraught,[5] one can see more clearly why

---

[4] Luzerne wrote to his government: "I found those States of the South and Center in the firm persuasion that the lands which extended to the Mississippi belonged to them, both by virtue of their charters and by divers acts of possession." *Ib.*

[5] Hunt, in his Introduction to the *Journal of the Continental Congress* for the year 1780, says: "The difficulties which beset the Continental Congress were almost overwhelming . . . On April 4th a committee reported that 'there is no money in the treasury and scarcely any provisions in the public magazines . . . On June 21st Congress was obliged to inform the States that they had failed to furnish any of the 25,000 men, who, it had promised the King of France, would be in the field to co-operate with the forces he was sending over. On August 3rd came a representation from the general officers in their own and the soldiers' behalf, that they were not paid and that no attention was given to their demands. On August 16th news was received of Gates' defeat at Camden; and on September 30th despatches arrived announcing Arnold's treason.' " Such were the clouds of gloom that were measurably cleared by the thunderbolt at King's Mountain, October 7th. During the period of darkened sky, Jones of Virginia said in Congress: "We shall see ourselves despoiled of our most beautiful territory, the lands washed by the Ohio, the Tennessee and the Cumberland, which flow through and water the richest country of the continent, and of the numerous population which possess it; and those whose labors have made it valuable will be forced to abandon it . . . We have not the strength to compel those colonists to give up a land rendered fit for cultivation by their hands and moistened by their sweat." Jones might have well added, "and by their blood."

the battle of King's Mountain was, in truth, the turning of the tide of adversity. Opposition to the demands of Spain and the suggestions and urgings of France grew even more determined; but Spain hesitated to carry the matter as far as an attempt at conquest of the West, east of the Mississippi.[6] As the Westerners were about to surround King's Mountain, Congress on October 4th, 1780, took a strong position in its instructions to Jay in Paris, which they were not sure could be long maintained. Referring to the West east of the Mississippi: "The people inhabiting those States, while connected with Great Britain and also, since the Revolution, have settled themselves at divers places to the westward near the Mississippi, are friendly to the Revolution and . . . Congress cannot assign them over as subjects of any other power."

There was much to justify this statement of the historian Bancroft: "We are come to the series of events which closed the American contest and restored peace to the world. . . . France was straining every nerve to cope with her rival [Britain] in the four quarters of the globe; Spain was exhausting her resources for the conquest of Gibraltar; but the incidents which overthrew the ministry of Lord North and reconciled Great Britain to America had their springs in South Carolina."

Many other historians have expressed the view that on the Southern campaigns launched by Clinton and carried forward by Lord Cornwallis, depended the integrity of the then existing British Empire.

When in 1782 the terms of peace were under consideration, the same argument was made by Rayneval as to America's non-right to the West. As France's representative he proposed this compromise:

A right line should be drawn from the eastern angle of the Gulf of Mexico which makes the division between the two Floridas, to Fort Toulouse, situated in the country of the Alabamos; from thence the river Locushatche [Coosa] should be ascended, from the mouth [source] of which a right line should be drawn to the Fort or Factory Quenassee; from the last place the course of the river Euphasee [Hiwassee] is to be followed till it joins the Cher-

[6] Carmichael, our representative in Madrid, poured into the ears of the Spaniards the assurance that it would be ages before the country along the Mississippi would be settled by Americans. His hearers knew better.

okee [Tennessee]; the course of this last river to be pursued to the place where it receives the Pelisippi [Clinch]; this last to be followed to its source, from which a right line to Cumberland River whose course is to be followed until it falls into the Ohio. The savages to the westward of the line described should be free under the protection of Spain; those to the eastward should be free and under the protection of the United States.

By looking over the chart we shall find that Spain would lose almost the whole course of the Ohio, and that the establishments the Americans have on this river would remain untouched, and that even a very extensive space remains to form new ones.[7]

Manifestly the Frenchman's purpose was to leave out the settlements on the Holston, the Watauga and Nolachucky, since to include them would quarrel with the *uti possidetis* rule, and that he did not know of, or preferred to ignore, the Cumberland settlements, south of that river. In fact, this proposal would have severed those settlements into two parts—a most impracticable thing.

To frustrate such attempts the American peace commissioners closed with Great Britain the treaty of 1783 independently of France, which treaty gave to America all the eastern part of the Great Valley above West Florida.

Aranda, negotiator for Spain, urged on Vergennes in 1782: "This Federal Government is born a pygmy. The day will come when it will be a giant—a colossus . . . The facility for establishing a new population on immense lands, as well as the advantages of a new government, will draw thither farmers and artisans from all nations. In a few years we shall watch with grief the tyrannical existence of the same colossus."

What Aranda so truly said also demonstrates that had Spain gained the region south of the Ohio, or even south of the Cumberland or the Tennessee, she could not have held it long against the hardy borderers who pushed ever farther westward and southward. What was yielded to Spain in 1783, the two Floridas, was not long kept out of the grasp of the land-loving Americans. What had been yielded by France to Great Britain in 1763 was held by the conqueror from the Americans for a little less than two decades.

Spain, as owner of the western bank of the Mississippi and

---

[7] It is evident that Rayneval used d'Anville's old French map in charting the boundaries.

claimant of the eastern bank, sought to hobble the expansion of
Western Americans by asserting an exclusive right to the navigation of that great highway of commerce to New Orleans and the
Gulf of Mexico.   From 1763 until 1779 the use of the Mississippi
had been open to the people of the western waters, first as British
subjects and then as American citizens; and they looked upon a
continuance as a right, recognized as such by the treaty with
Great Britain.   To hamper progressive settlements by the rest-
less and energetic Westerners, Spain next asserted a claim of right
to close the port of New Orleans and the mouth of the Mississippi
to American commerce.   The mere assertion of such a claim was
bound to cause bitter opposition; any attempt to enforce it, to
bring on a conflict of arms.   The assertion came from Madrid
in 1784 and began a wrangle which lasted for more than a decade
—into a period beyond that set for treatment in this volume.[8]

What the leaders of the Cumberland settlements did in our
period to meet this threat is recorded in another chapter.

---

[8] Winsor, *Critical and Narrative History,* VII, 152n.   To be consulted,
with profit, on this phase, are the work of our scholarly Tennessee historian, E. C. Burnett, *The Continental Congress,* and Van Doren's *Secret
History of the American Revolution.* Also, Johnson's *British West Florida,
1763–1783.*   None of these books was published at the time this chapter
was prepared—coming out too late to be used in writing it.

While this touched the people of the Cumberland more nearly than it
did those on the upper reaches of the Tennessee, it may be here noted
that a loaded flatboat belonging to Thomas Amis, of the Holston, was
seized at Natchez by the Spaniards.

CHAPTER XXXIII

LOOKING TO THE FUTURE

While the Revolutionary War formally closed in 1783, the events of the year which followed are briefly summarized. This, in order that there shall not be a gap between what is recorded in the *Dawn of Tennessee Valley and Tennessee History* and *History of the Lost State of Franklin.*

Of primary importance was the continued steady advance of settlements on the Cumberland and down the eastern valleys in what, as yet, was Greene County. Indeed, a few bold and reckless white men with their families crossed the French Broad.[1]

The attitude of the North Carolina government was too equivocal to win the confidence or even the respect of those living on the fringe of the western border. That State had not redeemed its pledge to deliver goods to be passed to the Cherokees in a treaty to be held for the purchase of the Indian lands above the French Broad and below, as far as the Big Pigeon, though the State had sold and granted lands there and received payment from settlers as if the State itself had concluded such a purchase from the Indians. On one subterfuge or another, the holding of a treaty was postponed—at last till April, 1785—which also passed by without an appearance of the promised goods.[2]

The two upper counties, Washington and Sullivan, particularly the former, suffered a drain of their inhabitants into the new county of Greene, and, to a less extent, into the Cumberland country. This was indicated by the allotment made by the North Carolina legislature of jurors for the first superior court from three eastern counties: Washington, fifteen jurors; Sullivan

---

[1] "People from the Nolachucky are improving lands over the French Broad." Col. Joseph Martin to Gov. Martin, Jan'y 25th, 1782. *N. C. St. Recs.,* XVII, 12–16.

[2] This treatment was one of the grounds of complaint validly leveled against North Carolina by the leaders of the movement for the State of Franklin.

twelve, and Greene twenty-one. Greene, at the time, covered the wide expanse of country outside the limits of the three other counties—Davidson being one of the three.

A superior court for all the counties in the West was established —for what was named "Washington District"—with Jonesborough as the judicial capital.[3] It is believed that for years only one session was held, because of the establishment by the State of Franklin of its own courts. The "capital" was made ready by the Washington County court which ordered the construction of a new courthouse, the specifications being: twenty-four feet square, diamond corners, hewn down after it is built up; nine feet high between the two floors; body of the house four feet above the upper floor; floors neatly laid with planks; shingles of the roof to be hung with pegs; a justices' bench; a lawyers' and clerk's bar; also a sheriff's box to sit in. Ramsey aptly says of Jonesborough of that day: "It was already distinguished as the oldest town established in the present Tennessee, the center of much of the intelligence and political influence in the new country."[4]

In the general assembly of North Carolina for the year 1784 were: Elijah Robertson, of Davidson; Wm. Cage and David Looney, of Sullivan; Joshua Gist and Alexander Outlaw, of Greene, and Charles Robertson (in the senate) and Landon Carter, of Washington. An ambitious effort was made to lay off and mark a road from Long Island of Holston to far-away Green Lick on Duck River and to French Lick on Cumberland River.

The route into Kentucky through Bean's Station, across Clinch Mountains and through Cumberland Gap was now frequently used, even by Virginians.[5] As late as 1784 the journey was a perilous one, as wily Chickamauga Indians lurked along the trail. For security, parties of large numbers formed, led by unencumbered horsemen, all traveling in single file. Another like group brought up the rear, with women, children and packhorses in between.[6]

[3] *N. C. Acts of 1784*, ch. 28.
[4] *Annals*, 281.
[5] A Federal highway now runs the same course.
[6] An interesting account of two such parties is given in Waddell, *Annals of Augusta County*, 316–18. One of these consisted of 300 from Augusta County, and at Bean's Station they were joined by 200 more from Carolina, three-fourths of all being women and children. At that Station they

Colonel John Sevier was raised to the rank of brigadier-general of the new District of Washington; and David Campbell was named assistant judge for the district.

The name of Nashborough was changed to Nashville, and Samuel Barton, Thomas Malloy, Daniel Smith, James Shaw and Isaac Lindsey were named by the legislature "directors to lay off and carry on" [7] the town. James Robertson was by an act granted first choice of four lots at four pounds, each.

The principal officers of the militia of Davidson County were: Anthony Bledsoe, colonel; Isaac Bledsoe, first major; Samuel Barton, second major; Kasper Mansker, George Freeland, John Buchanan and James Ford, captains.

Provision was made for the building of a court house, prison and stocks, Ephraim McLean, Andrew Ewin and Jonathan Drake, the commissioners; also for the establishment of a court of oyer and terminer for the trial of criminal cases, including felony cases. Davidson County was in Washington District.[8]

A flood of prospectors for lands and homes came into the Cumberland country and on the lower reaches of the Tennessee, a large majority of them being North Carolinians, most of them to settle on the military reservation,[9] the lower part of which was

---

were also joined by James Knox and his group, and the entire command was conceded to Knox. At the eastern base of Clinch Mountain signs of prowling Indians were observed and an attack in force at Cumberland Gap was expected, but none was made. The account of this journey is intensely interesting. It should be incorporated in full in any history of Grainger or Claiborne county.

[7] *N. C. Acts 1784*, ch. 47. The change from "borough" (English) to "ville" (French) seems appropriate, since the town site had been French Lick. The Act recites, "in honor of the patriotic and brave Gen. Nash." See n. p. Gen. Nash's name already appeared in Nashborough. Each purchaser of a lot was, by his deed, required to build a "framed or square-logged or brick or stone house, sixteen feet square at least and eight feet pitch in the clear, with a brick or stone chimney." These conditions were to be complied with within three years from the date of the conveyance. Samuel Barton was named the town treasurer.

[8] It so continued until Mero District was created in 1788 and named for Estevan Miro, Spanish governor at New Orleans, whose name was misspelled in the legislative act.

[9] "So that nine-tenths of the early population were North Carolinians." Clayton, *History of Davidson County*, 45. This is an over-estimate. Some valuable citizens were lost by the Holston and Watauga regions to Middle Tennessee in this period, most of them of Virginia birth.

rendered more inviting after the Chickasaw cession of 1783.

The three counties in the eastern part of the Tennessee country also now received accessions, principally from the Valley of Virginia.[10] Everywhere the future was viewed with hopefulness, and with confidence that in their part of the West a Commonwealth was in the offing. With two such great leaders as John Sevier and James Robertson such confidence was not unjustified.

In 1784–6 the North Carolina general assembly entered on a course of action with the evident intent to win the aid of the leaders and people of Davidson County—then of wide expanse—to the aiding of prominent men of Eastern Carolina in gaining choice lands in those regions which are now known as Middle and West Tennessee. The inhabitants of Davidson County were given preferential treatment—in marked contrast with what had been done for early settlers on the upper reaches of the Tennessee, on the Watauga and Nolachucky and Holston Rivers.

The first step was the exemption of the Davidson inhabitants from the payment of poll taxes in 1784; the raising of three companies (two hundred and one men) for the protection of the Cumberland settlements, compensation to be in warrants for lands west of Cumberland Mountains; and, particularly, the awarding to each of the first settlers on the Cumberland, or his heirs, a grant of 640 acres of land "without being obliged to pay any price for the same."

These favoring acts played a large part in the later history of the Tennessee country. It accounts for the lack of harmony between those who lived west of the Cumberlands and those who had earlier settled the region east of those mountains.

Speaking of this people of the Tennessee country, of their part in the development of the Mississippi Valley and of their influence in forming a frontier democracy, the greatest historian of the West, Frederick J. Turner, wrote: "Its center rested in Tennessee, the region from which so large a portion of the Mississippi Valley was settled by the descendants of the men of the Upper South." [11]

---

[10] Towards the close of 1784 Richard Henry Lee wrote a letter to Madison, in which he spoke of daily accounts of powerful migrations from Virginia southward and southwest, caused by land hunger and the hatred of heavy taxes. *Letters of R. H. Lee,* II, 300.

[11] *The Frontier in American History,* 192. Later on, in writing of An-

It has been this writer's purpose to demonstrate, at least partially, the correctness of Turner's conclusion.

This people could not pierce the future far enough to see that their sons would be called to fight another war with Great Britain; that one of their kind would soon appear among them to lead those sons to victory at New Orleans in 1815, and later give to the nation its "Jacksonian Epoch."

It was, of course, beyond the ken of those people, far-visioned as they were, to foresee that the East Tennessee Valley they were conquering, seizing and possessing, would, in far-off years, become once more a frontier but of a different sort. They could not look down the vista of time to oncoming generations and forecast that the national government would build great dams in the rivers and develop electric power which would bring to the region a host of migrants to make homes and join in a great industrial development—*of a modern frontier.*[12]

drew Jackson, he said: "He had the essential traits of the Kentucky and Tennessee frontier. It was a frontier free from the influence of European ideas and institutions. The men of the western waters turned their backs upon the Atlantic Ocean and with a grim energy and self-reliance began to build up a society free from the dominance of ancient forms."

[12] Common justice impels the recording here of a fact: the father of this frontier was a far-seeing Westerner, Senator George W. Norris, of Nebraska, who introduced the bill in Congress for the location of the Tennessee Valley Authority, and through several years of effort overcame opposition to the measure and secured its passage.

APPENDICES

APPENDIX A

Excerpt from the Virginia Gazette, of July 26, 1776

WILLIAMSBURG, *July* 26.

YESTERDAY afternoon, agreeable to an order of the Hon. Privy Council, the DECLARATION of INDEPENDENCE was folemnly proclaimed at the Capitol, the Courthoufe, and the Palace, amidft the acclamations of the people, accompanied by firing of cannon and mufketry, the feveral regiments of continental troops having been paraded on that folemnity.

Advices from Charleftown, which arrived here by exprefs, fay, that the Cherokee Indians have committed feveral outrages; which feems to be only a part of the capital and favourite plan laid down by his *moft excellent* and *clement* majefty, George the third, to lay wafte the provinces, burn the habitations, and mix men, women, and children, in one common carnage, by the hands of thofe mercilefs favages. It is to be hoped, however, that our frontier riflemen, joined to thofe of the Carolinas, will be able, before long, to ftrike fome blow that may intimidate the numerous tribes of Indiaus from falling into the meafures of the tyrant, and make a fevere, lafting, and falutary example, of the treacherous Cherokees ---By the fame exprefs, we learn that the army and fquadron under Clinton and Parker have remained tolerably quiet fince their late drubbing; but daily make fome alteration in the difpofition of the land forces, from one ifland to another, probably for the fake of water, of which deferters fay they are in great want, as allo that confiderable ficknefs prevails among them, and great difcontents, from hard duty and bad diet.

FACSIMILE REPRODUCTION OF THE EXCERPT

Copy of a Talk from Nath'l Gist to Oconastota
Raven, Dragging Canoe and Tassel

Brothers

When I parted with you last I promised to be
back before cold weather was done and according to your
desire have spoke to the great Warriors of the American
States for peace for you and now send by one of your
own people some of the Talks they gave me and have
several more good Talks to give when you came to this
place to treat ~ I also now send you two Strings of
Wampum that was delivered me by the delawares and
Shawanese for the Cherokees, desiring that they would
no more listen to the lying bad Talks Carried you by
some of their foolish people and the mingoes, for that
the delawares and Shawanese had brightned the Chain
of friendship with Virginia, have taken them by the hand
and will for ever live as brothers and be as one people
and that whoever is enemies to the American States
they will esteem as their Enemies and will go to War
with them accordingly ~

        Two Strings of Wampum

Brothers

Immediatly after I left the/Cherokee Country [p.322]
last fall I set out and travelled Northwardly as far as
New York during my journey I had an opportunity

Gist's first communication to the chiefs of the Cherokees. One copy,
doubtless that of the Dragging Canoe, reached Superintendent John
Stuart and found its way to the British Archives in London.

of seeing and talking with many great Council men and Warriors of America and now know their hearts is good to all the Red people their Neighbours if it is not their own fault — At last near New York I met with my old friend General Washington at the head of a great Army seen great numbers of prisoners he had taken of the people over the great Water at war with us and know that the King during the Cold Weather has lost four thousand five hundred men near New York before I left that and I do think they are all killed and taken before now as they were then surrounded in a little Spot Starving for bread and begging for peace —

All my Brothers listen attentively

I saw the great English Warriors Letter to General Washington begging peace as the French and Spaniards had begun a War over the great Water and that their Ships must go home to fight and save the Country where the King lives —

Brothers

If you now mind well what I say all may be well with you yet. I seen plenty of powder, Lead and other goods in Virginia and you may get enough after the peace is Confirmed and I think I can get the white people to forgive the / Murder you Committed the last Winter as I hope it was done by some foolish young men Contrary to the advice of the Head men.

you know all particularly my Comrade the Dragging Canoe that what I advised last year before you went to War was for your good, and would have saved the lives of many of your people, and saved your Towns from being destroyed ~

Now I again tell you this year it will be much worse than last unless you now make a peace when the good time is Come, as it is the last offer of peace you will get from Virginia; so don't blame me when hard times Comes again among you as I have now told you the truth and advised you for your good and now offer to shake hands with all my Brothers the Cherokees in behalf of Virginia ~

The bearer hereof or a runner sent from you with a white flag must Come to me here in twenty days that I may know whether you are Coming for peace or not, they shall be kindly treated and kept from harm

(Signed) Nath.ᶜˡ Gist

Great Island Fort
   28.ᵗʰ March 1777

[P.ᵃᵍᵉ 306]

Endorsed Great Island Fort / 28.ᵗʰ march 1777 / Copy of a Talk from / Nath.ˡ Gist at Oconastota / & other head Men of the / Cherokees ~ In M.ʳ Stuart's (N.ᵒ 17) of / 14.ᵗʰ June 1777.

APPENDIX C

Dr. Col°.

This moment, I met Capt. McCorkle, have seen the Letter he brings to you, it appears the Indians have actually struck, and kill'd a Man near the Fort at Watauga, and that a number of Tracks have been seen not fare distant therefrom, all making toward s^d Fort. From these sircumstances it is almost certain they cannot support much longer together without making an attack on some of our settlements. The Capt. Informs me that our strength near the Island (together with a Company waiting to be taken into Service) does not exceed two hundred and fourty; a small number I think to make head against the strength we have reason to expect against us: the number at Rye Cove is uncertain, as I can get no exact Acc^t. I hope you'l take every step you think will Expedite the March of the Companys now under Marching Orders.

I have examined the situation of the Lead Mines, and find it absolutely necessary to augment the strength at that Post to Thirty Men, which, together with the Neighbourhood that ought to assemble there, I hope may [be? MS torn] sufficient Guard to protect the Works which number of thirty, [MS torn] pper officers I hope you'l Immediately Order including those at Fort Chiswell, who must be sent there! I have directed a small Fort to be built round the Works, if Timber can be h^d convenient. Two hundred WT of the Powder at Fort Chiswell being good for nothing, proves to me the necessity of applying to some ajacent County to lend us some, till we can replace it from below, without which I am well satisfy'd our Country will brake up in a short time. I know of no better expedient, than to apply to Col°. Fleming for two hundred and fifty or three hund, and that to be guarded by the Men coming from that County, if they have not Marched before Col°. Flemming can be apply'd to, should that be the case, pleas sir, to order it to the Mines, where I hope the Guard will be sufficient to take care of it.

I have Wrote to Col°. Flemming to send 50 more Men, which, together with the Company's already call'd for, I hope may be sufficient, to cover our Frontier, until we can apply to the Executive Power.

But, should we be disappointed in geting one other Comp^y. from Botetourt, I hope you'l mak[e up? MS torn] a Company, off the

Waters of New River, and if agreeable to y[MS torn] the Comm^d. of it to Capt. Draper. The bad Powder at Fort Chiswell, I think ought to be sent out here to distribute among the Forts where the Inhabitants have geathered. it being all we can spare them at present, perhaps it may be worked over, and amended. I fear our men on Duty are much unguarded,—and consequently liable to surprise: but shall try as quick as possible to remedy that Evil. while writting many People come in, by whom I understand, many of the Men now at the Island expect to be Relieved in a Week or ten Days to secure their Harvest, the[re]fore must apply again to Col^o. Smith of Augusta for another Company. I beg to refer you to Capt. McCorkle for the Report of our Victory at Charlestown. I hope to here from you by all opportunities, and am, D^r· Col^o. your Most Obed^t. & Humb. Servt.

                                                    W Russell

            July 20th 1776
Addressed: On the Publick Service
            To Colo. William Preston
         favour'd by
      Capt. McCorkle
Endorsed: Col^o. Russell's
            Letter July 20th '76

(On the reverse of the letter is this note:)

Sir, Our Scouts this Moment some of them come in, W^m. Falling in particular, & have discovered the Tracks of about one hundred Indians, coming right along the Path from Browns, making towards our Fort; the Scouts then left the Road & push'd in, & as they came in they discovered the Tracks of several Parties, supposed to be 15 & 20 in a Party, all making towards the Fort. I am sure they will attack this Fort in the Morning. Myself & the other Officers is in good Spirits & will do all we can, & hope we will be able to give them a warm Reception & keep them Out, untill you can assist us with more Men.

                        Farewell
                        James Rober[t]son
                    —Draper MSS. 4 QQ 55

APPENDIX D

ATTA KULLAH KULLAH [2]

One of the Leaders of the Cherokees, who inhabited the banks of the
river Tennessee.

This Indian chief, better known among the whites by the appell-
tion of *Little Carpenter*, was born in the Big Island [3] of the French
Broad River (being the same island through which the Nolochuckie
war path formerly passed towards the Overhill towns) so long ago
that he recited various facts of ancient date (in 1777), the truth of
which was strongly corroborated by many respectable testimonies.
The place of his nativity, indeed, was then covered with stately and
venerable oaks, supposed to be coeval with the last century. This
warrior, who was reputed to be a deep and sound politician, took a
lead in many of the councils and treaties of his own countrymen: he
spoke well and had considerable influence. The Little Carpenter
professed uniformly to be a friend of the white people; and had, at
least, sagacity enough to persuade them he was sincerely so. But it
we are to believe the accounts of some contemporary countrymen,
who were entitled to equal credit, he was a sly, artful, cunning hypo-

---

[1] From the *Annual of Biography and Obituary*, 1820. (London.)
These sketches by Williams Tatham have been reprinted in America, only
in Williams, *William Tatham, Wataugan*, 21 *et seq.* Since that little
volume was in a severely limited edition (exhausted in the year of its
publication), they are reprinted here. The notes are by S. C. W.

[2] Usually spelled, Attakullaculla, from the Cherokee words, ata (wood)
and gulkalu (a word implying that something long is leaning against
another object); hence, "Leaningwood." Mooney, *Myths of the Cherokees*, 510. For other accounts of this great chief, see Drake, *Aboriginal
Races*, 373; Goodpasture, "Indian Wars and Warriors in the Old Southwest," *Tennessee Historical Magazine*, IV, p. 1, et. seq.; Mooney, *Myths*,
40; Hodge, *Handbook of American Indians*, 115; Logan, *History of Upper
South Carolina*, I, 490–515. Haywood at one place calls him by mistake,
"Little Cornplanter." He was one of the delegation of chiefs taken over-
seas to the British Court, by Alexander Cumings, in 1730. Williams,
Early Travels in the Tennessee Country, passim.

[3] Later called Sevier's Island, Ramsey, 263. A rendezvous of the
pioneers in their later wars against the Cherokees, *Ib.*, 272.

crite, who deceived both parties to serve his own views, and under the mask of friendship, he was often the secret stimulator of bloodshed.[4] Certain it is that he preserved his influence to a good age, and died a natural death in his own country, about the termination of, or a little after the American war.[5] Atakullahkullah was a man of small stature,[6] but when young was admitted, by those who had long known him, to have been as alert in the field as he was latterly in the council. He had several friends of a similar age and standing; of them it may suffice to mention *Oconistoto* and *Onitossitah*, or the *Corn Tassel*. The first of these was the chief king or emperor of all the Cherokee tribes and divisions; and the latter was reputed to be the best statesman, as well as the greatest orator, of their country.

OCONISTOTO [7]

This ancient chieftain was a strong, athletic, large man, pitted with smallpox, and of blunt, plain, downright manners, such as might be

---

[4] There is nothing to justify this suspicion. The Little Carpenter was the steadfast friend of the whites as far as their course against his people would allow. See sketches above referred to.

[5] Probably 1780.

[6] This accords with the description given by William Bartram in his *Travels in North America*. Bartram thus describes him: "The Cherokees' present grand chief or emperor (the Little Carpenter, Atta-kul-kulla), is a man of remarkable small stature, slender and of a delicate frame, the only instance I saw in the nation; but he is a man of superior abilities." Page 482. For Bartram's account of his interview with the Little Carpenter see pages 362–4. He was "half-king" or vice-king and not the king or emperor at this time, as Bartram states. The delineation given by Felix Walker in his *Memoirs* (p. 8) is yet more interesting. He attributes the name of "Little Carpenter" to this chief's possession of great diplomatic skill: "Like as a carpenter could make every notch and joint fit in wood, so he could bring all his views to fill and fit their places in the political machinery of his nation. He was the most celebrated and influential Indian among all the tribes then known; considered as the Solon of his day. He was said (1775) to be about ninety years of age; a very small man, and so lean and light-habited that I scarcely believe he would have exceeded more in weight than a pound for each year of his life. He was marked with two large scores of scarfs on each cheek; his ears cut and beaded with silver, hanging nearly down to each shoulder, the ancient Indian mode of distinction in some tribes, and fashion in others." Walker saw the Little Carpenter at the Treaty of Sycamore Shoals, March, 1775.

[7] Usually spelled, Oconostota, from the Cherokee (groundhog sausage) Mooney. For accounts of him, see Drake, ib., and Goodpasture, ib.; Hodge II, 105; Thwaites and Kellogg, *Dunmore's War*, 38; Mooney, 42, 207, 355; Hewat, *Historical Account*, II, 237, 243.

expected from a rough English countryman, who takes the shortest road to arrive at the truth. He made it his business to attend and listen to what passed in all treaties; and he took care to preface them with a candid acknowledgment that he was no speaker and not much of a statesman; but that he had a high confidence in the abilities of his nephew and representative (Savanooka, or the Raven of Chota) in these matters, and that he should set his hand to whatsoever he said, reserving to himself the privilege of putting him right if he went astray; this, indeed, was a liberty which he would take with any man, however great or powerful. The relator of these facts was once present, when one of the ancient inhabitants of Kentucky asserted a position concerning his purchase of that country, which the old warrior dissented from, and his reply may be exhibited here as a specimen of his manners. After commenting for some time on the term "sale of these lands" he spoke nearly as follows: "Why you know you are telling lies! We always told you these lands were not ours; that our claim extended not beyond Cumberland mountain; that all the lands beyond Cumberland river belonged to our brothers, the Chickasaws. It is true you gave us some goods for which we promised you our friendship in the affair, and our good will. These you have had according to bargain, and more we never promised you; but you have deceived your people!"

It was a favorite topic with the old king to recite military exploits of his youth; and the writer of this narrative was present at a singular conversation between him and Thomas Price,[8] a respectable old trader with the Cherokees, who had accompanied him in some unsuccessful expeditions in early life. Speaking of one of these against the Shawanees, Mr. Price reminded his majesty that they were beaten at a particular place on the river Ohio; and asked him if they had not been forced to retreat? "True, Thomas," replied the old man, "I confess that we had the worst of it; but they did not make us *run;* we only *walked very fast!*"

ONITOSITAH

Onitositah, or the Corn Tassel,[9] of the Cherokee nation of Indians,

---

[8] Price was an attesting witness to the deed of the Cherokees to Robertson, Trustee of the Watauga Settlers (1775). Ramsey, 120. Also mentioned in connection with the Little Carpenter, in a letter of Robertson to Governor Caswell, evidently written by William Tatham. Ramsey, 172. Price's home was in Washington County.

[9] Mooney (page 544) gives as the Cherokee equivalent Utsidsata (Corn Tassel). In his later years he was called by the whites, "Old Tassel," or "Old Corn Tassel." He had his residence at Chota. There seems to be no

though somewhat younger, was the leading counsellor of Oconistoto, and consequently his contemporary, as well as that of *Attahallah-kallah, Willanawaugh,* and the *Pigeon.* He added to the reputation of a profound Indian statesman and orator, the inestimable character of being uniformly respected for his integrity and truth; in this last point it was said of him by all of his acquaintances, that throughout a long and useful life in his own country, he was never known to stoop to a falsehood. The Corn Tassel was a stout, mild and decided man, rather comely than otherwise; and of a smooth and somewhat fat and inflated face.

At the treaty of Long Island, in July, 1777, he was the principal spokesman, and on the proposition of the American Commissioners that the Cherokees should cede a much greater extent of country than was agreed to in the result, the following able reply on his part is given from a memorandum of a gentleman who was present; [10] yet it is supposed to have been bereaved of much of its native beauty by the defects of interpretation; for the manly and dignified expression of an Indian orator loses nearly all its force and energy in translation.

SPEECH OF ONITOSSITAH

"It is a little surprising that when we entered into treaties with our brothers, the whites, their whole cry is *more land!* Indeed, formerly it seemed to be a matter of formality with them to demand what they knew we durst not refuse. But on the principles of fairness, of which we have received assurances during the conducting of the present treaty, and in the name of free will and equality, I must reject your demand.

"Suppose, in considering the nature of your claim (and in justice to my nation I shall and will do it freely), I were to ask one of you, my brother warriors, under what kind of authority, by what law, or on what pretense he makes this exorbitant demand of nearly all the

other sketch of this able chief. Materials for one appear in Haywood, Ramsey, *North Carolina State Records,* and *Calendar of Virginia State Papers.* Corn Tassel visited Philadelphia in 1787, for the purpose of laying before Congress, not then in session, the complaints of his people against the whites because of trespasses on the domain of the Cherokees. He met Benjamin Franklin, who gave a talk to the chief: "I am sorry that the Great Council Fire of our Nation is not now burning, so that you cannot now do your business there. In a few months the coals will be raked out of the ashes, and the fire will be again kindled. Our wise men will then take the complaints and desires of your Nation into consideration and take the proper measures for giving you satisfaction." (June 30, 1787.) Corn Tassel succeeded Oconostata in the principal chiefship.

[10] The gentleman referred to was William Tatham, himself.

lands we hold between your settlements and our towns, as the cement and consideration of our peace.[11]

"Would he tell me that it is by right of conquest? No! If he did, I should retort on him that *we* had last marched over his territory; even up to this very place which he has *fortified* so far within his former limits; nay, that some of our young warriors (whom we have not yet had an opportunity to recall or give notice to, of the general treaty) are still in the woods, and continue to keep his people in fear, and that it was but till lately that these identical walls were your strongholds, out of which you durst scarcely advance.

"If, therefore, a bare march, or reconnoitering a country is sufficient reason to ground a claim to it, we shall insist upon transposing the demand, and your relinquishing your settlements on the western waters and removing one hundred miles back towards the east, whither some of our warriors advanced against you in the course of last year's campaign.

"Let us examine the facts of your present eruption into our country, and we shall discover your pretentions on that ground. What did you do? You marched into our territories with a superior force; our vigilance gave us no timely notice of your manouvres; your numbers far exceeded us, and we fled to the stronghold of our extensive woods, there to secure our women and children.

"Thus, you marched into our towns; they were left to your mercy; you killed a few scattered and defenseless individuals, spread fire and desolation wherever you pleased, and returned again to your own habitations. If you meant this, indeed, as a conquest you omitted the most essential point; you should have fortified the junction of the Holstein and Tennessee rivers, and have thereby conquered all the waters above you.[12] But, as all are fair advantages during the existence of a state of war, it is now too late for us to suffer for your mishap of generalship!

"Again, were we to inquire by what law or authority you set up a claim, I answer, *none!* Your laws extend not into our country, nor

---

[11] This reference to the lust for lands on the part of the whites long continued to be much on the mind of Corn Tassel. In June, 1787, he wrote Governor Randolph of Virginia: "I observe in every treaty that we have made that a bound is fixed but that your people settle much faster shortly after a treaty than before. . . . Truth is, if we had no lands, we should have fewer enemies." *Calendar Virginia State Papers*, IV, 306.

[12] The mention of a fort at this place may have been the source of Colonel Arthur Campbell's suggestion (1780) to the same effect. Jefferson concurred with that view: "If you can effect this, a right should be reserved for building a fort at the confluence of Holston and Tennessee." February 17, 1781, *Writings of Jefferson*, I, 295.

ever did. You talk of the law of nature and the law of nations, and they are both against you.

"Indeed, much has been advanced on the want of what you term civilization among the Indians; and many proposals have been made to us to adopt your laws, your religion, your manners and your customs. But, we confess that we do not yet see the propriety, or practicability of such a reformation, and should be better pleased with beholding the good effect of these doctrines in your own practices than with hearing you talk about them, or reading your papers to us upon such subjects.

"You say: Why do not the Indians till the ground and live as we do? May we not, with equal propriety, ask, Why the white people do not hunt and live as we do? You profess to think it no injustice to warn us not to kill our deer and other game from the mere love of waste; but it is very criminal in our young men if they chance to kill a cow or a hog for their sustenance when they happen to be in your lands. We wish, however, to be at peace with you, and to do as we would be done by. We do not quarrel with you for killing an occasional buffalo, bear or deer on our lands when you need one to eat; but you go much farther; your people hunt to gain a livelihood by it; they kill all our game; our young men resent the injury, and it is followed by bloodshed and war.

"This is not a mere affected injury; it is a grievance which we equitably complain of and it demands a permanent redress.

"The great God of Nature has placed us in different situations. It is true that he has endowed you with many superior advantages; but he has not created us to be your slaves. *We are a separate people!* He has given each their lands, under distinct considerations and circumstances; he has stocked yours with cows, ours with buffaloe; yours with hog, ours with bear; yours with sheep, ours with deer. He has, indeed, given you an advantage in this, that your cattle are tame and domestic while ours are wild and demand not only a larger space for range, but art to hunt and kill them; they are, nevertheless, as much our property as other animals are yours, and ought not to be taken away without our consent, or for something equivalent."

SAVANOOKA [13]

Known among the Whites by the name of the Raven of Chota.

This warrior was by birth a Shawanee; but, by marriage, he belonged to the Cherokees with whom he resided; and he was the he-

---

[13] Savanucah (Ramsey) or Sawanugi (Cherokee for Shawnee) known by the whites as the Raven of Chota. In the treaty of purchase by the Wataugans (1775) he is called Savanucah, otherwise Coronoh. The name

reditary representative of the Cherokee Empire; but whether as the sister's son of Oconistoto or by marriage is not recollected by the writer, who was well acquainted with him.

He was a stout, manly, firm and dignified person; of an open, yet serious deportment, dark complexion, steadfast and comely countenance; and was reputed to be the most powerful man in the Cherokee nation at all athletic exercises.

He bore the reputation of a good warrior, and certainly was not inferior in council or oratorical abilities to any one of his tribe.

Notwithstanding his fame in war, he was naturally disposed to cultivate the enjoyments of peace; and he gave several strong proofs of this disposition in the campaign of 1776, when he commanded the left division of the Cherokees, professing openly his aversion to the conflict, and directing their mischief to objects short of murder, so far as he had power to extend his influence.

In the autumn of that year he came to the frontier garrison of the United States, accompanied by Ninatoogah (or the Bloody Fellow), a noted young warrior of the Cherokees, and a Chickasaw called Nahoolah (or the Little Owl), and two or three others, who spent the winter at the fort and laid the foundations of the next year's treaty. At that treaty, held in July following at the Long Island of Holstein, he was a principal speaker.

Little more can now be said of him, except that a circumstance happened during the treaty which fully evinced his power over the nation, and is somewhat descriptive of their obedience to superiors. While the Corn Tassel (Onitossitah) was speaking on a very interesting branch of the treaty, some of the Indians (who were encamped to the amount of about four hundred, in the island opposite, which was overlooked from the arbor where the assembly was held) had got so drunk and outrageous in camp that the women were busily employed in hiding guns, tomahawks and other weapons; and the whole encampment had become a scene of riot and confusion which disturbed the spectators of the treaty. The speaker on this ceased for a moment, on which the Raven arose from his seat and directed two young warriors, who composed a part of the audience, to step over and *tie* the rioters. They sprang immediately to a canoe, crossed the river, and in a few minutes quieted the camp as if nothing had hap-

---

of Raven "points out an indefatigable, keen and successful warrior" (Adair). It was a favorite name for the chiefs of the Cherokees; and was, therefore, for particularization followed by the name of the village in which the person bearing it lived. For further facts respecting the Raven, see Ramsey, Goodpasture, and *North Carolina Colonial Records*.

pened, and rejoined the audience who experienced no further interruption.

It may be ramarked that such an affray would have been harder to
quell under the boasted regulations of a civilized system, yet these
were savages!

APPENDIX E

LETTER OF JAMES ROBERTSON TO COMMISSIONERS LANIER AND
WINSTON

Washington District Oct 1777

Sirs.—

I had a Talk in Chota with the Indians on the 29th of September, when I had a letter sent me by Mr. Avery read and interpreted to a number of the warriors and chiefs of the Nation. I gave them a talk of my own in which I endeavoured to lay open to them the dangerous consequences that might attend their adhering too much to Cameron and those Ministerial tools, the Tories that had deluded and pressed them to a war before, and that they had found them false, and they would still be so. And the Indians seemed to be well pleased with the whole—at least to appearances; and I am of opinion that there is not the least danger of a lasting peace [1] with them at Chuckemago as well as those in the Upper Towns, though they complain much of the want of trade.

As I was going to the Nation I met with Capt. Martin, Agent for the State of Virginia, on this side of French Broad River, who told me he looked on my going into the Nation to be precarious and dangerous. He informed me that the Indians advised him to leave the Nation, and that they were afraid that he had staid too long; but when I got in I found the Indians all peaceable and friendly—though all the white people amongst them that were friends to us and the American cause on some pretense of danger had left the Nation— some of which has brought their familys, and others expect their women after them in a short time: except Fields,[2] who is armourer to the Indians, paid by the State of Virginia. I learnt amongst the Indians that some of them had left the Nation under pretense of getting goods which they said was to be sent to the Long Island for them from Virginia; and others stole away unperceived by the Indians and took their horses out of the range, about Little River, and so left the Nation. Amongst those fled in the manner before told are Ellis Harling, Francis Budwine, John Benge,[3] and one Hawkins.

---

[1] Seemingly, Agent Robertson meant to say "failure of a lasting peace."

[2] Founder of a family which was influential in the Cherokee Nation in later generations.

[3] Father of a Cherokee leader in later years.

Provisions are very scarce amongst the Indians. I was obliged to give ten pounds, Virginia currency, for a small steer. I carry a great part of my provisions from home with me; and a little does not serve, as I have a good many visitors. Capt. Martin is clear of that expense, having fifteen beeves given him by the State of Virginia.[4]

I should have gone down to the Assembly myself, but think it may be to the advantage of the State for me to return soon to the Nation. I am very doubtful that Cameron may have me taken prisoner, and any white people he knows to be friends to the American cause. I see no way to prevent it but by fixing a station either in [the] Upper Towns or at the Fork of the River[5] that might enable us to send a party down to the Chuckemoga, and take that party of Ministerial white people that is there. I understand there is about a dozen now, and Cameron is expected shortly. He has a house built; and we have not the least reason to think he will venture without a number of Tories, perhaps a hundred or more, as I am informed he has that many now with him in the Creek Nation.

One Inis,[6] that was an assistant commissary at Long Island, as soon as he returned to the Nation went to Cameron and still continues with him.

A few days before I got to the Nation, Cameron had sent his deputy at Chuckemago (with orders to give out to the Indians) that Philadelphia was taken, and fourteen thousands of the Provincials killed, and that America in six weeks time would be in ye hands of the English. All which I contradicted in my Talk the 29th of Sep't.

I think it would be necessary, if I should be continued as agent for the State any longer, that I be empowered to administer oaths, and take depositions when necessary. The Indians will not give up the horses, save two of my own, which were so poor I could not get them home, and have since lost them, and never expect to get them more.

At the conference above mentioned, Oconostoto, ye Little Carpenter and Willonowah were appointed by the council to pay his Excellency, the Governor of the State, and his council a visit, agreeable to the directions of Mr. Avery's letter; and they at that time sent a runner to the Middle Settlements and the Valley Towns to warn some of their chiefs to be ready there to go down with them.

---

[4] The contrast between the treatment by Virginia of her agent and that accorded by North Carolina to Robertson is to be remarked.

[5] The point of confluence of the streams (near present-day Lenoir City). This seems to be the first suggestion of a fort there. It may be that Col. Arthur Campbell based his advocacy of a fort in the Fork on what he had learned from Robertson.

[6] Colonel Innis mentioned in the text. See Index.

I am dubious that Capt. Price and his men may be prejudicial to the State, as I have reason to believe that there are some ill-disposed persons in that company; and I am well assured that there will be Indians on that Course a hunting, and I understand that they are frequently ranging below the bounds settled by the Commissioners, and threaten the Indians.

I beg leave to refer you to Col. John Carter [7] for further particulars. And, having nothing more of importance to inform you of, shall conclude with subscribing myself your obedient and very humble servant,

Jas. Robertson.

Colo. Lanier
Major Winston 17th Oct. 1777.

Draper MSS, KK, p. 32

[7] Who was on the point of leaving home for a session of the North Carolina general assembly.

APPENDIX F

(Col. Wm. Campbell to Col. Wm. Preston)

Major Gilbert Christians,[1] Dec.
15th 1780.

By an express I am informed that the trail of about 20 of the Enemy [Indians] was discovered yesterday 20 miles below this, making up the river. This I conclude may be the advance to a large Body; consequently, we will have fighting nearer than their Towns. I am sorry and ashamed of the tardy preparations of our Militia for War. They must exert themselves or the Country will be subjected to great desolation. I hope you will hurry the Men down as well provided for with provisions as possible. The Country below the North Fork abounds with Corn; consequently we need not starve.

Va. Mag. of History, XXVII, 317.

---

[1] Near Long Island of Holston. In later years the name of "Christiansville" was given to the neighborhood.

APPENDIX G

Perhaps General Nathanael Greene, above any other commander of American forces in the South, was in the best position to make an adequate and just appraisal of the quality of the troops from East and West North Carolina. What follows tends to show why the General was so persistent and insistent that the over-mountain riflemen return for "repeat-performances" east of the Alleghanies. His appraisal, made near the end of the war, did not lack frankness or incisiveness. Better still, it was based largely on personal observation of the troops in action on the field of battle. He wrote from his camp on Pee Dee River in South Carolina in June, 1781:

"The back country people are bold and daring in their make, but the people on the seaboard are sickly and indifferent militia."

An impulse cannot be restrained—to end this volume with a quere for the consideration of the students of the Revolutionary War:

What people of any other section, having a population and manpower the size of those on the western waters, contributed as much to the winning of that war as did the trans-mountain riflemen of Campbell, Shelby and Sevier and their alternates?

275

Abbott, Edward, 101
Abram, Chief Old, 38, 44
Adair, John, 126, 142, 144
Adair, Moses, 142
Adams, Lucretia, and family, 225
Allison, Charles, 165, 224
Allison, James, 124
Allison, John, 124, 164
Alston, Philip, 216
Alston, Thomas W., 216
Amis, Thomas, 7, 79, 206, 251
Anderson, Capt. John, 84, 126
Anthony, Jonathan, 103
Applegate, Thomas, 97
Aranda of Spain, 245, 250
Armstrong, Frank, 115
Armstrong, John, 215
Armstrong, Martin, 214, 244
Attakullakulla, Chief ("Little Car-
    penter"), 28, 36, 57, 63, 65, 67–68,
    74, 79, 189, 209–10, 263–66
Augusta County, Va., 8, 29, 253
Avery, Waightstill, 66–67, 85, 125,
    232, 271–72

Baker, Andrew, Jr., 75
Balfour (Belford), Col. Andrew, 124
Barley, John, 23
Barnett, Capt. James S., 137
Barton, Joshua, Sr., 22
Barton, Samuel, 178, 234, 237, 254
Bartrum, William, 264
Bates, Henry, 22
Bates, Henry, Jr., 22
Bates, William, 22
Battles, campaigns, and encounters:
    siege of Augusta, 202; Battle
    Creek massacre, 172; Beattie's Mill
    battle, 202; battle of Boyd's
    Creek, 182–87; battle of the Bluffs
    (Nashville), 175, 177–79; battle of
    Camden, 248; A. Campbell's In-
    dian campaign, 136–37, 182–91;
    Carter's Valley raids, 38, 42–44,
    62; battle of Cedar Springs, 131–
    32; Charleston, S.C., campaigns,
    32–34, 128, 217, 219, 223, 258;
    Chickamauga raids, 98, 211, 220,
    224; Chickasaw raids, 171–74;
    Christian's Cherokee campaign,
    48–60; Clinch River raids 43, 65,
    211; battle of Cowpens, 181; Cum-
    berland River raids, 175; Delaware
    Indian raids, 165; Eutaw Springs
    battle, 219; Freeland's Station
    raid, 174; battle of Guilford's
    Court House, 160, 193, 196, 198,
    217; Indian raids, 62, 100; siege of
    Jefferson Fort, 171–72, 236; Ken-
    tucky campaigns, 71–73, 81–82,
    93–97, 107; battle of King's Moun-
    tain, 65, 138–62, 180–81, 183, 195–
    96, 233, 248–49; battle of Long
    Island Flats, 38–42, 49; Lookout
    Mountain campaign, 206–8; battle
    of Long Cane, S.C., 202; raid on
    Mansker's Station, 176; Monck's
    Corner, S.C., engagement, 220;
    battle of Musgrove's Mill, 132–36,
    138, 141, 149, 155; siege of Fort
    Nashborough, 177–79; Northwest
    campaigns, 92–94, 96–98, 100;
    Powell Valley raids, 192; battle of
    Point Pleasant, 31, 40, 72, 146;
    Poor Valley raid, 44; Red River
    massacre, 172; Sevier's Indian ex-
    pedition, 193–94; E. Shelby's
    Chickamauga campaign, 91–99; I.
    Shelby's S.C. campaigns, 218–23;
    revolt against the Spaniards, 242,
    244; capture of Thicketty Fort,
    130; siege on Fort Watauga, 44–
    47; Williamson's Cherokee cam-
    paign, 130

Baulon, Gov., 100–1
Bean, Edmund, 88, 208
Bean, George, 88
Bean, Jesse, 208
Bean, John, 88, 208
Bean, Robert, 134, 181, 201, 208
Bean, Capt. William, 7, 22, 44, 67, 75, 84, 87–88, 92, 96, 129, 181, 187, 201, 208
Bean, Mrs. William, 44, 58
Bean, William, Jr., 44, 208
Belew, Benjamin, 111, 115
Bell, John, 216
Benge, Chief John, 78, 271
Benton, Jesse, 26
Benton, Robert, 103
Benton, Thomas Hart ("Old Bullion"), 26, 216
Big Bullet, Chief, 67
Big Creek settlements (Holston), 7, 16, 70, 78, 84, 92, 104, 206
Big Fool, Chief, 94
Big Island or Sevier's Island, 185, 187, 207, 263
Bird, Amos, 233
Blackburn, Robert, 97
Blackman, Shelby, 108
Blackmore, Capt. John, 111, 115
Blair, Hugh, 22
Blanca, Florida de, 245
Blankenship, John, 54
Bledsoe, Col. Anthony, 28, 77, 108, 118, 125–26, 145, 214, 225, 254
Bledsoe, Maj. Isaac, 108, 168, 192, 237, 254
Bledsoe family, 172
Blount, William, 28, 227, 230
Bloody Fellow; see Ninatoogah
Blountville, Tenn., 10
Bluff City; see Shoate's Ford settlement
Boat Yard, The, 110; see also Christianville; Long Island of the Holston
Bond, John, 194
Boone, Daniel, 10, 71, 102, 104
Boone, Squire, 72
Bostin, Joud., Sr., 22

Botetourt County, Va., 8, 29, 137, 261
Boundary lines, 2, 15, 23, 28, 60, 69, 76, 117–22, 126–27, 164, 213–15, 230, 232, 234, 249
Bounds, Jesse, 124
Bowman, Isaac, 116
Bowman, Col. John, 71, 73
Bowyer, Luke, 22, 46, 84, 86, 181
Boyd, Alexander, 187
Boyd, John, 115
Boyd, Joseph, 98
Boydston, William, 98
Braddock, Gen. Edward, 72
Brevard, 153
Bright's settlement, 147, 156
Briscoe, Capt. William, 28
Bristol; see Sapling Grove settlement
Brooks, George, 44
Brooks, William, 18, 23
Brown, Ezekiel (Zekle), 85
Brown, Jacob, 19, 22–23, 28, 67, 129, 181, 262
Brown, John, 18, 23, 97
Brown, Joseph, 22–23
Brown, Morgan, 34
Brown, Col. Thomas, 99, 149, 183, 200, 205, 208, 240
Bruster, E., 97
Bryan(t), John, 28–29, 36
Buchanan, Alexander, 108, 178
Buchanan, John, 108, 179, 254
Buchanan, Capt. William, 39
Buckingham, Thomas, 233
Budwine, Francis, 78, 271
Buford, Col., 141, 155, 158
Buller, Joseph, 22
Bullock, Leonard H., 63, 226
Bumper, Job, 23
Burke, Thomas, 139, 247–48
Burney, Simon, 236

Caffrey, John, 111, 115–16
Cage, William, 253
Cain, James, 115
Calloway, Col., 30
Calvatt, Frederick, 22, 64

Calvatt, Joseph, 23
Cameron, Alexander, 26, 28, 48, 50, 53, 55–58, 61, 65–67, 72, 78–79, 89, 91, 99, 101, 132–33, 171, 271–72
Campbell, Col. Arthur, 73, 77–78, 91, 120, 136–37, 140, 144–45, 182–91, 184, 187, 191, 199–200, 203, 206, 209, 267, 272
Campbell, Judge David, 254
Campbell, Jefferson, 78
Campbell, Capt. John, 39
Campbell, Col. William, 69, 136–37, 142–43, 145, 149, 154–56, 159, 177, 182, 184, 187–89, 196–99, 201, 274–75
Candler, Warren A., 160
Candler, Maj. William, 160–61
Carelton, Sir Guy, 101, 240
Carmichael, Mr., 249
Carter, Col. John, 7, 13, 16, 22, 27–29, 45, 62, 65–66, 75–79, 83–84, 88, 174, 184, 193, 205, 226–27, 273
Carter, Landon, 22, 128, 131, 190, 225–27, 253
Carter's Valley, 16, 38, 42–44, 47, 62, 69, 84, 92, 119, 125
Cartright, Robert, 112, 115
Caronah; see Savanooka
Caswell, Alexander, 97
Caswell, Gov. Richard, 29, 62–64, 83, 87, 89, 91, 117, 125, 127, 134–35, 185, 202–3, 211, 227, 230, 265
Catawba Indians, 193
Catron, Judge John, 106, 216
Chambers, Daniel, 115
Chambers, Robert, 97
Chambers, Samuel, 147, 160
Charleville, Jean du, 105
Cheatham, Gen. B. F., and family, 116
Cheney, Thomas, 97
Cherokee Indians, 1–2, 13, 15–16, 19–20, 24–31, 35–44, 46–71, 74, 76, 78, 82–83, 86, 89, 91–96, 99, 104, 118, 127, 130, 133, 136–37, 149, 167, 174, 180, 182–83, 189, 191, 199, 200, 206–7, 209–10, 215, 225,

228–29, 234, 237, 239–40, 252, 258–60, 265–72, 274
Chesney, Alexander, 140, 142, 147, 150, 155
Chester, Gov. Peter, 241
Chickamauga Indians, 36, 58, 61–62, 65, 72, 79, 82, 86, 89, 91–99, 111–13, 127, 129, 133, 136–37, 175, 177, 180, 182–84, 191–92, 199, 205–8, 210–11, 220, 224, 237, 239–40, 253
Chickasaw Bluffs (Memphis), 120, 241, 243–44, 246, 255
Chickasaw Indians, 35, 82, 93, 115–16, 165, 171–74, 191, 199, 234–44, 255, 265, 269
Chisholm, John, 75, 84, 126
Christian, George, 40
Christian, Col. Gilbert, 28, 53, 84, 92–93, 126, 188, 190, 274
Christian, Col. William, 31, 48–64, 66, 74, 117, 199, 201, 228, 240
Christian, William H., 215
Christianville, Tenn., 17, 28, 110, 184, 274
Chronicle, Maj. William, 154
Clark, Benjamin, 123
Clark, Col. Elijah, 130–31, 133–34, 148–50, 160–61, 188–89, 201–2
Clark, Col. George Rogers, 72, 81–82, 93–94, 96–98, 105–6, 120, 171, 236, 243–44
Clark, Henry, 75, 123, 126, 165
Clark, John, 131
Clark, Lardner, 7
Clark, Nathan, 126
Clark, William, 22, 75, 84
Clarksville, Tenn., 244
Clem, William, 97
Clement, Patrick, 207
Clement, W. L., 153
Cleveland, Col. Benjamin, 65, 70, 139, 148, 151, 153–54, 204
Cleveland, Robert, 139
Clinch River settlements, 43, 51, 110–11, 211, 227, 250
Clinkenbeard, John, 23, 101–2
Clinkenbeard, William, 102

Clinton, Gen. Henry, 24–26, 33, 153, 183, 187, 197, 249, 258
Clouse, Henry, 46
Cobb, Benjamin, 79
Cobb, Pharaoh, 79
Cobb, William, 79, 84, 88, 166
Cocke, Col. William, 12, 39–40, 59–60, 75, 77, 84–85, 122, 127, 130
Cockrill, John, 115–16, 176
Cockrill, Sterling R., 116
Coffey, Gen. John, 116
Colbert, Chief James, 35, 171, 242–43
Cole, James, 216
Cole, Stephen, 124
Colleton, Sir John, 222
Condley, John, 88
Connecort, Chief ("Old Hop"), 209
Coody, Archy, 111, 207
Cooper, James, 18, 23, 45–46
Copeland, Stephen, 233
Cornstalk, Chief, 31
Corntassel; see Onitositah
Cornwallis, Lord, 130, 137–38, 141–42, 152, 154, 160–62, 180, 183, 195–98, 219–20, 233, 249
Cotton, John, 112, 115
Coulter, John, 17
Cowan, John, 72
Cox, Abraham, 22
Cox, Edward, 22
Cox, John I., 22
Cox, John, Jr., 22
Cox, William, 22
Craighead, Lavenia Robertson, 104
Crawford, James, 147, 160
Crawford, Moses, 85
Crawford, Samuel, 85
Creek Indians, 24, 37, 56–57, 61, 64–65, 183, 192, 211, 239–40, 272
Creek War, 156, 237
Crockett, David, 22, 44, 62
Crockett, David (grandson of David), 62
Crockett, William, 22
Crugar, Col. J. H., 134, 149, 152–53, 160–61
Crutchfield, William, 115

Cruzat, Madame, and family, 242–43
Culbertson, Josiah, 133–34
Cumberland Compact, 168, 237
Cumberland settlements, 1, 39, 73, 100–5, 108, 114–16, 119, 171–73, 175–77, 179, 208, 211, 216, 225, 237, 244, 250–55, 272; see also French Lick settlement
Cumings, Sir Alexander, 263
Cummings, the Rev. Charles, 53
Cunningham, Christopher, 22
Cunningham, Christopher, Jr., 22

Dartmouth, Lord, 24, 26
Davidson, Gen. William Lee, 148–49, 159, 170, 180–81, 198, 233
Davidson County, Tenn., 233, 243, 253–55
Davie, William R., 125
Davis, 54
Davis, Capt., 129
Davis, John, 18, 23
Davis, Nathaniel, 194
Dawson, Elias, 97
Deaderick, David, 7
Dechard, Mr., 146
Dedman, Thomas, 22
Delaware Indians, 30–31, 82, 165, 238, 240
Demunbreum; see Montbrun, Jacques
DePeyster, Capt. Abraham, 155, 157–58
DePeyster, Gen. J. W., 154
DeSoto, 112
Detgavoret, John, 97
DeWitt, John H., 215
Districts: Miro, 254; Morgan, 232; Salisbury, 48, 75, 128, 149, 198, 232; Washington, 18–20, 23, 33, 62, 66, 75–76, 205, 253–54
Doak, the Rev. Samuel, and family, 10, 79, 145, 163–64
Dodd, William, 22
Donelson, Andrew J., 116
Donelson, Catherine, 111
Donelson, Gen. Daniel S., 116

Donelson, Col. John, 19, 104, 106, 110–12, 115, 167, 172, 175–76, 226–27, 230, 236–38
Donelson, John, Jr., 111, 115, 175
Donelson, Rachel (Mrs. Lewis Robards and Mrs. Andrew Jackson), 111, 116, 216, 226
Donelson, Stockley, 226
Dorherty, George, 98, 233
Douglas, John, 236
Dragging Canoe, Chief, 38, 41, 55, 57–58, 61–66, 79, 94, 177, 183, 205, 210–11, 259–60
Drake, Jonathan, 254
DuBuy, Maj., 196
Duncan, Capt. John, 84, 126
Duncan, Joseph, 88
Duncan, Rice, 22
Dunham, John, 22
Dunham, Joseph, 22, 185–86
Dunlap, Ephraim, 53, 85–86, 126
Dunlap, Maj. James, 131, 139, 202
Dunmore, Lord, 1, 40, 52
Dunmore's War, 1, 40, 102
Dunwoody, William, 233

Earnest, Felix, 233
Earnest, Henry, 233
Easley, James, 22
Eastley, James, 22
Eaton, Amos, 29, 38–39, 43, 115, 126
Edminston, William, 77
Elizabethton; see Sycamore Shoals
Elliott, Isabelle, 190
Elliott, Capt. James, 190
English, James, 233
Evans, Nathaniel, 124
Ewing, Andrew, 254
Ewing, Samuel, 54, 63

Fallen (a trader), 55
Falling, William, 36, 262
Featherstonaugh, Mr., 112
Ferguson, Col. Patrick, 85, 129–32, 135–37, 139–43, 147, 149–62, 183
Fields, Mr., 78, 271
Fincastle County, Va., 16–17, 29, 35–36, 60

Fleming, John, 97
Fleming, Col. William, 107, 236, 261
Fletcher, Richard, 23
Flint, Timothy, 108
Floyd, Col. John, 114, 240
Ford, Capt. James, 254
Forrest, Gen. Nathan Bedford, 216
Forts and stations: Asher's Station or Station Camp Creek, 168; Bean's Station, 253; Fort Blackmore, 110–11; Bledsoe's Fort (Sullivan County), 108; Bledsoe's Station (Middle Tennessee), 108, 168, 172; Boone's Fort, 72–73; Carpenter's Station, 107; Caswell Station (Knox County), 144; Caswell's Fort (see Fort Watauga); Carter's Fort, 65; Fort Charlotte, 25, 141, 152, 154, 180, 219; Fort Chiswell, 16, 30, 118, 261–62; Clinch River forts, 43, 110–11; Cumberland Gap Fort, 191–92, 226; Cumberland stations, 236–37; Donelson's Fort, 116, 168; Earl's Fort, 150; Eaton's Fort or Station (Sullivan County), 29, 38–40, 43, 115, 126; Eaton's Station (Middle Tennessee), 39, 168, 174, 179, 238; Freeland's Station, 168, 174, 216, 238; French Lick Fort, 214, 227, 237–38, 253; Gillespie's Station or Fort Lee, 29, 36–38, 45; Fort Grainger, 117, 191; Fort Jefferson, 171, 236; Kaskaskia Fort, 81–82, 93, 96, 116; Lenoir City fort site, 191; Fort Loudoun, 56; Fort Lee (see Gillespie's Station); Mansker's Station, 102, 107, 119, 168, 175–76, 238; Mauldin's or Mautey's Station, 238; Fort Moultrie, 33–34; Fort Nashborough (the Bluffs), 174–75, 177, 214, 238 (see also French Lick Fort); Fort Panmure, 242; Fort Patrick Henry (Sullivan County), 51–53, 63–64, 66, 69, 71, 74, 76, 97, 110, 112, 125, 127, 133, 172, 175, 260, 269; Fort Patrick Henry (Vincennes), 97; Fort Pitt, 93, 241;

Forts and stations (*cont.*)
  Pittsman's Station, 107; Fort
  Quenassee, 249; Robertson's Fort,
  70, 92; Shelby's Fort (Sullivan
  County), 29, 45; John Shelby's
  Station, 29; Strode's Station, 101;
  Thicketty Fort, 130; Fort Union,
  168; Fort,Toulouse, 249; Fort Wa-
  tauga (Fort Caswell), 13, 29, 37–
  38, 44–45, 51, 65, 261; Whitley's
  Station, 107; Fort Williams, 8, 13,
  65; Womack's Fort, 29, 47
Fox, Charles J., 197
Franklin, Benjamin, 266
Fraser, Maj., 134
Freeland, George, 104, 174, 216,
  237, 254
French Broad River settlements,
  229–30, 233, 252
French and Indian War, 18
French Lick settlement (Nash-
  borough) 7, 72–73, 100–8, 113–16,
  119–21, 167–69, 172, 174–76, 178,
  214, 234, 237–38, 253–54; *see also*
  Cumberland settlements
Friggs, J. C., 97
Friggs, Robert, 97
Fry, Joshua, 117

Gadsden, Col. Christopher, 33
Gage, Gen. Thomas, 26
Gaines, Gen. Edmund Pendleton, 17
Galvez, Bernardo de, 120, 242, 246–
  47
Gates, Gen. Horatio, 134, 135, 147–
  48, 181, 195, 248
Gay, Capt., 53
George III, 64, 70, 258
George, Capt. Robert, 236
Germain, Lord (George Sackville
  Germain), 25
Gibson, Capt. James, 181
Gilbert, William, and wife, 138
Gill, Peter, 178
Gillespie, George, 232
Gillespie, Thomas, 134
Gilliland, John, 124, 157
Gist (the tory), 50

Gist, Benjamin, 75, 84
Gist, Christopher, 63
Gist, Joseph, 185
Gist, Joshua, 253
Gist, Col. Nathaniel, 32, 50, 55–57,
  63–64, 66, 71, 259–60
Gist, Capt. Thomas, 129, 184–85
Goodan, Drury, 23
Gower, Capt. Abel, and family, 175
Gower, David, 176
Gower, Nancy, 112, 175
Graham, Lt. Col. John, 99, 153, 236
Graham, Joseph, 75, 153
Grampre, Carlos de, 100
Granville, Lord, 15, 76
Green, Gen. Nathaniel, 181, 195–97,
  199–200, 204, 215–19, 223, 232–33,
  275
Green, Thomas, 216
Greene County, Tenn., 98, 215, 232,
  252–53
Greeneville, Tenn., 7, 69, 83, 233
Greer, Alexander, 23
Greer, Andrew, and family, 22–23,
  65, 75, 84, 88, 166
Greer, Joseph, 23
Grimes, Col., 160
Grimes, Henry, 85, 87
Grimes, Joseph, 22
Grubbs, Mr., 88
Gwin, David, 115–16
Gwin, Senator William, 116

Haile, John, 22, 75
Hall, Capt. John, 237
Hall, Morgan, 108
Hamilton, Lt. Gov. Henry, 82, 93,
  95, 98
Hampton, Col. Andrew, 143, 151,
  153
Hampton, Capt. Edward, 161
Haney, Frank, 115
Hanging Maw; *see* Squallacutta
Hanley, James, 104
Hardeman, Thomas, 88
Hardin, John, 215
Hardin, Capt. Joseph, 51, 98, 233
Hardin, Mr., 98

Harlin, Ellis, 54, 57, 78, 89, 184, 271
Harrison, Gov. Benjamin, 228, 236–39
Harrison, David, 233
Harrison (Harmison), John, 97
Harrison, Mr., 77
Harrison, Reuben, 111, 115
Hart, David, 226–27
Hart, George, 22
Hart, Nathaniel, 114, 226
Hart, Thomas, 226
Harwood, William, 97
Hawkins, Matthew, 23
Hawkins, Mr., 78, 271
Hawkins, Sarah (Mrs. John Sevier), 46, 129
Henderson, Archibald, 66, 103, 148–49, 153, 203
Henderson, Nathaniel, 169
Henderson, Pleasant, 103, 169, 210
Henderson, Col. Richard, 19, 63, 68, 103–6, 114, 118–21, 164, 167, 169–70, 175, 177, 225–28
Henderson, Samuel, 118
Hendrix, David, 97
Henry, Hugh, Sr., 111–12, 115
Henry, Gov. Patrick, 48, 52–54, 56, 58–59, 62–64, 66, 81, 83, 89–94, 105–6; 228
Henry, Thomas, 115
Henry, Widow, 115
Hessians, 196, 220
Hibbet, John, 215
Hickey, David, 22
Hider, Michael, 23
Higgins, John, 97
Higgins, William, 75
Hightower, Oldham, 23
Hildebrand, Michael, 36
Hill, Col. William, 135
Hines, Thomas, 216
Hix, Abednago, 23
Hodge, Ambrose, 22
Hogg, James, 226
Holland, Maj. James, 138
Hollis, James, 126
Holliway, Capt. Charles, 124
Holly, John, 85–86

Holston River settlements, 1–3, 11, 13, 15–16, 18, 24, 26–28, 32, 34–35, 39, 47–49, 51, 53, 63, 67, 69, 73, 77, 81–82, 84, 92–93, 104, 108, 110, 125, 132, 136, 177, 183, 192, 228, 237, 240, 247, 250–51, 254–55; see also Long Island of the Holston
Honeycutt, John, 78
Hood, Robert, 233
Hopson, Edward, 22
Hoskins, Capt., 129
Hoss, Bishop E. E., 160
Houghton, Joshua, 23
Houghton, Thomas, 22, 75, 84, 166
Houston, James, 97, 233
Howard, Gen. John, 196
Howe, Sir William, 82
Hubbard, James, 208
Hudson, George, 23
Hudson, John, 94
Huger, Lt. Col. James Isaac, 33–34
Hughes, David, 22, 124
Hughes, Thomas, 22
Husband, Col. Vezey, 157
Hutchings, Capt. Thomas, 111, 115
Hutchins, Capt. John, and family, 111, 114

Indian towns, 26, 30, 36, 55–59, 61, 64, 78–79, 89, 91, 94, 98, 111, 188–90, 194, 206–11, 226, 231, 234, 237, 239–40, 265, 271–72
Inman, Capt. Shadrack, 133–34
Innis, Col. Alexander, 132, 134, 272
Iredell, Jane, 207
Ireland, Hans, 97
Iroquis Confederation, 30
Isbell, Godfrey, 128–29
Isbell, Zachariah, 22, 75, 84

Jack, Jeremiah, 231
Jack, Patrick, 231
Jackson, Gen. Andrew, 17, 102, 111, 116, 156, 216, 237, 256
Jackson, Mrs. Andrew; see Donelson, Rachel
Jackson, Samuel D., 203
Jarnigan, Thomas, 233

Jay, John, 248–49
Jefferson, Peter, 117
Jefferson, Gov. Thomas, 77, 81–83, 93, 95, 127, 136–37, 161, 171, 182–83, 191, 228, 267
Jennings, David, 97
Jennings, Jonathan, 115–16
Jennings, John, 112–13
Jennings family, 113, 116
Johns, Mr., 115, 172
Johnson (or Johnston), Ann; see Robertson, Ann
Johnson, Barrett, 97
Johnson, Capt., 161
Johnson, Uzal, 156
Johnston, Isaac, 75
Johnston, William, 226
Jones, Francis M., 138
Jones, John, 22, 248
Jones, Lewis, 23
Jones, Robin, 123
Jones, Thomas, 102
Jones, Willie, 25, 123, 205
Jonesborough, Tenn., 7, 79, 123–24, 181, 232, 253
Joslin, Col. Benjamin, 102
Judd's Friend; see Ostenaco
July 4th celebration (1777, first in the west), 70

Kennedy, Daniel, 79, 233
Kennedy, George, 178
Kentucky settlements, 1, 63, 69, 71–73, 81–82, 100–1, 105–7, 121, 176, 183, 240
Kerr (or Carr), John, 233
Kickapoo Indians, 171
Kincaid (or Kinnard), John, 43
King, John, 23
King, William, 42
King of France, 248
King of Spain, 243
Kingsport, Tenn.; see Boat Yard; Christianville; Long Island of the Holston
Kirkland, Moses, 25
Knox, James, 254
Kunoskeskie, 207

l'Abide, Don, 242
Lacey, Col. William, 154
Lackey, James, 124
Lambert, Jeremiah, 235
Lane, Aquilla, 88
Lane, Lt. Isaac, 87, 186
Lane, Tidence, 10, 87–88, 90
Lanier, Col. Robert, 66, 79, 199, 271, 273
Latman, Joseph, 97
Lee, Gen. Charles, 29, 33–34, 49
Lee, Henry, Jr. ("Light-Horse Harry"), 196, 198, 218
Lee, Richard Henry, 246, 255
Le Fevre, 100
Le Fevre, Isaac, 100, 102
Leiper, James, 178
Leslie, Maj. Gen. Alexander, 196
Lewis, Capt. Aaron, 92, 93, 95
Lewis, Col. Charles, 50, 52–53
Lewis, Gen. Daniel, 52–53
Lewis, Gideon, 139
Lindsay, Isaac, 234, 254
Linn, Andrew, 97
Linn, Daniel, 97
Linn, William, 97
Little Carpenter; see Attakullakulla
Little Fellow; see Ward
Little Owl; see Nahoolah
Litton, Catel, 97
Long, John, 43
Long, Richard, 97
Long Fellow; see Tuskegetchee
Long Island (Indian town in Alabama), 98
Long Island of the Holston (Kingsport), 2, 13, 15, 17, 28, 38, 40, 45, 51–53, 60, 62–63, 67–71, 74, 76, 79, 92, 94, 104, 110, 115, 117–18, 125, 127, 133, 175, 184, 191, 199–200, 206, 209, 217, 228–29, 237, 239, 253, 260–62, 266, 269, 271–72, 274
"Long Knives," 172, 209
Looney, Maj. David, 126, 165, 224, 253
Looney, Moses, 126, 224
Looney, Peter, 115
Love, Robert, 42–43

Love, Samuel, 43
Love, Gen. Thomas, 42–44, 46, 210
Love's settlement, 44
Lowry, Charles, 233
Lucas, Isaac, 178–79
Lucas, Maj. Robert, 22, 75, 84, 174, 226–27
Lumpkin, George, 7
Luske, Joseph, 22
Luttrell, John, 226
Luzerne, 246–48
Lyman, Gen. Phineas, 216
Lynn, Robert, 62

Madison, President James, 118, 255
Madison, the Rev. James, 118
Madison, Capt. Thomas, 39, 66
Madison, Capt. William, 53
Malloy, Thomas, 234, 237, 254
Maney, Martin, 124
Mansker, Gasper (or Casper), 102, 107, 119, 168, 176, 238, 254
Marion, Gen. Francis ("The Swamp Fox"), 220, 222
Martin, Gov. Alexander, 164, 205, 208, 227, 229–30, 252
Martin, Gen. Joseph, 36–37, 53, 70, 89, 92, 94, 112, 126–27, 182–84, 187–93, 199, 206–7, 209, 211–12, 227–28, 230, 237–39, 252, 271–72
Martin, Mrs. Joseph; see Ward, Betsy
Martin, William (son of Joseph), 187, 209–10
Massengill, Michael, 88
Matthews, Sampson, 228
Mauer, John, 97
Mauer, Thomas, 97
Maury, Matthew F., 216
Maxwell, George, 115, 126
Mayham, Col., 220–22
McArthur, Brig. Gen. Archibald, 240
McCall, James, 54
McCartney, Charles, 23
McCartney, Joseph, 23
McCay, Judge Spruce, 124–25, 232
McClain, Ephraim, 215, 254
McClure, Peter, 124

McCorkle, Capt. James, 261–62
McCormick, John, 22
McCroskey, John, 95
McDonald, John, 89, 95, 183, 190, 205, 240
McDowell, Col. Charles, 126, 129–32, 134–35, 138–40, 143–44, 147–48, 151, 153–54, 205, 207–8
McDowell, Maj. Joseph, 154
McElwee, James, 97
McGuire, Neely Cornelius, 208
McMahan, John, 75, 84
McNabb, David, 193
McNabb, John, 75, 84, 128–29, 181
McNabb, William, 84
McSpadden, William, 97
Memphis; see Chickasaw Bluffs
Menifee, James, 178
Miller, John, 146
Milligan, Samuel, and family, 87–88
Milton, Anthony, 97
Mingo-homa, Chief ("The Red King"), 238
Minton, Richard, 124
Miro, Estevon, 254
Mitchell, Joab, 22
Mitchell, Mark, 22
Mohawk Indians, 30
Montbrun, Jacques Timothe Boucher de (Demunbreun), 100–2, 105, 174, 207
Montgomery, John, 115
Montgomery, Col. John, 93, 96–97, 172, 236, 243
Moonshaw, Joseph, 178
Moore, Alexander, 40–42, 208
Moore, Anthony, 233
Moore, John, 22
Moore, Patrick, 130
Moore, Samuel, 45–46, 58
Moore, Capt. William, 51
Morgan, Gen. Daniel, 52, 148, 181, 204
Morgan, Col. Haynes, 52
Morgan, Isaac, 97
Morris, Daniel, 22
Morris, Gideon, 22
Morris, Groves, 22

Morris, Shadrack, 22
Moseley, Robert, 22
Mulherrin, James, 108
Mulherrin, John, 108
Mulkey, the Rev. Jonathan, 43, 216
Mulkey, the Rev. Philip, 216

Nahoolah ("Little Owl"), 41, 61, 95, 269
Nash, Gov. Abner, 137, 193
Nash, Gen. Francis, 149, 169–70, 234, 254
Nashborough (Nashville); see French Lick settlements
Natchez settlements, 242, 251
Nave, Teeter, 23
Navigation routes, 16–19, 110–11, 117, 245–46, 251
Neal, Archibald, 138
Neal, Jack, 138–39
Neal, James, 138
Neal, William, 138
Nealley, Buck, 97
Neave, John, 22
Neeley, Isaac, 115
Neeley, William, and family, 104, 172, 176
Newberry, William, 22
Newell, Samuel, 63
Newman, John, 233
Ninatoogah ("Bloody Fellow"), 269
Nolachucky (Nolichucky) River settlements, 1, 3, 8, 13, 15–16, 19, 21, 26–29, 32, 45, 47, 53, 65, 67, 124, 129, 132, 144, 183, 231, 247, 250, 252, 255
Norris, Senator George W., 256
North, Capt. George, 212
North, Lord, 249
Northwestern Indians, 81, 82, 99
Norton, Richard, 23

Oconostota, Chief, 57, 63, 66–68, 79, 183, 206, 208–10, 259–60, 264, 266, 269, 272
O'Gullion, Barney, 97
O'Hara, Gen. Charles, 196
Old Hop; see Connecort

Old Tassel; see Onitositah
Onitositah, Chief ("Old Tassel" or "Corntassel"), 63, 67–69, 118, 200, 207–8, 210–11, 259, 264–69
Oranda; see Aranda
Ostenaco (or Ostenau), Chief ("Judd's Friend"), 57
Ottawa Indians, 30
Outlaw, Alexander, 253
Overall, William, 23, 104
Owens, Senator Robert L., 37
Ownsby, Thomas, 43

Page, John, 49
Paine, Bishop and Mrs. Robert, 116
Parker, George, 97
Parker, Sir Peter, 24–25, 258
Parker, William, 95
Patrick, James, Sr., 72
Patterson, Capt. James, 129, 181
Patton, Mary, 143
Payne, Mr., 112, 115
Pebler, Elias, 22
Peck, Lt. Adam, 72
Pendergrass, Garrett, 97
Pendleton, Edmund, 17, 32
Pendleton District, 17–18, 28, 69, 84, 93, 125; see also Holston River settlements; Long Island of the Holston
Penny, James, 233
Perkins, Elisha, 97
Petit, Benjamin, 103
Peyton, Ephraim, and family, 108, 111, 113, 116
Phillips, Samuel, 141–42
Pickens, Gen. Andrew, 218
Pierce, John, 97
Pigeon, Chief The, 71, 266
Pinson, Aaron, 75
Piomingo, Chief, 174, 238–39
Pitt, William, 197
Plummer, Maj. Daniel, 157
Polk, Ezekiel, 214
Polk, President James K., 214, 216
Polk, Gen. Thomas, 32, 214
Polk, Col. William, 214, 227
Polson, Andrew, 97

Powell Valley settlements, 167, 192, 214, 225–27, 240, 261
Prather, Charles, 97
Preston, Col. William, 28–30, 32, 38, 63, 121, 182, 199, 262, 274
Price, Samuel, 97
Price, Capt. Thomas, 42, 65, 84, 265, 273
Pruett, Capt. William, 185
Purnell, Mrs., 115
Purviance, William, and family, 44, 62

Quigley, Patrick, 176

Rains, John, 107
Randolph, Gov. Edmund, 267
Rankin, William, 231
Raven, The; see Savanooka
Rawdon, Lord, 180, 217
Rawlings, Asahel, 233
Ray, James, 124
Rayneval, Gerard de, 245–46, 249–50
Raysdale family, 164
Red King, The; see Mingo-homa
Redbird, Chief, 40
Redd, John, 51, 56, 58
Reese, James, 124
Reeves, William, 22
Reid (or Reed), Maj. John, 237–38
Renfroe, James, 115
Renfroe, Joseph, and family, 115, 172
Renfroe, Moses, 115, 172
Reynolds, Maj., 124
Rhea, John, 92, 126
Rhea, the Rev. Joseph, 10, 53
Richardson, Capt. James, 32, 212
Ridley, Broomfield, 103
Roads and pathways, 2–4, 9–10, 38, 55, 78, 102, 104, 107, 114, 119, 123, 139, 143, 167, 176–77, 228, 253–54, 262
Robards, Mrs. Lewis; see Donelson, Rachel
Roberson, William, 22

Robertson (children of Col. James), 104, 115
Robertson (the younger brother of James), 87
Robertson, Ann, 47, 114, 116, 176
Robertson, "Black Charles," 78
Robertson, "Buffalo Charles," 78
Robertson, Col. Charles, 20, 22, 33, 64, 75, 77–78, 84, 91–92, 96–98, 115, 123–24, 129–32, 137–38, 145, 156, 160, 165, 181, 193, 195–96, 198, 253
Robertson, Edward W., 116
Robertson, Elijah, 22, 78, 85, 214, 253
Robertson, E. Sterling, 116
Robertson, Felix, 107, 174
Robertson, Col. James, 12, 21–22, 29, 32–33, 45–47, 53, 59, 64–65, 70, 73, 75, 78, 83–84, 87, 89, 91, 100, 102–9, 113–15, 119, 167, 173–75, 177–78, 184, 237–39, 244, 247, 254–55, 262, 265, 271–73
Robertson, Mrs. James (Charlotte Reeves), 10, 47, 115–16, 178
Robertson, John R., 173
Robertson, Joseph Randolph, 175
Robertson, Julius, 23
Robertson, Keziah, 156
Robertson, Lavinia, 104
Robertson, Mark, 23, 33, 104
Robertson, Mary (Gower), 175
Robertson, Samuel M., 116
Robertson's Colony (Texas), 12, 109
Robinson, John, 22
Roddy, James, 88, 186
Rogan, Hugh, 115, 176
Rogers, John, and family, 37, 113
Rogersville, Tenn., 7, 62
Rose, Ossa, 22
Ross, Chief John, 95
Rounsevall, David, 237
Rounsifer, M., 115
Ruddle, Isaac, 97
Russell, George, 18, 22, 75, 84, 88, 92, 123, 184, 208

Russell, Col. William, 45, 50–52, 74, 117, 213, 262

Rutherford, Gen. Griffin, 31, 48–51, 56, 62, 66, 91, 128, 214–16, 227

Rutherford, Henry, 214

Rutledge, Gov. John, 140–41, 204

Rye Cove settlement, 261

Sandusky, Emanuel, 3

Sapling Grove settlement (Bristol), 7, 16, 78, 142, 203

Savanooka, Chief ("The Raven"), 38, 43, 55, 57, 70–71, 89, 259, 265, 268–69

Sawyer, John, 97

Scott, Mr., 205–6

Sequoyah, Chief, 56, 63, 189, 207

Settlers: in Bean's Company, 87–88; in Davidson County Militia, 254; on first Greene County Court, 233; prominent in Greene County, 233; purchased first Jonesboro lots, 124; in Shelby's Company, 97; on first Sullivan County Court, 126; on first Washington County (N. C.) Court, 84; in 1780 Washington County Militia, 128–29, 181; on Washington District Court, 75; signing Washington District (1776) N. C. Petition, 22–23; in Watauga Association, 75

Sevier (the younger brother of John), 87

Sevier, Abram, 212

Sevier, Charles Robertson, 156

Sevier, James (son of John), 131, 158, 184, 194, 208

Sevier, Jefferson, 203

Sevier, Gen. John, 8, 12, 18, 22, 26, 29, 35–36, 45–46, 53–54, 75, 83–85, 87–88, 124, 126, 128–29, 131, 139, 142–45, 147, 154, 156–57, 159–62, 164, 166, 177, 181, 184–89, 193–95, 199–201, 203, 205, 207–8, 211–12, 217–20, 223, 225, 229–30, 233, 254–55, 275

Sevier, Mrs. John; see Hawkins, Sarah; Sherrill, Catherine

Sevier, Robert, 23, 33, 85, 92, 124, 128, 131, 141, 147; and family, 156, 158–59, 199

Sevier, Maj. Valentine, 23, 54, 75, 84, 128–29, 131–32, 157, 193–94, 208

Sevier, Valentine, Jr., 54

Sevier's Island; see Big Island

Shane, the Rev. John D., 101

Sharp, Benjamin, 38, 41–42

Sharp, William, 66, 125

Shaw (Shor or Schror), James, and family, 103, 216, 234, 237, 254

Shawnee Indians, 30–31, 73, 82, 192, 240, 265

Shelby, Gen. Evan, 7, 16, 29, 32, 45, 47, 52–53, 59, 62–63, 69, 74, 78, 81, 84, 91–92, 94–99, 111, 118, 127, 136, 190, 199–200, 224, 240

Shelby, Maj. Evan, Jr., 47, 69, 97, 158

Shelby, Col. Isaac, 12, 41, 66, 94, 97, 126, 129–36, 138–39, 141–45, 148–49, 151–52, 155–56, 158–62, 181, 195, 200, 203–6, 211, 214, 217–23, 237–39, 275

Shelby, Capt. James, 39, 41, 84, 92, 97, 238

Shelby, John, 29, 32, 75, 97, 126

Shelby, John, Jr., 84

Shelby, Moses, 142, 181

Sherrill, Adam, 22, 186

Sherrill, Catherine ("Bonnie Kate," Mrs. John Sevier), 46–47, 129, 144–45, 203

Sherrill, Samuel, 22, 46–47

Sherrill, Samuel, Jr., 22

Shoate, Emanuel, 22

Shoate's Ford settlement (Bluff City), 2, 47, 78, 237

Siler, Henry, 22

Simpson, Thomas, 18, 23, 75

Slaughter, Francis, 97

Smallwood, Gen. William, 180

Smith, Col., 262

Smith, Gen. Daniel, 53, 108, 118–21, 215, 234, 254, 262

Smith, Ezekiel, 78

Smith, Capt. James, 22, 137

46-129

Smith, Samuel, 126
Smith, William, 134, 208
Smith, Capt. William Bailey, 71–73,
    81–82, 114, 118–19, 121
Snoddy, William, 124
Snodgrass, William, 92, 97
Spenser (Spencer), Thomas Sharp,
    103
Springstone, William, 112, 184
Squallacutta, Chief ("Hanging
    Maw"), 183, 199, 207–8
Stalnacker's place, 49, 51
Starr, Caleb, 54
Starr, Emmett, 36–37
Stedman, Mr., 25
Stewart, Gen. Alexander, 222
Stewart, Thomas, 112, 115
Stewart, Thomas, Jr., 112
Stinson, Capt. James, 128–29, 181,
    185, 193, 233
Stockton, Thomas, 233
Stone, William, 88
Stoner, Michael, 102–3, 175
Stuart, Mr., 115
Stuart, Charles (brother of Henry
    and John), 241
Stuart, Henry, 24–28, 30–32, 35, 241
Stuart, James, 66, 84, 88, 123–24
Stuart, John, 35, 50, 53, 58, 66–67,
    82, 99, 241, 259
Sullivan, Gen. John, 126
Sullivan County, N. C. and Tenn.,
    78, 126, 128–29, 144, 163, 165, 181,
    187, 189, 192, 204, 206, 208, 224–
    25, 232, 252–53
Sumner, Gen. Jethro, 213
Sumpter, Gen. Thomas, 153
Swanson, Edward, 104, 178–79
Sweet, Benjamin, 97
Sycamore Shoals (Elizabethton),
    19, 37, 68, 144–45, 167, 225, 264

Talbot, Matthews, and family, 79,
    84, 143, 201
Tarleton, Lt. Col. Banastre, 158,
    196–97, 204
Tassell, The; see Onitositah
Tate, Robert, 88
Tate, Samuel, 88

Tatham, William, 8–10, 13–14, 18,
    19, 22, 29, 35, 45, 64, 68, 210, 214,
    263
Tatum, Absolom, 214
Taylor, Andrew, 79
Taylor, Christopher, 79, 124, 147
Taylor, Capt. John, 150
Taylor, Mr., 10
Taylor, Nannie, 37
Taylor, Gen. Nathaniel, 79
Telford, G. W., 163
Terrapen; see Tuckasee
Terrill, Obediah, 119
Thomas, Isaac, 27–28, 35–36, 38,
    53–54, 91, 184, 187, 193, 207–8
Thompson, Capt. James, 38–39, 53
Thompson, Thomas, 108
Thompson family, 38
Timberlake, Lt. Henry, and family,
    36–37, 71
Timpany, Maj. Robert, 152–53
Tipton, Jonathan, 23, 128–29, 181,
    185–86, 188, 193
Titus, Ebenezer, 237
Todd, Charles S., 220, 223
Todd, Col. John, 207
Tom, William, 97
Tonyn, Gov. Patrick, 83
Tories, 16, 24, 32, 35, 60–61, 80, 85–
    88, 100–1, 125, 131, 141, 143, 147,
    159–60, 180, 202, 206, 216, 224
Treaties: Chickasaw (1783), 236–
    38, 241, 245; Hopewell (1785),
    225; Lochabar (1770), 2, 15, 28,
    127; Long Island of the Holston
    (1777, Avery), 13, 66–70, 104, 199,
    229, 266; (1781) 62–63; (1783)
    239; Sycamore Shoals (1775,
    Transylvania Purchase), 120–21,
    166–67, 170, 226–28, 264
Trimble, Capt. William, 128–29, 181
Tryon, Gov. William, 35
Tuckasee, Chief ("The Terrapen"),
    209
Turnbull, John, 216
Turner, Frederick, J., 255–56
Turner, John, 242
Turnley, George, 97
Turpin family, 115, 216

Tuskegetchee, Chief ("Long Fellow," brother of Nancy Ward), 36

Vance, David, 147
Vance, Patrick, 53
Vance, Terry, 53
Vaughan, Frederick, 23
Vergennes, 245–46, 250
Villars, Don Bathasar de, 242
Vincent, Thomas, 92

Waddell, John, 23
Walker, Felix, 19, 32, 33, 209–10
Walker, Col. John, 32–34
Walker, Dr. Thomas, 66, 118–21, 164
Wallace, William, 126
Walton, Maj. Jesse, 65, 79, 84, 88, 91–92, 123–24, 185, 201–2
Ward, Betsy (Mrs. Joseph Martin), 37, 189
Ward, Bryant, 37
Ward, John, 186
Ward ("Little Fellow," son of Nancy Ward), 36
Ward, Nancy ("The Ghigan"), 36–37, 45, 184, 189, 191, 200, 209, 231
Ward, Nannie, 36
Ware, the Rev. Henry, 10
Washington, Gen. George, 18, 56, 63, 71–72, 95, 162, 182, 206, 214
Washington County, N. C. and Tenn., 83, 123, 126, 128, 144, 165–66, 189, 204, 206, 208, 217, 225, 232–34, 252–53
Washington County, Va., 69, 77–78, 144
Watauga Association, 7, 19–20, 75
Watauga River settlement, 1, 2, 7, 13, 15–20, 24, 26–27, 29, 32, 34, 48, 53, 65, 67, 81–82, 132, 144, 177, 180–81, 183, 247, 250, 254–55; see also Sycamore Shoals
Watee, Gen. Stand, 37
Watts, Chief John, 187, 205, 207
Wear, Samuel, 97, 208
Webster, Lt. Col. James, 196
Wells, Heydon, 237
Wells, Joseph, 97

Wells, Zachariah, 104
White, John, 115
White, Richard, 84
White, Soloman, 115
White, Zachariah, 178
Wilkes County, N. C., 23, 201
Willenawah, Chief, 79, 266, 272
Williams, Daniel, 108
Williams, Edmund, 225
Williams, Col. James, 132–33, 152
Williams, Jarret, 23, 36
Williams, John, 103, 226
Williams, Lt. Col. Joseph, and family, 50, 52, 58–59, 65, 117–18, 148, 153–54, 199, 228
Williams, Lucretia Adams, 225
Williams, Sampson, 108
Williams, Capt. Samuel, 128–29, 131, 181
Williams, William, 232
Williamson, Gen. Andrew, 56, 130
Willing, Capt. James, 241
Willis, Henry, 10, 235
Wilson, Benjamin, 84
Wilson, George, 42
Wilson, Isaac, 23
Wilson, Joseph, 75, 84, 128–29, 181
Wilson, Samuel M., 103
Winn, Gen. Richard, 141
Winston, Maj. Joseph, 50, 66, 79, 148, 154, 271, 273
Winters, Moses, 43
Wise, Gov. Henry A., and family, 116
Witcher, Capt. William, 52
Witherspoon, James, 164
Womack, Jacob, 22, 29, 47, 75, 78, 84, 88
Wood, Michael, 84
Woods, John, 123–24
Woods, Richard, 233
Wright, Col. Gideon, 180

Yancey, John, 124
Yearly, Isam, 87
Young, Charles, 40, 42
Young, Robert, and wife, 40, 42, 67, 157

THE UNIVERSITY OF TENNESSEE PRESS
KNOXVILLE

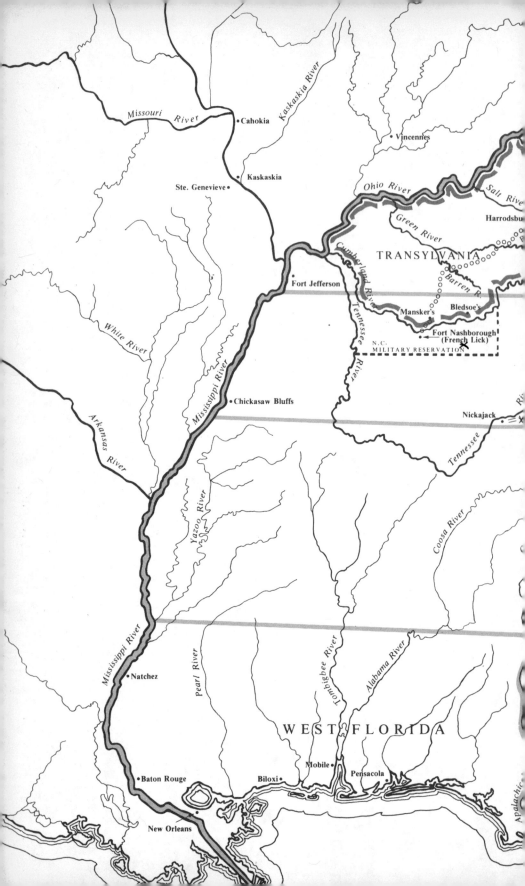

Missouri River

• Cahokia

• Vincennes

Kaskaskia River

Ohio River

Salt River

Green River

Harrodsbu

• Kaskaskia

Ste. Genevieve •

TRANSYLVANIA

Cumberland River

Barren R.

• Fort Jefferson

Mansker's

Bledsoe's

White River

Mississippi River

Tennessee River

• Fort Nashborough
(French Lick)

N.C.
MILITARY RESERVATION

Arkansas River

• Chickasaw Bluffs

Nickajack
×

Tennessee R.

Yazoo River

Coosa River

Pearl River

Tombigbee River

Alabama River

• Natchez

WEST FLORIDA

• Mobile

• Pensacola

• Baton Rouge

Biloxi •

Apalachic

New Orleans